Library of
Davidson College

WEAK STATES IN THE INTERNATIONAL SYSTEM

Weak States
in the
International System

MICHAEL HANDEL

*Research Associate, Harvard
Center for International Affairs
and
The Hebrew University, Jerusalem*

FRANK CASS

First published 1981 in Great Britain by
FRANK CASS AND COMPANY LIMITED
Gainsborough House, Gainsborough Road
London E11 1RS, England

and in the United States of America by
FRANK CASS AND COMPANY LIMITED
c/o Biblio Distribution Centre
81 Adams Drive, P.O. Box 327, Totowa, N.J. 07511

Copyright © 1981 Michael Handel

Written under the Auspices of the
Center for International Affairs, Harvard University

British Library Cataloguing in Publication Data

Handel, Michael
    Weak states in the international system
    1. International relations
    I. Title
    327'.35   JX1395

ISBN 0-7146-3117-5

All rights reserved. No part of this publication may be reproduced, stored in a retrieval system, or transmitted in any form, or by any means, electronic, mechanical, photocopying, recording, or otherwise, without the prior permission of Frank Cass and Company Limited.

Typeset by A-Line Services.
Printed in Great Britain by T. J. Press (Padstow) Ltd.
Padstow, Cornwall

To My Mother
and
In Memory of My Father

Contents

	Page
List of Tables	ix
List of Figures	xi
List of Illustrations	xiii
Acknowledgments	xv
Introduction	3

Chapter I. Definitions and Characteristics of the Weak States — 9
  The Great Powers — 11
  The Middle Powers — 23
  The Weak States — 30
  The Mini States — 47
  Summary: The Ideal Type of the Weak State — 48

Chapter II. Internal Sources of Weakness and Strength of the Weak States — 67
  The Geographical Position of Weak States — 70
  The Military Position of Weak States — 76
  The Utility of Military Strength for the Weak States — 90
  Summary — 103
  A Note on Passive Resistance (Nonviolent Action) by Weak States — 104

Chapter III. External Sources of Weakness and Strength of the Weak States — 119
  Formal Alliances between Weak States and Great Powers — 121
  Patrons and Clients: A Perspective on Weak State-Great Power Relations — 131
  Weak States and the Benefits of Collective (Public) Good — 148
  Alliances of Weak States — 153

Chapter IV.	**The Position of Weak States in Different International Systems**	169
	The Weak States and the Great Powers' Spheres of Influence	171
	Weak States in a Balance-of-Power or Multipolar System	175
	Weak States in Bipolar Systems	187
	Maneuvrability in a Nuclear World	195
	Problems of Nuclear Weapon Acquisition by the Weak States	197
Chapter V.	**The Economic Position of the Weak States in the International System**	217
	Sources of Economic Weakness	220
	Modifications, Qualifications and Caveats	229
	The Application of Economic Pressure against Weak States	236
Conclusions		257
Appendix A	A Note on the Domestic Sources of the Foreign Policy of Weak States	261
Appendix B	The 'New' International Norms of Conduct among States and the position of Weak States	265
Appendix C	The Potential Impact of Modern Military Weapons Technology on the Military Position of Weak States	277
Bibliography		287
Index		313

Tables

	Page
1. Military and Economic Strength of Great Powers 1971	15
2. Highest and Lowest Great Powers by Military and Economic Criteria	18
3. Military and Economic Strength of Middle Powers 1971–1972	25
4. Highest and Lowest Middle Powers by Military and Economic Criteria	27
5. The Military and Economic Strength of Weak States	32
6. Economic and Demographic Data on Mini States 1973	49
7. Total Military Aircraft Production of the Four Major Powers 1939–1944	82
8. OPEC Foreign Investment 1974–1977	218
9. Relation between Size of Country and Country Export Concentration	221
10. Per Cent Commodity Share in Country Total Export by Value, 1965 (for African States)	222
11. Latin America's Exports (1959)	223
12. Germany's Percentual Share in the Trade of Southeastern European Countries	227
13. Serbian Exports in 1906 and 1907	237
14. Decline in U.S.-Cuban Trade After Castro's Rise to Power	238
15. Geographic Distribution of Cuban Exports	239

Figures

	Page
1. A Continuum of States	11
2. Middle Powers by Population and GNP per capita	24
3. Elements Determining the Strength of a State	69
4. Total Strength of Weak and Powerful States Compared	70
5. Mobilized and Potential Power of Weak and Powerful States Compared	80
6. A Typology of Weak State Alliances	121
7. Correlation between Degree of Equality and Benefits Derived in Great Power-Weak State Relationship	134
8. Distribution of Alliance Commitments, 1946–1965	157

Illustrations

	Page
A Small State (Czechoslovakia) Threatens Germany	73
Fulfillment (Austria Beaten by Serbia)	96
Bravo Belgium! (The Belgians Blocking the Road of the German Armies Invading France)	98
The Power Behind (Russia Supporting Serbia against Austria)	125
Who Is Australia's Next Patron?	140
The Two Constrictors (Russia and Germany)	170
United States' Sphere of Influence	174
The Helpers League (Persia Divided between Great Britain and Russia)	178

Acknowledgments

For their time and patience, I would especially like to thank Professor Stanley Hoffmann, Professors Samuel P. Huntington and Karl W. Deutsch of Harvard, and Klaus Knorr of Princeton, who in addition offered helpful ideas and incisive comments. Above all, I would like to thank Professor Thomas C. Schelling of Harvard University for his original suggestions and for the stimulating conversations during my work on the book.

As always, one's friends help shoulder and lighten the burden. For assistance and support beyond the call of friendship, I especially wish to thank Richard K. Betts of Lowell House, who is now at the Brookings Institution—my most relentless and valued critic, who kept me going even when I was in a weak state; and Diane (Daniela) Lynn Saltz, the archeologist who collaborated with the "enemy upstairs" to polish my English and who helped me in innumerable other ways. I would also like to thank Donal Cruise O'Brien for his kind help and good company. Amos Perlmutter has inspired much of my reading and has introduced me to many new directions in my research.

Appendix C was written as part of a larger study supported by a Ford Foundation grant for research on International Security and Arms Control.

Last but not least, I am indebted literally and figuratively to Harvard University and the Department of Government for their generous support between 1969 and 1974. In the final analysis, it is the generosity of Harvard University and the traditional hospitality of the United States' universities to foreign students that can make such research possible.

... right, as the world goes, is only in question between equals in powers, while the strong do what they can and the weak suffer what they must.

> Thucydides, *The History of the Peloponnesian War,* Book V, chap. 17.

Introduction

The studies of modern diplomatic history and the theories of international relations have usually been based on the relations among the great powers: Britain, France, Prussia/Germany, Russia, and the United States. The available works are already exhaustive, but the output continues.[1] The study of the weak states, on the other hand, has been sorely neglected. This work is an attempt to look at the international system through the eyes and experiences of the weak states.

Methodologically, I have focused my attention at the level of analysis referred to by Kenneth Waltz as the "third image"[2] and by Graham Allison as the "rational actor" model (model 1).[3] The "third image" concentrates on the primacy of the international system for determining foreign policy. The "rational actor" model assumes that states are unitary, purposive, value-maximizing calculators.

While most of the existing theories of international relations can be readily applied to the behavior of weak states in the international system, the overall weakness of these states must be taken into account. Although the differences between the constraints which affect weak and powerful states can be overemphasized, several distinctions are important.

Domestic determinants of foreign policy are less salient in weak states. The international system leaves them less room for choice in the decision-making process. Their smaller margin of error and hence greater preoccupation with survival makes the essential interests of weak states less ambiguous. Kenneth Waltz's "third image" is therefore a most relevant level of analysis.

Moreover, because of the reduced scale of complexity of

bureaucratic and decision-making structures of weak states, there are *usually* fewer bureaucratic influences on foreign policy making, which makes Allison's "rational actor" model more appropriate.

Therefore it has been suggested that "the most obvious fact about small powers is that their foreign policy is governed by the policy of others. It follows that the student of small power policy, even more than the student of great power policy, must concentrate on the environment in which his subject exists".[4]

The available studies of weak states in international relations employ two basic methodological approaches. One is a "horizontal section," namely an attempt to develop general theories for the position and conduct of weak states in the international system. The other is a "vertical section," a study in depth of the foreign policy of one (or a few) weak state(s) in a given period of history. This work comes closer to the first category, attempting to find some general insights and observations on the behavior and position of the weak states in international relations.

Each method has its advantages and disadvantages. The more general the theory, the greater the number of countries that must be taken into account. But the more countries studied, the less the possibility of achieving a deep and meaningful analysis of each specific case. Whatever is gained on the theoretical level might result in the loss of richness in detail. Samuel Huntington referred to the same problem in *The Soldier and the State* as follows: ". . . understanding requires theory; theory requires abstraction; and abstraction requires the simplification and ordering of reality".[5] On the other hand, even if one were to exhaust the literature on any given country, one would surely reach the point of diminishing returns because so much of the information is repetitive and so little new knowledge can be gained.

In this work, I have attempted to analyze all the available theoretical literature on weak states in international relations, as well as to look into as many case studies as possible. Many of the theories in this growing body of literature can be accepted, but a sizeable number must be rejected, since they generalize too much from unique cases. Too many generalizations are also made for a given historical period and then cavalierly applied to another.

The historical period and the structure of the international system in which the position of weak states is examined are of great importance. The position of the weak European countries for most of the nineteenth century (excluding the Napoleonic wars and Prussia's war with Denmark) was relatively secure, while the weak states *outside* the European system had to face the dangers of European imperialistic policies and very often could not maintain their independence. Although the weak European countries were not recognized as equal until the end of the First World War, and most of the important decisions in international politics were made by the Concert of Europe and later the great powers, the actual existence of the weak states was rarely at stake. During the decade or so that preceded the First World War, the competition among the great powers for the allegiance of the weak states considerably enhanced the bargaining power and maneuverability of the latter. After the First World War the position of the weak states further improved, as they achieved almost complete formal-legal equality in the League of Nations, while at the same time the great powers grew weaker.

The rise of the revisionist powers in the 1930s, however, marked the lowest point in the security of the weak states since the Napoleonic wars. Their security and very survival were directly threatened and many predicted their disappearance. This trend continued after the Second World War and at the beginning of the Cold War as the great powers —especially the USSR—tried to establish control over what they regarded as their spheres of influence. On the other hand, most of the African and Asian states have freed themselves from the grip of the powers and considerably improved their position *vis-à-vis* the great powers, a process which continues today.

It is therefore possible to distinguish between cycles of security or insecurity, influence or impotence of the weak states in the international system. The position and relative security of any weak state must be gauged in terms of the specific international system in which it is operating.[6]

A further impediment to arriving at more general

pronouncements on the position and behavior of weak states in the international system is that, even at the same period in history, weak states located in different areas have different neighbors and thus face different problems. This indicates the central importance of the geographical location of weak states. Therefore, studies of Finland, Czechoslovakia, Belgium, Poland, Hungary and Israel stress problems of survival and vulnerability, while works on Portugal, New Zealand, Chile, and even Switzerland and Sweden emphasize their relative safety and capacity to hold their own against the powers.

In like manner, two basic approaches are evident in the theoretical discussions on weak states. One stresses their preoccupation with problems of survival and their limited freedom of maneuver. The other approach tends to inflate the influence of the weak states out of proportion to their real power. On the whole, I find myself taking a position somewhere in between the two. Weak states have not disappeared *en masse* as Treitschke and his followers and some social Darwinists predicted in the last quarter of the 19th century.[7] But neither can the weak states ever afford to relax their vigilance on matters of security, nor bask in the protection and good will of the powers. Even more than the powerful, the weak must be continuously on the alert. Any error in judgment can be fatal, "as those who are weak hang on a single turn of the scale."[8]

In fact, very few weak states have disappeared from the international scene during the last century. Weak states have demonstrated a remarkable capacity to survive despite all the dangers they faced due to their lack of power. The worst "enemy" of the weak states has been national unifications, such as in Germany and Italy. This process accounts for the "disappearance" of most of the weak states. When Karl Haushofer predicted the disappearance of the small countries, he recommended that they unify with the larger states: ". . . we may say that small states have a constantly decreasing chance of independent survival".[9] During the First and Second World Wars many weak states were temporarily occupied but they re-emerged after the war. Since the end of the First World War, but especially after the Second, the number of weak independent states has grown continuously. In the 20th century, the only weak states which have disappeared are the Baltic States. Others, such as the East European States after the Second World War, and perhaps Finland, have lost much of their freedom of action in the international system, as well as much of their freedom to determine their own internal affairs. Having retained their national framework and cohesion as separate political entities, however, they can at least maintain the hope of regaining complete independence sometime in the future.

In this book, I have attempted to present a balanced account not only of the weaknesses and vulnerability of weak states, but also of the positive capabilities which they can develop to compensate for their deficiencies, i.e., those conditions under which their security is endangered and those under which it is enhanced. Many of the problems faced by the weak are also, to a lesser extent, shared by the more powerful. It must be remembered that if weakness and strength were *absolute* rather than *relative,* and fixed rather than dynamic qualities, the result of each conflict and collision of interests between weak and powerful states would always end in favor of might. For, as Professor Schelling has observed,

> "Bargaining power," "bargaining strength," "bargaining skill" suggest that the advantage goes to the powerful, the strong, or the skillful. It does, of course, if those qualities are defined to mean only that negotiations are won by those who win. But, if the terms imply that it is an advantage to be more intelligent or more skilled in debate, or to have more financial resources, more physical strength, more military potency, or more ability to withstand losses, then the term does a disservice. These qualities are by no means universal advantages in bargaining situations; they often have a contrary value.[10]

Given the broad scope of this book, there were certain subjects in the field which could justify a whole study on their own, such as guerrilla warfare as the weapon of the weak, the position of weak states in regional integration projects, the role of multinational corporations in weak states, etc. Rather than treat them superficially, I preferred to leave them to other times, or other hands.

NOTES

1. Italy, Japan and other states could be added to the list. It is tempting to suggest that the number of books, articles, monographs, and other publications devoted to a given state, at different periods in history, can serve as a quantitative indicator to its power, rank and position in the international hierarchy and to the impact of a state on the international system.

    For example, the literature on the Hapsburg Empire's foreign policy during the 19th century and up to the outbreak of the First World War is voluminous. The literature on Austrian foreign policy since the end of the First World War is quite limited. The works on Mussolini's foreign policy are quite extensive, whereas the literature on post-Second World War Italian foreign policy is minimal. The research on Germany's foreign policy on the eve of the First World War or on Hitler's foreign policy cannot be read by a single researcher; the literature on the Weimar Republic's foreign policy, a low point in German power, can easily be read by anyone.
2. Kenneth N. Waltz, *Man, the State and War* (New York: Columbia University Press, 1968), pp. 159–186.
3. Graham T. Allison, *Essence of Decision* (Boston: Little, Brown & Co., 1971), pp. 10–38.
4. Quoted in J. E. Spence, *Republic Under Pressure: A Study of South African Foreign Policy* (London: Oxford University Press, 1967), p.6. See also Richard Kennaway, *New Zealand's Foreign Policy 1951–1971* (Wellington: Hicks Smith, 1972), pp. 153–155.
5. Samuel P. Huntington, *The Soldier and the State* (New York: Vintage Books, 1969), p. vii.
6. For an interesting analysis of historical international systems, see Richard N. Rosecrance, *Action and Reaction in International Politics* (Boston: Little, Brown & Co., 1963) and Kyung-Won Kim, *Revolution and the International System* (New York: New York University Press, 1970). However, both concentrate mainly on the position and interrelationship of the great powers.
7. See, for example, Gertrude Himmelfarb, *Darwin and the Darwinian Revolution* (New York: Norton, 1968), pp. 412–431; also Richard Hofstadter, *Social Darwinism in American Thought* (Boston: Beacon Press, 1971), pp. 170–200.
8. Thucydides, *The History of the Peloponnesian War* (New York: E. P. Dutton, 1950), p. 405.
9. Karl Haushofer, quoted in Andreas Dorpalen *The World of General Haushofer: Geopolitics in Action* (Port Washington, N.Y.: Kennikat Press, 1966): "Small Countries have no Right to Exist" p.220.
10. Thomas C. Schelling, *The Strategy of Conflict* (New York: Oxford University Press, 1969), p. 22.

CHAPTER I

Definitions and Characteristics of Weak States

If the notion of war were unknown in international relations, the definition of "small power" would have no significance; just as in the domestic life of a nation it has no significance whether one man is less tall or has a weaker physique than his fellow citizen.

Laszlo Reczei[1]

The term "smaller country" seems to be reserved for large countries with small populations, small countries with large populations, small countries with small populations, and sometimes countries of any size that mostly mind their own business in world affairs.

Herbert Goldhamer[2]

Humpty Dumpty: "When *I* use a word, it means just what I choose it to mean—neither more nor less."

Lewis Carroll[3]

The behavior of states in the international system is largely determined by the power relations and differentials among them. Order within the system is continually threatened by the possibility that some states will resort to force or war in order to improve their relative positions. Because states frequently do coerce one another—or threaten to do so—it is important to analyze their respective capacities to protect, maintain, or further their national interests.

The traditional theories of international relations take the unequal distribution of strength among states into account by recognizing the existence of a pecking order of states based upon five gradations: super powers, great powers, middle powers, small powers (states), and mini-states.

The term "small power" appears frequently in the literature,[4] and it has a long tradition of usage. Yet it is a self-contradictory term, both semantically and logically. The main characteristic of weak states is, indeed, their *lack* of power or strength, and hence they are continuously preoccupied with the question of survival.

Raymond Aron refers to the semantic problem as follows:

> We avoid here the common expression "small powers", so as not to introduce a confusion in vocabulary. The use of the word *power* to designate the actors and not merely the capacity of the actors is self-explanatory. The rivalry of power being part and parcel of international life, we identify the actors and their capacity for action, and establish a hierarchy of actors as a function of their capacity.[5]

Aron, like the German scholars, employs the phrase "small state" (*Kleinstaat*) which, though more logical than "small power" (*"Kleinmacht"* would sound absurd!), is not entirely satisfactory. In the study of international relations, it is not the *size* of a state which matters, but rather its relative strength. Strictly speaking, a small state should be small in area. This term, however, has been applied to countries with enormous territories, such as Saudi Arabia, Chad, Mongolia, Libya, and Mauritania. To be exact, the expression "small state" should be used to describe only those states which both lack strength and are small in territory.

The term "weak states" has been adopted here because it

can be applied not only to small, weak states but to countries of considerable area which are, nevertheless, weak and therefore vulnerable. When the term "small states" appears within quoted material, it should be understood to mean "weak states."

The international power hierarchy—super powers, great powers, middle powers, weak states, and mini-states—might be illustrated by a pyramid in which the lowest layer, representing the weakest states, would include the greatest number of states. But it is more accurate to depict this hierarchy as a continuum:

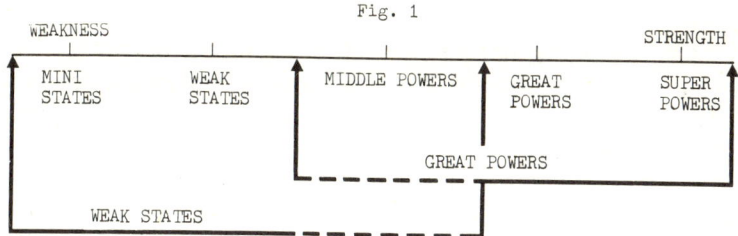

Fig. 1

This study will focus on weak states, those on the left side of the continuum (or the bottom layers of an imaginary pyramid).

The Great Powers

The simplest definitions of weak states are negative. For example: "A small state is any state in the international system that does not belong to the category of the powers...."[7] An explanation similar to that lexicon definition has been given by Paul Herre:

> ... within the European historical development one should treat as Small States all those states which in the prevailing political system do not belong to the Great Powers.[8]

Other German scholars have simply referred to weak states as *Nichtgrossmachten* (non-great powers).[9]

Such definitions fail to characterize weak states positively; nor do they reveal enough about the great powers to make a derivative definition of weak states possible.[10] It is necessary, therefore, to define the term "great power." Historically, there has been general agreement on what states are in the great-power category, and since this class is limited in number, common denominators are more readily apparent.

In modern times, the possession of nuclear weapons distinguishes the great powers from the rest of the states.[11] It is obvious, though, that prior to 1945 nuclear weapons could not have served as a criterion. Thus the standards used to define the great powers, as well as other states in the international system, are not static or permanent. Technological breakthroughs, changes in values, changes in perception by the states involved, and victories and defeats all lead to changes, often rapid and unexpected, in the power classification of states.[12]

The changing nature of such a definition becomes clear when one considers the growing number of states which may produce nuclear and conceivably even thermonuclear weapons, and thus join the hitherto exclusive atomic club of the great and super powers. The capability of additional countries to produce nuclear weapons also indicates the possibility of upward mobility in the international hierarchy.[13] Yet would the production of nuclear weapons by countries like Sweden, Israel, Switzerland, Brazil, and Egypt turn them instantly into great powers? The answer is obviously no. Under certain conditions, that achievement might add to their military power, bargaining leverage, and prestige; but under other conditions the development of nuclear weapons could lead to the imposition of pressures that might actually weaken rather than strengthen their position.[14]

The super powers at the extreme right of the continuum can be differentiated from the more numerous great powers by their nuclear development: the quantity of nuclear weapons available to them (abundance and overkill versus sufficiency);[15] technological advancement in terms of miniaturization of nuclear devices; the sophistication of their delivery system; differences in their second strike capability; and their ABM and MIRV capabilities. In the future, however, different technological criteria may be suggested to differentiate between the super powers and the great powers, such as their space programs, which are out of the reach of any great power.

It is clear that more than one set of criteria is needed to

define the position of a state in the international system. Nuclear weapons, the criterion used so far, will probably come to be only a necessary, not a sufficient, condition to determine whether a country can be classified as a militarily great or super power. The same thing is true of the other commonly used criteria.

Historically, the single most important yardstick for the measurement of military power has been the population size of a given state. This remained the basic standard for evaluating the military might of states well into the industrial-technological age. Indeed, until the outbreak of the First World War, despite all technological advances "the Balance of Power was directly affected by the population changes that took place during the period [among the major powers]."[16] The larger the population, the larger the army a state could put into the field, and God usually favored the largest number of battalions.

Of course, organizational qualities and the tactical skill of great captains of war could, to a certain extent, help compensate for small populations. This accounts for the temporary rise of less populous states to the ranks of the great powers of their times—states like the Netherlands, Sweden under Gustav Adolf, and Prussia under Frederick the Great.[17] Population size, then, is a necessary but not a sufficient condition for classifying a state as a great power.

Quite a few states whose populations are as great as or greater than those of Great Britain, France, West Germany, Japan—countries such as India, Indonesia, Brazil, Mexico, Nigeria, Italy—are not accepted as great powers. Indeed, a highly populated state cannot always utilize the manpower available to it. Although China's population is at least three times greater than Russia's, the Chinese army is smaller than that of the USSR and not so well equipped. It is much more difficult for a state that is less developed economically and socially to expand and equip a modern military force than it is for a modern industrialized society to do so.

In the 1970s, what counts is not the absolute size of a population but rather the so-called "effective population",[18] that is, the part of the population which can be armed and educated to operate modern sophisticated weapons. Additional criteria must therefore be introduced to correlate a nation's population with its economic, industrial, and social capacity.[19] Two major indicators are the Gross National Product (GNP) and the GNP per capita.

The overall GNP enables one to compare the absolute size of the economic output of a country with that of any other state. This index, however, is not completely satisfactory for the measurement of a state's relative power. Canada with a population of 21.4 million produces a GNP of 78.1 million dollars, as compared with India, whose population reaches 553.8 million but which has a GNP of only 52.9 million dollars.[20] Similarly, Israel with a population of 3 million has the same GNP as Egypt with a population close to 34 million.[21] Therefore a country's GNP must be measured and corrected against the size of its population.

This correction can be made partly by measuring the GNP per capita,[22] which indicates a country's level of education, productivity, and industrialization, and hence furnishes a better idea of its capacity to provide its armed forces with modern equipment, to maintain its weapon systems, and to mobilize its manpower. To use the same countries mentioned above, the GNP per capita for Canada is $3,651, whereas that for India is less than $100. Israel's GNP per capita is $1,897, while Egypt's is only $220.[23]

The second problem with the GNP index is that the absolute size of a GNP may not reveal much about the structure of an economy. A relatively large GNP *can* be based primarily on agricultural products, whereas a small GNP can be based on modern sophisticated industry. Even when two industrial countries are being compared, the industry of one may be better geared to the production of military hardware than the industry of the other.[24]

Thus further information on the economic structure of a country is needed in order to evaluate its real strength. Here data can be acquired on such specific criteria as a country's steel production, energy consumption, energy reserves, and motor vehicle industry (see Table 1). For a state to qualify as a great power, it has to rank very high in all or most of these categories. Table 2 gives the ranges of the nations classified as super and great powers in the early 1970s.

TABLE 1
MILITARY AND ECONOMIC STRENGTH OF GREAT POWERS 1971

	STATES	Population (millions)	Area (thousand sq. km.)	GNP (billion $)	GNP (per capita ($))	Armed Forces (millions)	Military expenditures (billion $)	Nuclear weapons in 1973	Petroleum reserve (million metric tons)	Gas reserve (billion cubic meters)
SUPER POWERS	USA	205.3	9,363	976.8	4,758	3.066	77.80	10,000+	5,144	7,895
	USSR	242.8	22.402	497.0	2,047	3.535	65.00	10,000+	8,203	18,010
GREAT POWERS	CHINA	836	9,596	120.0	143	3.100	10.00	256	n.a.	n.a.
	JAPAN	103.4	370.07	197.2	1,907	0.250	1.50	—	3	16
	W. GERMANY	61.7	247.97	185.5	3,006	0.484	6.20	—	79	388
	U.K.	55.8	244.04	121.0	2,168	0.390	5.90	10,000+	396	1,126
	FRANCE	50.8	547.02	145.9	2,872	0.506	6.00	6,336	14	205

TABLE 1 (continued)

STATES	Coal reserve (billion metric tons)	Uranium reserve (metric tons)	Energy production (millions metric tons)	Energy consumption (million metric tons)	Energy consumption (kg. coal metric per capita)	Pig iron (thousand metric tons)	Crude steel (thousand metric tons)	Ship production (thousand gross tons)	Merchant marine (thousand gross tons)
SUPER POWERS									
USA	1,100,000	226,800	2,029.19	2,327.64	11,244	75,722	109,265	482	15,204
USSR	4,121,603	n.a.	1,250.26	1,112.19	4,531	89,256	120,660	n.a.	16,774
GREAT									
CHINA	1,011,000	n.a.	n.a.	n.a.	561	27,000	17,000	n.a.	2,676
JAPAN	19,248	2,400	49.47	341.90	3,267	74,635	88,557	11,992	34,929
W. GERMANY	70,000	—	175.51	320.06	5,223	30,223	40,314	1,649	8,516
U.K.	15,500	—	176.01	306.68	5,507	15,416	24,175	1,239	28,625
FRANCE	2,800	40,800	54.22	201.48	3,928	18,694	22,859	1,112	7,420

TABLE 1 (continued)

		Motor Vehicles production (thousands)
SUPER POWERS	USA	8,505.0[a] 2,053.1[b]
	USSR	529.0[a] 862.3[b]
	CHINA	n.a.
GREAT POWERS	JAPAN	3,717.9[a] 2,104.8[b]
	W. GERMANY	3,696.8[a] 277.8[b]
	U.K.	1,741.9[a] 458.6[b]
	FRANCE	2,694.0[a] 342.2[b]

Sources:
United States Arms Control and Disarmament Agency, *World Military Expenditures 1971* (Washington, D.C., July 1972), p. 50; *United Nations Statistical Yearbook 1971* (New York, 1972), passim; Karl Deutsch, *The Analysis of International Relations* (Englewood Cliffs, N.J.: Prentice Hall, 1968), p. 33

n.a. = not available
a = Passenger car
b = Commercial vehicle

TABLE 2

HIGHEST AND LOWEST GREAT POWERS BY MILITARY AND ECONOMIC CRITERIA, 1971

Population (in millions)	835	China	50.8	France
Area (in thousand sq. km.)	22,402	USSR	244	UK
GNP (in billion $)	976.8	US	120	China
GNP per capita (in $)	4,758	US	143	China
Armed Forces (in millions)	3.535	USSR	0.25	Japan
Military Expenditures (in billion $)	77.8	US	1.5	Japan
Nuclear Weapons	10,000+	US–USSR–UK	none	Japan–W. Germany
Petroleum Reserve (in million metric tons)	8,203	USSR	3	Japan
Gas Reserve (in billion cubic meters)	18,010	USSR	16	Japan
Coal Reserve (in million metric tons)	4,121,603	USSR	2,800	France
Uranium Reserve (in metric tons)	226,800	US?	2,400	UK–W. Germany
Energy Production (in million metric tons)	1,250.26	US	49.47	Japan
Energy Consumption (in million metric tons)	2,327.64	US	201.48	France
Energy Consumption per capita (in kg. coal)	11,244	US	561	China
Pig iron (in thousand metric tons)	89,256	USSR	15,416	UK
Crude Steel (in thousand metric tons)	120,660	USSR	17,000	China
Ship Production (in thousand gross tons)	11,992	Japan	482	US
Merchant Marine (in thousand gross tons)	34,929	Japan	2,676	China
Motor Vehicle Production (in thousands)	8,505.0	US		
	2,104.8	Japan		China?

Source: Table 1

The variations among the great powers are tremendous. But it is relatively easy to separate the two super powers from the rest. Their populations are over 200 million. Their GNP's exceed 500 billion dollars. (Each has over 15 per cent of the world's total GNP!)[25] They control extensive territories which enhance their second strike capabilities and give them more room for strategic maneuvering and defense.[26] Their standing armies are over 3 million in size and their military budgets are at least 60 billion dollars. Finally, they are the only states so far to develop a serious space research program.

It is also noteworthy that the two super powers are the only great powers which control very large reserves of energy (especially oil), making them less dependent on other states and hence less susceptible to pressures from oil-producing countries. Their steel production is well above the 100 million ton mark. Both super powers have reached a level of saturation in the production of nuclear weapons and highly sophisticated delivery systems. None of the other great powers even approaches these figures. Such quantitative indicators seem sufficient to separate the super powers from all the rest of the great powers.

Moving in the other direction and using most of the same categories, one does not always find such striking differences between the great powers and the middle powers. On certain criteria, in fact, the middle powers score as high as the great powers. The middle powers are not necessarily smaller in territorial size or population than the great powers. The middle powers' standing armed forces may even be larger than those of the great powers but the latter are usually more modern, and of course Great Britain and France have nuclear weapons. Despite the impressive economic and military capacity of the great powers, the quantitative indicators do not separate them clearly enough from the middle powers. Therefore it is necessary to supplement these statistics on the great and super powers with a set of nonquantitative criteria.

Historically, the super and great powers have been the great military powers, with the exception of China. Although China was very weak militarily, she still could not be completely subdued because of her large population and territory. At some point in history, each of the great powers successfully passed the test of a major war—or else, after initial victory, was defeated only by an enormous coalition. Those which *failed* the test of battle—Germany and Russia after World War I, Japan and Germany after World War II, and China before the Korean War—were temporarily considered *not* to be great powers. "The test of a Great Power then is the test of strength for War."[27]

Some definitions of the super and great powers reflect this idea:

> ... a super power is one over which the joint military efforts of *all* non-super powers would be unable to achieve a military victory, because the latter are not likely to survive a nuclear onslaught; in other words: super power = militarily invincible power.[28]
> ... a Great Power was a state which could insure its own security against all comers.[29]
> A state may be defined as a Great Power if its total destruction would require a coalition of all other states to accomplish.[30]
> [A great power is] a state which cannot be defeated in war by any other state or coalition of states without it exacting comparable costs from its opponents.[31]

All these definitions are variations on one theme—the capacity of a super or great power to defend itself under even the most adverse conditions. Thus the inability of France and Great Britain to defend themselves exclusively by their own efforts in the First and Second World Wars was a sign of their decline as great powers.[32] It follows that one of the major characteristics of a weak state is the inability to secure its own existence, especially against a great power, or even against another weak state supported by a major power.[33] Since the second half of the twentieth century, however, the great powers have been dependent (to varying degrees) on the military aid and support of the United States, especially for aircraft and electronic technology, and they have been protected by the American nuclear umbrella.

So, despite their large standing armies, nuclear weapons, and sophisticated military industries, even the great powers are, in the final analysis, incapable of completely securing their own independence against a super power. To the extent that this dependence on the super powers is increasing, the gap between the super powers and great powers is widening. At the same time, the line dividing the great powers from weaker countries is becoming less distinct.

Another important qualitative characteristic of the great powers frequently found in the literature is the *worldwide* scope of their interests, as contrasted to the more limited interests of the less powerful nations.[34]

> In the case of a big power its interests, the very *conditions* of its self-preservation, the safeguarding of its security and great power status reach beyond its frontiers; therefore its basic foreign policy consists of protecting and safeguarding its *sphere of interests.* Some of the conditions ensuring its existence *within* its frontiers lie *beyond* them . . . . For a great power, therefore, there exists a sphere of influence beyond its borders; any interference with this constitutes a danger, just like interference within its frontiers—naturally, it will defend itself against such interference.[35]

The global perception of the great powers is partly a function of their ability to act on a worldwide scale to defend their interests. It would also be advantageous for any weak state to actively defend and secure its survival and interests well beyond its own borders, but it does not have the strength to do so.[36] Ironically, the conditions which most vitally affect the existence of a weak state lie outside its borders to an even greater extent than for the great powers. These conditions of self-preservation, in fact, are primarily the influences exerted by the great powers themselves.

Robert O. Keohane has suggested defining states on the basis of the scope of their influence on the international system. He refers to the great powers as "system-determining" states.

> A great power is a state whose leaders consider that it can alone exercise a large, perhaps decisive impact on the international system.[37]

The weaker the state, the less its influence on the international system[38] and the greater the impact of the great powers upon it.

This difference in the scope of interests between the great powers and the weak states has been reflected in international law and organizations since the Congresses of Vienna (1815) and Aix la Chapelle (1818) which made a formal distinction between states of *general interests* (system-wide interests) and states with limited interests.[39] A similar distinction was made at the Versailles Peace Conference of 1919.[40] All states which were recognized as powers (Principal Allies) were assigned permanent seats in the Council of the League of Nations.[41] Later, the great powers were given permanent seats in the United Nations Security Council as well as the right of veto.

The power of veto is sometimes accepted as an important means of distinguishing between the great powers and all other states.[42] The value of this criterion is limited, however. It can quickly turn into an anachronism which does not reflect the real division of power and prestige among the great nations. Thus, although West Germany and Japan have power at least equal to that of France and Great Britain (except for nuclear weapons), they cannot exercise the right of veto for obvious historical reasons. Conversely, for years the Republic of China (Taiwan) had a permanent seat and veto in the Security Council, but could hardly have been considered a great power.

It is important to note that although the right of veto belongs exclusively to the great powers, the use of veto power is by no means confined to them. In fact, on most occasions the veto has been used by the great powers on behalf of their weaker clients when their interests happened to converge. For many weak states the veto is a regular weapon in their diplomatic arsenal, which they have learned to manipulate and take for granted. Many weak states enjoy the right of veto in the Security Council; for example: the Arab countries (on the Middle Eastern question), African states (in relation to colonial questions), and the East European states. A Soviet memorandum makes this practice clear:

> The right of veto in the hands of the Soviet Union is an important guarantee of the independence and sovereignty of smaller states. The Arab and other independent states know from their own experience how in the Security Council the Soviet Union opposes attacks by the imperialist states on newly independent states.[43]

The characteristics that make the super and great powers a separate and distinct class become even clearer when this group is contrasted to the middle powers and weak states.

The Middle Powers

The middle powers belong to a category which is somewhat difficult to define. On the whole, they exhibit the characteristics of the weak states, rather than those of the great powers. They are "the upper crust of the non-great."[44] Trudeau has referred to Canada as "the largest of the small powers."[45] The middle powers can be divided into two main types: those with relatively small populations but highly developed and efficient economies (I), and those which are highly populated but economically less developed (II).

The first group (I) can be subdivided further into two classes. One includes states such as Canada and Australia which have never been considered powers but which control large territories with enormous reserves of natural resources. In addition to their present advanced economies, they have great potential for future growth. The second subdivision consists of states whose economic performance is currently impressive but which are declining in relative power. Examples are Italy and perhaps Spain (on the lower border of middle powers). Some scholars have included West Germany and Japan in this class,[46] while Great Britain and France may have to be added in the future.

The second main group (II) encompasses presently underdeveloped countries with large and rapidly growing populations and sizable territories. Under certain favorable conditions, they could advance up the international scale of economic and military power. Brazil is the best example,[47] but countries such as Mexico and India might be included as well.

As one moves down the hierarchy of power in the international system, it becomes more difficult to decide which states fit into each category of power. Indeed, there is very little consensus about which states should be considered middle powers.

A book on the middle powers issued by the Deutsche Gesellschaft für Auswärtige Politik in Bonn[48] includes such widely different states as West Germany, Sweden, Italy, Yugoslavia, Israel, South Africa, India, Pakistan, Indonesia, Australia, Japan, Canada, Mexico, and Brazil.[49] Such a selection is arbitrary at best. In the first place, if states of the size and power of Israel, Sweden, and Yugoslavia are included, then why not add the Netherlands, Turkey, Spain, Czecho-

Fig. 2

	Population	
GNP	Small	Large
Low	Weak states	Middle powers (II) (usually low GNP per capita)
High	Middle powers (I) (usually high GNP per capita)	Great powers

slovakia, and a good many others? Secondly, on what basis have West Germany and Japan been included in the group? They are far ahead of the other states economically and in other ways. To give another example, Jean-Luc Vellut considers Poland a middle power.[50] But Poland can hardly pursue an independent foreign or domestic policy despite its economic achievements, sizable population and area, and large armed forces and military expenditure. The reason it is difficult to decide which countries are middle powers is that there are no common denominators. (For relevant statistics on the middle powers, see Tables 3 and 4).

In his article on smaller states, Vellut suggests the following quantitative definition: a middle power is a state with a population of at least 50 million or a GNP of at least 10 billion dollars (as of 1958).[51] On the basis of an annual GNP of 10 billion dollars, a number of weak European states would have to be added to the list of middle states in the early 1970s. Such an updated list would include Bulgaria (GNP $11.1 billion), Czechoslovakia ($32.9 billion), and Hungary ($15.3 billion). Yet these countries have only limited control over their internal

TABLE 3

MILITARY AND ECONOMIC STRENGTH OF MIDDLE POWERS 1971–1972

COUNTRY	Population (millions)	Area (thousand sq. km.)	GNP (billion $)	GNP per capita $	Armed forces (thousands)	Military expenditures (billion $)	Petroleum reserve (million metric tons)	Gas reserve (billion cubic meters)	Coal reserve (billion metric tons)	Uranium reserve (metric tons)
ARGENTINA	24.1	2,776	23.8	987	144	0.510	279	206	450	9,100
AUSTRALIA	12.7	7,686	43.46	2,639	73	1.30	241	395	16,000	19,700
BRAZIL	93.2	8,512	35.4	379	225	1.00	113	26	10,675	900
CANADA	21.0	9,976	78.1	3,651	83	1.90	1,126	1,571	61,000	210,500
INDIA	547.3	3,280	52.9	96	1,200	1.80	98	6	106,260	—
INDONESIA	132.4	1,491	10.73	81	375	0.286	1,459	147	845	—
IRAN	30.8	1,648	15.09	489	211.5	2.010	8,265	3,681	1,000	—
ITALY	54.0	301	91.8	1,713	413	2.50	40	142	—	1,400
MEXICO	50.7	1,972	39.45	778	71	0.281	397	—	3,466	1,200
SPAIN	33.8	504	32.4	959	281	1.20	22	—	2,830	10,000

TABLE 3 (continued)

COUNTRY	Energy production in 1971 (million metric tons)	Energy consumption in 1971 (million metric tons)	Energy consumption per capita (kg. coal)	Pig iron (thousand metric tons)	Crude steel (thousand metric tons)	Ship production (thousand gross tons)	Merchant marine (thousand gross tons)	Motor vehicle production (thousands)
ARGENTINA	37.63	41.75	1,773	861	1,951	—	1,401	196.0[a] 55.0[b]
AUSTRALIA	75.78	68.21	5,359	5,765	6,800	79	1,185	374.5[a] 78.0[b]
BRAZIL	20.39	47.70	500	4,686	5,997	149	1,885	363.0[a] 152.4[b]
CANADA	223.70	201.38	9,326	8,010	11,040	32	2,381	1,096.8[a] 279.4[b]
INDIA	84.91	102.52	186	6,740	6,175	14	2,650	50.0[a] 43.4[b]
INDONESIA	62.33	15.39	123	—	—	—	619	n.a.
IRAN	317.29	26.66	895	—	—	—	181	39.0[a] 13.2[b]
ITALY	26.26	145.04	2,682	8,727	17,452	813	8,187	1,701.1[a] 116.0[b]
MEXICO	59.20	64.70	1,270	2,428	3,784	—	417	158.6[a] 53.6[b]
SPAIN	16.54	55.08	1,614	4,956	7,782	916	4,300	460.0[a] 69.2[b]

n.a. = not available
a = Passenger cars
b = Commercial vehicles

Sources: United States Arms Control and Disarmament Agency, *World Military Expenditure 1971* (Washington, D.C., July 1972);
United Nations Statistical Yearbook 1972, 24th issue (New York, 1973);
London Institute for Strategic Studies, *The Military Balance 1972* (London, 1973).

TABLE 4
HIGHEST AND LOWEST MIDDLE POWERS BY MILITARY AND ECONOMIC CRITERIA, 1971–72

Population (in millions)	547.3	India	12.7	Australia
Area (in thousand sq. km.)	9,976	Canada	301	Italy
GNP (in billion $)	91.8	Italy	10.73	Indonesia
GNP per capita (in $)	3,651	Canada	81	Indonesia
Armed Forces (in thousands)	1,200	India	7	Mexico
Military Expenditures (in billion $)	2.5	Italy	0.28	Mexico
Petroleum Reserve (in million metric tons)	1,459	Indonesia	22	Spain
Gas Reserve (in billion cubic meters)	3,681	Iran	—	
Coal Reserve (in million metric tons)	106,260	India	—	
Uranium Reserve (in metric tons)	210,500	Canada	—	
Energy Production (in million metric tons)	317.29	Iran	16.59	Spain
Energy Consumption (in million metric tons)	145.04	Italy	15.39	Indonesia
Energy Consumption per capita (in kg. coal)	9,326	Canada	123	Indonesia
Pig Iron (in thousand metric tons)	8,727	Italy	—	Indonesia & Iran
Crude Steel (in thousand metric tons)	17,452	Italy	—	Indonesia & Iran
Ship Production (in thousand gross tons)	916	Spain	—	
Merchant Marine (in thousand gross tons)	8,187	Italy	181	Iran
Motor Vehicle Production (in thousands)				
Passenger Cars	1,701.1	Italy	?	Indonesia?
Commercial Vehicles	279.4	Canada	?	Indonesia?

Source: Table 3

and external affairs, and no freedom to change diplomatic alliances. Rumania ($26.5 billion) and Finland ($12.6 billion) would also fall into this category, although their freedom of action is limited to what is considered proper behavior by their powerful neighbor.

The defense of some other countries—Belgium ($35.5 billion), Denmark ($20.3 billion), Greece ($12.2 billion), Netherlands ($44.8 billion), and Norway ($15.1 million)—is mainly in the hands of an extra-continental power. These states cannot conceivably defend themselves by their own efforts. It is clear from their present national goals and ambitions that they perceive themselves as weak rather than middle states. The same holds true for such neutral countries as Switzerland ($30.6 billion), Austria ($20.4 billion), and Sweden ($42.3 billion).

Obviously, to set the minimum threshold of a middle power at the 1958 $10 billion GNP figure (in an article written in 1967) makes very little sense. Acceptance of this definition would engender a veritable inflation of middle powers. Marshall R. Singer, for instance, assigns no less than twenty-one nations to what he calls group II states, although he does not call them middle powers.[52] Of course, the minimum GNP could be raised to $15 or even $30 or $40 billion, but on what basis would one choose a figure? And how long would such a gauge remain useful?

Vellut's second criterion, a population of at least 50 million, is no less problematic. Some states with very high populations but very low absolute GNP's, extremely low per capita GNP's, and underdeveloped economies can only be considered as weak states. Examples are Indonesia (population 132,400,000 million, GNP $10.73 billion), Bangladesh (population 76,000,000, GNP $3.5 billion), and Pakistan (population 69,800,000, GNP $4.7 billion). Clearly, quantitative criteria are not sufficient in determining which states belong to the middle-power group.

As usual, a host of traditional pseudo-definitions exist for this group of powers. Carsten Holbraad defines a middle power "simply" as

> a state occupying an intermediate position in a hierarchy based on power . . . a country much stronger than the small nations though

considerably weaker than the principal members of the states system.[53]

How much stronger? Stronger by what criteria? Which are the small nations, and how are they defined?

The German group has performed the usual "trick." First they have decided which states are middle powers, and then they have created a suitable definition. "We understand a middle power to be a state which plays a political role within the limits of its own region."[54] This is, of course, an intuitive and impressionistic answer. What defines a region? How is a state's influence in a given region evaluated? What about "regional powers without a region" (Canada)? What is Japan's region?

Another definition has been suggested by Keohane:

> A middle power is a state whose leaders consider that it cannot act effectively by itself, but may have a systemic impact in a small group or through an international institution.[55]

Accordingly he calls middle powers "system-affecting states."[56] But the acceptance of such a definition would force the inclusion of a large number of states whose strength does not justify calling them middle powers. For example, Syria, Egypt, Israel, Uganda, Serbia (1914), Montenegro (1914, in the Balkan League), and Cuba have or had an important impact on their respective regions and occasionally beyond, but still they cannot qualify as middle powers on a worldwide scale.

Other definitions stress the importance of the middle powers to the great powers in the larger worldwide balance of power. Unlike the weak states, these are countries whose defection from one "camp" to another could seriously undermine the existing balance of power. In other words, their strength and potential strength are of more than marginal value to the great powers.[57] They are, therefore, states "whose behavior must be taken into account by the major powers in their key decisions...."[58]

Unfortunately, reality does not conform to this description. On important matters, the super powers do not hesitate to reach decisions over the heads of the great powers, not to mention the middle powers. The United States, despite the direct effect of her decisions on Canada during and on the eve of the Cuban missile crisis, did *not* consult that country. Nor did the US seriously consult Australia in regard to its policy in Vietnam. And even worse, Russia did not hesitate to invade Czechoslovakia, a fraternal communist country.

Still other definitions focus on the capacity of the middle powers to produce nuclear weapons on relatively short notice,[59] and therefore would include as middle powers

> those industrialized or semi-industrialized nations capable of making the $10–20 billion allocation over a five-to-fifteen year period to develop a significant nuclear force.[60]

As the number of weak states achieving the scientific and technical knowhow to develop nuclear weapons grows, and as new and cheaper processes are developed to produce the fissionable material necessary, this definition, if accepted, would become obsolete. Nor would every weak state acquiring nuclear weapons automatically turn into a "roaring mouse."

There is obvious difficulty in finding a simple and satisfactory definition of a middle power. The more criteria used, and the more known of a state's past and the promise of its future, the better can one decide on its inclusion in that class. In the final analysis, the decision will remain partly intuitive—in some degree a matter of taste.

The Weak States

Now the stage has been set for the main concern of this study—the problem of defining and characterizing the weak states. As a class these states score considerably lower than the middle states on a *combination* of the criteria used above. Occasionally, however, a weak state will score fairly high on one or even two factors. The weak states, of course, form the largest class of states and have the most diverse membership—facts which make it still more difficult to assign them any common denominator other than their overall relative weakness. Nevertheless, it will become clear that some of the weak states are not totally lacking in strength.

Some books of considerable importance on the position of the weak (small) states in the international system have made no attempt to define them.[61] Either a general consensus on the nature of the states has been assumed, or else the discussions included *implicit* definitions, expressed in the choice of states discussed and in the analysis of their various characteristics and problems.

Many scholars have tried to suggest an upper limit for weak states in terms of their population. Thomas Masaryk and Sir J. A. R. Marriott saw as weak all those European states whose populations were under 20 million.[62] R. P. Barston set his maximum at 10–15 million.[63] An even lower cut-off point of 10 million has been suggested by Simon Kuznets.[64]

David Vital has refined this approach by proposing one limit for developed weak states (10–15 million) and another for underdeveloped ones (20–30 million).[65] Combining population with GNP, Vellut postulates three classes of "small powers":

1) 10–50 million population and/or 2–10 billion GNP.
2) 5–10 million population and/or 1–2 billion GNP.
3) below 5 million population and below 1 billion GNP.[66]

(Most of the last class will be referred to below as *mini-states*.)

All such limits are highly artificial. For example, in *The Power of Small States,* Annette Baker Fox calls countries such as Turkey and Spain small (weak) states, but Vital, Barston, and Kuznets do not even consider them because each has a population of over 30 million. Yet in terms of their overall capabilities, these countries quite clearly fall short of the middle powers, and they are usually referred to as weak or small states.

Raising the upper population limit might solve the problem of classifying the states that fall between these definitions, but obviously size of population cannot serve as a satisfactory criterion. Bangladesh with close to 72 million people must be considered a weak state, while Australia with a population closer to 13 million is best regarded as a middle power.

The use of multiple criteria[67] in evaluating the position of weak states leads to a better understanding of their relative strength. On the whole, weak states score relatively low on most of the criteria used here. And the larger the combination of criteria employed, the lower the weak states score in comparison to the great and middle powers (see Table 5).

TABLE 5
THE MILITARY AND ECONOMIC STRENGTH OF WEAK STATES

	Population (millions) 1973	Area (thousand sq. km.) 1973	GNP (billion $) 1973	GNP per capita $ 1973	Armed forces (thousands) 1973	Military expenditures (millions $) 1973	Petroleum reserve (million $) 1971
EUROPE							
ALBANIA	2.23	0.028	1.07	480	38	118	13
BELGIUM	9.71	0.030	28.71	2,960	89.6	990	—
BULGARIA	8.54	0.110	7.02	820	152	301	38
CZECHOSLOVAKIA	14.50	0.127	30.79	2,120	190	1,336	68
DENMARK	4.96	0.043	17.02	3,430	39.8	568	—
FINLAND	4.68	0.337	11.92	2,550	39.5	231	—
GERMANY (EAST)	17.05	0.107	34.89	2,190	132	2,031	—
GREECE	8.97	0.131	11.23	1,250	160	580	38
NETHERLANDS	13.19	0.040	34.60	2,620	112.2	2,102	479
NORWAY	3.90	0.324	12.22	3,130	35.4	665	7
POLAND	32.50	0.312	29.40	1,212	287	2,200	—
PORTUGAL	20.47	0.092	7.05	730	204	425	—
RUMANIA	9.71	0.237	15.22	740	170	528	198
SWEDEN	8.11	0.449	34.38	4,240	750	1,883	—
SWITZERLAND	6.32	0.041	22.99	3,640	600	799	43
YUGOSLAVIA	20.72	0.255	15.18	730	240	826	
ASIA							
AFGHANISTAN	14.58	0.647	1.14	80	84	35	—
BURMA	29.57	0.678	2.43	80	149	91	5
IRAQ	9.75	0.434	3.56	370	101.8	338	4,420
ISRAEL	3.01	0.020	6.60	2,190	300	1,474	—
PHILIPPINES	37.91	0.300	9.16	240	42.7	95	—
SAUDI ARABIA	7.48	2.149	4.01	540	42.5	1,090	18,737
SOUTH KOREA	31.84	0.098	9.14	290	633.5	476	—
SRI LANKA	12.84	0.650	1.26	100	12.5	29	—
TAIWAN	14.88	0.036	6.44	430	503	700	—
THAILAND	37.34	0.514	7.82	210	180	293	—
TURKEY	36.16	0.780	12.16	340	477	812	26
VIETNAM (NORTH)	21.60	0.158	2.16	100	578	584	—
VIETNAM (SOUTH)	18.80	0.173	4.35	230	572	379	—

DEFINITIONS AND CHARACTERISTICS

TABLE 5 (continued)

	Gas reserve (billion cubic meters) 1971	Coal reserve (million metric tons) 1971	Energy production (million metric tons equiv. of coal) 1971	Energy consumption (million metric tons equiv. of coal) 1971	Energy consumption per capita (kg. equiv. of coal) 1971	Crude steel (thousand metric tons) 1971	Merchant marine (thousand gross registered tons) 1971
EUROPE							
ALBANIA	—	—	2.12	1.40	634	—	—
BELGIUM	—	1,796	11.18	61.57	6,116	12,449	1,192
BULGARIA	28	1,147	14.80	34.41	4,008	1,947	742
CZECHOSLOVAKIA	11	11,573	81.79	95.92	6,615	12,064	103
DENMARK	—	—	—	26.45	5,327	471	4,020
FINLAND	—	—	1.31	20.30	4,334	1,025	1,630
GERMANY (EAST)	—	50	84.10	107.49	6,308	5,350	1,198
GREECE	—	—	3.92	13.01	1,470	210	15,329
NETHERLANDS	2,498	2,394	64.15	66.89	5,069	5,083	4,972
NORWAY	396	166	8.67	20.29	5,189	863	23,507
POLAND	85	45,741	163.80	143.24	4,374	12,738	925
PORTUGAL	—	26	1.02	7.14	805	386	2,013
RUMANIA	250	590	62.78	60.90	2,975	6,803	446
SWEDEN	—	90	6.51	49.35	6,089	5,263	5,632
SWITZERLAND	—	—	4.01	22.63	3,575	532	212
YUGOSLAVIA	44	319	23.13	33.03	2,973	2,256	1,588
ASIA							
AFGHANISTAN	—	85	3.54	0.47	27	—	—
BURMA	3	21	1.15	1.93	68	—	—
IRAQ	566	—	110.07	6.34	650	—	121
ISRAEL	—	—	8.23	8.16	2,710	120	698
PHILIPPINES	—	105	0.37	11.32	298	—	925
SAUDI ARABIA	1,818	1,185	295.35	7.87	988	—	—
SOUTH KOREA	—	—	12.95	27.94	860	2,180	1,057
SRI LANKA	—	—	0.10	2.07	163	—	—
TAIWAN	—	—	—	—	296	40	108
THAILAND	—	—	0.39	10.47	—	—	—
TURKEY	9	1,335	11.01	18.65	516	1,312	743
VIETNAM (NORTH)	—	1,000	3.48	3.56	290	—	—
VIETNAM (SOUTH)	—	1,000	—	5.46	—	—	—

TABLE 5 (continued)

	Gas reserve (billion cubic meters) 1971	Coal reserve (million metric tons) 1971	Energy production (million metric tons equiv. of coal) 1971	Energy consumption (million metric tons equiv. of coal) 1971	Energy consumption per capita (kg. equiv. of coal) 1971	Crude steel (thousand metric tons) 1971	Merchant marine (thousand gross registered tons) 1971
AFRICA							
ALGERIA	4,417	20	52.99	7.26	492	31	—
EGYPT	57	—	19.81	9.69	282	300	243
ETHIOPIA	—	—	0.03	0.81	32	—	—
GHANA	—	—	0.36	1.65	192	—	166
LIBYA	767	—	173.18	1.15	571	—	—
NIGERIA	283	350	99.81	3.33	59	—	99
SOUTH AFRICA	—	72,465	58.83	71.71	2,895	4,739	511
TUNISIA	18	—	5.33	1.34	255	86	—
UGANDA	—	—	0.10	0.73	72	—	—
ZAIRE	—	73	0.56	1.73	77	—	—
LATIN AMERICA							
CHILE	66	218	9.08	15.09	1,516	607	382
COLOMBIA	—	12,500	21.36	13.90	638	239	232
CUBA	—	—	0.26	9.97	1,152	140	398
GUATEMALA	—	—	0.03	1.33	250	—	—
PARAGUAY	—	—	0.02	0.35	142	—	—
PERU	85	2,334	5.27	8.70	621	94	446
URUGUAY	—	—	0.18	2.80	958	—	143

TABLE 5 (continued)

	Population (millions) 1973	Area (thousand sq. km.) 1973	GNP (billion $) 1973	GNP per capita $ 1973	Armed forces (thousands) 1973	Military expenditures (millions $) 1973	Petroleum reserve (million $) 1971
AFRICA							
ALGERIA	14.43	2.381	5.26	360	63	100	1,283
EGYPT	34.08	1.001	7.54	220	298	1,737	138
ETHIOPIA	25.25	1.221	1.99	80	44.57	40.5	—
GHANA	8.85	0.238	2.25	250	18	30.4	—
LIBYA	2.01	1.759	2.93	1,450	25	145	3,695
NIGERIA	56.51	0.923	7.84	140	157	242	1,351
SOUTH AFRICA	22.74	1.221	18.36	810	100	716	—
TUNISIA	5.24	0.163	1.67	320	24	28.7	53
UGANDA	10.14	0.236	1.34	130	12.6	26.4	—
ZAIRE	19.32	2.345	1.75	90	50	84	—
LATIN AMERICA							
CHILE	9.99	0.756	7.55	760	60	174	15
COLOMBIA	22.32	1.138	8.18	370	63.2	92	—
CUBA	8.57	0.114	4.39	510	108.5	290	—
GUATEMALA	5.43	0.108	2.12	390	10	—	—
PARAGUAY	2.45	0.406	0.68	280	14.9	19	—
PERU	14.01	1.285	6.65	480	54	240	69
URUGUAY	2.92	0.177	2.20	750	21	77	—

Sources: World Bank Atlas 1973 (Washington, D.C., 1974); *United Nations Statistical Yearbook 1971* (New York, 1972); *The Military Balance 1973–74* (London: The Institute for Strategic Studies, 1973), pp. 74–75; United States Arms Control and Disarmament Agency *World Military Expenditures 1971* (Washington, D.C., July 1972).

A number of non-quantitative definitions of weak states also appear in the literature. Whereas one of the most important characteristics of the great powers is their military strength and capacity for self-defense, the weak states are continually preoccupied with the question of survival. They have difficulty in defending themselves against the great and middle powers, against a coalition of weak states, or even against a single weak state.

The small states are characterized by their military weakness.[68]

> ... a Small Power is a state which recognizes that it cannot obtain security primarily by use of its own capabilities, and that it must rely fundamentally on the aid of other states, institutions, processes, or developments to do so; the Small Power's belief in its inability to rely on its own means must also be recognized by the other states involved in international politics.[69]
>
> Unlike the larger members, however, none of the smaller NATO countries is able to present a credible coverage of its security needs, even in the conventional sector.[70]
>
> The large-small distinction is based on the degree to which a country can credibly cover its own security needs at any given period of time.[71]
>
> A small state . . . is a state which is *unable to contend in war with the great powers* on anything like equal terms. Unfortunately for the small states, their relative military strength has progressively declined during the past century, and very sharply since World War I, as only the large industrial countries can afford the new types of armaments. Their military weakness made them diplomatically weak. As a result they played an insignificant role in world politics. The great powers generally ignored them as vassals rather than as equals.[72]

It should not come as a surprise, therefore, that some scholars have referred to weak states, often derogatorily, as *consumers* rather than producers of security.[73]

In most of these definitions and descriptions, the weak states are contrasted, either explicitly or implicitly, with the great and super powers and not with *other weak states*. Here lies the danger of this approach. One should not compare apples and pears. Since the gap between the military capacities of weak states and great powers is so pronounced, such definitions are merely statements of the obvious. It would be much more meaningful to compare weak states with other weak states.[74]

In this century, weak states have fought one another, thus endangering their own existence, no less than have the great powers.[75]

> It is, in any case, usually more important for a small state to provide for its defence against possible enemies in its own subsystem (e.g. Israel) than to defend itself against a super power.[76]

Between weak states, the enormous gap in power disappears. They can and do successfully defend themselves against one another.

Not Russia but the Arab states are the greatest danger to Israel (and vice versa). For India it was Pakistan rather than China. For Bulgaria during the second Balkan War it was Serbia, Greece, Rumania, and Turkey. For Paraguay it was Bolivia in the Chaco War. For Hungary between the World Wars it was Czechoslovakia, Rumania, and Yugoslavia. For Kuwait it is Iraq, and for Iraq it is Iran. Therefore, when speaking of the ability or inability of a weak state to defend itself, one must immediately ask, "Against whom?"

Another fallacy is the claim that weak states in the modern world have only defensive capabilities and must renounce the use of power to achieve offensive goals.

> In summary, we can describe the small state as a state which, because of its lack of power, is unable to achieve [has to renounce] its political goals vis-a-vis most other states.[77]
>
> The states called "small powers" generally have—can only have—defensive ambitions. They seek to survive *as such* . . . the nations called "great powers" desire to possess the capacity that we have called offensive.[78]

The "weakness" of weak states is frequently mistaken for peacefulness, nonaggressiveness, and the desire to maintain the status quo. In his classic statement on the peaceful nature of weak states, H. A. L. Fisher has overly idealized the noble motives of such highly cultured societies as ancient Greece, Florence, Geneva, Goethe's Weimar, and Holland.[79] It is obvious that many of today's (and yesterday's) weak states are far from his ideal of the cultured city-state. But from the moral point of view:

> There is little evidence that small states are more peaceable than great powers. It is rather that the former are less militarily effective than the latter, not more peace loving.... If the exercise of state power is ever morally questionable we cannot help noticing that small states exercise it as readily as they can. There seems little evidence that the political initiatives of small states, however constrained, are characterized by a greater delicacy of scruple, or perceptibly more prudence, than those of greater neighbors... we may reach the conclusion that the belief in the superior virtues of small states is a romantic illusion.
>
> Small states, in short, are great powers writ small. They behave as much like great powers as they can. Nor should we blame them for this. They belong to an international order which requires them to exercise what power they have.... Nor can they escape from this international order without ceasing to exist as states. Any distinctiveness in small state behavior arises not from any qualitative difference between small states and others but from the limitations their smallness places upon their capacity to implement significant decisions in foreign policy.[80]

Naturally it is often in the interest of weaker states to appear more virtuous and moral than the more powerful states.

Others apparently feel that weak states pursue a de facto policy of nonaggression for pragmatic reasons.

> If Small States are on the whole internationally less sinful than Great Powers it is not because they are more saintly but because they are less apt to be successful sinners.[81]
>
> ... small nations have no imperial ambitions—not because they are better than any other nations in any way, but because the actual facts of their situation bar them from imperialistic ambitions.[82]
>
> Small States can obviously be just as aggressive and expansionist as Great Powers, even if they cannot pursue such a policy as effectively.[83]

But there is no reason why weak states cannot be effectively aggressive *against other weak states*.

The belief in the pacific nature of weak states is largely based on modern European history. Countries such as Belgium, the Netherlands, Portugal, and Denmark had to be content willy-nilly with the status quo in Europe. But this did not prevent their aggression and expansion *outside* the European continent. In the 1970s an increasing number of dissatisfied weak states are actively pursuing policies aimed at changing the status quo in their favor. In other words, there is no direct correlation among size, relative power, and aggression. The aggressive behavior of states must be explained by other factors.[84]

In like manner, the strength of the great powers has been confused with aggression and imperialism. For example, Quincy Wright has concluded,

> There seems to have been a positive correlation between the warlikeness of a state and its relative power. The "great powers" in all periods of history have been the most frequently at war, and the small states have been the most peaceful . . . . The more important reason for the excessive belligerency of great powers, however, lies in the structure of the balance of power, which practically assures that all great powers will enter wars which threaten the balance in order to preserve it, a responsibility which smaller states do not have.[85]

Even if his conclusions are valid for the earlier part of this century, they do not necessarily hold for the present. Jorge Dominguez has found a considerable increase in the number of recent wars involving weak, underdeveloped states. But the concomitant increase in the number of weak states might necessitate some amendment of his conclusion.[86]

In general, weak states must take defensive positions against the great and super powers. Occasionally, however, a weak state takes a *limited offensive* posture against a great or super power, often defying it with a certain degree of success. In fishing disputes, Iceland and Peru have successfully resisted British and American pressures. North Korea challenged the United States with impunity, and went unpunished in the Pueblo incident. Serbia risked the wrath of Austria before World War I.

It is not accurate to minimize the offensive capabilities of weak states and to imply that aggression is the prerogative of the powers alone. For, paradoxically, the use of coercive force by the super powers is of diminishing value. The powers have to bow to the "new norms" of international conduct which not only stress nonviolent means of coercion, but above all insist that the initiation of force by a super or great power

against a weak state is an act reminiscent of imperialism and colonialism, and hence is taboo.

In a competitive world, where the great powers do not want to alienate the weak states, the powers' ability to use force has become very limited indeed, as can be seen in the following incidents: the failure of the French and British in Suez in 1956 and their reluctant withdrawal from imperial possessions; the inability of the United States to coerce the Cuban government or to win the war in Vietnam; and Russia's acceptance of the distasteful revisionism of Rumania and Albania.

Even more than the weak states, the great powers are confined to defensive uses of power. (Events in Santo Domingo in 1965 and in Czechoslovakia in 1968 were exceptions.) Moreover, the super powers must behave with cautious constraint because their mutual nuclear deterrence has led to mutual neutralization and stalemate.[87] To a large extent, the opposite conclusion is true for weak states: they have more opportunities for and fewer restraints on the application of force.

Furthermore, the dilemma of security and survival is not the exclusive problem of weak states.[88] Japan, West Germany, Italy, and China (in the 1950s) all had or still have to depend on the nuclear and conventional power of the United States (and Russia). Also, for the acquisition of modern, sophisticated weapons they must rely on the super powers whose research abilities are much more advanced and whose production costs are lower.

For a long period, before the development of intercontinental and submarine-based missiles, even the security of the great powers (especially the United States) was based on the cooperation and good will of other states in permitting the use of their territory for bases, early warning systems, and so forth. The United States still depends on Canada's benevolence for the maintenance of its Distant Early Warning System (DEW line).

The ability of all states to defend themselves by their own efforts is a relative one. The super and great powers can do so better than the weak states, but they are not totally self-reliant.

Other characterizations of weak states stress the fact that because of their general military and economic weakness, they do not weigh heavily in the international balance of power. Hence their shifting from one side to another is of no consequence to the overall balance among the great and super powers. Some scholars consider the weak states to be simply *quantités négligeables*.[89]

> The small state (or minor or tertiary) power, in other words, is that state which, in the long term, in itself and as a satellite or client or close ally—i.e. as a non-autonomous participant in international politics—can constitute no more than a dispensable and non-decisive increment to a primary state's total array of political and military resources, regardless of whatever short-term, contingent weight as an auxiliary (or obstacle) to the primary power it may have in certain circumstances.[90]

Wilhelm G. Grewe, for example, suggests that from the point of view of the great powers, the difference between middle powers and weak (small) states may be stated as follows: the defection of a middle power might prove critical to the balance of power, but if a weak state switched sides, it would not upset the balance. For example, he proposes that the "defection" of Cuba to the Socialist camp (or Russian orbit) was of no importance to the United States.[91] I disagree. Whatever the importance of Cuba's action, the American reaction did not indicate indifference towards its "defection." On the contrary, the United States was forced to swallow a bitter *fait accompli*.

It is true that the value of a single weak state may be minimal. But if a weak state shifts its position, there is always the possibility that this action will have a contagious or catalytic effect on other weak states. Therefore, for psychological as well as political and military reasons, it is in the best interests of a super power to prevent such a move, whether by force or by positive rewards.

Indeed, the United States' intervention in Lebanon, Santo Domingo, and South Vietnam—actions stemming from this "Domino Theory"—as well as the Russian invasions of Hungary and Czechoslovakia, indicate the importance attributed to weak states in the world balance of power.

While it is true that states such as Guatemala, Honduras, Paraguay, Ceylon, Uganda, and Luxembourg are of little obvious significance to the great powers, countries such as

Saudi Arabia and Kuwait, which control enormous oil reserves, can no longer be considered of marginal worth. Even though the value of foreign military bases is on the decline, such weak states as Malta and Iceland are also of considerable strategic importance.

In like manner, Cuba as a base for Soviet submarines, missiles, and ideology so close to the United States, or Egypt as the opinion leader in the Arab world, can affect the perceived or actual balance of power, even if not critically. Therefore, it cannot be said that weak states are of little or no value, but only that they are *less important than the middle powers* for maintaining the balance of power.

It has been observed that the range of interests of the super and great powers is characteristically global. At the same time, most of the literature agrees that the range of interests and influence of the weak states is relatively limited. Annette Baker Fox combines their marginal importance to the great powers with their limited range of interests.

> We can think of small states as those whose leaders (as well as those of other powers) recognize that their own state's political weight is limited to a local arena rather than to the global one, that they are dependent upon outside political forces for much of their security, and that their particular state's interests may be dispensable in the eyes of one or more great powers.[92]
>
> Small powers are almost by definition "local" powers whose demands are restricted to their own and immediately adjacent areas . . . the power of the small state is narrow in "domain" however much or little may be its "weight."[93]

In other words, the outlook of weak states and their leaders is provincial or parochial.[94] "Where the great affairs of the world impinge on them directly, the leaders of a small power will therefore generally find themselves operating in the light of their own regional interests, conflicts and fears."[95]

This narrower outlook has considerable merit. All scholars agree that because weak states are able to focus their attention on a limited range of foreign policy problems, they have a relative advantage over decision-makers in the super and great powers. Policy-makers in weak states have a closer knowledge of issues involved and fewer distractions. But when weak states are faced with problems of a much wider scope or with issues *directly* involving the great or super powers, the information available to them is often inferior, so that they find themselves dependent on intelligence supplied to them by the powers.[96]

During the Middle Eastern wars of 1967 and 1973, the Israelis and Arabs could concentrate their attention on the local crises. On the other hand, on these occasions the United States' leaders had to contend with the problems of Vietnam, Russia, European "allies," SALT talks, and complicated domestic difficulties, as well as the Middle Eastern issues. Russia was in the same predicament.

For weak states, the question is often simply, "Is it good or bad for us?" They can then try to act on the answer to the best of their abilities. But for a super power, the most appropriate action in one part of the world might actually weaken its position elsewhere. Thus the overriding consideration in Finland's foreign policy is to achieve a modus vivendi with the USSR and to tailor its policy accordingly. But for Russia, Finland is only one problem—one problem with lower priority than the Middle East, China, the United States, or Eastern Europe.[97]

> Possibly the main advantage a small power's foreign minister has over his great-power colleague is that he is not obliged to adopt a position on every international issue that arises.[98]

Despite their generally narrower focus, there are specific subjects on which even the weak states can have worldwide interests. Norway and Greece have farflung maritime interests,[99] Israel has expressed concern for the welfare of Jews in all countries, and Spain may still have an influential position in Spanish-speaking Latin America. These interests can be political or cultural, but unlike the hegemonial powers, weak states do not have the muscle to protect worldwide interests, and thus they are limited by the goodwill of the other countries involved.

Attempts have been made to define the behavior of weak states as relatively passive and reactive in contrast to the more active and dynamic roles of the great powers. One frequently finds them referred to as "objects," "pawns," and "vassals."[100] More sophisticated works take into account the bargaining leverage of the weak states and the frequent instances of their manipulating great powers for their own ends, and thus avoid such belittling metaphors. Nevertheless, some scholars still see passivity as a major trait of weak states.

Michael Brecher differentiates between two components in the conduct of foreign policy of a given state: an *initiating* element and a *reactive* element. The policy of each state is a mixture of the two. Usually, the more powerful a state is, the more the initiating element is evident in its foreign policy. Professor Brecher, however, does not completely exclude the possibility of initiative by weak states, generally on a regional level.[101]

Other discussions of the passivity of weak states are unfortunately more simplistic.

> For smaller powers this normally is more a matter of reacting to situations created by others over whom they have little or no control, than it is of taking the obvious and direct measures that would, on the face of it, seem the simplest way of getting what they want. Not all of the smaller powers fully recognize the limitations on their abilities to take initiatives and see them through. But a moment's reflection on recent international history will reveal at least that the non-greats' main activities have been to respond to situations presented to them by those more powerful than themselves and that most of their decisions have been on how to deal with situations they had little or no part in creating.[102]

Attempts to determine whether small or weak states are more passive than large and powerful states continue to preoccupy scholars. These attempts, however, may prove an unproductive area of research. Whether a human being is active or passive, an introvert or an extrovert, has nothing to do with his physical strength, height, or weight. The same is true of states. Efforts to correlate states according to their strength or size with such Jungian terms as "acquiescence", "withdrawal oriented", "activist involvement", or "inner directed" are sterile for a number of reasons:

1) The question of passivity or activity might be more of a question of "national style" or "national character" than of size or stage of development. Thus Danish passivity in foreign affairs may be attributed more to national character than to the size of Denmark.

2) Often it is the leader of a state and his character or ambition that shape the style and activity of a country's foreign policy. Ghana under Nkruma, Indonesia under Sukarno, France under de Gaulle, Uganda under Amin, Cuba under Castro, are examples which display an active and often aggressive style in their foreign policies. A leader's activity in world affairs may have nothing to do with the size or strength of his country, but more with his own personality.

3) A country may be very active in some areas of interest, but less so in others. It may be active on a regional basis but passive on the global level, or vice versa. Often passivity or activity is not determined by the country itself, but forced upon it by the behavior and policies of its neighbors. New Zealand is a small state whose passivity is dictated not by its size but by its remote location. Cuba is small and weak but pursues an active and often offensive foreign policy . . . perhaps due to Castro's restless character, its revolutionary ideology, or Russian pressure.

It will prove more productive to find a correlation between foreign policy and ideology, a leader's character, a state's geographic location, and its regional problems. Size and stage of development may have little bearing on a pursued plan of foreign policy.[103]

A corollary of the assumed passive behavior of weak states is that they cannot affect the structure of the international system, since this framework is an external "given."

> Great powers determine the nature of systemic patterns; as such they can alter the system or perhaps merely ignore its imperatives without suffering grievously. Small powers on the other hand are much more limited in their freedom by the nature of the systemic structure. For the most part they are dominated by the system, in the sense that the opportunities they have are dependent on the kind of system which exists. They can rarely create their own opportunities.[104]

Even if one agrees that the nature of the international system is primarily determined by the number of great powers and their interrelationships, weak states are by no means impotent, helpless victims of the system. On the contrary, they are quick to take advantage of the opportunities arising from the nature of any given international system. They learn to manipulate the competition between the great powers to their own ends, and in this way they exert a considerable influence, even if not a critical one, on the system itself.

It is therefore difficult to accept the generalization that weak states tend to be more passive than great powers. Such a statement confuses the limited strength of the weak states, their light "weight" on the balance of power, and their occasional support of a convenient status quo (for example, in Europe) with passivity and resignation. Because weak states lack the strength to sanction and reward, fewer viable policy options may be open to them. But this condition is not the same thing as passivity.

The degree to which a country has an effect on the international system is not an indication of activity or passivity. The United States' isolationism between the World Wars might be regarded as a passive static policy, but it nevertheless had considerable effect on the international system. Conversely, within the limits of their strength, weak states such as Yugoslavia, Cuba, Albania, Israel, and the Arab countries have pursued highly active and ambitious foreign policies; and these countries have not failed to leave their mark on the international system. Slogans such as the "power of the weak,"[105] "tyranny of the weak,"[106] "weak but not meek,"[107] "the big influence of small allies,"[108] and "the tail that wags the dog" all indicate the greater than marginal influence of the weak states on the international system and the big powers.

Because interstate warfare is not frequent in this age of nuclear deterrence, the actual and potential economic strength of a state, which often reflects its military power, becomes more important for determining its rank in the international hierarchy. Weak states may therefore be defined in economic terms.

> . . . [it] seems preferable to define a small nation as one which, while depending comparatively heavily upon foreign trade both for supplies and sales markets, makes only a modest contribution to the aggregate flow of international trade . . . a nation is small from the point of view of foreign trade when its dependence on foreign markets is relatively great but its contribution to them small in absolute terms.[109]
>
> . . . most small countries have a more specialized export industry

than large countries. This follows from the distribution of natural resources over the world surface, from regional differences in climate and traditions, and from advantages in specialization and large-scale production. It is easy to find examples where agricultural or forest products, fish, ore, oil or shipping dominate the exports of small countries. Large countries are less likely to have all their export eggs in one or a few baskets. There is, therefore, an *a priori* likelihood that small countries will more often find themselves for periods in a favorable or unfavorable situation as regards the trends and potentialities of their dominating exports.[110]

Economically, as militarily and politically, the weak states are at a serious disadvantage when compared with the great and middle powers. But even here, as we shall see below in chapter five, they can find ways to compensate for their weakness.

The Mini States

> You will find us only on the very best atlases, because we are the smallest country left in Europe—and when I say country, I don't mean principality or grand duchy. I don't mean a haven for gambling or income tax evasion—I mean self-respecting country which deserves, and sometimes achieves, a colour of its own on the map—usually a dyspeptic mint green, which misses the outline of the frontier by a fraction of an inch, so that one can almost hear the printer saying damn. Our population is so small, that it's not worth counting.
>
> Peter Ustinov,
> *Romanoff and Juliet,* Act I.

The last (and least) group of states in the international hierarchy of power are the so-called "mini"- or "micro"-states. The problems of defining the mini-states are as complicated as those encountered in defining the larger and more powerful states.[111]

Most of the mini-states have a very small population as well as very little territory. Exceptions would be states with a rather large population concentrated in a limited area (over four million in Hong Kong and two million in Singapore), or alternatively, relatively large territories that are very sparsely populated (such as Mauritania). Many of these mini-states are still colonial dependencies, though a large number of them have by now attained an independent or semi-independent status. Many are isolated islands. Most of them have common and serious economic problems resulting from their lack of material and human resources. Clearly the question of self-defense is irrelevant, as none of these states can effectively defend itself by its own devices against even the weakest of other states.

Jacques Rapaport differentiates the mini-states from the weak states by setting an upper limit of one million inhabitants.[112] Patricia Blair sets the population maximum at 300,000,[113] while Stanley de Smith draws the line at 150,000.[114]

There is no need to go into further detail on the mini-states since this study is not concerned with the weakest of all states, but with weak states in general. Methodologically, all the criteria that apply to weak states apply even more readily to the mini-states. Table 6 lists some of the best-known mini-states and their characteristics.

Summary: The Ideal Type of The Weak State

The foregoing discussion has made one thing clear—that it is impossible to define any of the groups of states in the international hierarchy in one concise, precise, and elegant statement. In terms of strength, states are not static entities. Their position on the continuum is constantly being challenged, tested, and changed.

This dynamic situation cannot be captured by a simple set of measures; instead, a very large set of criteria must be used. Some are easily quantified, while others are highly intuitive and qualitative, yet no less important. After all, much of the foreign policy behavior of the various states is based on intuitive evaluations by policy-makers in trying to assess the relative strength and position of the opposition, including judgments on national morale, quality of leadership, scope of interests, organization, and the other states' perception of relative strength.

The main danger lies in simplistic attempts to evaluate the relative position of states in the international system by con-

TABLE 6
ECONOMIC AND DEMOGRAPHIC DATA ON MINI-STATES 1973

MINI-STATE	Population	Area (sq. km.)	Population density (per sq. km.)	GNP (million $)	GNP per capita	UN membership
COCOS IS.	618	14	44	n.a.	n.a.	no
CONGO BRAZZAVILLE	1,123,000	842,000	1.3	300	267	yes
CYPRUS	640,000	9,251	69	700	1,093	yes
GABON	494,000	267,667	1.8	340	688	yes
GAMBIA	370,000	11,295	33	50	135	yes
GREENLAND	47,000	2,175,600	.002	90	1,870	no
HONG KONG	4,045,000	1,034	3,912	3,650	902	no
ICELAND	206,000	103,000	2	510	2,475	yes
KUWAIT	830,000	17,818	47	3,200	3,855	yes
LUXEMBURG	339,000	2,586	131	1,060	3,126	yes
MALDIVE IS.	110,000	298	369	10	91	yes
MALTA	330,000	316	1,044	280	230	yes
MAURITANIA	1,190,000	1,030,000	1.2	200	848	yes
MONACO	23,035	1.5	15,357	n.a.	n.a.	no
SAN MARINO	12,100	61	198	n.a.	n.a.	yes
SINGAPORE	2,110,000	581	3,632	2,530	1,199	yes
SOUTH W. AFRICA (NAMIBIA)	589,000	824,292	0.7	n.a.	n.a.	no
TRINIDAD AND TOBAGO	1,030,000	5,128	201	970	942	yes

Sources: *World Bank Atlas 1973* (Washington, D.C., 1974), passim; Jacques Rapaport et al., *Small States and Territories: Status and Problems* (New York: Arno Press, 1971), pp. 59–78.

centrating primarily, if not exclusively, on those characteristics which are relatively easy to quantify and tabulate neatly, while neglecting to take into account many really important—but somewhat intuitive—criteria. The tendency to focus on what is measurable results from the desire, shared by many social scientists, to find clear-cut, unambiguous answers and definitions where they do not exist, in other words, to define the indefinable. Unfortunately, this intolerance towards ambiguity limits their understanding of many a social—or in this case international—phenomenon, for its essence is to be found precisely in its ambiguity and uncertainty. Indeed, as Hans Morgenthau (and Hobbes long before) has shown, one statesman's inability to evaluate another's real strength correctly is at the root of all power politics (both domestic and international); hence there is a continuous struggle to obtain additional strength to assure a larger margin of safety.[115]

This is why diplomacy and the study of international politics is still more of an art than a science. While the beauty of a formula in the natural sciences lies in its clarity, precision, and the use of a minimum number of variables, the more precise a social scientist wishes to be, the larger the set of "variables" (criteria) he must use in order to approach a social truth. To that degree, his description becomes more complicated and less elegant. It is the essence of politics—a situation of antagonism and conflict—that ambiguity and uncertainty are dominant traits and cannot be eliminated.

Furthermore, the study of politics deals with relative as well as absolute phenomena. As long as scholars employ terms which have no universally accepted definitions—"imperialism," "power," "intervention," "small states," and so on—international relations cannot be an exact science. The general meaning of such terms is obvious to all, until an attempt is made to clarify the meaning and reach an exact understanding.

Since this study deals with relative, not absolute phenomena, it is readily apparent that no state is entirely strong or wholly weak. The United States could not win the war in Vietnam on its own terms, nor could it shape or even influence Cuba's foreign policy after Castro took over. The Soviet Union has to tolerate many provocations from weak countries such as Albania, Yugoslavia, or Rumania; it cannot translate its over-

DEFINITIONS AND CHARACTERISTICS 51

whelming power into total political influence over these countries.

The weak states are not entirely weak. They have important internal sources of strength which they have learned to use to their advantage. They have also learned to manipulate the strength of the great powers on their own behalf, and to draw on this external source of strength to further their own national interests. And yet, when the chips were down, the USSR did not hesitate to attack Finland, annex Estonia, Latvia, and Lithuania, or divide Poland with Germany. Similarly, the United States sacrificed Taiwan's interests in the United Nations, coerced South Vietnam into an undesirable peace (from South Vietnam's point of view), and forced Israel to make concessions to the Arabs.

But all in all, the great powers are still more powerful than they are weak, and the weak states are characterized by their relative weakness, not strength. Weak states do not usually "twist the arms" of the big powers. Saudi Arabia cannot occupy the United States, even though it can refuse to sell its oil, while the United States could conceivably occupy Saudi Arabia. The USSR can invade Czechoslovakia, which can only resist passively and cannot invade the USSR in turn.

In evaluating the *relative* strength or weakness of a state, its geographic location must be taken into account. The position or ranking of a state should not be compared with *all* others. States cannot be ranked like football teams in one international league. In such a rating system, Canada and Mexico would clearly be middle powers. But a perusal of Canadian and Mexican literature on their own foreign policies makes it clear that both states are frustrated and overwhelmed by their giant neighbor, next to whom they feel dwarfed. Their political, economic, and military dependence on the United States makes them perceive themselves as much weaker than they really are.

Similarly, although earlier in this century Poland ranked quite high and had a semi-permanent seat in the League of Nations Council in recognition of its middle-power status, it was in a vulnerable geographic location, squeezed in between two hostile giants whose only common interest was their desire to partition Poland for the fourth time. The country was also in conflict with all its smaller neighbors, which depreciated its real strength.[116]

Ireland is a weak state in absolute terms but has no threatening enemies. Israel's armed forces are large in absolute terms but small in relation to the combined forces of the Arab states. The power of a state is thus best measured not against all other countries, but in relation to its neighbors, and by the degree to which the strength at its disposal matches its national goals and ambitions.

Since no single definition of a weak or powerful state is completely satisfactory, it is necessary to find a methodological substitute that will better reflect the complex problem of characterizing the relative power of states. Such an alternative method must take into account the enormous power differentials between the strong and the weak states, while at the same time acknowledging that the line between strength and weakness is not always easy to distinguish in reality.

To solve this methodological quandary, I propose the construction of two ideal types,[117] one of the "almighty" super power and the other of the weak state. In the model below, the characteristics preceded by an asterisk are questionable, as I have already explained.

CRITERIA	THE WEAK STATE	THE STRONG STATE
POPULATION	Very small	Very large
AREA	Very small	Very large
ECONOMY	1. GNP small in *absolute* terms. 2. Little or no heavy industry. 3. High degree of specialization in a narrow range of products. 4. Small domestic market, hence high dependency on foreign markets for imports and exports. 5. R and D very low in absolute terms.	1. GNP very high in absolute terms. 2. Very large, highly developed heavy industry (including weapons). 3. Very high degree specialization in large variety of products. 4. Very large domestic market, hence little dependence on foreign export/import trade. 5. R and D very high in absolute terms.

DEFINITIONS AND CHARACTERISTICS

CRITERIA	THE WEAK STATE	THE STRONG STATE
	6. High dependence on foreign capital.	6. No dependence on foreign capital.
MILITARY POWER	1. Cannot defend itself against external threats by its own strength; high or total dependence on external help.	1. Can defend itself by its own power against *any* state or combination of states; very little reliance on external support.
	2. Total (or very high) dependence on weapon acquisition in foreign countries.	2. Has full array of nuclear weapons and their delivery systems.
	3. A high proportion of strength always mobilized or at its disposal; longer-range *war potential* very low.	3. Domestic production of all weapons systems. 4. Large standing armies, combined with very high war potential.
THE INTER- NATIONAL SYSTEM	1. Limited scope of interests (usually to neighboring and regional areas).	1. Worldwide (global) interests.
	2. Little or no influence on the balance of power (or the nature of the system).	2. Weighs heavily in world balance of power; shapes the nature of the international system.
	*3. Mainly passive and reactive in foreign policy.	*3. Pursues a dynamic and active foreign policy.
	*4. Tends to minimize risks, especially vis-a-vis the powers.	*4. Tends to maximize gains (rather than minimize risks).
	*5. Can be "penetrated" relatively easily.	*5. Relatively difficult to "penetrate" (depends on nature of the internal political system).
	*6. Strong support for international law and norms and of international organizations.	*6. Low regard for international law and organizations; prefers power and summit policies.

*Characteristics frequently found in the literature with which I do not entirely agree. See text above.

These two ideal types are exaggerated abstractions of reality. Although a given state may approximate to one of the ideal types, it can never be identical with it. In reality, any one state is a mixture of characteristics found in each model. The relative strength of these opposing qualities determines whether a given country has more in common with the ideal weak state or the ideal super power. The great advantage of the ideal type method is that it reflects the complexity of the situation without simplifying it—that it stresses the relative qualities of each type of state rather than dealing in absolutes.

In only two of the many books I have read on weak states have I encountered even an embryonic suggestion concerning an ideal type of the weak state. Neither author makes any attempt to construct an actual model. B. H. M. Vlekke, in his introduction to Van Campen's *The Quest for Security,* speaks of the problems involved in the study of weak states:

> The diversity [among weak states] is so great that the question may be asked whether it is permissible at all to speak of the *"average small state."* It is possible, however, to describe an *imaginary small state* on the basis of those characteristics which are common features of many existing small states.[118]

Maurice East suggests the abstraction of a "conventional model" of a small state's behavior, which includes seven somewhat overlapping patterns exhibited by weak states. Some of the characteristics he gives for weak states are invalid, and he does not fully develop his model.[119]

NOTES

1. Laszlo Reczei, "The Political Aims and Experiences of the Small Socialist States," in August Schou and Arne Olav Brundtland (eds.), *Small States in International Relations* (Stockholm: Almquist and Wiksell, 1971), p. 76.
2. Herbert Goldhamer, *The Foreign Powers in Latin America* (Princeton: Princeton University Press, 1972), p. 237, n. 29.
3. Lewis Carroll, *The Annotated Alice* (Cleveland: The World Publishing Company, 1970), p. 269.
4. Note the following titles: David Vital, *The Inequality of States: A Study of the Small Power in International Affairs* (Oxford: Clarendon

Press, 1967) and *The Survival of Small States: Studies in Small Power/Great Power Conflict* (London: Oxford University Press, 1971); Robert L. Rothstein, *Alliances and Small Powers* (New York: Columbia University Press, 1968).
5. Raymond Aron, *Peace and War* (New York: Frederick A. Praeger, 1967), p. 55, n. 13.
6. The only work which systematically uses the term "weak states"— without, however, trying to clarify or define its meaning—is Marshall R. Singer, *Weak States in a World of Powers* (New York: The Free Press, 1972). But by "weak states" he apparently means "less developed states." It must, however, be noted that there is at least an economic basis for this confusion between weak and underdeveloped states as has been suggested by Väyrynen:

". . . small and underdeveloped powers are systematically worse off than great or rich countries . . . small size and low level of development have the same influence".

See Raimo Väyrynen, "The Position of Small Powers in the West European Network of Economic Relations," *European Journal of Political Research* (June 1974), p. 149.
7. *Schweizer Lexikon* (Zurich: Encyclios Verlag, 1947), IV, 964. For a similar definition see also *Brockhaus Enzyklopädie* (Wiesbaden: F. A. Brockhaus, 1970), X, 251.
8. Paul Herre, *Die Kleinstaaten Europas und die Entstehung des Weltkrieges* (München: C. H. Becksche Verlagsbuchhandlung, 1937), p. vii.
9. William E. Rappard, "Small States in the League of Nations," *Political Science Quarterly,* 49 (December 1934), 545. See also David Vital's article, "The Analysis of Small Power Politics," in Schou and Brundtland (eds.), *Small States in International Relations,* p. 15; and Jens Boyesen, "Contributions of Small Powers to the Alliance," in Edgar S. Furniss, Jr. (ed.), *The Western Alliance: Its Status and Prospects* (Columbus, Ohio: Ohio State University Press, 1965), p. 107.
10. For a similar discussion see David Vital, *The Survival of Small States,* p. 5.
11. See David Vital in Schou and Brundtland (eds.), *Small States in International Relations,* p. 15; also Vital, *The Survival of Small States,* p. 5; and Jorge I. Dominguez, "Mice That Do Not Roar," in *International Organization,* 25 (Spring 1971), 175.
12. For example, one qualification of a great power prior to World War II was the possession of colonies and overseas dominions. Obviously such a criterion is now out of date. In the case of some weak European states, a strange duality developed. They were powerless to defend themselves on the European continent against the powers— and yet controlled enormous colonial territories overseas (mainly Belgium, Holland and Portugal). To a large extent those territories were a source of weakness rather than power, as they were coveted by the great powers who continually devised plans to divide these colonies among themselves. See the chapters on Belgium, Holland, and Portugal

in Herre, *Die Kleinen Staaten Europas;* also Amry Vandenbusch, *Dutch Foreign Policy since 1815: A Study in Small Power Politics* (The Hague: Martinus Nijhoff, 1959).

13. For a brief discussion of mobility in the international system see Carsten Holbraad, "The Role of Middle Powers," in *Cooperation and Conflict*, 6 (1971), 78; also Singer, *Weak States in a World of Powers*, pp. 57–88; Michael David Wallace, *War and Rank Among Nations* (Lexington, Mass.: Lexington Books, D. C. Heath, 1973), p. 22.

    For a discussion of downward mobility, see Gustavo Lagos, *International Stratification and Underdeveloped Countries* (Chapel Hill: The University of North Carolina Press, 1963). Lagos suggests the neologism "*atimia,*" which stands for the loss or deterioration of status (p. ix and chapter 1). Also Raimo Väyrynen, "Stratification in the System of International Organizations," *Journal of Peace Research*, 4 (1970), pp. 291–310.

    The Netherlands, Spain, Portugal, and Sweden were once great powers. Russia declined after the 1905 war with Japan, rose afterwards, and then along with Germany, experienced a short decline after World War I. Germany, Japan, and Italy were weakened after the Second World War but have regained their strength. After World War II and until the early 1950s, Canada was considered a major power, due to the temporary decline and exhaustion of the European powers, but is now relegated to the ranks of the middle powers. See Peter C. Dobell, *Canada's Search for New Roles* (London: Oxford University Press, 1972), p. 1; and J. L. Granatstein (ed.), *Canadian Foreign Policy Since 1945: Middle Power or Satellite?* rev. ed. (Toronto: Copp Clark, 1970), p. 2.

14. According to Rothstein, weak states can find themselves in a weaker position after producing nuclear weapons for the following reasons: (a) the danger of a pre-emptive strike by one of the powers; (b) growing pressure from a super power (especially one to which it is allied) to bring such weapons under its control or eliminate them altogether under threat of withdrawal of support; (c) the prohibitive price of producing nuclear weapons might lead weak states to neglect the development of their conventional forces. Rothstein, *Alliances and Small States*, pp. 265–323. Opposing views are offered by the Swiss strategist Gustav Däniker, *Strategie des Kleinstaats* (Frauenfeld: Verlag Huber, 1966), and by Pierre Gallois, *The Balance of Terror* (Boston: Houghton Mifflin Co., 1961).

15. See Karl Deutsch, *The Analysis of International Relations* (Englewood Cliffs: Prentice Hall, 1968), p. 33, Table 6.

16. A. J. P. Taylor, *The Struggle for Mastery in Europe 1848–1918* (Oxford: Oxford University Press, 1968), pp. xxiv–xxv. See also Rothstein, *Alliances and Small Powers*, pp. 12–21.

17. See Klaus Knorr, *Military Power and Potential* (Lexington, Mass.: D. C. Heath, 1970), chap. 4, pp. 119–136; also his *War Potential of Nations* (Princeton: Princeton University Press, 1956), pp. 99–160.

18. Nadav Safran, *From War to War* (New York: Pegasus, 1969), pp. 256–265.
19. A detailed analysis of the economic power of states is not attempted here; for standard discussions see, among others: Karl Deutsch, *The Analysis of International Relations,* chap. 3, pp. 21–39; and, by Klaus Knorr: *The War Potential of Nations* (New York: Basic Books, 1973); *Military Power and Potential* (New York: Basic Books, 1973); and *Power and Wealth* (New York: Basic Books, 1973).
20. Data based on United States Arms Control and Disarmament Agency, *World Military Expenditures 1971* (Washington, D.C., July 1972), p. 50.
21. Michael Handel, *Israel's Political-Military Doctrine* (Cambridge, Mass.: Harvard University Center for International Affairs, Occasional Paper No. 30, July 1973), p. 7.
22. If the "good life" is one of the most important goals of the modern state, then some of the weak states have done at least as well as any of the super or great powers. Sweden surpassed the US in GNP per capita in 1973 for the first time, as did West Germany. See *Boston Globe,* July 15, 1973, pp. 60–61. Kuwait, Quatar, and Abu Dahbi will each have GNP per capita in excess of $10,000 in 1974. *New York Times,* March 20, 1974, pp. 53, 59.
23. Data based on *World Military Expenditures 1971,* p. 50. See also Annette Baker Fox, "The Small States in the International System 1919–1969," *International Journal,* 24 (Autumn 1969), 753.
24. See Herman Kahn and Anthony J. Wiener, *The Year 2000* (New York: Macmillan, 1968), pp. 132–133n.
25. Deutsch, *The Analysis of International Relations,* p. 37.
26. On territory as a condition for great-power ranking, see George Liska, *International Equilibrium* (Cambridge, Mass.: Harvard University Press, 1957), pp. 25–26.
27. Taylor, *The Struggle for Mastery in Europe,* p. xxiv. This axiom of international affairs can be found in any text book. See, e.g., Quincy Wright, *A Study of War* (Chicago: Chicago University Press, 1942), I, 268; and Raymond Aron, *Peace and War,* p. 60.
28. Laszlo Reczei, in Schou and Brundtland (eds.), *Small States in International Relations,* p. 73. See also George Liska, *Alliances and the Third World* (Baltimore: Johns Hopkins University Press, 1968), p. 16.
29. Rothstein, *Alliances and Small Powers,* p. 296.
30. Heinrich von Treitschke, *Politics* (New York: Macmillan, 1916), II, 607.
31. Vital, *The Survival of Small States,* p. 5.
32. One indication of Great Britain's decline as a world power is the gradual disappearance of the Royal Navy from the high seas. Before World War II, the British Navy consisted of 7 aircraft carriers, 15 battleships, 60 cruisers, and nearly 200 destroyers. It has now only 7 aircraft carriers (one in reserve), 1 cruiser, and 15 destroyers. Not one new aircraft carrier has been built since the end of the Second World

War. See C. J. E. Harlow, *The European Armaments Base: A Survey,* Part 2, *National Procurement Politics* (London: Institute for Strategic Studies, July 1967).

33. Robert O. Keohane, "Lilliputians' Dilemmas: Small States in International Politics," *International Organization,* 23 (Spring 1969), 293.
34. William E. Paterson, "Small States in International Politics," *Cooperation and Conflict,* 4 (1969), 122. Max Weber, *Economy and Society* (New York: Bedminster Press, 1968), II, 912.
35. Laszlo Reczei, in Schou and Brundtland (eds.), *Small States in International Relations,* pp. 74–75. As A. J. P. Taylor said of the Austrian Empire on the eve of the First World War, "Only the Austrian Empire had no concerns outside Europe: this was a sign of weakness, not a source of strength" (*The Struggle for Mastery in Europe,* p. xxii). Similarly Britain's withdrawal from "East of Suez" was a sign of its decline as a world power.
36. For a similar view, see Stanley Hoffmann, *Gulliver's Troubles* (New York: McGraw Hill, 1968), p. 57.
37. Keohane, "Lilliputians' Dilemmas," pp. 295, 296; also Jean-Luc Vellut, "Smaller States and the Problem of War and Peace: Some Consequences of the Emergence of Smaller States in Africa," *Journal of Peace Research,* 2 (1967), 252, 253; Stanley Hoffman, *Gulliver's Troubles,* p. 57; Arthur Andrew, *Defence by Other Means—Diplomacy for the Underdog* (Toronto: Canadian Institute of International Affairs, 1970), p. 24; Liska, *International Equilibrium,* pp. 24–25, 35.
38. Keohane, "Lilliputians' Dilemmas," p. 296.
39. Inis L. Claude, *Swords into Plowshares,* 2nd ed. (New York: Random House, 1961), p. 24; Carsten Holbraad, *The Concert of Europe* (London: Longmans, 1970), chap. 1, pp. 15–61; Edwin DeWitt Dickinson, *The Equality of States in International Law* (Cambridge, Mass.: Harvard University Press, 1920), pp. 296–301.
40. Dickinson, *The Equality of States in International Law,* pp. 348–378; H. W. V. Temperley (ed.), *A History of the Peace Conference of Paris,* I (London: Oxford University Press, 1969), 249.
41. See F. P. Walters, *A History of the League of Nations* (London: Oxford University Press, 1965), pp. 45–46.
42. See Vellut, "Smaller States and the Problem of War and Peace," p. 255. He chose the veto right at the UN as one of the criteria for being a great power.
43. Sydney D. Bailey, "Veto in the Security Council," *International Conciliation,* January 1968, no. 566, pp. 45–46. For a full list of vetoes cast see Sydney D. Bailey, *Voting in the Security Council* (Bloomington: Indiana University Press, 1969), appendix 6, pp. 159–221.
44. Andrew, *Defence by Other Means,* p. 29. On the relative position of middle powers, see also Hoffmann, *Gulliver's Troubles,* pp. 56–57.
45. Dobbel, *Canada's Search for New Roles,* p. 3.
46. In general, Deutsche Gesellschaft für Auswärtige Politik, Bonn, *Mittlere Mächte in der Weltpolitik* (Opladen: C. W. Leske Verlag, 1969).

47. Gustavo Lagos emphasizes the position of Brazil as a middle power, both in world politics and in Latin America mainly because of its future promise: "It is the image of the future potentiality of the high real status it is called to occupy within the international system, that explains its constant striving for an international policy of prestige." Lagos, *International Stratification,* p. 143.
48. *Mittlere Mächte in der Weltpolitik,* pp. 7–12, 145–155.
49. *Ibid.* Dominguez, "Mice That Do Not Roar," p. 175, also includes Czechoslovakia and Poland. Vellut, "Smaller States and the Problem of War and Peace," p. 255, adds East Germany, Argentina, and Nigeria. Singer, *Weak States in a World of Powers,* p. 65, adds the Netherlands, Belgium, Philippines, Switzerland, Rumania, and Denmark. All in all, the number of states included among the middle powers according to different definitions is 25. This is by no means a final list. See also Carsten Holbraad, "The Role of Middle Powers," in *Cooperation and Conflict,* 6 (1971), 77–90.
50. Vellut, "Smaller States and the Problem of War and Peace," p. 255.
51. Vellut, "Smaller States and the Problem of War and Peace," p. 255. Dominguez, "Mice That Do Not Roar," p. 176, suggests a minimum GNP of 20 billion, but even this higher limit seems to be dated.
52. Singer, *Weak States in a World of Powers,* p. 65.
53. Holbraad, "The Role of Middle Powers," p. 78.
54. *Mittlere Mächte in der Weltpolitik,* p. 8. See also Holbraad, "The Role of Middle Powers," p. 81.
55. Keohane, "Lilliputians' Dilemmas," p. 296. See also Dominguez, "Mice That Do Not Roar," p. 176.
56. Keohane, "Lilliputians' Dilemmas," p. 295.
57. Wilhelm G. Grewe, *Spiel der Kräfte in der Weltpolitik* (Düsseldorf: Eion Verlag, 1970), p. 28.
58. Dominguez, "Mice That Do Not Roar," p. 175.
59. *Ibid.,* p. 176.
60. William Schneider, Jr., in Holbraad, "The Role of Middle Powers," p. 81.
61. For example, Annette Baker Fox, *The Power of Small States* (Chicago: University of Chicago Press, 1967); Singer, *Weak States in a World of Powers;* V. V. Sveics, *Small Nation Survival* (New York: Exposition Press, 1970); Trygve Mathisen, *The Functions of Small States* (Oslo: Universitetforlaget, 1971).
62. T. G. Masaryk, *The Problem of Small Nations in the European Crisis* (London: University of London, Athlone Press, 1966); p. 23. J. A. R. Marriott, *Federalism and the Problem of the Small State* (London: Allen and Unwin, 1943), p. 62. In a slightly earlier article, Marriott chose an upper limit of 13 million. Marriott, "The Problem of the Small State," *The Fortnightly,* vol. 151, no. 902 (February 1942), p. 134.
63. R. P. Barston, "The External Relations of Small States," in Schou and Brundtland (eds.), *Small States in International Relations,* pp. 41, 43, 50.

64. Simon Kuznets, "Economic Growth of Small Nations," in E. A. G. Robinson (ed.), *Economic Consequences of the Size of Nations* (New York: St. Martins Press, 1960), p. 14.
65. Vital, *Inequality of States*, p. 8.
66. Vellut, "Smaller States and the Problem of War and Peace," pp. 254–256.
67. The problem of assigning relative weight to each criterion is not discussed here. For such attempts, see F. Clifford German, "A Tentative Evaluation of World Power," in *Journal of Conflict Resolution;* Jack Sawyer, "Dimensions of Nations: Size, Wealth and Politics," *American Journal of Sociology*, 72 (1967), 145–172; J. P. Cole, *Geography of World Affairs*, 4th ed. (London: Penguin Books, 1972), pp. 68–74, 370–373. For a different attempt to rank states according to their diplomatic status, see J. David Singer and Melvin Small, "The Composition and Status Ordering of the International System 1815–1940," *World Politics*, 18 (January 1966), 236–282 and "The Diplomatic Importance of States 1816–1970: An Extension and Refinement of the Indicator," *World Politics*, 25 (July 1973), 577–599.
68. Arnold Wolfers, *The Small Powers and the Enforcement of Peace*, Yale Institute of International Studies, August 1943, p. 3 (mimeo.). In all fairness, it must be mentioned that Wolfers later became aware of the improved bargaining position of the weak states in the postwar bipolar world. It was he who coined the term "the power of the weak." See Arnold Wolfers, *Discord and Collaboration* (Baltimore: The Johns Hopkins Press, 1962), p. 111.
69. Rothstein, *Alliances and Small Powers*, p. 29.
70. Nils Orvik, "NATO: The Role of the Smaller Members," *Atlantic Community Quarterly*, 4 (Spring 1966), 92.
71. Orvik, "NATO, NAFTA and the Smaller Allies," *Orbis*, 12 (Spring 1968), 455.
72. Amry Vandenbosch, "The Small States in International Politics and Organization," *The Journal of Politics*, 26 (1964), 294 (my emphasis). Raymond Aron agrees with this judgment of the relative decline in this century of the power of the weak states: "The industrial character of the war nevertheless contributed . . . towards making the big even bigger and the small even smaller, in other words to widen the gap between first-class and second-class powers." Raymond Aron, *On War* (London: Secker and Warburg, 1958), p. 57. See also E. H. Carr, *Conditions of Peace* (New York: Macmillan, 1943), p. 52, and Morgenthau, *Politics Among Nations*, p. 343.
73. See, for example, Vandenbosch, "Small States in International Politics," p. 301. The weak states have often been accused, especially after the outbreak of the Second World War, of creating power vacuums that invite aggression. For such claims, see for example Elam J. Anderson, "Is the Small State Doomed?" *Institute of World Affairs*, 17–18 (1939/1940)), 250; also Trygve Mathisen, *The Functions of Small States*, p. 23. During the Second World War many scholars came to the defense of the weak states on this issue. For example, Arnold Wolfers,

DEFINITIONS AND CHARACTERISTICS 61

"In Defense of the Small Countries," *Yale Review*, Winter 1944, pp. 201–202, 210–220. Also Dr. Hubert Ripka, *Small and Great Nations* (London: Czechoslovakia Ministry of Foreign Affairs Information Service, 1944), p. 9.

74. States have to be compared with other relevant states. ". . . most of the smaller nations, and indeed many of the larger ones, will tend to view their status in the context of a regional subsystem. The U.A.R. will probably make status comparisons with Israel or Iraq; it is very unlikely that she will do so with Brazil or Norway . . . ." Wallace, *War and Rank Among Nations*, p. 20.

75. For a similar observation see Klaus Knorr, *On the Uses of Military Power in the Nuclear Age* (Princeton: Princeton University Press, 1966), p. 170.

76. William E. Paterson, "Small States in International Politics," *Cooperation and Conflict*, 4 (1969), 120. See also Singer, *Weak States in a World of Powers*, p. 410; Annette Baker Fox in a review of Vital's book, *The Inequality of States*, in *International Journal* (1968), 623; also Lagos, *International Stratification*, p. 98.

77. Thomas Fleiner, *Die Kleinstaaten in den Staatenverbindungen des Zwanzigsten Jahrhunderts* (Zurich: Polygraphischer Verlag, 1966), p. 27. A similar definition is suggested by L. G. M. Jaquet, "The Role of Small States within Alliance Systems," in Schou and Brundtland (eds.), *Small States in International Relations* (p. 58): ". . . a small state is a state that is neither on a world scale nor on a regional scale able to impose its political will or protect its national interests by exerting power politics."

78. Aron, *Peace and War*, p. 83.

79. *Studies in History and Politics* (Oxford: Clarendon Press, 1920), pp. 161–179. For similar idealizations, see Fridtjof Nansen, "The Mission of the Small States," *The American-Scandinavian Review*, 6 (1918), 9–13; and Alfred Cobban, *The Nation State and National Self-Determination*, rev. ed. (New York: Thomas Y. Crowell, 1970), p. 292.

80. Robert Purnell, *The Society of States: An Introduction to International Politics* (London: Weidenfeld and Nicolson, 1973), pp. 98–99.

81. Rappard, "Small States in the League of Nations," p. 574.

82. Carl J. Hambro, "The Role of the Smaller Powers in International Affairs Today," *International Affairs*, 15 (March-April 1936), p. 172.

83. Herbert Tingsten, *The Debate on the Foreign Policy of Sweden 1918–1939* (London: Oxford University Press, 1949), p. 303.

84. One hypothesis is this: "The greater the inconsistency between a nation's capabilities and the reputational status accorded it in the international system, the greater the likelihood that it will engage in conflict behavior." Wallace, *War and Rank Among Nations*, p. 18.

85. *A Study of War*, II, 848–849. Wright supports this contention with statistical evidence, *ibid.*, I, 220–222.

86. Dominguez, "Mice That Do Not Roar," p. 178.

87. For a development of this argument see Stanley Hoffmann, *Gulliver's Troubles*, part I; Knorr, *On the Uses of Military Power in the Nuclear Age;* and Oran R. Young, *The Intermediaries: Third Parties in International Crises* (Princeton: Princeton University Press, 1967), p. 367. The opposing view is best represented by Kenneth N. Waltz, "International Structure, National Force, and the Balance of World Power," *The Journal of International Affairs*, 21 (1967), 215–231.
88. Keohane, "Lilliputians' Dilemmas," p. 293.
89. Ripka, *Small and Great Nations*, p. 6.
90. Vital, *Survival of Small States*, p. 9. See also his "Analysis of Small Power Politics," in Schou and Brundtland (eds.), *Small States in International Relations*, pp. 18–19; and his *Inequality of States*, p. 36. Also Grewe, *Spiel der Kräfte in der Weltpolitik*, p. 28; Aaron Wildavsky and Max Singer, "A Third World Averaging Strategy," in Aaron Wildavsky, *The Revolt against the Masses* (Basic Books, 1971), pp. 463–482. On the whole, Wildavsky agrees with Vital, but he suggests that in unstable systems weak states may have influence out of proportion to their real power: "In a 'stable' system, small causes have small effects that generate countervailing influences which return the system to its former equilibrium. In an unstable system, small causes have large effects that throw the system into ever greater disequilibrium as (appropriately) in a nuclear chain reaction" (p. 465).
91. Grewe, *Spiel der Kräfte in der Weltpolitik*, p. 28.
92. Fox, "The Small States in the International System 1919–1969," *International Journal*, 24 (1968/1969), 751, n. 3.
93. Fox, *The Power of Small States*, p. 3, n. 3. See also Barston, "The External Relations of Small States," in Schou and Brundtland (eds.), *Small States in International Relations*, p. 41; William E. Paterson, "Small States in International Politics," p. 122; Stanley Hoffman, *Gulliver's Troubles*, p. 57; Bjol, *The Power of the Weak*, p. 159.
94. An excellent example of the small states' provincialism and their narrow, even egocentric, outlook can be cited from Herre:
    Balkan statesmen have rarely been able to look beyond the Balkans. They have seen very clearly only the interlocking relationships between European big-power politics and their own parochial Balkan politics and have consciously taken them into account in pursuing their national aims. It was the practice of turning the big powers into instruments of the small states about which the Serbian prime minister, Pashitch, spoke almost cynically, after the end of the Balkan Wars in August 1913, to the Serbian chargé d'affaires in Berlin: "I could have risked a European war during the First Balkan War in order to acquire Bosnia, but since I feared that we would then be forced to make considerable concessions to Bulgaria in Macedonia, I first wanted to secure Macedonia for Serbia and only then proceed to annex Bosnia and Herzegovina."
    Die Kleinen Staaten Europas, p. 374 (quoting Boghischewitsch). My translation.
95. Vital, *The Inequality of States*, p. 29.

96. This dependence on information from the super power is an even more acute problem for the middle powers, whose interests are regional and hence more often interwoven with those of the super powers. The intelligence services of the middle powers cannot match their extended range of interests. For Australian dependence on United States intelligence, see H. G. Gelber, *The Australian American Alliance* (Baltimore: Penguin Books, 1968), pp. 26, 39; H. G. Gelber (ed.), *Problems of Australian Defence* (Melbourne: Oxford University Press, 1970), chap. 6; H. G. Gelber, *The USA and Australia*, p. 89; Max Teichmann (ed.), *New Directions in Australian Foreign Policy: Ally, Satellite or Neutral?* (London: Penguin Books, 1969), p. 87. For Canada, see examples in Harold von Riekhoff, "Nato: To Stay or Not to Stay," in Stephen Clarkson (ed.), *An Independent Foreign Policy for Canada* (Toronto: McClelland and Steward, 1968). See also Jon B. McLin, *Canada's Changing Defense Policy 1957–1963: The Problems of a Middle Power in Alliance* (Baltimore: Johns Hopkins Press, 1967). He cites an interesting example (pp. 100–101): " '. . . Canada was victimized by changing U.S. strategic intelligence estimates. This is indeed a general problem, since Canada depends almost entirely upon the U.S. for information upon which to base such estimates . . . . Canadians have . . . had the expensive not to say the humiliating experience of producing for about half a billion dollars a fighter interceptor designed for use against bombers, only to be told that the main threat was from ballistic missiles; and have proceeded to scrap the interceptor, only to be told that there *is* a threat from bombers after all'." McLin is quoting from James Eyars, *Northern Approaches: Canada and the Search for Peace* (Toronto: Macmillan of Canada, 1961), p. 34. Vital, *The Inequality of States*, pp. 23–24, argues that weak states are at a disadvantage in the collection of information, and suggests that cooperation with a great power is the best solution.
97. See Erling Bjol, "The Power of the Weak," *Cooperation and Conflict*, 3 (1969), 161.
98. Andrew, *Defence by Other Means*, p. 53. Also Annette Baker Fox, "Small State Diplomacy," in Stephen D. Kertesz and M. A. Fitzsimmons, *Diplomacy in a Changing World* (South Bend, Ind.: University of Notre Dame Press, 1959), p. 340.
99. See Edward Hambro, "Small States and a New League: The View Point of Norway," *American Political Science Review*, 37 (August 1943), 907; also J. J. Holst, in Schou and Brundtland (eds.), *Small States in International Relations*, p. 199.
100. For example: Holbraad, "The Role of the Middle Powers," p. 77; Andrew, *Defence by Other Means*, p. vii; Herre, *Die Kleinen Staaten Europas*, p. vi; Vandenbosch, "The Small States in International Politics and Organization," p. 294.
101. See Michael Brecher, *The Foreign Policy System of Israel* (New Haven: Yale University Press, 1972), pp. 15–16.
102. Andrew, *Defence by Other Means*, pp. 37–38, 55. See also Lagos, *International Stratification*, p. 95; Laszlo Reczei, "The Political Aims

and Experiences of the Small Socialist States," p. 75, and J. J. Okumu, "The Place of African States in International Relations," p. 149, in Schou and Brundtland (eds.), *Small States in International Relations;* and B. H. M. Vlekke in his introduction to S. I. P. Van Campen, *The Quest for Security* (The Hague: Martinas Nijhoff, 1958), pp. vii–viii.

103. For two recent attempts to correlate size and development with active/passive foreign policy, see Patrick L. McGowan and Klaus-Peter Gottwald, "Small State Foreign Policies: A Comparative Study of Participation, Conflict and Political and Economic Dependence in Black Africa", *International Studies Quarterly*, Vol. 19, No. 4. December 1975, pp. 469–500; and Peter Hansen, "Adaptive Behavior of Small States: The Case of Denmark and the European Community", *Sage International Yearbook of Foreign Policy*, Vol. II, Patrick J. McGowan, ed. (Beverly Hills: Sage Publications 1974), pp. 143–174.

104. Rothstein, *Alliances and Small Powers*, p. 182.

105. Arnold Wolfers, *Discord and Collaboration*, p. 111.

106. Astri Suhrke, "Gratuity or Tyranny: The Korean Alliances;" *World Politics*, 25 (July 1973), 508.

107. Fox, "The Small States in the International System, 1919–1960," p. 761 (quoting Peter Calvocoressi).

108. This is the title of an article by Robert O. Keohane, "The Big Influence of Small Allies," *Foreign Policy*, 2 (Spring 1971), 161–182.

109. G. Marcy, "How Far Can Foreign Trade and Customs Agreements Confer Upon Small Nations the Advantages of Large Nations?" in Robinson, *Economic Consequences of the Size of Nations*, p. 268. There are, as always, some exceptions to this rule. Great Britain, though considered a great power, relies relatively heavily on both imports and exports. This indeed has considerably weakened and undermined Britain's position (*ibid.*, p. 267).

110. I. Svermilson, "The Concept of the Nation and Its Relevance to Economic Analysis," *ibid.*, p. 12. Also Kuznets, *ibid.*, pp. 15–16.

111. A substantial amount of literature has been published on these states in recent years. Patricia Wohlgemuth Blair, *The Ministate Dilemma*, Occasional Paper no. 6 (New York: Carnegie Endowment for International Peace, October 1967); Burton Benedict (ed.), *Problems of Smaller Territories* (London: University of London, the Athlone Press, 1967); Stanley A. de Smith, *Microstates and Micronesia* (New York: New York University Press 1970); Jacques Rapaport, Ernest Muteba, and Joseph J. Therattil, *Small States and Territories: Status and Problems* (New York: Arno Press, 1971); Sir Hilary Blood, *The Smaller Territories* (London, 1958); Dieter Ehrhardt, *Der Begriff des Mikrostaats* (Aalen: Scienta Verlag, 1970); Arvidis Ziedonis, Jr., Rein Taagepera, and Mardi Valgemäe, *Problems of Mininations' Baltic Perspective* (San José: Association for the Advancement of Baltic Studies, Inc., 1973).

112. For an excellent methodological discussion also relevant to the problems of defining the large powers, see Rapaport et al., *Small States and Territories: Status and Problems*, especially the introduction and the

annex by Professor Charles L. Taylor of Yale University, "Statistical Typology of Microstates and Territories: Towards a Definition of a Microstate," (pp. 183–202).
113. Blair, *The Ministate Dilemma,* p. 3.
114. de Smith, *Microstates and Micronesia,* p. vii.
115. Hans J. Morgenthau, *Politics Among Nations,* pp. 150–164, 202–213. Thomas Hobbes, *Leviathan,* ed. Michael Oakeshott (New York: Collier Books, 1962), p. 80.
116. For Polish diplomatic history between the two World Wars, see Anna M. Cienciala, *Poland and the Western Powers 1938–1939* (London: Routledge and Kegan Paul, 1968); Bodhan B. Budurowycz, *Polish-Soviet Relations 1932–1939* (New York: Columbia University Press, 1963); Roman Debicki, *The Foreign Policy of Poland 1919–1939* (London: Pall Mall Press, 1963); Piotr S. Wandycz, *France and Her Eastern Allies 1919–1925* (Minneapolis: The University of Minnesota Press, 1962); Harold von Riekhoff, *German-Polish Relations 1918–1933* (Baltimore: Johns Hopkins University Press, 1971); Josef Korbel, *Poland Between East and West* (Princeton: Princeton University Press, 1963); Henry L. Roberts, "The Diplomacy of Colonel Beck," in Gordon A. Craig and Felix Gilbert, *The Diplomats 1919–1939* (Princeton: Princeton University Press, 1953), chap. 19, pp. 579–614.
117. Julius Gould and William L. Kolb (eds.), *A Dictionary of the Social Sciences* (New York: Free Press, 1967), p. 312. See also Max Weber, *Economy and Society,* 1 (New York: Bedminster Press, 1958), 19–22; and Judith Janoska-Bendl, *Methodologische Aspekte des Idealtypes: Max Weber und die Soziologie der Geschichte* (Berlin: Duncker und Humblot, 1965); Abraham Kaplan, *The Conduct of Inquiry* (Scranton: Chandler, 1964), pp. 82–83. Instead of the term "ideal type" the term "paradigm" may be used.
118. Introduction by B. H. M. Vlekke, p. viii, in S. I. P. Van Campen, *The Quest for Security: Some Aspects of the Netherlands' Foreign Policy 1945–1950* (The Hague: Martinas Nijhoff, 1958).
119. Maurice A. East, "Size and Foreign Policy Behavior: A Test of Two Models," *World Politics,* 25 (July 1973), 557.

CHAPTER II

Internal Sources of Weakness and Strength of the Weak States

Melians. But we know that the fortune of war is sometimes more impartial than the disproportion of numbers might lead one to suppose; to submit is to give ourselves over to despair, while action still preserves for us a hope that we may stand erect.

Athenians. Hope, danger's comforter, may be indulged in by those who have abundant resources, if not without loss at all events without ruin; but its nature is to be extravagant, and those who go so far as to put their all upon the venture see it in its true colours only when they are ruined; but so long as the discovery would enable them to guard against it, it is never found wanting. Let not this be the case with you, who are weak and hang on a single turn of the scale; nor, be like the vulgar, who abandoning such security as human means may still afford when visible hopes fail them in extremity, turn to invisible, to prophecies and oracles, and other such inventions that delude men with hopes to their destruction.

Melians. You may be sure that we are as well aware as you of the difficulty of contending against your power and fortune, unless the terms be equal. But we trust that the gods may grant us fortune as good as yours, since we are just men and fighting against unjust, and that what we want in power will be made up by the alliance of the Lacedaemonians, who are bound, if only for very shame, to come to the aid of their kindred. Our confidence, therefore, after all is not so utterly irrational.

Thucydides, *The History of the Peloponnesian War,* book V, chapter XVII, para. 102–104.

Four different elements determine the strength of a state. They are *geographical data*, for example the area of the territory and the nature of the frontiers; *material data*, for instance the absence or presence of natural resources and industrial capacity (technological development and capital); *human resources*, such as the size of the population, ethnic homogeneity and social integration (cohesion and unity), national character and morale; and *organizational capabilities* (or in Raymond Aron's terminology, the "collective capacity for action"), such as the structure and stability of political institutions, administrative capabilities, the qualities of command and military preparedness (military decision-making), the quality of diplomacy, and capacity for adaptation.[1] There is no need to discuss all the elements of strength in relation to the weak states; instead attention will be focused on those which have a special impact on the international position of the weak states.

The elements of strength just mentioned constitute the sum total of the *internal* or domestic sources of strength available to a state. But the behavior and conduct of states, like that of individuals or social groups, cannot be studied in isolation— in a social or political vacuum.[2] States have the capacity to interact with one another and hence, on most occasions, to avail themselves of an external source of strength. The only realistic way to evaluate the might of a state, therefore, is to combine its internal and external sources of strength. (Instead of "internal and external sources of strength," the terms "direct and indirect sources" or "autonomous and derived sources" could be used.)

TOTAL POWER OF A STATE = INTERNAL POWER (MOBILISED and POTENTIAL) + EXTERNAL POWER

One of the major differences between a weak state and the great powers is the relative combination of these two available sources of strength. As the preceding chapter pointed out, the weak states have on the whole fewer resources, and they are unable to resolve their defense problems by their own strength. It follows therefore, that on most occasions the external sources of strength available are more crucial for the weak states and

INTERNAL SOURCES OF WEAKNESS AND STRENGTH 69

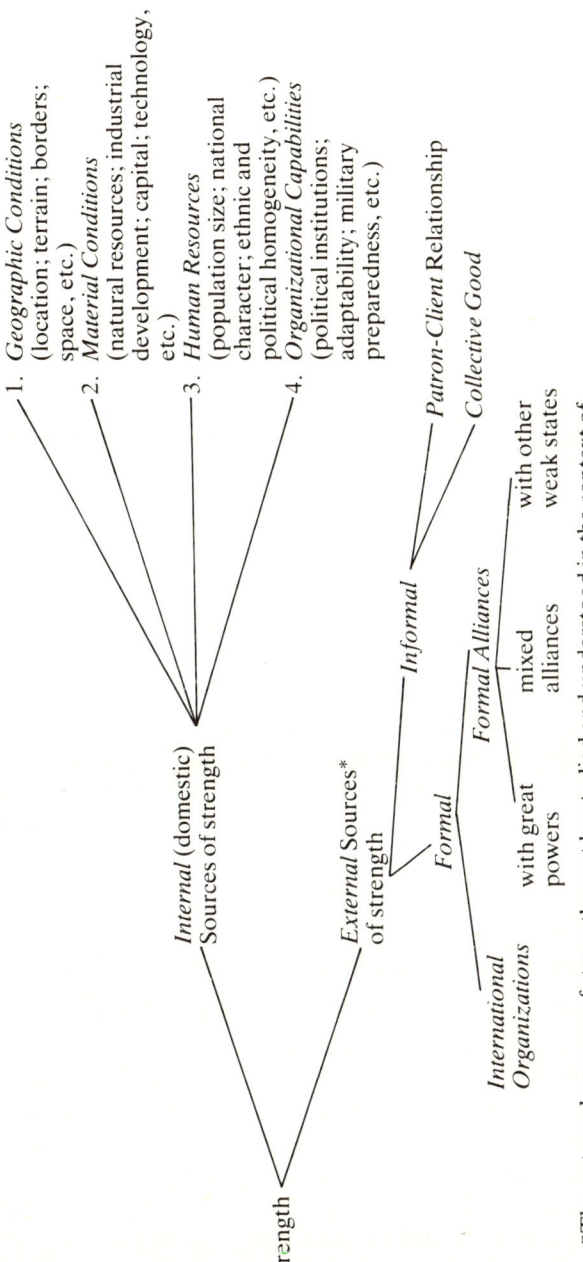

Fig. 3. Elements Determining the Strength of a State

*The external sources of strength must be studied and understood in the context of
a) the different types of international systems and different problems and opportunities they present to the weak states
b) the changing norms of conduct in international relations (especially between the great powers and the weak states), mainly the growing democratization of international affairs and the decline in the legitimacy of outright use of coercion and force.

constitute a relatively greater part of their total strength than is the case for the great powers. This situation can be presented as in Fig 4.

Fig. 4 Total Strength of a State

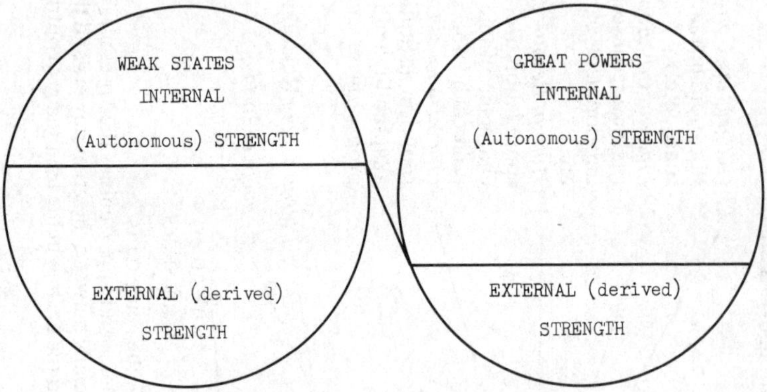

```
         WEAK STATES                          GREAT POWERS
         INTERNAL                             INTERNAL
     (Autonomous) STRENGTH                (Autonomous) STRENGTH
     ─────────────────────                ─────────────────────
       EXTERNAL (derived)                   EXTERNAL (derived)
           STRENGTH                              STRENGTH
```

This chapter will discuss the internal sources of power of the weak states, stressing two elements: (1) their geographic situation and its impact on their strength and international position, and (2) their military strength, which is a combination of two or more of the elements of strength (geography, materials, human resources, organizational capabilities). The next chapter will examine the availability of external strength to the weak states, the techniques and circumstances under which they can "draw on" and "borrow" the strength of other states, and how they can manipulate and retain it.

The Geographical Position of Weak States

Geography is a prime constraint on the weak states' survival. Since they usually control a relatively small territorial space, the probability of finding a large and well balanced variety of natural resources is lower than for larger states. The weakness of the weak states' economies bears a direct relationship to their greater dependence on the importation of foreign raw materials. The smaller territorial size also has important implications for the military and strategic situation.[3] States controlling only a small space are more vulnerable to attack, especially

INTERNAL SOURCES OF WEAKNESS AND STRENGTH 71

surprise attack. Having no strategic depth, strategic withdrawal is out of the question; they have little or no room to maneuver and face the danger of being quickly overrun; they are unable to "trade space for time" in order to reorganize their defenses and continue to fight. The loss of the first battle can mean the loss of the whole war. Therefore, "the small power . . . must await the enemy at the gates, at the outer limits of its vital centers . . . . Defense in depth is not a viable strategy."[4] Thus weak (small) states in danger of attack have to maintain relatively large standing armies, for they have little time to mobilize. For the weak (or territorially small) state at war, the distance between the front line and the rear is obviously smaller than for other states. In the 1970s, Israel is a typical example of such a vulnerable state.[5] In the past, two such states in the European system were Belgium and Czechoslovakia.

On occasion large territorial space can pose equally serious problems for a weak state if the territory is sparsely populated. This is the case with Australia. Despite exceptional luck as one of the few countries in the world whose strategic frontiers correspond to its national boundaries,[6] it faces serious defense problems in case of war. Its population (12.7 million—about fortieth in the world—see Table 3, Chapter I) is relatively small in relation to its territorial size (7,686 thousand square kilometers, or the sixth largest in the world) and its coastline frontier (almost 12,200 miles).[7] Iceland, a much weaker state, finds itself in a similar situation, as its Foreign Minister, Agnar Kl. Jonsson, has stated: ". . . with a comparatively small population [195,000] in so large a country [103,000 square kilometers], it would have been completely impossible to obtain any defense system."[8] Mauritania faces a similar situation with a small population (1,050,000) and a very large territory (1,030,700 square kilometers), which makes it for "all intents and purposes beyond [its] power to maintain even symbolic control of [its] frontiers. Genuine defense of the national frontiers against incursion is almost entirely ruled out."[9] This anomaly helps to explain why Rousseau's first advice on reform to the Poles was to limit the size of their territory.[10]

Among the most important elements determining the international position of a weak state is its geographic location.

Weak states which are on the periphery of the international system (or their own subsystem) are in a much better position than those which are located in the center of their relevant system, that is, in between, or "in the way of," the great powers. Countries such as Belgium, Czechoslovakia, Poland, Hungary, Israel (Palestine) have historically been the victims of their central geographic position—strategic highways for great powers on the march. On the other hand, countries such as Ireland, Sweden, Portugal, Chile, or New Zealand have been far away from the centers of conflict and have successfully avoided direct conquest and war for years. New Zealand, for example, is "remote from the habitual trouble spots of the world. Within a 2,000 km. radius of Israel there are about 20 countries. Within the same radius of New Zealand, only the south eastern tip of Australia intrudes."[11] Annette Baker Fox, in her study of the diplomacy of weak states during the Second World War, found that the location of a small state was among the crucial factors for keeping such countries out of the war. She concluded that "the greater the distance the small state was located from a direct line between belligerents" the better was its chance of staying out of the war.[12]

Closely related to the location of a weak state is the question of its strategic importance *for other states,* especially the great powers. Finland's control of some islands and territory which could block the sea routes to Leningrad, as well as the closeness of its border to Leningrad (within artillery range), has made it the object of Russian desire. Finland is typical of a weak state which does not pose a direct threat to a great power, but which may pose an *indirect* threat through its inability to prevent occupation by a second great power—by a state that might threaten the first great power. During the Second World War Russia wanted to control the Baltic states in order to preempt any possibility of their being occupied by Germany.[13] The Russians, fearing that the Germans would conclude "cat and mouse" (unequal) treaties with the Baltic states, were afraid of becoming the victims of what they called indirect aggression.[14] (The Russian government knew well what to fear, for it projected its own intentions on the Germans.) "We cannot permit small states to be used against the USSR. Neutral Baltic states—that is too insecure."[15] Russian fears can be

INTERNAL SOURCES OF WEAKNESS AND STRENGTH 73

easily understood in the light of the almost uncontested German occupation of Denmark and Norway, and later Belgium, Holland, and Luxemburg.

Russian fear of power vacuums created by the weak states was not totally unjustified.[16] After the First World War the countries whose establishment was meant to isolate Russia—the famous "cordon sanitaire"—could easily have turned into a springboard for aggression by the powers against Russia. The strategic location of Czechoslovakia vis-à-vis Germany—as Bismarck said, Bohemia is the key for the control of Central Europe—was not an asset to the Czechs. The Germans were less afraid of the Czech state itself than of a coordinated effort between Czechoslovakia and another power (namely, France). They saw the country as an "aircraft carrier" in the middle of Europe.[17]

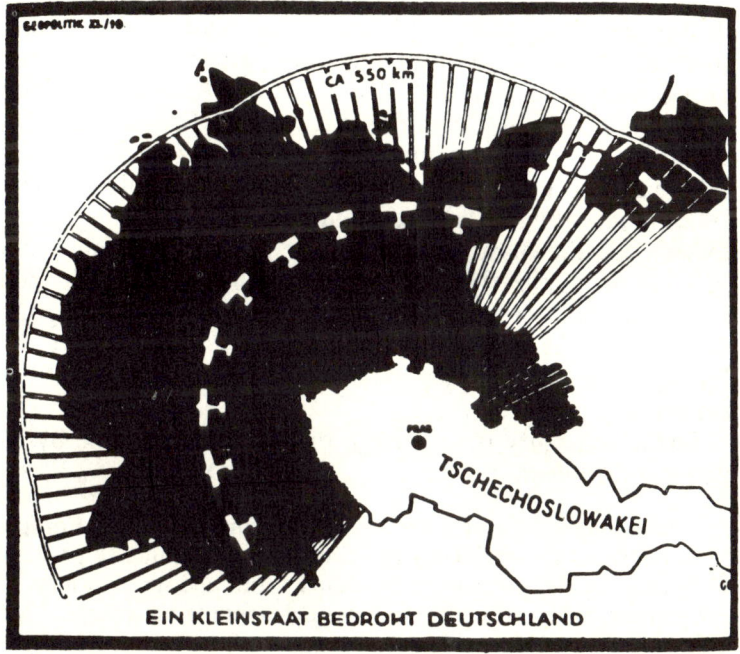

A Small State Threatens Germany.
The air-threat to Germany by Czecho-Slovakia. Almost all of Germany can be reached by Czech bombing planes in two hours.

Source: Derwent Whittlesey, *German Strategy of World Conquest* (New York: Farrar and Rinehart, 1942), p. 140.

In a similar way, Turkey's control of the Bosphorus made her a prize greatly coveted by Russian diplomats. Egypt's control of the Suez Canal was no doubt responsible for British occupation until 1956, and something similar can be said for the US interest in Panama (the Canal Zone), and of Danish control over the entrance to the Baltic.[18] Strategic location is both an asset and a liability; in wartime it can endanger the integrity of a weak state.

Belgium's location, as the best route to invade France, made it the victim of the German war machine. Its strategic importance for Great Britain led the British to guarantee its independence, though they could not prevent it from being overrun and occupied twice.[19] In the same way Portugal's strategic importance for the control of the sea lanes to Great Britain has helped it to secure British defense.[20]

Also important for the weak state's position is the nature of its terrain and borders. Switzerland's mountainous terrain (combined with a determined army) prevented a German attack during the Second World War.[21] Albania's difficult terrain and lack of a common border with Russia may have deterred a Russian attempt to intervene in its affairs when Albania defected to the Chinese People's Republic.[22] The Italians who fought the Greeks in 1940 learned through hard experience the disadvantages of the Albanian terrain for a modern mechanized force.[23] Similarly, the Finns were helped by the difficult terrain on their border with Russia during the Winter War. Highly unsuitable for tank warfare, it gave the lightly armed and highly mobile Finnish infantry units the relative advantage.[24]

Swiss neutrality is to a large extent made possible by its geographic location:

> Dominating the mountainous center ground of Western Europe, Switzerland maintained a most advantageous military position from the point of view of both land forms and internal lines of communication. It controlled strategic mountain passes that led into Italy, and shared border with four of the great powers. Its armies, long trained in the defense of its difficult terrain, were prepared to offer hard-core resistance to any potential enemy. Few states aspiring to hegemony could have afforded the expenditure of resources required to dislodge them, especially when

Switzerland's commitment to perpetual neutrality made it unnecessary. Finally, it is doubtful whether the other great powers would have allowed Switzerland to be occupied, and thereby have risked the danger of the conquering state or coalition of states controlling its mountain passes and borders.[25]

The Chilean borders have proved very useful for defense. Chile has the character of an island: the impassable Andes which form its eastern border with Argentina, the Atacama Desert to the north on the border with Peru, and the Pacific Ocean to the west and south "have minimized the possibility of a surprise invasion."[26] If Cuba were not an island ninety miles from the United States, it might have shared the fate of some of Mexico's territory. Difficult borders and terrain have considerably enhanced the survival of weak states such as Andorra, San Marino, Nepal,[27] Afghanistan, and Mongolia.

Another way of looking at a country's vulnerability or nonvulnerability is to examine what has been called by geographers "border pressure." In considering this one takes into account the number of neighboring countries with which a common border is shared, their relative population ratios, their military strength, and their political intentions. Israel, for example, touches Egypt, Jordan, Syria, and Lebanon.

> ... Israel has a ratio of 1:13 with all four neighbors positively hostile to it .... Czechoslovakia with 14 million against 360 million (including both the USSR and West Germany) has a ratio of roughly 1:26 .... Switzerland with 6 million has neighbors West Germany (58 million), France (50), Italy (52), and Austria (7), a ratio of 6:167 or an index of 1 to 28 .... The Mongolian People's Republic (1 million) adjoining China (720 million) plus the USSR (236 million) has an extremely high index, nearly 1:1000.[28]
> Such balances are measures only of potential pressure, but they may give a rough index of "hidden" feelings of being enclosed and threatened on the part of the politicians and even whole peoples.[29]

Border pressure explains the predicament of Poland (between the two World Wars), "which remained on bad terms with no less than four of her six neighbors—Germany, Russia, Lithuania and Czechoslovakia."[30] It also clarifies the position of Yugoslavia, bordering on seven other states, "a larger number than any other country in Europe except Germany. The demarcation of each of these boundaries was disputed, apart from the 100 miles shared with Greece."[31]

The possible geographic advantages and disadvantages of the weak states can be summarized as follows:

Possible Advantages	Possible Disadvantages
1. Large territory: (a) a higher probability of including a larger and more balanced variety of natural resources; (b) more room for strategic maneuver.	1. Small in size: (a) lower probability of a large and balanced variety of natural resources; (b) a serious strategic disadvantage.
2. Combination of natural, easy-to-defend borders and difficult or impassable terrain.	2. Lack of easy-to-defend natural borders, and terrain conducive to fast advancement of troops.
3. Geographic isolation (an island) or a low number of adjacent and weaker neighbors preferably nonhostile ("low border pressure").	3. Large number of bordering countries, more powerful and with conflicting goals ("high border pressure").
4. Located on the periphery of the relevant system or subsystem. Distant from the active center of the system. Nonstrategic location.	4. Central location in a system or subsystem (in conflict). Location of strategic importance to the powers.

The Military Position of Weak States

> "One Finn may be worth ten Russians but what do we do when the eleventh comes along?"[32]

The need of the weak states to maintain military forces is not always self-evident. It is clear that a weak state which faces the danger of being attacked by *another weak state* must build up its military strength for it has an excellent chance of defending itself successfully. But the situation is less clear when a weak state has to face a great power or any state stronger than itself. Since there is a consensus among most scholars that a weak state cannot defend itself by its own efforts against any of the great powers, why should a country such as Denmark, Holland, Belgium, Sweden, or Switzerland invest scarce human and material resources in building up its military forces?

In the past, weak states have on occasion given up hope of defending themselves by their own efforts and have decided to invest only a minimum effort in their military forces. Adopting a doctrine known as "defense nihilism," they have put their faith in neutrality, which they have considered to be the best preparation for war.[33] This doctrine won adherents in Norway, Sweden, and particularly in Denmark before the First World War. "In 1916 the Defense Nihilists sought to destroy the seaward fortifications of Copenhagen."[34] Before the Second World War a similar attitude was epitomized by the Danish saying, *"til hvad kan det nytte?* (what's the use?)"[35] Such an attitude is a dangerous one for the weak state. In times of tension and war, a neighboring great power may fear that the weak state, being a power vacuum in military terms, will fall easy prey to the great power's enemies—and thus serve as a base against it. In addition to the example given earlier of Russia's fear of "indirect aggression" through the power vacuum of the Baltic states and Finland, there was Germany's fear during the First and Second World Wars concerning Holland, Norway, and Denmark.[36] This kind of fear, felt by two or more great powers surrounding a weak state, may turn into a self-fulfilling prophecy by leading one of the powers (or even two, as was the case in Norway during the Second World War[37]) to occupy the weak state in order to prevent occupation by its adversary. Hitler's war directive for the occupation of Norway (and Denmark) explains the preemptive nature of the operation:

> The development of the situation in Scandinavia makes it necessary to prepare for the occupation of Denmark and Norway by formations of the Armed Forces ('Case Weser—exercise'). This would *anticipate* English action against Scandinavia and the Baltic . . . .[38]

Admiral Doenitz gave a similar explanation:

> There were indications that the enemy also was planning military operations against Norway. It was these indications which finally led to the decision to *forestall him by means of a counter-stroke*. In these circumstances there was, therefore, always *the possibility that the enemy might act before we ourselves had had time to complete our operations.*[39]

In like manner the French high command feared an imminent German attack on France via Belgium and thus made plans to meet the Germans on Belgian soil.[40] Switzerland was a similar case during the First and Second World Wars, as was Sweden in the Second World War as a result of its coveted ore deposits.[41] However, through their strength and determination the Swiss and Swedes successfully deterred such attempts. Iceland, on the other hand, became a victim of its weakness and fears when in 1940 the British government occupied it following the German occupation of Norway and Denmark.[42]

During the Second World War such power vacuums led to accusations that the weak states created unstable and "tempting" situations that encouraged aggression and war.[43] There was more than a grain of truth to these accusations. On the other hand, weakness *per se* in *more stable situations* does not lead to aggression. After all, Germany attacked Belgium and Holland not because of their inherent weakness but because it was at war with France and Great Britain, and the two small countries happened to be located on the strategic highway to France. Power vacuums created by the weakness of the weak states are not the usual cause for an all-out war between the great powers. Such wars break out over much more substantial calculations of the changes in balance of power or as a result of the hegemonial and aggrandizing aspirations of the great powers. But once a general war between the great powers has broken out, the existence of power vacuums, such as those mentioned above, can extend the war to larger areas not included among the original goals of the belligerents.[44]

It becomes clear, therefore, that in order to minimize the chance that war will spread, and to *deter* preemptive attacks, the weaker states should try to develop their military power to a level sufficient to reduce the fear of the great powers concerning a power vacuum. What problems face the weak states in developing military forces? How useful are such forces in wartime?

The first major problem faced by the weak states is their relatively smaller populations. They have more difficulty in mobilizing large armies in time of war, and their human resources are relatively limited and exhaustible. The traditional and only way of overcoming this problem has been to try to mobilize a larger proportion of the population. The Military

Participation Ratio (MPR)[45] of the weak states is very often much higher than that of the great powers. This may explain the rise of the Kingdom of Prussia in the 17th century, at a time when military power was almost exclusively measured by number of soldiers.

> The disproportion between the army and the population of the country was flagrant in 1740; at the death of Frederick William I, Prussia with its 2,240,000 inhabitants maintained 80,000 soldiers, a number equal to that of Austria with her sixfold population; and even the French army was only one and a half times as strong, although Louis XV had nine times as many subjects. At the death of Frederick II [the Great] when the population of Prussia had risen to 6,000,000, the peace strength of the army was 200,000 men, rising to 250,000 at the close of the century.[46]

Weak countries such as Sweden, Switzerland, or Israel have very large armies in relation to the size of their populations. They can develop large armies without suffering an overwhelming burden by building up their reserve system. Reserves can be called up on short notice, and their quality and training are almost equal to that of the regular units. Because these countries are highly developed economically, their *effective population* (those who can serve in a modern army) is very high. Other weak countries that are less developed economically also maintain very large standing armies; for example, the Republic of Vietnam, Republic of Korea, Republic of China, Turkey, Democratic Republic of Vietnam, and North Korea. (See Table 5, Chapter I.)

Both developed and underdeveloped weak countries have one thing in common: their mobilized armies (regular plus reserve) cannot usually be much further expanded. In other words, due to the limits of available manpower, their war potential is relatively low. Because of geographical (as well as other) considerations they have to concentrate their forces in the very early stages of a war to prevent a *fait accompli* from which they could not recuperate. After concentrating all their troops in the early stages in order to meet overwhelming odds, they cannot further expand their military forces. This is clearly stated in Marshal Mannerheim's memoirs: "In the final phase of the War [the Winter War] our weakness was not therefore on the material plane but in the lack of trained manpower."[47]

Whereas a weak state has to fight from the very beginning with all or most of its war potential mobilized, a great power which starts with only part of its forces mobilized and suffers initial defeats can still fall back on its large war potential, both human and material. The very high MPR rate of some of the weak states poses another serious difficulty. In full mobilization the economy can be brought practically to a standstill because of the high proportion of men in service. It is, of course, very difficult for weak countries to mobilize such extensive forces for extended periods. They could be brought close to ruin without a shot being fired. This is why, if the superiority of the adversary is not overwhelming, a weak state can be tempted to strike first in order to prevent the consequences of prolonged mobilization.[48] During World War II the Greeks found themselves in the predicament of having to mobilize their forces for an extended period against the Italians.

> ... it was not unreasonable to suppose that any prolonged state of Greek mobilization without actual fighting would serve the Italian plans of wearing Greece down before actually going to war against her. In fact, if the Greek armed forces were to remain mobilized for a considerable period of time without doing any actual fighting, any prolongation of this situation might result in a complete unsettlement of the general life of the country, might weaken the morale of the armed forces and cause the material of mobilization to wear out permanently.[49]

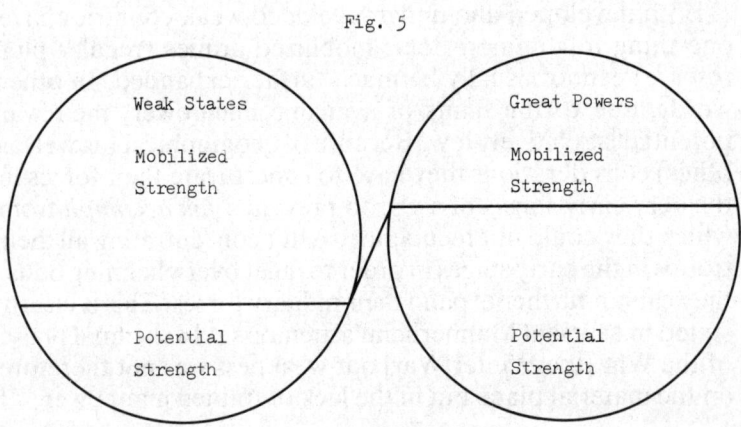

Fig. 5

The great powers, on the other hand, can mobilize very large forces against a weak state without affecting their own economies adversely. They can fight, so to speak, with one hand tied behind their backs.

This difference in proportion between mobilized and potential strength on the part of the weak states and the great powers also holds good for their military equipment. A weak country such as Israel can have an air force similar in size to that of a country such as Italy or France, but whereas the large countries can increase their air forces by a considerable degree over an extended period of time, Israel would not be able to do so.[50] Yet there is one fact concerning military preparedness that gives an advantage to the weak state with a high rate of mobilization: the great amount of time necessary to expand, organize, equip, and in particular to train pilots for a modern air force. This time factor gives the mobilized, trained, and experienced weak state an initial opportunity to achieve either military or diplomatic results. Nevertheless, the differences in relative *material potential* between the weak states and the great powers are enormous. Unlike the great powers, the weak states usually cannot produce the most sophisticated weapons; if they can, such production is possible only in limited quantities. In this area the weak countries are highly vulnerable and dependent on external help. The most difficult type of war for a weak state to pursue against a stronger state or combination of states, therefore, is a prolonged war of attrition. The best type of warfare for the weak state is a short war of movement—or a guerrilla war.

The war potential of the great powers is a "quantum jump" over anything the weak states can ever hope to achieve in any military effort.[51] A few examples will give an idea of the dimensions involved. Before and during the Second World War, Germany produced 1,170 U-boats of which 863 became operational; it lost in sea action and in ports no less than 753 U-boats.[52] The number of military aircraft produced during the Second World War by Japan, Germany, the United Kingdom and the United States is shown in Table 7.

This table demonstrates the enormous war potential of the great powers and their capacity to expand production as the Second World War continued. All the great powers expanded

TABLE 7

TOTAL MILITARY AIRCRAFT PRODUCTION OF THE FOUR MAJOR POWERS, 1939–1944[53]

Year	Japan	Germany	United Kingdom	United States
1939	4,467	8,295	7,940	2,141
1940	4,768	10,826	15,049	6,019
1941	5,088	11,776	20,094	19,433
1942	8,861	15,556	23,672	47,836
1943	16,693	25,527	26,263	85,898
1944	28,180	39,807	24,461	96,318
Total	68,057	111,787	117,479	257,645

Source: Irving Brinton Halley, *Buying Aircraft: National Procurement for the Army Air Forces,* United States Army in World War II Special Studies (Washington, D.C.: Department of Army, 1964), p. 555.

their output of military aircraft by a factor of at least three, while the United States increased its production by a factor of almost fifty! The United States was a super power before the end of World War II.

Between 1939 and 1945 the Russians produced no less than 126,398 tanks, tank destroyers, and mobile artillery pieces.[54] In the 1960s and 70s the United States lost over Indochina no less than 8,572 helicopters and planes—3,706 planes and 4,866 helicopters. The total cost of the air war was 16 billion dollars.[55]

The quantitative dimensions of these war efforts are beyond the material capacity of a weak state. The Greeks fighting the Italians successfully in 1940–41 had no tanks and only a very small air force.[56] The Finns fought the Russians during the Winter War of 1940, also with great success, but with hardly any planes or tanks. The Russians, on the other hand, concentrated or had available at least 2,500 aircraft (they lost 725 to the Finns), as well as 5,000 to 6,000 tanks (of which they lost at least 1,600).[57] A similar comparison could be made for North Vietnam and the United States. Finally, during the so-called war of attrition of Israel along the Suez Canal, the loss of five

INTERNAL SOURCES OF WEAKNESS AND STRENGTH 83

Phantom F-4's in one day nearly resulted in a national trauma. It is doubtful whether the leaders of a great power can appreciate the meaning of such an event for a weak state.

The difficulties of building an effective military force in a weak state are almost overwhelming, and yet on most occasions the utility of such forces cannot be doubted. The price tag on the maintenance and development of up-to-date armies is enormous. Beyond paying salaries and financing routine maintenance of equipment and hardware, most of the military investments of modern armies are directed toward research and development of modern weapons and the purchase of such weapons. Obviously a weak state cannot invest the sums of money necessary for the development of the major modern weapons systems, especially aircraft, aircraft engines, missiles, and tanks. The most important weapons systems call for the investment of enormous sums in R & D in *absolute* terms.[58] The weak states, and sometimes even the great powers, cannot afford to support such costly projects. If they try to do so, either for reasons of prestige or in order to become independent of external sources (which is practically impossible), their best move is to invest in the development of one or two weapons systems, with the almost inevitable result of neglecting other procurement programs.

Not only is the price tag on R & D beyond the reach of most weak states, but it is also necessary for them to maintain large enough production lines to reduce the cost of the weapons systems developed. Even the British have failed in their efforts to produce the TSR-2 after making enormous investments in its design; earlier they failed to develop the Blue Streak missiles.[59] Most great powers—not to mention weak states—purchase their major aircraft in the United States or produce them locally under license. This holds true for such great powers as Japan, West Germany, Great Britain, and to a lesser extent France. The material development of the Chinese People's Army has declined because of its inability to purchase both know-how and weapons abroad.

In the last decade or so, even a super power like the United States has faced serious difficulties in paying for the development and production of modern aircraft and other larger projects, of which the C-5A is only one example.[60] This fact is evident in the reluctance of Congress to allocate the necessary funds for the development of a new tactical fighter-bomber or interceptor for the 1980s. Such a situation points up the advantages of using the ideal-type approach to the description of states rather than closed definitions. In terms of weapons development, production, and procurement, most of the great powers are demonstrating a fair share of the traits of weak states: for example, inability to produce by their own efforts some important weapons needed for self-defense, and growing dependence on the aid and goodwill of a foreign super power.[61] Even the super power is beginning to drift away from the ideal type of the all-powerful state.

What holds true for the great is obviously true for the weak. No weak state in need of maintaining a modern military force can be considered independent of external military aid. The Canadians long ago discovered that they could not develop their own modern weapons systems for a reasonable price, and they have had to reconcile themselves to purchasing sophisticated, heavy, modern weapons in the United States.[62] The Australians have been victimized in a rather different way. They had to decide well in advance of production, or even testing, whether or not to acquire the F-111. After they decided to purchase the aircraft, its cost became much higher than originally anticipated. (And the Australians had not been clever enough to fix the price in the contract!) Secondly, malfunctions and other development problems delayed delivery for years, which left a gap in Australia's defense. The performance and reliability of the F-111 was still in doubt in 1974.[63]

Another problem is faced by weak states—or rather, by all states which must purchase their weapons abroad. Imported weapons are designed for the needs of the power that produces them and are not specifically tailored for the use and needs of the importing states. Canadians, having a country with large and empty spaces and a hard climate, prefer an interceptor with two engines rather than one, to give extra safety in case of engine trouble.[64] The tanks the Russians produce are mainly designed for cold climates and Russian terrain—not for the hot Middle Eastern deserts. Most American aircraft carry a heavy load of electronic gear, which is not needed by a country such as Israel. The main exception to this rule concerns aircraft designed for export, such as the Mirage 5 (actually designed by Israel) and the Freedom Fighter F-5.

Many of the highly developed weak states, such as Belgium, Finland, Czechoslovakia, Holland, Israel, Sweden, and Switzerland have successfully developed and produced excellent light, medium, and occasionally heavy weapons. Among the non-communist countries, only Israel has developed an operational sea-to-sea missile, which proved its effectiveness during the October 1973 war. It has also produced a highly successful air-to-air missile.[65] Since before World War I, the famous Czech Skoda factories have been producing a complete range of weapons. The Swedes also manufacture high-quality artillery, tanks, and fighter-bombers (the J-35 Draken and the Viggen).[66] But even Sweden and Israel must depend on outside technology, especially that of the United States, for jet engines and certain sophisticated electronic systems.[67] And it must be remembered that none of these developed weak states can produce sufficient quantities of weapons for self-defense in the event of an all-out war.

The success stories of these countries are in no way typical of other weak states, which are almost totally dependent on weapons purchased abroad. Even such middle and great powers as Canada, India, Australia, Italy, Japan, and West Germany assemble aircraft under license and with technical assistance from one of the super powers.

What all these efforts have in common is a high degree of explicit or implicit dependence on the super powers. Indeed, there are very few countries in the world today that can design and produce a powerful modern jet engine from scratch. An autonomous capability in this area is thus an important indication of the military as well as the industrial potential of a nation.

Clearly, the capability of the weak states to produce their own weapons is the exception rather than the rule. A major source of strength for most states in the world must be *external;* the capability to purchase weapons abroad is a crucial factor. Most of the weak states have little or no problem in acquiring modern weapons if they are members of the right alliances or have enough resources to buy in a highly competitive market. The dependence of the weak states on this external source of strength becomes problematical only when they are faced with political difficulties and cannot easily obtain the weapons they need. Israel in the 1950s was a good example of this predicament. Israelis still worry about their dependence on foreign weapons suppliers, a situation which explains their almost desperate attempts to produce domestically as many weapons as possible going far beyond cost-benefit considerations.[68]

The weapon-producing countries—usually the great powers of course—have innumerable opportunities to influence and put pressure on the weak countries. The weak states, especially when they are in conflict with other states, are dependent on loans and financial aid to buy weapons; they depend also on the continued supply of spare parts, and many of them rely on aid to train their soldiers to use these weapons.

> In overall terms, the creation of modern and effective armies in African states increases their dependence on the outside world— the arms are expensive and have to be produced abroad and the cost of importing specialists and technicians is very high.[69]
> What counts is that the military of the weaker state become equipped with and trained to handle the hardware of the Power, creating a high degree of dependence on the supplier for training, parts, and replacements. This is exactly what the Powers mean when, in seeking to sell military equipment to weak countries, they speak of "standardization of equipment" and "joint acceptance of strategic and tactical concepts and doctrine through the use of common hardware."[70]

There is little doubt that the selling of weapons to weak states is one of the most important, and perhaps one of the most efficient means available to the powers in their struggle for hegemony.[71] In very much the same way as the pusher is ready to supply the potential addict with his first doses of heroin in order to make him a dependent, the great powers use special techniques to promote weapons sales in certain areas or under certain circumstances. The difference is that weapons sales are even more addictive: the addict can buy his heroin from any pusher, but a country can get its spare parts only from the original source. This phenomenon has developed to such an extent that since the mid-fifties the great powers have been involved in what is called "preemptive supply."

Having received arms, the recipient country becomes, in some degree, militarily dependent upon the supplying country, which can then demand favors or threaten to withhold spares or further supplies if the recipient does not comply with its interests. Alternatively the supplying country may simply be interested in preventing another supplier from achieving this kind of relationship; this is known as *preemptive supply*.[72]

The so-called preemptive selling is necessary in certain cases to safeguard U.S. security interests ... in [Jordan and Iran], the U.S. sale was made fundamentally to avoid the serious danger of a radical shift in the orientation of the recipient country through the introduction of Soviet arms, training missions and other instruments of influence ....[73]

The bargaining power of weak states before an arms deal is usually high, for the great powers compete for political influence and hegemony, as well as economic profits. Thus Iran or Jordan can pretend to inquire into the possibility of acquiring weapons from the USSR in order (a) to obtain better financial conditions and better bargains on weapons from the United States, and (b) to make the United States sell them advanced weapons it would not have sold otherwise.[74] This is a common technique for other weak states—Saudi Arabia, Turkey, Greece, and Yugoslavia. But once these countries have bought weapons systems (even at a good "bargain price"), they are hooked and lose much of their room for maneuver. After years of training on American equipment, it is impossible to switch over quickly to Russian equipment. Not only would such an attempt require a long period of adjustment, but it would be prohibitively expensive; and the country would find itself highly vulnerable and exposed during the transition.

A good example was Jordan's ploy in May 1976. The Jordanians were interested in purchasing a substantial number of US anti-aircraft missiles, but the American government was reluctant to approve the sale. The Russians, however, were quick to make a generous offer. The Soviet Union was prepared to sell to Jordan a comprehensive air defense system, complete with anti-aircraft missiles. The sale would be made unconditionally, while the Americans insisted that the missiles be installed only in static *defensive* positions. King Hussein accordingly approved a visit by the Soviet Deputy Defense Minister and Commander of the Air Force, Marshal Pavel Kotachov. Kotachov was received in Jordan with much pomp and circumstance, no one suspecting that the Soviet Marshal would *not* return with a signed order for the anti-aircraft system.

Jordan was merely going through the motions of a complex bargaining maneuver; Hussein wanted to induce the United States to sell the desired number of missiles under the best obtainable conditions. The Soviet Union, anxious to exploit even the slightest chance of military penetration into Jordan, unwittingly became an instrument of small-state blackmail. The Jordanians, in the end, did acquire the American missiles they desired on excellent terms.

The great powers have not been reluctant on occasion to use weapons pressures in order to exert influence. The French government embargoed the supply of weapons to Israel, unofficially, in the aftermath of the Six Day War, and officially a year later. During the 1970 war of attrition, the United States, Israel's alternative source of weapons, suspended the provision of arms to Israel for a time in order to make it accept an unfavorable cease-fire. Similarly, there is little doubt that the Russians can exert pressure on Arab countries because they are the Arabs' main suppliers. Neither the United States nor Russia hesitated to impose an embargo on arms to India and Pakistan in 1965.

In what way and to what extent can the weak states minimize this dependence on the great powers? Theoretically, it can be done, though only to a limited extent, by domestic production. In reality, as modern weapons become more expensive and sophisticated, fewer and fewer weak states are able to produce their own armaments. Another method is the attempt to spread purchases across different countries. This, however, raises serious problems of standardization and logistics. Even if one state were to supply the aircraft and another the tanks, only one of them would need to refuse spare parts for the whole military machine to collapse.

Some weak states, especially in Africa, have preferred to purchase their weapons from other weak states and to have their armed forces trained there. Israel, Yugoslavia, and Belgium, among others, have trained the armies of Burma, Ethiopia, Kenya, Uganda, and Ghana.[75] The difficulty is that if weak states are in need of highly sophisticated weapons, this alternative is not open to them. Israel and Egypt can get the ultra-sophisticated weapons they need, and in sufficient quantities, only from the super powers. Even if major suppliers, such as Great Britain or France, could supply large quantities of modern weapons to weaker states, such as Israel or the Arab countries, they cannot, unlike the super powers, guarantee the large quantities of weapons the weaker states would need given the attrition rate during a modern war, such as the October 1973 War. Nor can they, in case of need, quickly airlift the weapons and ammunition needed. Also, the weak states supplying weapons are not above imposing their own embargos. Sweden, for example, refused to supply Australia with ammunition for Swedish anti-tank weapons used in the war in Vietnam.[76] Dependence on foreign weapons suppliers can be reduced somewhat, but only marginally.

Another dimension that limits the capability of weak states militarily is the enormous expense of war itself. As already mentioned, the most difficult type of war for a weak state to fight is the prolonged modern war of attrition. The cost of ammunition, of fuel, of spare parts, is prohibitive and would quickly bring even the most developed weak state to a standstill. The price of weapons and ammunition for refurbishing the Israeli army after the October 1973 war, plus other costs incurred by the war, has been well over 5 billion dollars (75 per cent of the projected 1973–74 GNP), to say nothing of the loss in Israel's economic output and the decline in the growth of its GNP. In terms of weapons supplies, Israel had to be bailed out by the United States,[77] just as the Arab states had to be bailed out by the Soviet Union. The cost of the war to Israel has been 30 to 40 per cent of its yearly GNP, and it could be much higher. The United States, on the other hand, fighting in Vietnam with one hand tied behind its back, never spent over 3 per cent of its GNP per year. In the words of Klaus Knorr:

> ... the larger the national economic capacity of a state, the less it will be absorbed by a military effort of a given size in terms of resource demands. The fact that the United States could fight a sizeable war in South Vietnam in 1967 at a budget outlay then amounting to little more than 3 per cent of the GNP—which

clearly did not tax its *economic* capacity very much—simply reflects on the country's huge economic military potential. The same kind of war would have strained the resources of a smaller power with a potential similar to that of France or the United Kingdom.[78]

Now, however, when even wars between minor powers have to be fought with great quantities of industrially produced ammunition, including explosives delivered by aircraft that consume vast amounts of fuel, the antagonists quickly run out of the means to continue fighting in the absence of supplies from abroad—which is to say, in the absence of positive involvement by other and wealthier countries. This is why the 1965 war between India and Pakistan ended in 17 days.[79]

To maintain an effective—rather than symbolic—military force, even in times of peace, is a much heavier burden for a weak state than for a great power. This is reflected by the fact that the *only* states that spend over 10 per cent of their GNP are the weak states. Thus in 1970 only Laos, North Vietnam, Cambodia, the Republic of Vietnam, Iraq, Egypt, Jordan, Syria, Albania, North Korea, Saudi Arabia and Israel spent over 10 per cent (and up to 25 per cent) on defense.[80]

The Utility of Military Strength for the Weak States

> ". . . if the only choice was between submission with loss of independence, and danger with the hope of preserving that independence, in such a case it is he who will not accept the risk, that deserves blame, not he who will".
> Thucydides, The History of the Peloponnesian War, Book II, Chapter VIII, paragraph 62.

The military strength of a state can be effective in two different ways: (1) if it succeeds in the ultimate test of battle, when its military forces achieve the ends for which they were designed; (2) if it projects an image of power sufficiently deterrent to prevent war. Successful deterrence can be achieved *only* if a country has invested a considerable effort to build up its military strength and demonstrates the readiness to fight for its defense if necessary. Without these two prerequisites deterrence can easily fail, and in times of conflict the small state can find itself at war.

From the point of view of the weak states there are two basic types of war. The first is war between a weak state and another weak state of comparable power (or between any combination of weak states). The second is war that occurs *directly* or *indirectly* between a weak state and a great power. Wars of the first type are quite rare. Usually the great power can be found in modern wars—backstage if not in front of the lights. Examples of wars only between weak states are the Balkan Wars (Bulgaria, Greece, Montenegro, Serbia, Turkey, and later Rumania) and the Chaco War (Bolivia and Paraguay).[81] As for direct wars between a great power and a weak state, there have been those between Russia and Finland (1940); Italy and Abyssinia; and Germany against Denmark and Norway.

Between these two extremes lie conflicts such as the Six Day War and the October 1973 War in the Middle East, in which the super powers took an active but *indirect* role by encouraging or instigating one of the belligerents, supplying weapons, or threatening intervention on behalf of their client if the war went the wrong way. Thus even if the super powers did not send their soldiers to the area, the outbreak and outcome of the conflict cannot be understood without taking their decisions and conduct into account. Other examples include the *direct* intervention of a super power on one side and the *indirect* support of another great power on the other (for example, the Korean War and the war in Vietnam). In each case it is the intensity of great-power involvement that is the crucial element in determining the shape and direction of the war. The less intense this involvement, the shorter on the whole is the time span of such wars. (Compare the duration of the Balkan Wars, the Chaco War, and the Middle Eastern Wars with the First and Second World Wars, the Korean War, and the Vietnam War.)

The utility of military force for a weak state in conflict or potential conflict with more or less equal states is obvious. Through it the weak state has a good chance to defend itself successfully and to beat back an attack by other weak states. Conversely, a weak state can use its military strength to enforce its will against other weak states. There is therefore little need in such cases to justify the investment. The reason for a weak state to build up its military strength against a great power is less obvious. The weak country already knows that it can neither win a war in the long run nor hold out successfully in the initial stages. In spite of this obvious result, however, it is still necessary for the weak state to avoid becoming a power vacuum which could cause one or more of the great powers to intervene preemptively. It must also avoid becoming just a defenseless prey.[82]

There are two additional reasons for utilizing military strength in a confrontation between a weak state and a great power. First, a weak state needs to be able to hold out long enough to prevent a quick takeover, or until external help from other states can be obtained. Second, and more interesting, is the development of military power by a weak state in order to *deter* stronger states from attacking it.

> The greatest danger for a small country is that of being speedily overrun by a Great Power, thus establishing a *fait accompli*, which the other Powers would be inclined to accept, for fear of being exposed to an atomic [or any other] conflict, for an objective which, in itself, is of no great importance.[83]
>
> It is among other issues a major task of the Swiss Army to be capable to fight long enough on its own, so as *to win the necessary time* until the real support *from the outside* can be prepared.[84]

The longer the Finns could hold their own during the Winter War, the greater the chance that Great Britain, France, and perhaps even Sweden would come to their aid.[85] Indeed, the chances of allied intervention on Finland's behalf increased considerably as it continued to resist. This fact helped the Finns achieve relatively mild peace conditions at the bargaining table in Moscow. Similarly, Sweden, fearful of Soviet expansion, has decided to maintain both a position of diplomatic neutrality and an army strong enough to hold out until the Western powers can come to its rescue.[86]

Clearly, if a weak state is facing the danger of being overrun by superior forces, the longer it can resist, the better are its chances of receiving help. If it is rapidly overwhelmed through lack of determined resistance, help from another power would come too late or might not be offered at all. If Israel had been overrun within three or four days in October 1973, then no amount of external military aid could have helped. That it held out and fought back successfully eventually led to the supply of American material aid. If South Korea had been completely and quickly overrun by North Korean troops in 1950 (as almost happened), the United States might have considered intervention impractical and too costly.

Conversely, if Czechoslovakia had decided to resist the enforcement of the Munich Agreement, it might have deterred Germany. The Czechs had excellent defense lines and a well equipped and trained army.[87] In addition, as hindsight reveals, the German Generals objected to such a war because of inadequate preparation and the fear of engaging the British and French on the Western front with only screening forces. Even if deterrence had failed, the Czechs might have been strong enough to hold out for a couple of months, or until the British and French entered the conflict. It must be admitted, though, that even if the British and French had had large enough forces to attack the Germans on the Western front while they were at war with the Czechs, they lacked the necessary determination, as they demonstrated during the Polish campaign a year later.

Nevertheless, the Czechs' behavior throughout the crisis and their decision not to fight did little to pull the British and French into a war on their side. The Czechs were *too rational;* unlike the Finns and Greeks or the North Vietnamese, they were not ready to take a chance in a battle which they did not think they could win in the long run. The Finns or North Vietnamese, perhaps less calculating and more emotional, were ready to fight against overwhelming odds and ultimately fared better.

Although the Finns lost twice, their determined resistance brought them admiration and respect, and perhaps their toughness made them less attractive as potential satellites. (They might have been too difficult to control.) Thus the Finns maintained their independence, though it was limited by a tacit understanding with Russia concerning the "do's" and "don't's" of conducting foreign affairs. The North Vietnamese fought a bitter and prolonged war against the French and the United States, but they prevailed and achieved many of their goals.

It is true that both the Finns and the North Vietnamese paid dearly for their eventual successes. During the Winter War and Second World War, 90,000 Finns were killed, out of a population of little more than four million.[88] Over 900,000 North Vietnamese and Viet Cong were killed during the Vietnam War.[89]

More interesting than the need of the weak state to gain time in case of attack is the problem of deterrence. How can a weak state deter a great power, if it is well known that the weak state will eventually lose the battle to its antagonist? The secret of deterrence lies in the weak state's ability to exert such a high price from the aggressor power that victory becomes too costly. The weak state will profit immensely if another, more central conflict is going on in the international system. Not only has it a better chance of getting help from another large power, but the calculations of the attacking power will become more complicated. If the weak state succeeds in extorting a high price from the attacker, that price will probably be higher than a simple sum of the losses suffered. The great power will probably find itself much weaker *vis-à-vis* its *main* opponents—other great powers.

First, the great power can lose a large amount of war material, manpower, and even precious time. Secondly, even after winning the conflict, it may have to maintain a substantial number of troops in the occupied territory—troops which cannot be used elsewhere in more important theaters of war. This situation can be called *tertius gaudens,* because the real benefactors of such a conflict are the third parties who are saving their strength for the major confrontation. A similar strategic logic lay behind Grossadmiral Alfred von Tirpitz's famous "Risk Theory." He wanted to build up the German Imperial Navy to a strength sufficient, not to dominate the high seas, but to inflict such heavy damage on the British Navy that it would be helpless against the navies of third parties, such as the French, Italians, or Russians, or a combination of their forces. His idea, it seems, was not so much to challenge the British Navy to a duel as to deter it from participating in a coalition against Germany, as well as to force Britain to make colonial concessions.[90] The British, whose psychological reaction the Germans totally misjudged, developed in return their "two-power standard" doctrine—that British naval power must always match at least the combined strength of the two next most powerful navies.[91] It is possible, of course, for the weak states to develop a comparable risk theory of their own.

The price exacted by a weak state from an attacking great power can be very high indeed, disproportionate to any expected gains. (This is referred to in nuclear strategy as "proportional deterrence.") A great power tends to underestimate the strength of the weak state under attack; in particular, it often fails to perceive the weak state's determination to fight back, out of desperation and lack of alternatives. Thus great powers have often suffered severe blows, at least initially. This happened to the Austrians, who underestimated the Serbs, to the Russians *vis-à-vis* the Finns, to the Italians against the Ethiopians and Greeks, and to the Americans against the North Vietnamese.

In September and November 1914 the overconfident Austrians were seriously beaten in their first major battle with the Serbs. They lost half of their attacking forces: 227,000 were killed, wounded, or taken prisoner out of an army of 450,000, and the rest had to retreat across the Danube by December 1914.[92]

The Russians were severely beaten during the first phases of the Winter War. Mussolini, in fact, described Russia as "not a power but a weakness,"[93] an epigram which described Italy's position even better. In the words of Max Jacobson:

> The Finnish campaign, far from being a painless local operation, had developed into a major war which had become a serious drain on Soviet resources, caused uneasiness among the population, and tied down the Red Army in a secondary direction at a time when the European war might at any moment present the Soviet Union with fresh dangers. Nor was this all: by the end of January, it had become apparent that Zhdanov's insistence on gaining strategic advantages in the North, instead of improving Russia's defenses against Western intrusions, was inviting an intervention from the West and thus endangered the success of Stalin's policy of keeping out of the "Second Imperialist War."[94]

Russia's poor performance during the Winter War probably made her more vulnerable. The Red Army lost a considerable amount of credibility, which may have contributed to Hitler's decision to attack Russia the next year.[95]

PUNCH, OR THE LONDON CHARIVARI.—December 23, 1914.

FULFILMENT.

Austria. "I SAID ALL ALONG THIS WAS GOING TO BE A PUNITIVE EXPEDITION."

Mussolini's attack on Greece less than a year later ended in an even worse disaster. Not only could the Italians not bring their superiority in manpower and matériel to bear on the battlefield; they were eventually pushed back into Albania and found themselves on the defensive against the Greeks. The Italians had to be bailed out of a humiliating defeat by the Germans. In the process, however, the Germans lost crucial time (over four weeks) in their Balkan operations, which delayed them in beginning the Russian campaign.[96]

If time is of crucial importance, prolonged struggle by a weak state can also be crucial. Belgium's determined resistance to the German's execution of the Schlieffen Plan during the first week of the First World War delayed the Germans by as much as a week, which made possible the "miracle on the Marne."[97] In the eyes of the French and British, this feat earned the Belgians a relatively more important place at the Versailles Conference than was given to other weak states. Great powers hope that a weak ally, if attacked, will resist as long as it can. This view was expressed by President Roosevelt to the American ambassador to Yugoslavia on the eve of the German invasion of that country:

> I think we should find some means of getting across to the Prince Regent and others that the United States is looking not merely to the present but to the future, and that any nation which tamely submits on the grounds of being quickly overrun would receive less sympathy from the world than a nation which resists, even if this resistance can be continued for only a few weeks.[98]

There are many other examples of the weakening of a great power through campaigns with weak states. The German-Polish campaign was not a primary one, but nevertheless it involved the loss of considerable matériel.[99] That loss was worth eight months of production at a time when the Germans had weakened their defenses on the Western border with France. Had the British and French decided to attack while the Germans were occupied in Poland, it might have cost the Germans dearly.

During their attack on Norway the Germans lost a substantial part of their navy to Norwegian and British resistance, which left their surface fleet crippled for the rest of the war. Shirer summarizes the situation:

[In relation to British losses,] German naval losses were comparably much heavier: ten out of twenty destroyers, three of eight cruisers, while the battle cruisers *Scharnhorst* and *Gneisenau* and the pocket battleship *Luetzow* were damaged so severely that they were out of action for several months. Hitler had no fleet worthy of mention for the coming events of the summer. When the time to invade Britain came . . . this proved to be an insurmountable handicap.[100]

Another result of the Norwegian campaign was that the Germans had to tie up a very substantial number of troops in Norway, not only to control the local population but mainly to stem a possible invasion.

. . . it took between 300,000 and 400,000 soldiers to garrison Norway. These were perhaps not first-rate troops, but they could have been used elsewhere. The German military experts have not all agreed that the invasion was worth the loss when viewed from the angle of the whole war's direction rather than as a single operation.[101]

. . . Norway, which a reinforced corps had conquered, took an army plus vast expenditure of material to defend . . . it was a stone around [Germany's] neck . . . . The economic assets [iron ore, etc.] . . . all these were valuable, and yet none of them had a discernible influence on the outcome of the war . . . . He [Hitler] poured in troops and material there on a scale which far surpassed the need and drained strength from more active theaters . . . .[102]

The same phenomenon recurred in Yugoslavia. The Yugoslav army, one of the largest in Europe, totalled 1,457,000 men when fully mobilized—thirty infantry divisions, one guards division, and three cavalry divisions.[103] Nevertheless, it surrendered to the German invading forces within a week, due mainly to internal divisions between the Serbs and Croats. Nevertheless, once partisan warfare broke out, it took no fewer than 160,000 German soldiers (approximately nineteen divisions) to garrison the country.[104]

Early in the nineteenth century Napoleon had learned a similar lesson from the Peninsular War in Spain. The Spanish war, which was not of major importance for Napoleon to begin with, drained his resources and eventually became one of the major causes of his defeat.

> ... Spain was the least successful satellite kingdom. Its cost far outweighed the contributions of the others. By the end of its life, in June 1813, it had cost the empire 300,000 casualties, almost 4,000,000,000 reals (over a billion francs) in specie, and untold amounts in matériel, armament, munitions, and supplies. If the Spanish adventure were not responsible for Napoleon's downfall, as he himself suggested more than once, it surely lessened the empire's chances of surviving the shock of defeats in Russia.[105]

Spain is the classic example in modern times of the relative advantage of a weak state in the operation of guerrilla warfare against a numerically and materially superior enemy. At times the Spanish tied down nearly 300,000 French soldiers through their guerrilla activities and with the direct military intervention of 50,000 British troops commanded by Wellington. This demonstrated the enormous potential of guerrilla warfare conducted both within familiar terrain and with the active cooperation of a sympathetic population.

The same lesson had to be learned by Americans in Vietnam. The United States employed the bulk of its combat units, navy, and air force in Vietnam but achieved only meager results. With its forces tied up in Vietnam in 1967–1968, the United States would have found it difficult to intervene in other more important areas should it have been necessary— in the Middle East in 1967 or perhaps in Europe or Korea.

All these events are examples of *failures* by the weak states to deter an attack by a great power; yet they demonstrate why the attempt to deter should have been made. Even though the weak states' *direct* contribution during the Second World War was relatively small, the forces they attracted and engaged and the time they gained for the great powers were of vital importance to the outcome of the war.

In some cases, of course, weak states, by their own *internal* strength, have successfully deterred an attack by a much stronger state. The most obvious examples are the two armed neutrals of Europe, Switzerland and Sweden. Both have shown their determination to fight back if necessary against any invading army. They have invested considerable amounts of money and energy in the development and maintenance of efficient military machines. They have made it clear by their actions and preparations that they would put up stiff resistance against any possible invader. The British military attaché in Switzerland made this point in a report dated 17 November 1909. He wrote that any army trying to invade or pass through Switzerland's territory would lose so much strength and momentum in terms of time, expenses, material, and manpower as to render such an attempt unprofitable.[106] A similar statement was made to the German Kaiser when he was attending Swiss Army maneuvers in September 1912.[107]

The Swiss as well as the Swedes made it clear that they would not allow their territories to become power vacuums to attract preemptive attacks. Edgar Bonjour in his study of Swiss neutrality discusses this point:

> The strategic location of Switzerland exposed it, at the outbreak of the war [WWI], to the danger of the belligerents marching through its territory. Each of the Swiss task forces had to make its presence felt throughout the Federation's territory by threatening the invader from the flanks and rear. Had the Swiss border not been under heavy protection, the warring parties would have almost been forced to undertake military operations in Switzerland in self-protection, or at least to take precautionary measures in order to be able to confront their adversary on Swiss territory to protect their open flank. Under such conditions the Swiss Federation could have forcibly been turned into another European theater of war. Yet, because Swiss arms provided sufficient border defense, they enabled the belligerents to depend on Switzerland and spare (free) their troops.[108]

During the Second World War the Swedes built their military force up to 600,000 soldiers (including reserves), as well as creating a strong navy and air force.[109]

The Swiss and Swedish defense policies are well summarized in a Swedish defense memorandum:

> The defense has to be so strong that the costs to defeat Sweden are out of proportion as compared to the strategic advantages which an aggressor might attain. It is equally important that the Great Powers should have confidence in Sweden's will and capability to defend herself. If Sweden were attacked or exposed to hard political pressure by an adversary and if any of the Great Powers should have doubts about Sweden's will to fight, this Great Power might be tempted to take the first step itself and, by attacking Sweden, try to prevent the adversary from obtaining

bases on Swedish territory . . . . No part of the country must be surrendered without stubborn resistance.[110]

In a major conflict, as experience has gone to show, even the Great Powers must plan the use of their resources, large though they are, and they cannot afford to throw in overwhelming troop concentrations against a minor secondary object. Accordingly we are building up a defence which has naturally not much of a chance of surviving against a concentrated attack by a Great Power but which, nevertheless, may be rather troublesome to overcome if Sweden is a secondary objective.[111]

Sweden and Switzerland are by no means the only weak states to have deterred a powerful aggressor. Holland's ability to mobilize an army of up to 450,000 soldiers may have helped it maintain its neutrality during the First World War.[112] Yugoslavia's readiness to use force between 1948 and 1952 to resist a possible attack by Russia may have been responsible for deterring such an invasion. Similarly, Rumania's declared intention to defend itself against Russian intervention may have helped prevent a Russian attack in September 1968.[113]

The successful defense policies of Sweden and Switzerland cannot be followed by all weak states, mainly for two reasons: geographic location and financial burden.

The geographic location of Sweden and Switzerland on the periphery of confrontation, in areas not essential for fighting and of little consequence for military maneuver, helped these countries during the two world wars. Belgium and Poland, on the other hand, though neutral, heavily armed, and determined to fight, could never have stayed out of a major European conflict from the very first days. They were the victims of their strategic location.

The burden of maintaining efficient, well equipped, modern armed forces (such as the Swiss and Swedish forces) is very heavy, even during peacetime. It has been pointed out "that armed neutrality involves a financial burden out of proportion to the revenue of a small country, which is not in the position to purchase the whole series of indispensable weapons."[114]

The Australians, who have considered the option of armed neutrality,[115] have also realized that, whatever its advantages or disadvantages, they would have to allocate a considerably larger amount of resources to defense.[116] Indeed, neutral countries, unlike some of the weaker NATO allies or non-aligned states, cannot accept free foreign military aid. On the other hand, even if neutrality is a heavy financial burden, this burden is not beyond the reach of many states. Despite that burden, Switzerland and Sweden are among the richest countries in the world. It seems a price worth paying if a state can keep out of war for as long a time as Sweden and Switzerland. But it should be added that many weak states have spent a higher proportion of their GNP for defense than those two countries, without being able to avoid war. This fact indicates the exceptional importance of a weak state's geographic location.

Summary

One of the major differences between the weak states and the great powers is that the weak states rely much more heavily on *external* strength when they are fighting against other weak states supported by a great power, or directly against a great power. This greater reliance on external aid in times of conflict is the result of the much smaller war potential of the weak states as compared to that of the great powers. The weakness of the weak states forces them to keep a higher rate of mobilization in order to survive the first blow from a stronger power. The possibilities of renewing or expanding their strength from their own resources if the war continues are limited, whereas the great powers can afford to mobilize during the conflict. The weak states' dependence on external aid for their weapons and spare parts makes them highly vulnerable to external pressure in times of war.

The utility of maintaining strong armed forces against enemies of comparable strength is self-evident. Therefore, attention has been focused on unequal conflicts between weak states and great powers. At first glance, it would seem illogical for a weak state to resist an attack by a great power, an attack whose outcome is already known. But even under unfavorable conditions it still makes sense for a weak state to fight back: either to hold out until external help arrives, or to inflict such heavy damage on the attacking state that the attack proves unprofitable. Therefore it is logical for a weak state to maintain large enough forces to *deter* a possible attack by a great power.[117] However, the conventional goal of military forces at war, namely the desire to achieve a decisive victory, is out of the question. The goal of a weak state fighting a great power is not total victory, but successfully to deter or evade war, to survive, and to inflict costly damage on the attacker.[118]

Most of the examples given have been taken from the history of the Second World War—from a different international system—but the lessons are still valid for a nuclear world. The Russian invasion of Czechoslovakia in the summer of 1968 discounted the possibility of forcible resistance by the Czechs;[119] nevertheless, the Russians might not have been so ready to intervene had they expected the Czechs to fight back as the Hungarians did in 1956. Similarly, American difficulties in Vietnam have demonstrated that in the nuclear age the determination of a weak state (supported by other powers) to fight back is as meaningful as ever. This last example demonstrates the unrealistic nature of the ideal type. The super power is not always capable of winning in a confrontation with a weak state. The super power is not almighty and the weak states are not all weak.

A Note on Passive Resistance (Nonviolent Action) by Weak States

V. V. Sveics has suggested recently, in a study of the problems of survival of the weak states,[120] that since they have no chance of holding out militarily, they ought to transfer the contest "to the political area" where the "strategic success against aggression must be sought."

> ... many a small state can achieve a decisive political victory even in the "nuclear age."
> The political superiority of a small nation can be exploited to defeat a militarily stronger aggression.
> Small nations can rely on the political nature of conflicts to escape the ruinous course of military campaigns—destruction and defeat —without direct or indirect surrender.
> It [political or nonviolent resistance] can be adjusted to any kind of outside pressure—from the strongest to the weakest. Its flexibility is practically endless.

> The main characteristic of the modern era of warfare turned out to be the ascendency of politics over war.
> Since its [the weak state's] greatest strength is political, it rallies to defeat the invader politically.
> A correct strategy for small nations is to apply their national strength in a political struggle, where most advantages favor the defending community. Correctly utilized, it may insure national survival.[121]

Similar quotations could be given *ad nauseam*. The book is an exaggerated if not naive presentation of nonviolent resistance as the panacea for the weak state. It is a study in a vacuum. Sveics focuses on the potential of nonviolent resistance while neglecting to examine the other side, namely resistance by force. Nor does he examine the failures of nonviolent resistance, which are at least as numerous as its successes.

The basis for Sveics' enthusiasm is the Czechs' successful resistance of the Russian invader for seven long months.[122] He overlooks the end, which was probably inevitable: the "victory" of the Russians by splitting the Czech leadership and finding enough supporters to run the country. Any occupying power, especially if it is ruthless, can discover counter tactics and countermeasures against passive resistance. Despite the limited success of Norwegian and Danish[123] passive resistance to the Germans during the Second World War, they had to be freed by the allies. In Poland and Yugoslavia, where the Germans behaved much more ruthlessly, passive resistance was out of the question. Passive resistance comes *after* a defeat, not before one. The build-up of strong military forces by a weak state, plus its readiness to employ guerrilla or partisan warfare tactics after being occupied by a power, *combined* with passive or nonviolent resistance wherever possible, seems to be the best preparation for fighting or deterring a great power. Under favorable conditions passive resistance can be an important addition to the arsenal of the weak states, but it is never a substitute for internal military strength or external support. Up to a point, and under highly favorable conditions,[124] the citizens of a weak state can go their own way, developing a state within the occupied state, but such a situation cannot last indefinitely. The resort to arms is inevitable.

Nonviolence is not a modern invention.[125] Had it been as

efficient a panacea for the weak states as Sveics claims, guerrilla and partisan warfare, wars of liberation, and all the rest would have been unnecessary. History teaches a different lesson: a nation is never so solidly united that it can resist the divisive techniques of the occupying enemy, which range from psychological warfare, controlling the mass media, bribing and rewarding, to punishing and executing.

A prerequisite for successful resistance on the part of a weak state is the homogeneity of the population. Similar ethnic, national, and political views are of great importance in determining the capacity of the country to withstand external pressures or actual warfare. Sweden's ethnic homogeneity helped it to face German pressure during the war. Conversely, Yugoslavia's relatively large army was defeated within a week due to internal divisions between the Serbs and Croats.[126] Similarly, Czechoslovakia's lack of a homogeneous population undermined its capacity to resist German pressure. Unity of the people is a necessary condition for a national strategy of nonviolence.

It must be noted, however, that on many occasions the nonhomogeneity of a state does not hinder its military resistance to an invading enemy. Finland and Israel are intensely divided politically. Although political divisions had led to near-exhaustion, both countries put up stiff resistance on the battlefield. Perhaps their capacity for self-defense would have been even greater had they been united politically. Switzerland is a heterogeneous society, linguistically and culturally, that has demonstrated political unity in face of danger.

This issue of the relation between homogeneity and the capacity of weak states to defend themselves demonstrates the difficulty in formulating general laws to describe the behavior of weak states. Similar conclusions can be reached from opposing observations: under certain conditions, homogeneous and heterogeneous weak states can fight equally well. The most that can be said is that heterogeneous or internally divided countries, such as Finland, Israel, and Switzerland, whose citizens, despite all differences among themselves, accept their state as a legitimate framework of political action, and who are willing to play according to the rules of the game, will prevail in the face of danger. In other words, despite the existence of centrifugal disruptive forces, the centripetal unifying forces are stronger, where there is agreement on the benefits of living together in one political system. In the cases of Czechoslovakia and Yugoslavia, on the other hand, the opposing national groups did not recognize the legitimacy of the state and would have preferred to see the country divided into different autonomous states.

NOTES

1. This summary is based mainly on a discussion in Aron, *Peace and War*, pp. 52–54; on Knorr, *Military Power and Potential;* and Knorr, *War Potential of States*, pp. 40–41.
2. My approach is exactly the opposite of David Vital's. He prefers to analyze the weak states in isolation and chooses his case studies accordingly:

    ... the present attempt at an analysis of the political viability of the small state has been cast in terms of the isolated, maverick, unaligned power, the small power *alone*—the state which can rely least on outside help and sympathy and which, by virtue of its situation, is compelled to make its own decisions on the basis of its own understanding of that situation and such resources as are available to it. (Vital, *Inequality of States*, p. 6).

    ... it is only when acting alone—rather than in concert with other, greater states—that the small power can be said to be pursuing an external policy which is in any sense of a class with the external policies of great powers and capable of being compared with them. And it is only when the small power is unaligned and unprotected that the full implications of, say, maintaining or failing to maintain a modern defence establishment can be seen. (*Ibid.*, p. 5).

    His paradigm is then the strategically isolated state.

    ... the isolated state is one which is free to reverse such political ties as it may have when its intrinsic interests so dictate. (Vital, *Survival of the Small States*, p. 9).

    See also *ibid.*, p. 10, and Vital in Schou and Brundtland (eds.), *Small States in International Relations*, p. 20.

    This approach is methodologically unsound. The normal situation in international relations is the capacity of weak (as well as strong) states to combine their forces and enhance their own power. If anything, the "strategically isolated state" is the exception. See a similar criticism in Annette Baker Fox, "Intervention and the Small State," *Journal of International Affairs*, 22 (1968), 247; also Annette Baker Fox, a book review of Vital's *Inequality of States*, in *International Journal*, 23 (Autumn 1968), 623; also Paterson, "Small States in International

Politics," *Conflict and Cooperation,* p. 120. The study of the social sciences differs from chemistry, biology, and physics precisely because it is impossible to isolate and treat separately the variables involved. We can isolate and separate viruses, bacteria, or chemical elements, but we cannot study states or social groups of any kind as if they were isolated in a laboratory.

Such isolation is of course impossible for any human activity, including the interaction between states. See, for example, Karl Popper, *The Poverty of Historicism,* 3rd ed. (New York: Harper Torchbooks, 1964), chap. 1, pp. 5–24. On the contrary, we are *interested in the interaction and combination of forces in the study of politics.* Vital himself admits the impossibility of determining what part of a nation's power "it owes to its own resources and what to its partners." (*Inequality of States,* p. 5). This is exactly why we cannot study isolated states. Not only can we not differentiate completely the two sources of power, no such isolated state even exists.

This could easily be proved, even by the examples Vital chooses: Finland 1939–1940, Czechoslovakia 1938–1939, and Israel since the Six Day War. Indeed, all of these states were or are relatively isolated but not completely so. Finland improved its bargaining position *vis-à-vis* the Russians by the chance of British and French intervention on its side. See, for example, Marshal Mannerheim, *The Memoirs of Marshal Mannerheim* (New York: E. P. Dutton and Co., 1954), pp. 365, 376. To a certain extent, Finland could weaken Russian extremism by drawing on world sympathy, by pressures on Russia at the League of Nations, and its final expulsion from the League, as well as sympathy and some aid from the fascist states. Czechoslovakia was in a bad situation because it momentarily lost the *external support* it had had for years from its allies (especially France and the Little Entente); it did not try to draw on Russian power, which was offered to it, as Vital himself shows. And as for Israel, it is clear that without American military and financial aid it would have faced a very critical situation; but it can draw on American external help and cannot therefore be considered isolated. In an earlier period Israel benefited from Russian support (1948), and later had French support (1956). The effectiveness of external help is not measured by the number of countries with which a weak state is associated.

Vital claims that only when acting *alone* does a weak state follow a policy resembling that of the great powers. Yet on most occasions the great powers themselves do not proceed completely alone in the formation of their foreign policy. For a weak state, the real art of foreign policy is to learn to break its isolation, to manipulate and draw on the strength of other states. We cannot judge the actions of a weak state by the same criteria with which we judge the great powers. Vital's statement that "the isolated state is one which is free to reverse such political ties as it may have when its intrinsic interests so dictate" is meaningless. If a state is isolated it cannot reverse its political ties because it does not have any. If it is free to choose its new allies, this

freedom means very little because it cannot easily find allies (as Vital himself shows). Such a state usually has little alliance value to offer, and it is considered a liability rather than an asset by most potential allies. Therefore it generally has to be satisfied with whatever allies it can find.
3. See Vital, *Inequality of States*, p. 60, and the discussion, pp. 58–61.
4. See Panayotis Pipinelis, "Integration, Detente, and the Small Countries," *Nato Letter*, 15 (November 1966), 10.
5. Handel, *Israel's Political-Military Doctrine*, pp. 1–6.
6. See David Martin, "Armed Neutrality," in Max Teichman (ed.), *Aspects of Australia's Defense* (Melbourne: The Political Studies Association, Monash University, 1966), p. 80.
7. T. B. Miller, *Australia's Defence* (Melbourne: Melbourne University Press, 1969), 2nd ed., p. 28.
8. Agnar Kl. Jonsson, "Iceland's Place in the World—The Foreign Policy of Iceland," *Nato Letter*, 14 (January 1966), 10.
9. Vital, *Inequality of States*, p. 126.
10. What, gentlemen, is the business you are about? Reforming the government of Poland, which is to say: giving to the constitution of a large kingdom the stability and vigor of that of a tiny republic. You should first ask yourselves, before laboring to accomplish that purpose, whether your efforts can possibly be successful.

    Large populations, vast territories! There you have the first and foremost reason for the misfortunes of mankind, above all the countless calamities that weaken and destroy polite peoples. Almost all small states, republics and monarchies alike, prosper, simply because they are small, because all their citizens know each other and keep an eye on each other, and because their rulers can see for themselves the harm that is being done and the good that is theirs to do and can look on as their orders are being executed. Not so the larger nations: they stagger under the weight of their own numbers . . . . I cannot possibly repeat it too often: . . . The reform you ought to undertake first would be that of your territory; your vast provinces will never admit of the circumspect administration of the small republics. If you wish to reform your government, then, begin by narrowing your frontiers, though perhaps your neighbors intend to do that for you. It would certainly be a great misfortune for the dismembered parts, but a great blessing for the body of the nation. [Jean-Jacques Rousseau, *The Government of Poland*, trans. Willmoore Kendall (New York: Bobbs-Merrill, 1972), part V, pp. 25–26].

    See also Edward Sieber, *Die Idee des Kleinstaats bei den Denkern des 18. Jahrhunderts in Frankreich und Deutschland* (Freiburg in Baden: C. A. Wagner, 1920), p. 28.
11. Cole, *Geography of World Affairs*, p. 69. See also similar observations in Knorr, *Military Power and Potential*, pp. 31–39; and Reg Harrison, *New Zealand Foreign Policy*, in R. P. Barston (ed.), *The Other Powers: Studies in the Foreign Policies of Small States* (New York: Barnes and Noble, 1974), pp. 287–288.

12. Fox, *Power of Small States*, p. 184. Also her "Small State's Diplomacy," in Stephen D. Kertesz and M. A. Fitzsimmons, *Diplomacy in a Changing World*, pp. 349–350. An interesting indication of the predicament of the weak states is to be found in the large number of books entitled "... *Between East and West*." See bibliography.
13. See Albert N. Tarulis, *Soviet Policy towards the Baltic States 1918–1940* (South Bend, Ind.: University of Notre Dame Press, 1959).
14. *Ibid.*, pp. 115–116.
15. *Ibid.*, pp. 154–155, quoting Molotov.
16. *Ibid.*, p. 168.
17. See C. A. Macartney and A. W. Palmer, *Independent Eastern Europe* (New York: St. Martins Press, 1966), p. 302.
18. See Jan Klenberg, *The Cap and the Straits: Problems of Nordic Security*, Occasional Papers, No. 18 (Cambridge, Mass.: Harvard Center for International Affairs, 1968).
19. For Belgium's position, see Herre, *Die Kleinen Staaten Europas*, chap. 4, pp. 179–266; Jane Kathryn Miller, *Belgian Foreign Policy between Two Wars 1919–1940* (New York: Bookman Associates, 1951); and David Owen Kieft, *Belgium's Return to Neutrality: An Essay in the Frustrations of Small Power Diplomacy* (Oxford: Clarendon Press, 1972).
20. For Portugal, see Herre, *Die Kleinen Staaten Europas*, chap. 2, pp. 84–103.
21. See Edgar Bonjour, *Geschichte der Schweizerischen Neutralität*, II (Basel: Helbing und Lichtenhahn, 1963), 559–676.
22. William E. Griffith, *Albania and the Sino-Soviet Rift* (Cambridge, Mass.: The M.I.T. Press, 1969), p. 3; also Nicholas C. Pano, *The People's Republic of Albania* (Baltimore: Johns Hopkins Press, 1968), pp. 3–5.
23. See a description of this campaign in General Alexander Papagos, *The Battle of Greece 1940–1941* (Athens: J. M. Scazikis Alpha, 1949).
24. See, for example, James E. McSherry, *Stalin, Hitler and Europe*, II (Cleveland: World Publishing Co., 1970), 45; also Mannerheim, *The Memoirs of Marshal Mannerheim*, chaps. 14–15 and 17–18, pp. 322–391, 415–490; also Richard W. Condon, *The Winter War* (New York: Ballantine Books, 1972).
25. David E. Bohn, "Neutrality—Switzerland's Policy Dilemma: Options in the New Europe," *Orbis*, Vol. 25, No. 2. Summer 1977, pp. 339–340.
26. Robert N. Burr, *By Reason Or Force: Chile and the Balancing of Power in South America 1830–1905* (Berkeley and Los Angeles: University of California Press, 1965), pp. 14–15.
27. For Nepal's unique position see Leo E. Rose, *Nepal's Strategy for Survival* (Berkeley: University of California Press, 1971); and Leo E. Rose and Roger Dial, "Can a Ministate Find True Happiness in a World Dominated by Protagonist Powers?—The Nepal Case," in Wayne Wilcox (ed.), "Protagonist, Power and the Third World: Essays

on the Changing International System," *The Annals*, no. 386 (November 1969), pp. 89–101.
28. Cole, *Geography of World Affairs*, p. 378 (also pp. 376–379).
29. *Ibid.*, p. 378.
30. Alan Palmer, *The Lands Between* (New York: Macmillan, 1970), p. 184.
31. *Ibid.*, p. 165.
32. Max Jacobson, *Finnish Neutrality* (London: Hugh Evelyn, 1968), p. 87, quoting a popular Finnish war novel.
33. S. Shepard Jones, *The Scandinavian States and the League of Nations* (Princeton: Princeton University Press, 1939), pp. 13–17. Part of the reason for this attitude was the rise of the liberal and especially the labor parties, which identified military expenditure with support of the "military class" which they viewed as reactionary. Neglect of their defense systems was the result. These attitudes are still very much alive in Denmark.
34. *Ibid.*, p. 15.
35. Car-Ivar Lindgren, "Small States' Freedom of Action and Responsibility for International Stability under the Super Powers' Nuclear Umbrella," Center for International Affairs, Harvard University, April 1969, p. 20 (mimeo.).
36. See a similar discussion in Herre, *Die Kleinstaaten Europas*, p. 156.
37. For the preemptive attacks on Norway, see Fox, *Power of Small States*, chap. 4, pp. 78–107; T. K. Derry, *The Campaign in Norway* (London: HMSO, 1952); Winston Churchill, *The Second World War*, Vol. I, *The Gathering Storm*, pp. 9–16; E. A. Ziemke, *The German Northern Theater of Operations 1940–1945* (Washington, D.C.: Department of the Army Pamphlet No. 20–271, 1959).
38. Hitler's war directive no. 10 quoted from H. R. Trevor-Roper (ed.), *Blitzkrieg to Defeat: Hitler's War Directives, 1939–1945* (New York: Holt, Rinehart and Winston, 1971), p. 23; my emphasis; also William L. Shirer, *The Rise and Fall of the Third Reich* (New York: Simon and Schuster, 1960), p. 681 (chap. 20).
39. See Admiral Karl Doenitz, *Memoirs: Ten Years and Twenty Days* (Cleveland: World Publishing Co., 1969), p. 76; italics mine. For the mutual considerations of a preemptive strike, see Derry, *The Campaign in Norway*, pp. 22–24. Hitler himself objected for a long time to the invasion of Norway; he thought that a neutral Norway offered greater advantages to Germany than it did to Great Britain. Churchill, then the First Lord of the Admiralty, perceived this and suggested to the cabinet that England mine the Norwegian coast. The German Admiralty (OKM) was the main body advocating the occupation of Norway, as an essential condition for German submarine operations in the North Sea and the Atlantic. German naval authorities thought it was one of the greatest mistakes of World War I not to have occupied Norway, for that led to the closure of the German High Seas Fleet in its home port. See Vice Admiral Wolfgang Wegener, *Die Seestrategie des Weltkrieges* (Berlin: Mittler, 1929); Sven Tägil, "Wegener, Raeder

and the German Naval Strategy: Some Viewpoints on the Conditions for the Influence of Ideas," *Cooperation and Conflict*, 2 (1967), 102–112; Derry, *Campaign in Norway*, pp. 16–17.
40. For Gamelin's so-called "Dyle" Plan, see William L. Shirer, *The Collapse of the Third Republic* (New York: Simon and Schuster, 1969), pp. 581ff., and his *Rise and Fall of the Third Reich*, pp. 717ff.
41. See Fox, *Power of Small States*, chap. 5, pp. 108–146; also Derry, *Campaign in Norway*, pp. 10–11.
42. Donald E. Neuchterlein, *Iceland, Reluctant Ally* (Ithaca, N.Y.: Cornell University Press, 1961), pp. 20–26.
43. See Wolfers, "The Small Powers and the Enforcement of Peace," pp. 3–6; and his "In Defense of the Small Countries," *Yale Review*, 33 (Winter 1944), 201–220.
44. See Ripka, *Small and Great Nations*, p. 8.
45. Stanislav Andreski, *Military Organizations* (Berkeley and Los Angeles: University of California Press, 1968), pp. 33–35.
46. Constantin de Grünwald, *Baron Stein, the Enemy of Napoleon* (London: Jonathan Cape, 1936), p. 61.
47. Mannerheim, *Memoirs*, pp. 324, 372.
48. A good example is Israel. See Handel, *Israel's Political-Military Doctrine*, pp. 33, 66.
49. Papagos, *Battle of Greece*, p. 246.
50. The Israeli Air Force with about 543 modern jet fighters and fighter-bombers is larger than the air force of Italy or Great Britain. See *Maariv*, 25 May 1972; also *The Military Balance* for 1978–1979.
51. See Vital, *Inequality of States*, pp. 61–63.
52. Doenitz, *Memoirs—Ten Years and Twenty Days*, app. 6, p. 489. For the German war effort see Burton H. Klein, *Germany's Preparation for War* (Cambridge, Mass.: Harvard University Press, 1959); for the British war effort see M. M. Poston, *British War Production* (London: HMSO and Longmans Green, 1952).
53. Irving Brinton Halley, *Buying Aircraft: National Procurement for the Army Air Forces*, United States Army in World War II, Special Studies (Washington, D.C.: Department of the Army, 1964), p. 555.
54. John Milson, *Russian Tanks 1900–1970* (Harrisburg, Pa.: Stackpole Books, 1970), p. 180
55. *Newsweek*, 27 August 1973, p. 31; and Raphael Littauer and Norman Uphoff (eds.), *The Air War in Indochina*, rev. ed. (Boston: Beacon Press, 1972), p. 283. Another interesting difference of dimension between the great powers and the weak states is their respective losses in war. The number of sailors lost during the Second World War with the sinking of the British battleship Hood was 1,338, with the Glorious, 1,229; with the German battleships Bismarck, 1,977, and the Scharnhorst, 1,803; with the Italian battleship Roma, 1,254, and the Japanese Yamato, 2,498. Data from Siegfried Breyer, *Battleships and Battle Cruisers 1905–1970* (Garden City, N.Y.: Doubleday, 1973), pp. 161, 168, 293, 299, 359, 383. The number of Israeli soldiers killed in the October 1973 war was 2,412. *Haaretz*, 9 December 1973, p.1.

56. Papagos, *Battle of Greece*, pp. 390–391.
57. Mannerheim, *Memoirs*, p. 369.
58. Vital, *Inequality of States*, pp. 63–77. See also Ulrich Albrecht, "The Costs of Armamentism," *Journal of Peace Research*, 10 (1973), 265–283.

    Moreover large R & D efforts and scientific innovations are easier in larger countries where the absolute number of scientists is much larger, and hence there is a better chance for a scientific breakthrough. Evidence for this is the proportionately high number of Nobel prizes given to scientists from the larger states. As can be seen, the trend in favor of the larger states has become even stronger since the Second World War:

    The Nationality of Nobel Prize Winners in Science from 1901 to 1966
    (In Percentages)

States	1901–1950	1951–1966
Very Large States		
United States (plus the USSR)	16.5 (17.7)	50 (58)
Large States		
Great Britain, France, Germany	52.4	33
Small States		
Switzerland, Holland Sweden, Austria	18.9	2.3
Other States	11	6.8

    Source: J. Ben David, *Fundamental Research and the Universities* (O.E.C.D., 1968), Chapter 5, p. 26.
    For a study of R & D problems in smaller states see M. Carmi, *Research and Development in Small Developed Countries with Special Reference to Israel* (Israel: R & D Council, 1977), Mimeographed.

59. See Stephen Hastings, *The Murder of the TSR-2* (London: Macdonald, 1966).
60. See Ernest Fitzgerald, *The High Priests of Waste* (New York: Norton, 1972); Berkeley Rice, *The C-5A Scandal* (Boston: Houghton Mifflin, 1971).
61. See Albrecht, "Costs of Armamentism."
62. McLin, *Canada's Changing Defense Policy 1957–1963*, pp. 60–100. This is mainly a study of the failure of the AVRO CR-105 Arrow, whose price was prohibitive in comparison to planes that could be bought in the United States:

    > The Chiefs of Staff came to the conclusion that it did not make military sense to purchase aircraft at a cost of $8 million each when we could maintain aircraft with similar performance from the end of an American production line at a cost of something about $2 million each (p. 83).

    The cancellation of the AVRO CR-105 Arrow "was a traumatic

experience" and a "blow to [Canadian] national morale." See John Sloan Dickey, *The United States and Canada* (Englewood Cliffs, N.J.: Prentice Hall, 1964), pp. 68–69.

63. A small customer cannot expect to exert any meaningful control over the escalation of prices of foreign-produced weapons systems. See Ian Bellany and James Richardson, "Australian Defense Procurement," in H. G. Gelber, *Problems of Australian Defense* (Melbourne: Oxford University Press, 1970), p. 248.

> The cost of the aircraft [F-111] has steadily mounted, until it is now considerably more than double the original estimate. Worse (from Australia's point of view) is the fact that Australia signed the contract for the F-111 without taking elementary precautions on price rises. In other words we contracted to buy them whatever they cost and (within some limits) however they performed. There is not yet a confident delivery date. T. B. Millar, *Australia's Defense* (Melbourne: Melbourne University Press, 1969), p. 119.

64. McLin, *Canada's Changing Defense Policy,* pp. 62–63.
65. See Handel, *Israel's Political-Military Doctrine,* pp. 45–46, 62–63. On Israeli military industries, see *Armed Forces Journal,* vol. III, no. 2 (October 1973), esp. pp. 80–90. (This issue is devoted to the study of Israeli armed forces.)
66. Ingemar Dorfer, *System 37 Viggen: Technology and the Domestication of Glory* (Oslo: Universitets forlaget, 1973). This is an excellent study not only of the problems of weapon acquisition processes in general, but of the special weapon acquisition problems of a weak though highly developed state.
67. *Ibid.,* esp. pp. 107–111.
68. Handel, *Israel's Political-Military Doctrine,* pp. 62–63.
69. John J. Okunin, "The Place of African States in International Relations," in Schou and Brundtland (eds.), *Small States in International Relations,* p. 152.
70. Singer, *Weak States in a World of Powers,* p. 289.
71. For an interesting discussion see Ulrich Albrecht, *Der Handel mit Waffen* (München: Carl Hanser Verlag, 1971), esp. chap. 5, "Rüstungsexporte und Machtpolitik," section 5.1, "Hegemonialpolitik durch Sanktionen," pp. 123–135. This was Germany's policy toward the Balkan countries between the two World Wars. See Albert O. Hirschman, *National Power and the Structure of Foreign Trade* (Berkeley: University of California Press, 1969), p. 38.
72. *The Arms Trade with the Third World,* SIPRI (Stockholm International Peace Research Institute) (Stockholm: Almquist and Wiksell, 1971), p. 19 (see also pp. 24–25).
73. *Ibid.,* p. 25. See also Albrecht, *Der Handel mit Waffen,* chap. 5, sect. 5.2, pp. 135–161.
74. *The Arms Trade with the Third World,* p. 63.
75. *Ibid.,* pp. 63–65; also Singer, *Weak States in a World of Powers,* p. 275; Alvin Z. Rubinstein, *Yugoslavia and the Nonaligned World* (Princeton, N.J.: Princeton University Press, 1970), pp;. 52–53.

Diversification is also important, so that the weak state may avoid the danger of creating a narrow military elite loyal to the ideas of one foreign country. This has happened to Latin American armies, whose officers have been trained in the United States almost exclusively since the end of the Second World War. *Arms Trade with the Third World*, p. 63.

76. Sweden refused to supply ammunition for use in Vietnam; but some was eventually obtained through a third party. T. B. Millar, *Australia's Foreign Policy* (Sydney: Angus and Robertson, 1968), p. 169.
77. Interview with Ephraim Dovrat, Economic Advisor to the Minister of Finance, "The War Cost," *Israel Magazine*, 6 (1974), 22–26. See also Kenneth Hunt, "The Military Lessons," *Survival* (January/February 1974), p. 5:
   The intensity of the fighting and the amount and complexity of the equipment involved left both sides critically dependent on outside supplies, the Arab countries completely so . . . . So neither Egypt nor Israel will now dare embark on a war on this scale again without the assurance of full external support . . . . The scope for political leverage by the two super powers has been much increased.
78. Knorr, *Military Power and Potential*, p. 42. In 1968 the United States spent 30 billion dollars on the war in Vietnam. Cole, *Geography of World Affairs*, p. 129.
79. Louis J. Halle, "Does War Have a Future?" *Foreign Affairs*, 52 (October 1970), 28.
80. See *World Military Expenditures 1971*, p. 6, chart V. This is also suggested by Robinson in *Economic Consequences of the Size of Nations*, pp. 235–236.
81. For the Chaco War see William R. Garner, *The Chaco Dispute* (Washington, D.C.: Public Affairs Press, 1966); Leslie B. Rout, *Politics of the Chaco Peace Conference 1935–1939* (Austin: University of Texas Press, 1970); David H. Zook, *The Conduct of the Chaco War* (New Haven: Bookman Associates, 1960).
82. See also Daniker, *Strategie des Kleinstaats*, p. 144.
83. Jacques Freymond, "The Foreign Policy of Switzerland," in Joseph E. Black and Kenneth W. Thompson (eds.), *Foreign Policies in a World of Change* (New York: Harper and Row, 1963), p. 155.
84. Daniker, *Strategie des Kleinstaats*, pp. 133–134 (my emphasis).
85. "Finland's power of resistance raised the possibility that the Western great powers would eventually be attracted to its side, for Finland's cause proved not so desperate as to make such aid futile." Fox, *Power of Small States*, p. 59.
86. Samuel Abrahamsen, *Sweden's Foreign Policy* (Washington, D.C.: Public Affairs Press, 1957), p. 88. The Swedes tried to have their cake and eat it too. They wanted to and did maintain their neutrality, though they ultimately relied on their calculations of a "collective good"—"free" aid from the West. However, they took their military preparations more seriously than did other European weak states

enjoying the automatic support of the "collective good" of American help in NATO.
87. The Czech army was perhaps the strongest among the weak states' armies; when fully mobilized, it had 1,250,000 men, 700 tanks, 2,200 field guns of all calibers, 1,200 aircraft of which at least 600–700 were firstline aircraft. Vital, *Survival of Small States,* pp. 26–27. The Czechs had an industrial output roughly equal to that of Italy, which was considered a power, and they had a larger military industry. See Ripka, *Small and Great States,* pp. 6–7.
88. Jacobson, *Finnish Neutrality,* p. 20.
89. *Time,* Aug. 27, 1973, p. 34. See also Chalmers Johnson, *Autopsy on Peoples' War* (Berkeley and Los Angeles: University of California Press, 1973), pp. 47–48.
90. See E. L. Woodward, *Great Britain and the German Navy* (London: Frank Cass, 1969), esp. chaps. 1 and 2, pp. 19–66. (This is still the classical study of the Anglo-German naval race, though it was published originally in 1935!) See also Jonathan Steinberg, *Yesterday's Deterrent: Tirpitz and the Birth of the German Battle Fleet* (New York: Macmillan, 1965); Paul M. Kennedy and Edward Wegener in Herbert Schottelius and Wilhelm Deist (eds.), *Marine und Marinepolitik in Kaiserlichen Deutschland 1871–1914* (Düsseldorf: Droste, 1972), pp. 178–210, 236–262; Robert J. Art, *The Influence of Foreign Policy on Seapower: New Weapons and Weltpolitik in Wilhelminian Germany* (Beverly Hills: Sage Publications, 1973), pp. 14–25; Arthur J. Marder, *From Dreadnought to Scapa Flow,* Vol. I, *The Road to the War 1904–1919* (London: Oxford University Press, 1960), esp. chaps. 4 and 5, pp. 105–185; also Sidney B. Fay, *The Origins of the World War,* I, 2nd rev. ed. (New York: Free Press, 1966), chap. 4, pp. 233–245. See also Robert L. Rothstein, *Alliances and Small Powers,* pp. 280–281, esp. n. 16.
91. For the British two-power standard, see Arthur J. Marder, *From Dreadnought to Scapa Flow,* pp. 123–125.
92. See Cyril Falls, *The Great War 1914–1918* (New York: Capricorn Books, 1959), p. 54; B. H. Liddell Hart, *A History of the World War 1914–1919* (Boston: Little Brown, 1935), p. 205; Girard Lindsley McEntee, *Military History of the World War* (New York: Charles Scribner, 1937), p. 142.
93. Quoted in Max Jacobson, *The Diplomacy of the Winter War* (Cambridge, Mass.: Harvard University Press, 1961). p. 219.
94. *Ibid.,* p. 217.
95. *Ibid.,* p. 219.
96. On this point see Papagos, *Battle of Greece,* p. 386; Pipinelis, "Integration, Detente and the Smaller Countries," *NATO Letter,* p. 10. William Shirer describes Hitler's decision to attack Greece and Yugoslavia as "probably the most catastrophic single decision" in his career. *Rise and Fall of the Third Reich,* p. 824.
97. See Miller, *Belgian Foreign Policy between the Two Wars,* p. 23.
98. Quoted in J. B. Hoptner, *Yugoslavia in Crisis, 1934–1941* (New York: Columbia University Press, 1962), p. 298.

99. Anna M. Cienciala, *Poland and the Western Powers 1938–1939* (London: Routledge and Kegan Paul, 1968), p. 249.
100. Shirer, *Rise and Fall of the Third Reich*, p. 711. See Ziemke, *German Northern Theater of Operations 1940–1945*, p. 109, for similar comments.
101. Fox, *Power of Small States*, p. 103.
102. Ziemke, *German Northern Theater of Operations 1940–1945*, pp. 315–316.
103. Hoptner, *Yugoslavia in Crisis, 1934–1941*, p. 160. This is one of the very best studies of the foreign policy of weak states.
104. Alan Palmer, *The Lands Between*, p. 273.
105. Owen Connelly, *Napoleon's Satellite Kingdoms* (New York: Free Press, 1969), p. 263. The Japanese experience in China between 1937 and 1940 was similar.
106. Herre, *Die Kleinen Staaten Europas*, p. 294.
107. *Ibid.*, p. 293.
108. Bonjour, *Geschichte der Schweizerischen Neutralität*, II, 637–638. The Swiss army on the eve of the First World War included at least 250,000 soldiers of the first line (*ibid.*, p. 638). See also *ibid.*, p. 293.
109. Abrahamsen, *Sweden's Foreign Policy*, pp. 49–50; Fox, *Power of Small States*, chap. 5, pp. 108–145; Commander William W. Long, "Can Sweden Defend Herself?" *U.S. Naval Institute Proceedings*, 93 (September 1967), 48–49; Nils Andren, *Power Balance and Non-Alignment* (Stockholm: Almquist and Wiksell, 1967), chap. 4.
110. Quoted in Long, "Can Sweden Defend Herself?" p. 51.
111. Swedish Prime Minister Erlander, quoted in Vital, *Inequality of States*, p. 153.
112. C. J. E. Harlow, *The European Armaments Base: A Survey*, II (London: Institute for Strategic Studies, 1967), 51.
113. See A. Ross Johnson, "Yugoslav Total National Defense," *Survival* (March/April 1973), pp. 54–58, for the current Yugoslav doctrine of deterrence.
114. Jacques Freymond, "The Foreign Policy of Switzerland," in J. E. Black and K. W. Thompson (eds.), *Foreign Policies in a World of Change*, p. 163.
115. See Teichmann, *Non-Alignment—A Policy for Australia;* also David Martin, "Armed Neutrality," in Max Teichmann (ed.), *Aspects of Australia's Defence* (Melbourne: Political Studies Association, Monash University, 1966), pp. 61–76, 79–88.
116. See, for example, H. G. Gelber, "Some Western Determinants of Australian Foreign Policy," in Max Teichmann (ed.), *New Directions in Australian Foreign Policy—Ally, Satellite, or Neutral?* (Penguin Books, 1969), p. 93.
117. Fox differentiates between *external* and *internal* conditions conducive to the strengthening of a weak state's position. The first condition among those controlled by the weak states themselves is the readiness to meet force by force. *Power of Small States*, p. 184.
118. See Daniker, *Strategie des Kleinstaats*, pp. 44–54.
119. According to the *New York Times* of November 2, 1968. This point

was inferred from the relatively small number of Russian troops participating in the invasion—25 divisions in all.
120. Sveics, *Small Nation Survival* (New York: Exposition Press, 1969).
121. *Ibid.*, pp. 41, 48, 51, 64, 87, 97, 265.
122. See also, for example, Thomas W. Wolfe, *Soviet Power and Europe 1945–1970* (Baltimore: Johns Hopkins Press, 1970), pp. 381–382.
123. See Magne Skodvin, "Norwegian Non-Resistance during the German Occupation," and Jeremy Bennet, "The Resistance against the German Occupation of Denmark 1940–1945," in Adam Roberts (ed.), *Civilian Resistance as a National Defense* (Baltimore: Penguin Books, 1967), pp. 162–181 and 182–203.
124. Under less favorable conditions, such as the execution of hostages or counter terrorism, nonviolent resistance becomes a much more difcult task. Being occupied by a Western liberal country such as the United States or Great Britain is a totally different experience from occupation by Nazi Germany or Soviet Russia under Stalin and his heirs.
125. The most comprehensive study is that of Gene Sharp, *The Politics of Nonviolent Action* (Boston: Porter Sargent, 1973).
126. Hoptner, *Yugoslavia in Crisis*, pp. 247–292.

CHAPTER III

External Sources of Weakness and Strength of the Weak States

> So they stood, each with a foot placed at an angle as a brace, and both shoving with might and main, and glowering at each other with hate. After struggling till both were hot and flushed, each relaxed his strain and Tom said: "You are a coward and a pup. I'll tell my big brother and he can thrash you with his little finger, and I'll make him do it, too."
> "What do I care for your brother? I've got a brother that's bigger than he is—and what's more he can throw him over that fence, too."
> [Both brothers were imaginary.]
> "That's a lie."
> "You saying so, don't make it so."
>
> Mark Twain[1]

> Symbiosis—Association of two different organisms . . . which live attached to each other, or one as a tenant of the other, and contribute to each other's support.
>
> Oxford English Dictionary

Although weak states can achieve much in the conduct of foreign policy through the mobilization of internal sources, their relatively low strength potential clearly limits their maneuverability. When they confront a great power, or another weak state (or coalition of weak states) supported by a great power, their internal strength is not sufficient to withstand external pressures for any extended period of time. Under such circumstances, the weak states must turn to external sources of power for help.

> There is another difference between large and small states. The great power does not really have to ask whether it ought to mortgage its independence; the alliances it negotiates may well restrict its freedom of action but do not force it into dependence. A small power, when it establishes a hierarchy of the risks it must minimize, must choose between security and independence whenever it cannot simultaneously curtail the rights that threaten both.[2]
>
> The small nation must look for the protection of its rights to the assistance of powerful friends; only thus can it hope to oppose with a chance of success an attempt to violate its rights.[3]

Weak states must learn to "draw on" or "borrow"[4] the strength of other states. They will try to manipulate and commit, if they can, the strength of other states (mostly great powers), in order to secure their own interests. There are two major ways in which the weak states can recruit the support of other countries. They may either enter into a *formal* alliance with other states, or they may reach an *informal*, though not necessarily less helpful, understanding with partners sharing common interests.[5] Three types of formal alliances can be found, two bilateral and one multilateral. A so-called unequal bilateral alliance is one formed between a weak state and a more powerful state, usually a great power. An equal bilateral alliance includes states of more or less equal strength.[6] The third possibility, the mixed multilateral alliance—for example, the Warsaw Pact—includes other weak states as well as a great power or powers. Since the major influence is exerted by the great or super powers, a multilateral alliance could be classified as a subcategory of the equal bilateral alliance.[7]

Fig. 6.

	Formal Alliances	Informal Support
With Other Weak States	The Little Entente; The Balkan League 1912;	Arab or African "Solidarity"
With a Great Power	NATO; Warsaw Pact; ANZUS; CENTO; SEATO	U.S.-South Korea 1950; France-Israel, 1956; USSR-Egypt, 1956

Formal Alliances between Weak States and Great Powers

This section will examine all the types of formal alliances made by *free choice* between weak states and great powers. It is not concerned with alliances or pacts concluded under pressure or threats from a great power—the so-called "cat and mouse" treaties or "Al Capone alliances,"[8] such as those concluded between the USSR and the Baltic States in September and October 1939,[9] or most of the 329 bilateral treaties, agreements, and protocols signed by the USSR and the East European countries in the ten years preceding the Warsaw Pact.[10]

The attempt of a weak state to augment its own internal strength with external strength—that of another state, usually a more powerful one—is a result of necessity, not preference.[11] Whatever the inherent dangers of treaties between unequal partners, a weak state under the threat of a great power will choose the lesser of two evils—an alliance with another great power—in order to reduce the overwhelming pressures upon it.[12] Machiavelli's advice[13] to the prince of a weak state to avoid aligning himself with a more powerful state *whenever possible* is very sound under normal conditions, that is, when a weak state is not threatened by more powerful forces. But Machiavelli himself recognized that such advice is of little practical value in extraordinary circumstances. The major question for many if not most weak states is not whether they should enter into an alliance with a stronger power. It is, rather, how to obtain the external aid of another powerful state, how to commit the other power to support their interests, how to make sure that the help will arrive when needed, while at the same time maintaining their integrity and not becoming too dependent on the great power's good will and support. For many weak states, this is the *normal* way of life rather than the exception.

The dangers of alliances with a great power have been exaggerated as a result of certain actions by the USSR: its dictation of treaties and pacts in the 1940s to the Baltic States; its occupation of eastern Europe and the forced signing of treaties with those states; and its reluctant withdrawal from Iran after the Second World War. When treaties are made by the *free choice* of two unequal partners, the issues of maintaining the sovereignty, independence, and integrity of the weak state are secondary. For Taiwan, South Korea, South Vietnam, Israel, Egypt, and many Western states, concern and danger lie in the opposite direction—in the withdrawal of troops or aid by the super power, which could be far more dangerous to a weak state than the presence of the great power. The primary question is, then, how can the weak states strengthen the commitment of a great power to their interests, and what are the limits upon such efforts? Secondarily, what can they do to minimize the dangers of such unequal alliances?

From the point of view of the stronger ally, it is an advantage to leave its commitment somewhat ambiguous in order to avoid manipulation by the weaker state.

> . . . to restrain yet not alienate its allies, a state may want to prevent them from being confident that it will fulfill its obligations . . . . While nations generally want to be known as trustworthy, and deserting an alliance undermines credibility, a nation will lose bargaining leverage if their allies are sure they can count on it to live up to its original commitments to enter and stay in war.[14]

The simplest and most common way for weak states to commit a great power to support their interests is to make the great power sign a formal defense treaty with them, or to give clear, unambiguous promises of support in case of military attack.[15] Securing a formal treaty with a great power is not an easy task, especially if the weak state faces imminent danger. Moreover, treaties and declarations of support do not necessarily guarantee that such support will be forthcoming. It is, therefore, in the interest of the weak states to use additional means to buttress the great power's written and oral commitments.

If a weak state receives an ambiguous commitment of help, it will try at first to clarify the commitment with the supporting great power. If no positive results can be achieved, the weak state will very often clarify the verbal commitments *unilaterally*, in such a way as to favor its own interests. The great or super power can do very little about this, short of openly repudiating the weak state's actions and thus further diluting its own commitments. Usually, therefore, a power does not react at all.

A prime example is Castro's behavior before the Cuban Missile Crisis. Cuba had an ambiguous Russian promise of support, which Castro wanted to clarify and strengthen. In July 1960, reacting to President Eisenhower's decision to reduce the sugar quota for Cuba that year by 700,000 tons, Khrushchev said:

> In a figurative sense, if it became necessary, the Soviet military can support the Cuban people with rocket weapons . . . . [16]

Castro wanted a less ambiguous promise and tried to turn the Russian "figurative" missiles into real ones.

> . . . Khrushchev spoke of rockets only "figuratively," Castro chose to believe him literally . . . in his speech on July 10, 1960 the Cuban leader omitted the "symbolic" nature of the rockets Khrushchev had promised in the event of a U.S. attack on Cuba. Twice during the same month, the Soviet Premier made clear the real meaning of his promise, by substituting the phrase "all needed help" in case of aggression in place of the threat of rockets. Disregarding this, Castro, in the first manifesto to Latin America, known as the Declaration of Havana, gratefully acknowledged "the support of Soviet rockets."[17]

Castro's attempts to strengthen Russia's commitment to the defense of Cuba were not unsuccessful, for USSR prestige was at stake. Despite the Russians' deliberate ambiguity regarding their readiness to come to Cuba's aid in case of attack, they could not show their annoyance with Castro's "rattling Soviet rockets"[18] by denying their intention to aid Cuba. This would have weakened Cuba's position and perhaps even invited an attack on it, which would have been against Russian interests.

The Republic of China (Taiwan) stationed a large number of troops on the offshore islands of Quemoy and Matsu, taking advantage of the United States' inability, at that time, to undermine the position of the Republic of China. The great power was pressured into supporting Taiwan's continued control of the offshore islands despite their lack of strategic value for the United States.[19]

> ... Chiang's primary aim in putting large numbers of troops on the offshore islands was to ensure American participation in their defense. President Eisenhower subsequently remarked, "We had the feeling that he wanted to reinforce them so heavily with personnel that it would be difficult, indeed, for us not to go right to their defense quickly, even if there were only a local attack."[20]

Another important tactic of the weak states in their effort to win a great power to their side is their appeal to public opinion in the strong state. They try to "penetrate" the domestic system of the great power.[21] Although it would seem that the great powers should find it easier to penetrate the weak states, rather than the other way around, the weak states can and do "penetrate" the domestic systems of the powers.[22] One is tempted to say that this method is the weapon of the weak.

The weak states try very hard to cultivate public opinion in the countries whose support they want to secure. The Balkan Slavic states, especially Serbia, have tried for long periods to make use of the pan-Slavic sentiments of the Russian public.

> ... the Balkan states had no intention of allowing Russia to restrict their freedom of action, and they did not always take official warnings too seriously, for they believed that St. Petersburg's interests in the Balkans and pro-Slav public opinion would oblige Russia to save them, if need be, from the wrath of the Turks and Austrians.[23]
>
> There was always the possibility of a strong popular appeal to Russian public opinion, and the Balkan statesmen were counting on unofficial Russia, if events took a bad turn for the Slav cause.[24]

Similarly, the Poles and Czechs campaigned in the United States and elsewhere during the First World War for support in establishing Polish and Czech states. In the years after the

EXTERNAL SOURCES OF WEAKNESS AND STRENGTH

THE POWER BEHIND.

Austria (*at the ultimatum stage*). "I DON'T QUITE LIKE HIS ATTITUDE. SOMEBODY MUST BE BACKING HIM."

Second World War, the Republic of China (Taiwan) was very active in lobbying and building up American public opinion in its favor.[25] (Lobbying for public favor is different from lobbying in narrower political circles, such as in parties and in Congress.) The Israelis have done their best not only to recruit the support of American Jewry and to lobby in Congress, but also to influence American public opinion in general.

Care must be taken not to overemphasize the importance of appeals by the weak states to public opinion in the stronger countries. Despite Israel's generally successful appeal to American public opinion, the Eisenhower administration brought overwhelming pressure in order to force an Israeli troop withdrawal from the Sinai Peninsula in 1957. Public opinion may not help Israel in the future when similar decisions have to be made. In France, Great Britain, West Germany, and even in Yugoslavia, the public perhaps favors Israel's position in the Middle East; but that does not change the foreign policies of these governments towards Israel. Similarly, when the United States government decided on a rapprochement with Red China, all the mythical power of the Chinese lobby did not help the Republic of China, which found itself deserted.

Besides their attempts to influence public opinion in their favor, the weak states try to strengthen the commitment of a great power by inducing it to station troops and maintain bases on their territories. The intention, of course, is to have the troops of the great power act as a "trip wire"[26] and guarantee automatic intervention if the weak state should be attacked. If after Munich (or preferably even before Munich) the Czechs had been able to persuade the British and French to station troops on their soil—despite the obvious difficulties involved—the Czechs might have been in a much better position to deter German aggression. The United States' stationing of troops in South Korea or Taiwan is seen as the most important US guarantee of the independence of those states. The withdrawal of American troops could only be interpreted as a relaxation or weakening of the US commitment, whatever oral or written guarantees might be given. The same holds true for the American presence in Europe.

Whatever Machiavelli's dictum would suggest, Russia's

attempt to station troops and missiles in Cuba, whether by its own or Cuban initiative, was most welcome as a "trip wire" and as a major indication of Russia's readiness to protect Cuba against the United States. This is the only case I know of in which a super power has been forced out of such a situation by another super power. The circumstances were unusual in that the Russians were caught in the process of laying the "trip wire." Usually, it is dismantled at the initiative of the great power itself, as, for example, in the United States' decision to withdraw troops from Taiwan.[27]

The Australian government's permission for the United States to build an important naval communication center in the North West Cape, despite the danger that this would turn Australia into a target for nuclear attack, was clearly given under the assumption that the presence of such a base would increase the United States' commitment to defend Australia in case of attack.[28] The establishment of American air bases in Turkey was a sign of greater American interest in defending its Turkish ally against Russian encroachments.

Finally, weak states can strengthen the commitment of a great power by establishing a *symbolic value*[29]—a reputation as a "bastion of democracy," a model of a "harmonious alliance," or a staunch resister of aggression. The weak state in the alliance gives the great power an opportunity to demonstrate a benevolent attitude toward *all* weak states. Finland, for example, reflects the positive Russian image and thus commits Russia to continue its exceptional policy toward her. A similar effect may be achieved by strengthening commercial ties with the great power and by admiring and emulating its culture.

Although alliances with strong states offer many advantages for weak states under duress, they can also carry some drawbacks. The greatest danger is implicit in an alliance with a neighboring state, for that great power might not be ready to terminate the alliance once the reasons for its existence have disappeared. Such are the alliances between the USSR and the Baltic and East European states. Yet these alliances were not made by the free choice of the weak states. The USSR would have occupied their territory directly if they had not agreed to these "Al Capone" alliances. Not only did the weak states have no choice about signing the treaties offered them, but they could not align themselves with any other great power. The Russian alliances were forced on the weak neighboring states *after* Russia had concluded its Non-Aggression Pact with Germany on August 23, 1939.[30] This pact divided eastern Europe into new spheres of influence, which prevented the weak Baltic states from seeking help from Germany, the only other available power. Whether or not the weak states had voluntarily aligned themselves with Russia, they would have faced a similar fate—incorporation by force into the USSR. In agreeing to sign, they hoped to gain time— a diplomatic technique often employed by weak states as a last resort.

The only weak states which escaped mutual treaties with the USSR after the Second World War without bringing on permanent Russian occupation were those that could counterbalance Russian pressure with the strength of another great power. This was true of Iran in 1946, and of Yugoslavia between 1948 and 1955.

The danger that great powers will try to secure a permanent presence or bases in the weak state's territories has declined in the missile age because the value of such bases has depreciated. In turn, this means that the bargaining power of many weak states has decreased. The great powers, having relinquished their colonial possessions and imperial ambitions, no longer need "coaling stations" and "strategic bases" to secure the imperial routes. It is in the interest of the weak, no less than the ex-imperial powers, to keep these routes open. The shoe is on the other foot: it is the weak states (South Korea, Taiwan, South Vietnam) which are trying to find a way to secure the permanent presence of the great powers on their territory.

A piece of advice frequently given to the weak states has been to choose powerful but *remote* allies.[31] This advice is not always sound. Greater distance would not necessarily save a weak state from encroachment by a great power, and even if it did, that distance might mean a less certain military commitment in case of attack by a common enemy. Cuba's great distance from the Soviet Union clearly minimized the chance of direct Soviet help in times of crisis. Belgium, on the other hand, felt more assured of British help because of its proximity to Great Britain.

Another danger is that very often, while acquiring protection against an immediate or local danger (the prevention of which is of primary importance), the weak state may find itself facing new and unexpected threats. It may become involved in the conflicts of the great power (depending on the nature of the alliance); or, if the great power has acquired bases on the weak state's territory, it may find itself on the target list of another power with which it has no direct conflict. The way to minimize this last danger is to allow the establishment of such bases for defensive purposes only. In that way the small state can retain some measure of control over the use of the bases, not allowing nuclear weapons to be stationed there or, as the Norwegians have done, not allowing the establishment of bases at all in peacetime.[32]

A danger of a completely different nature, which is not often mentioned, is the threat to the cultural integrity of the weak state posed by the presence of a large number of foreign troops on its soil. The smaller the weak country and the larger the number of troops stationed there, the greater the danger. An interesting example is Iceland. During the Second World War the troops of Great Britain and later of the United States constituted a considerable fraction of the total population.[33] They influenced the local culture considerably, to the resentment of many Icelanders. Even in 1968, the 7,000 Americans based in Keflavik were the equivalent of 4 per cent of the population.[34] Similar situations have resulted from the presence of American troops in South Vietnam, South Korea, and other weak states. One of the ways to limit the impact of such a cultural shock is to confine the foreign troops to their bases, though this can create tensions between the troops and the local population.[35]

If the weak states often find themselves endangered by the great powers, the great powers are not totally immune from influence by the weak states. The danger of losing control of the situation is also faced by the great powers, though perhaps not to the same degree. On the whole, the weak states have been clever in obtaining the backing of stronger states in order to achieve their own ends, usually without compromising their independence. This is by no means, as is sometimes implied, a new phenomenon characterizing the bi-polar or post bi-polar world.

It often happens that the weak states manipulate a great power in the direction of their interests, more than the other way around. In fact, it is no longer clear whether the tail is not wagging the dog.[36] Hans Morgenthau has warned the great powers against falling into such traps:

> NEVER ALLOW A WEAK ALLY TO MAKE DECISIONS FOR YOU
> They [the Powers] lose their freedom of action by identifying their own national interests completely with those of the weak ally. Secure in the support of its powerful friend, the weak ally can choose the objectives and methods of its foreign policy to suit itself. The powerful nation then finds that it must support interests not its own and that it is unable to compromise on issues that are vital not to itself, but only to its ally.[37]

This has been said of Russia's position during the Balkan Wars:

> The Russian statesmen had patronised the Balkan League in order to lead it; they ended by having the leadership taken from their hands although the partnership remained intact. Pressed by the independent and determined action of the Balkan governments they trimmed their sails accordingly and handled the diplomatic situation adroitly.[38]

A similar case was illustrated when the Polish government stubbornly refused, despite British and French pressure, to allow Soviet troops to fight on Polish soil should Germany attack Poland. This caused considerable delays in British and French negotiations with the Soviet Government during the summer of 1939. It eventually contributed to the collapse of British-French-Russian conversations, and to the formation of the Soviet-Nazi Pact. Had the British and French pressured the Polish government by threatening to withdraw their military support, the Poles would have had no choice but to agree, or to face the German army alone. Instead, Chamberlain did "exactly what for more than a year he had stoutly asserted that Britain would never do; he had left to another nation [Poland] the decision whether his country would go to war."[39]

Such a situation has been referred to by Rothstein as "reverse potentiality,"[40] meaning that a weak state can reverse the direction of an alliance despite its greater weakness and often because of it. Rothstein quotes A. J. P. Taylor to that effect:

> When one state is completely dependent on another, it is the weaker which can call the tune: it can threaten to collapse unless supported, and its protector has no answering threat to return.[41]

Such a categorical statement should be taken with a grain of salt. Although the situation it describes can occur, it is by no means common; the great power that handles its diplomacy correctly is never short of the means to dictate its will. Threatening to collapse has been called in bargaining theory "coercive deficiency,"[42] and it happens when "a person or country has lost the power to help himself, or the power to avert mutual damage—the other interested party has no choice but to assume the cost of responsibility."[43] In international relations this can happen only when the continued existence or support of the weak state is of outstanding importance to the great power—when the power feels it cannot do without it, or that its loss would lead to the withdrawal of other states from its alliance system. This could happen in a "tight bipolar" system with intense competition, or in a situation where power is so evenly distributed that any change in the delicate balance would be regarded as significant.

These complications demonstrate the advantage of the ideal-type method of definition. The weak states are in greater need of the external help furnished by an alliance than are the great powers. Concluding an unequal alliance usually means accepting some dangers and liabilities along with the benefits. The dangers are not equally distributed. They seem to be heavier on the side of the weak states; but they also exist for the great powers. The powers are not immune to weak states' manipulations and are not always all-powerful, while the weak states drawing on the strength of the great can gain more influence than their intrinsic domestic importance would seem to warrant.

Patrons and Clients: A Perspective on Weak State—Great Power Relations

In some instances, the relationship between a great power and a weak state can take on a less favorable form from the weak state's point of view. The weak state can still get protection or material aid in time of need, but in return it has to render services which considerably limit its freedom of action and decision on a large variety of international issues. On almost every issue it has to follow the great power's lead and continuously try to please it. Sometimes the weak state is asked to do so; sometimes, on its own initiative, it tries to guess what the great power would like it to do.

Thus, for example, Cuban soldiers have been Soviet partners for some time in Africa, where Cuba has as many as 40,000 men, including some of its best fighter pilots. The Cubans deny that they are acting as Russian pawns; but they receive Russian aid amounting to $2 billion a year, and when the USSR switched support of Ethiopia, Cuba followed suit, even though it had previously trained and supported the Somalis.

A patron-client relationship is one type of informal relationship between unequal partners. The approach to patron-client relationships that is followed in comparative government can be used heuristically to study unequal relations between states in the international system. The main characteristics of patron-client relations as they appear in the literature of comparative government can be summarized as follows:[44]

1. They are instrumental relations between actors of unequal power and status (a superior patron and an inferior client). They are based on reciprocity (as distinguished from pure coercion) in the exchange of material goods or protection for services, loyalty, and deference to the patron. Most often there is an imbalance in these relations favoring the patron, despite the reciprocity involved in the process. The relation in its pure form is conditional in character.

2. The exchange is mutually valued by both parties. Coercion, manipulation, and authority can exist implicitly in the background but are not dominant. The power imbalance is not so great as to permit a pure command relationship. The relations are a balance between voluntarism and coercion.

3. The Patron: The bargaining power of the patron is by definition greater than that of the client. The resources he has and the protection he can offer usually have a strong monopolistic element. The patron assembles clients on the basis of his ability to assist them.

4. The Client: The client usually has a moral or contractual obligation which binds him to the patron. His position is determined by (a) the availability of other patrons who can render the same protection or material support, and the mobility of the clients between alternative patrons; (b) the degree to which the patron is dependent on his client's services.

Despite the frequent references in the literature of international politics to the relations between patrons and clients, no systematic attempt has been made to apply the paradigm of patron-client relations to the analysis of the relations between states. The reason is clear. The unequal nature of the patron-client relationship is contrary to the accepted norms of international conduct. Therefore both sides try to cover it up, and that makes it all the more difficult to study or document.[45]

As between individuals, so also patron-client relations between states may be of different degrees of intensity, dependence, and exploitation. They can range from an almost symbiotic relationship to a situation of almost unilateral exploitation.

The Romans systematically extended the model of their domestic patron-client relationships to their imperial policies.

> Roman notions of foreign client polities and the Roman view of the relationship between empire and client were rooted in the traditional pattern of patron-client relationships in Roman municipal life. The essential transaction of these unequal relationships was the exchange of rewards (*beneficia*)—accorded by the patron—for services (*officia*) performed by the client. Discrete gradations of the inquality between empire and client were recognized, though with the continuing increase in Roman power a divergence often developed between the formal and the actual relationship. By the later stages of the process, a client king whose formal status was that of a "friend of the Roman people" (*amicus populi Romani*)—a title suggesting recognition for services rendered "with a lively sense of favours still to come," but with no connotation of subservience—was generally no more than a vehicle of Roman control.[46]

It appears, then, that the Romans gradually developed a patron-client relationship close to unilateral exploitation. It gave only a low degree of benefits to client states which were actually closer to being protectorates or satellite states than members of a true alliance.

The major functions of client states were to help Rome protect the Empire's extended border from invasion, to maintain their own internal security, and to send auxiliary forces to fight beside the Romans. While Rome needed the help of its client states, it was careful to keep them at an optimal strength: strong enough to protect themselves and help the Romans, but too weak to threaten Roman interests.

Under the *Pax Romana,* no client was entitled to expand at the expense of a fellow client without explicit sanction from Rome. "It was understood that Roman interests were best served by maintaining local balances of power between nearby clients, so that the system could keep itself in equilibrium without recourse to direct Roman intervention."[47]

Maintaining this order was not always possible as client rulers had their own ambitions, backed by a military force. The Roman client states in the East could have invoked the countervailing power of Parthia to upset the regional balance of power.

Many of the elements in the Roman pattern of patron-client relations were found in the British Empire and, more recently, in the Soviet Union's relations with East European states.

Fig. 7

Correlation between Degree of Equality and Benefits Derived in Great Power-Weak State Relationship

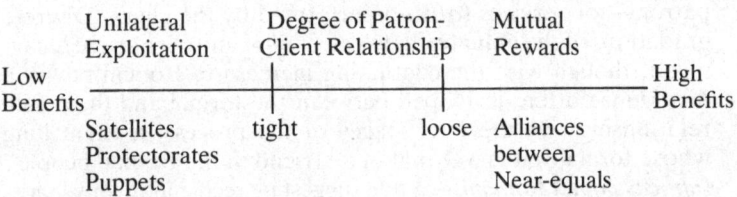

In international relations, the main characteristic of the relations between patrons and clients is their informality; they are much less rooted in tradition and less uniform in character than formal alliances.[48] In every instance, however, the client state makes decisions regarding its foreign policy with one ear to the wishes of the great power. These wishes do not have to be explicitly or formally presented to the client. On most occasions, patron-client relations in the international arena of the 1970s are characterized by the *tacit understanding* of the client state, which knows what is expected of it by the great power and adjusts its policy accordingly.

In the ideal form of patron-client relations (i.e., the non-coercive form), the client state voluntarily sets its own limits on action and makes decisions in support of the great power, hoping by such acts either to get immediate positive rewards from the great power or to accumulate goodwill and credit for the future. If the behavior of the weak state is designed only to placate[49] the great power rather than to gain some kind of positive rewards, its intention is to prevent the imposition of negative sanctions. This has been the case with Finland's behavior towards the USSR. The Finns voluntarily set their own limits on the conduct of foreign policy so as not to adopt any position which could offend the USSR; they try to follow the course most favorable to the USSR. They do so in order to maintain Russian good will and to forestall Russian military, political, or economic sanctions.[50]

The client state can develop what biologists call *synchronism*. They describe the behavior of the pilot fish (*Naucrates ductor*) as following the shark as a piece of iron does a magnet, obeying instantly the incessant and irregular changes of direction shown by the shark.[51] This phenomenon is not unknown in international politics.[52] For example, the Hungarian mission to the League of Nations in the early thirties coordinated its speeches with those of Germany, and the same must have been true for Albania and Italy.[53] The coordination of policy does not have to be explicit, and it can be minimal. Up to the mid-sixties, the United States could rely on the support of the Latin American countries at the United Nations. (These states were usually referred to as "safe votes.")[54] France today can count on the vote of its ex-African colonies in the United Nations. Israel in the late fifties and early sixties, being dependent on the supply of French weapons, voted with the French on all issues, including some on which Israel would have preferred to take a different position, such as the French nuclear tests or French policy towards Algeria. Israel was not pressured by the French to do so, but it decided to support France for reasons of loyalty (always a strong element in non-coercive patron-client relations), obligation, and in order to cultivate good relations. In like manner, one would expect Taiwan, South Korea, and South Vietnam to vote with the United States.

At times over-zealous loyalty can become embarrassing. Marshall Singer cites the following example:

> I was once told by a representative of one of the Powers at the United Nations that he wished the delegates of his country's associated states would not always vote with his country on every minor issue because it exposed those delegates to charges of being "satellites" of the Power, and created the impression that the Power was forcing them to vote as they did. He cited a number of instances in which he was approached by delegates from weaker associated states asking him how his country intended to vote on an issue before they would decide how their delegation would vote. These delegates presumably did so because they *thought* that the Power wanted them to vote the way the Power was going to vote.[55]

The same situation is reflected in the comments of a Central American delegate:

> We believe strongly in the necessity for the United States to have hegemony of advice in the American continent. We cannot afford to have another nation in a better position than the United States. We try to harmonize our policy with the United States' point of view, in the interests of regional solidarity.[56]

In the United Nations, a political arena in which mutual favors are traded, there is a large variety of patron-client relationships. The weak states, for example, exchange their political support of the great powers in the General Assembly for the guarantee of a great-power veto in the Security Council, and have thus achieved the veto right *de facto*. The weak states may also get other favors, such as economic aid and military support, in return for their loyalty.[57]

A client state behaves like a politically penetrated system. It takes decisions on foreign affairs *as if* a foreign state were participating in its decision-making process. By its own choice it sacrifices some freedom of action. In such relationships the known "leader [patron] may use military bases supplied by smaller allies for operations that have nothing to do with alliance business and which these allies may sense as disadvantageous to themselves."⁵⁸

In extreme cases a weak state may be militarily or politically penetrated to the extent that the great power is actually present in the decision-making process; but then the influence of the great power is gained by direct threats or coercion. Such circumstances are not illustrative of patron-client relations but of protectorates, puppet states, or satellites.⁵⁹ The threat of force is always present, and the voluntary element of co-operation is absent. The weak state does not enjoy the benefits of reciprocal aid, nor can it decide to switch to another patron or quit the "arrangement" which has been forced upon it. In such cases the great power usually employs its own local agents, quislings, or parties. This was true of Japan's Manchukuo, the German protectorates during the Second World War, and the Soviet satellite system established after the Second World War. The weak states must accept the great power's military forces, march in step politically with the dominating state, imitate its political system, and accept unfavorable terms of trade. Germany traded in this way with its protectorates, and the USSR forces East European satellites to buy from Russia products which might be cheaper and of better quality if purchased elsewhere.

The situation is not always so clear cut. Between the world wars Albania became an Italian client. The Italians gave the Albanians several loans, which they were supposed to repay not in money but in political loyalty.⁶⁰ Due to its exceptional weakness, Albania always seems to be a client of one great power or another.⁶¹ Its patrons have been successively Italy, Germany, Yugoslavia, the USSR, and China. The Yugoslavs' attempts to attract Albania into their orbit demonstrate that "no country seems to be too small or too poor to be a patron."⁶² Similarly, "India, a major recipient of economic assistance, has provided aid to Ceylon, Nepal, Tanzania and Indonesia."⁶³

India has tried to exert political and economic pressure to make Nepal its client. Because Nepal's transit trade is dependent on India and 90 per cent of its foreign trade is exchanged with India, it is very sensitive to Indian wishes, and has had to adapt its political stand accordingly. When Nepal deviated from what the Indians perceived as sympathetic or friendly policy, it was immediately brought under Indian economic pressure. "The first question the Nepal government must ask itself in formulating policy . . . is: how will this affect relations with India?"[64] In the early fifties no such thing as an autonomous Nepalese foreign policy existed. "On a number of occasions, the Nepal government not only tamely followed New Delhi's guidance but actually took the initiative in seeking it."[65] India reluctantly agreed that Nepal should enter the United Nations, where obviously it would have to vote along with Indian interests, as, for example, on the Kashmir question.

But India did not encourage Nepal to broaden its diplomatic relations with too many states. Later the two countries formally agreed that they ought to coordinate their foreign policies, in particular toward Tibet and China.[66] This meant, of course, that Nepal had to consult India on all important foreign policy decisions, but not vice versa. When it first established diplomatic relations with China, a resident embassy was *not* established in Katmandu, as the result of Indian "wishes." Earlier Nehru had stressed to the Chinese that Nepal must be acknowledged as an Indian sphere of influence and that Chinese recognition of the state should first be coordinated with India.[67]

Until the mid-fifties, Nepal had what was euphemistically called "special relations with India" (i.e., Indian patronage), but gradually the Nepalese have tried to shift to an "equal friendship with all."[68] This has been done through their "diversification policy," in accordance with which they established diplomatic relations first with the United States and France and later with the USSR and the Afro-Asian countries. Thus the Nepalese tried to counterbalance India's influence. Up to a point they have been successful and have set their own limits. However, in the last resort this policy is limited.

The Nepalese are dependent on India's goodwill for their transit trade, and even if they want to and are able to diversify their foreign markets, they can do so only with Indian cooperation.[69] Their economic and financial position is inevitably tied to India's. Inflation there means inflation in Nepal, and there is little the Nepalese can do about it. India has further control through the training of Nepalese officers in Indian military schools.[70] When, in 1962, it felt that Nepal's foreign policy was directed against Indian interests, the government did not hesitate to support Nepalese rebels by imposing an economic blockade.⁷¹ Whatever Nepal might do to improve its position *vis-à-vis* India—counterbalancing its influence, diversifying its economy, improving the road to China—in the last resort its position is determined by its geographic isolation and its dependence on India for access to the rest of the world.

Patron-client relations are not limited to the relations between a great power and a weak state. Weak states can try to behave as patrons of even weaker states. Poland has tried to control and influence the Baltic states; Egypt has tried to patronize and lead the Arab world. One can often find dual layers of patronage. Until 1948 Yugoslavia was dependent on Russian aid and was considered a Russian client state, while at the same time it tried to patronize Albania. Brazil was at times a client of the United States, but this did not stand in the way of its efforts to make Paraguay its client.

Patron-client relations also develop between the super or great powers and the middle powers. Then the relationships are not so intense. They are to a large extent a function of the *feeling* of constraint on the part of the middle power. Finding itself following too closely the policy of a super power, the middle power becomes afraid of losing its own identity (which is always a psychological problem present in patron-client relations) because it has not developed its *own* distinct foreign policy. The best examples of this type of relationship are Australia and Canada.

Traditionally the Australians have sought security and conducted their foreign policy in the company of great and powerful friends. Australia has usually been the faithful ally of greater powers, a voluntary partner whose influence was never equal to that of the great or super power.

> ... America can, and Britain may, be able to take decisions which affect Australia in important ways while Australia *can exercise no comparable countervailing pressure*. This in turn makes the effort to *pile up credit* in Washington, while rational enough as far as it goes, an essentially Sisyphean effort to which there can be no logical end. The commitment to secure American goodwill is open-ended, while American reassurance to Australia can never, in the nature of things, be complete.⁷²

Source: T. B. Millar, *Australia's Foreign Policy* (Sydney: Angus and Robertson, 1968), frontispiece.

Source: Cover design of H. G. Gelber, *The Australian American Alliance* (Baltimore: Penguin Books, 1968).

Australia's foreign policy has traditionally been a direct function of other states' behavior and decisions.[73] "In 1914 Andrew Fisher pledged Australian support 'to the last man and the last shilling,' and in 1939 Mr. Menzies declared Australia to be automatically at war with Germany because Britain was at war with Germany."[74] Australia was accused of developing "habits of dependency and fear"[75] which led to the policy of "never disagreeing with Britain in public over foreign policy [which] has been transferred to the United States."[76]

The motivation for Australia's behavior (other than loyalty to the Anglo-Saxon world) has been the desire to commit and obligate Great Britain, and later the United States, to come to its aid if it is attacked. In their short history the Australians have specifically feared Japan, China, and Indonesia. They are generally afraid of an attack by any one of the over-populated Asian countries against their own large, under-populated territory. As an investment in the future, "Australia is taking out an insurance premium, putting a deposit in a bank from which it may later wish to borrow, paying its 'club fees'."[77]

Australia's behavior towards the United States has been referred to by Gelber as based on the American "Lafayette Syndrome", i.e., to help the U.S. now in return for its gratitude and readiness to help in the future.[78] This also explains Australia's decision in 1965 to send its troops to fight in Vietnam.

> Australia has, for example, argued that the obligation to support the U.S. is a major reason for her presence in Vietnam. Indeed, it can be plausibly argued that her interest in maintaining and strengthening the U.S. alliance would require the dispatch of an Australian contingent *even if* the Australian government believed America's Vietnam commitment to be a mistake or likely to fail.[79]

New Zealand followed a similar policy. No American pressure was necessary to encourage its participation in Vietnam. Like the Australians, New Zealand wanted to "invest in the future" by morally obliging the United States to come to its aid should the need arise. Minister of Justice J. R. Hanan stated in May 1965, "never was there a more obvious time for us to stand up by the United States, if we are to rely on the United States for support should we face aggression". The New Zealand Prime Minister made a similar point: "If we are not prepared to play our part now, can we in good conscience expect our allies to help later?" Sending a token amount of troops to fight in Vietnam was not sheer altruism, but a calculated investment in the United States' goodwill.[80]

Similar considerations have dictated the presence of other American clients in South Vietnam—South Korea and the Philippines, for example, furnished token aid to demonstrate their good will, hoping later to cash in on the so-called "Lafayette Syndrome".

Another interesting pattern of patron-client relations developed between South Korea and the United States during the Vietnam War. While both sides benefited from this type of mutual dependence, it seems as if Korea gained more from services she rendered her patron, at least in the short run, than would usually be the case.[81]

All in all the South Korean government sent to Vietnam a force of 47,872 soldiers who fought effectively alongside the United States Armed Forces. What motivated it to send such a large force to South Vietnam? The reasons were "(1) a sense of obligation to repay the military help Korea had received from other countries during the Korean War; (2) the desire to strengthen the alliance with the United States; (3) interest in potential financial benefits; (4) the prospect of gaining international prestige; and (5) recognition that the security of South Vietnam was related to South Korea's own".[82]

The first two motives are quite similar to those of Australia and New Zealand, for example, in their attitudes toward the United States—especially their intention to strengthen a US commitment to them and to obligate her to come to their aid in the future by helping her in the present.

"The foremost reason for South Korea's decision to send combat troops to Vietnam was to be found in her desire to prevent the weakening of the U.S. security commitment in Korea and, if possible, to further strengthen it".[83] South Korea ". . . used the circumstances as an opportunity to solidify America's security commitment," it tried to get ". . . more and greater public verbal commitments, as well as to create a military and political situation in which the United

States would find it difficult to back out in case of a military confrontation in Korea".[84]

In addition to the strengthening of the American commitment to Korea's security, the Koreans have derived further economic benefits as a result of their participation in the Vietnam war, amounting between 1965 and 1969 to $546 million—16 per cent of Korea's total foreign receipts or about 2 per cent of the GNP for the same period.

> Earnings for the entire period of Korean participation (1965–1973) are estimated to have been at least 1 billion, without counting the increase in direct U.S. economic and military aid to Korea. The "Vietnam earnings" became available during a critical stage in Korea's economic development, when large amounts of international liquidity were needed for the rapid expansion of export industries.[85]

An indication of Korea's improved bargaining position vis à vis the United States was the great increase in American military aid. While Korea received from the United States during the five years between 1961 and 1965 a total sum of $815 million (an average of $163 million a year), it received during the next five years of its participation in the Vietnam war (1966–1971) a total sum of $1,681 million (or an annual average of $336 million). In addition the Korean government has secured an American promise (1971) to support a five-year program to modernize the Korean armed forces at an estimated cost of $1.5 billion.[86]

Because its contribution to the US war effort in Vietnam was so important, South Korea considerably increased its bargaining leverage over the United States by frequently threatening to withdraw its troops unless it received certain additional benefits. To a certain extent, however, the temptation to use the situation for "blackmail" must have weakened the United States' goodwill in the longer run. In Schelling's words ". . . in various crises governments have been able to extort a good deal out of the United States at the price of warning the United States that it had better reduce the degree of the relationship before the next crisis".[87]

Canada, a much more powerful country than Australia, has also developed a client attitude toward the United States, though to a lesser extent. In Canada, this approach is referred to as the "affiliation strategy."

> The affiliation strategy requires a small power to adopt a great power as its leader in international affairs. The small power will then seek to acquire some measure of influence over the course of events through its relation to a great power—an influence which it believes it could not have on the same events if acting independently. To augment its influence the small power will support the major policies of the great power to which it affiliates and refrain from taking initiatives of its own that would create open conflict. If the small power disagrees with the great power, it will neither openly declare its opposition nor do what it can to counteract the policy; it will, instead, seek to use its general support of the aims of the great power as the grounds for claiming the right to have its views taken into consideration by the decision-makers of the great power. Independence of action is limited to those areas in which the interests of the great power are not at stake. Britain's rapid decline as a great power after the war has been completed by her adoption of the affiliation strategy toward the US. Canadian foreign policy is also grounded at the present time in an affiliation strategy toward the United States which provides the major premise for quiet diplomacy.[88]

Canada's "affiliation strategy" resembles Australia's "faithful ally" policy and is similarly criticized as "pre-disposed by habit"[89] and "regressive rather than constructive." And furthermore, it is

> ... not only regressive, it is also futile. It is premised on the assumption that by being a "good ally" (one that does not oppose any major policy of the US), Canada will acquire influence in Washington. But any senior American government adviser ... always has more influence on decision-making than the Canadian ambassador who represents the people of Canada ....[90]

Canada's self-perception in relation to the United States often approximates that of a client state *vis-à-vis* a patron state. It has been observed that "Canadian policy exhibits more of the characteristics of a satellite than of an independent state. The United States ... is the planet around which the Canadian moon revolves with heavenly regularity."[91]

> Is a country sovereign when 70 per cent of its trade is with one country which is far greater in power? Can a country be considered

sovereign when most of its economy is owned by foreign interests, and in particular by one super-power? Can a territorial state be considered a nation when it has no separate culture, when its mass media and communications are heavily dominated by the same large foreign state? In all important areas, Canada is a "colony" of a great power, the United States. Only today, with the dissolution of the traditional empires of the 19th century, the appropriate word is "satellite."[92]

Instead of becoming the third power in the alliance [NATO], Canada was relegated to a role in the Greek chorus.[93]

We are the sheep and the State Department is the shepherd.[94]

As already mentioned, the problem of identity maintenance in patron-client relations is a crucial problem for the client. It is a major one for Canadians, who besides being geographically close to the United States, share a common language and culture. (For cultural and linguistic reasons, Mexico can maintain its identity more easily than Canada.) The Canadians are so preoccupied with their identity problem (or to be more exact, with justifying their separate identity from the United States) that they often give the impression of taking a position opposing that of the United States as a matter of principle rather than of interest.

> ... Canada has a great problem of national identity. Canadians ... are constantly asking themselves the question who they are. They are constantly in need of demonstrating to themselves and others how they differ from the United States. This appears ... to be something which gives Canadian policymakers an interest, having this psychological origin, in striking attitudes which are different from those of the United States, *for their own sake*. This is not an element in Australian policy.[95]

When compared to Australia, Canada is in most respects in a better bargaining position *vis-à-vis* the United States. Not only is it more powerful but it also has more room to maneuver because its security is closely tied to that of its neighbor. Its importance in this field gives Canadians a certain freedom to criticize the United States which the Australians lack.[96]

On the other hand, Canada's economy is so closely connected to that of the United States that it is continually aware of the possibility of economic reprisals, should its policy thwart American interests.[97] Because almost 70 per cent of Canadian trade is with the United States, Canada could be considered an economically penetrated system. In this context, however, it should be pointed out that

> Economic dependence can conceivably *increase* the political power of the dependent nation vis-à-vis the nation upon which it depends—at least on some issues. Consider the case of American investment in Canada. The United States has, in effect, placed hostages on Canadian soil.[98]

For both Australia and Canada, their position as client states (if they can be so described) is the result of free choice. Both countries have decided to cooperate with the United States and to "accumulate credit", even sacrificing some of their own freedom of action, because such cooperation serves their own interests. These two patron-client relationships come very close to being alliances between equal states. Certainly both countries are, on the objective level, members of an equal, or nearly equal, alliance. It is only psychologically that they perceive themselves to be clients. To a large extent this perception is the natural result of the identical interests shared by these countries and America, which cause them repeatedly to take the same positions as the United States. Identity or individuality is created by *differentiation of character* and opinions, not by continuous harmony, by stressing differences rather than similarities. Each of these two states, therefore, feels the need to assert its own identity in contrast to that of the United States.

> It is, after all, our external contacts that help define the image of ourselves, and if that image is always to be weak and accommodating, and if we can never find some independent way to express our view of the world, then we have little future as an independent country.[99]

In Canada's case there is a strong need to justify its existence as a separate political and national entity. "The central problem of pan-Canadian nationalism has been the need to find a reason for the country's existence."[100] Due to the need to assert their own international identity[101] and self-respect, both Canadians and Australians have seriously considered the option of non-alignment or armed neutrality.[102] Yet both countries, so far, have decided to continue their alliances and cooperation with the United States. This is a clear indication of the benefits they derive from the partnership.

These cases of patron-client relations between states reveal a great range in the intensity of such relations. They vary from the mutually rewarding relationships between the United States and Canada and Australia, based on mutual respect and a high degree of equality, through the middle position of Finland *vis-à-vis* the USSR, with the weak country enjoying most of the attributes of a sovereign state and yet being informally constrained in its freedom of maneuvering and alignment in the international system, to the India-Nepal relationship of the fifties, which was based on formal agreement and permitted only limited freedom of action to the near-vassal state.

The psychological problems of identity can be found in the background of all patron-client relations. In Western societies, but also in many Asian societies, an exaggerated degree of dependence results in resentment and hatred, rather than in a sense of moral obligation, gratitude, or commitment.[103] The degree to which various weak states develop tolerance of foreign intervention or agree to accept foreign penetration varies considerably.[104] The degree of tolerance is a function of three variables. First, the historical experience and geographical location of the weak state are significant. Persia, for example, has been accustomed in modern history to external patronage and penetration.[105] Second, there is the question of culture, whether Western or non-Western, and the impact of one upon the other. Finally, the nature and intensity of penetration by the foreign power affect the weak state's degree of tolerance. A communist penetration might be total, producing a complete *Gleichschaltung* with the communist system and its philosophy, whereas a Western penetration might be primarily political or economic.

The psychological dimension is also present in relationships between the great powers and some of the African and Asian states. Sometimes, as in the case of the French patronage of sub-Saharan Africa,[106] the weak state develops a psychological need for the patronage of a foreign power. Mannoni describes this phenomenon in the personal relations between colonizers and natives.[107] As he says, "Colonization has always required the existence of the need for dependence. Not all peoples can be colonized: only those who experience this need."[108] In some instances such dependence can give the weak state a sense of security and protection, not only because of military assistance and political support, but perhaps mainly in the area of economic aid. Hence the weak states that wish to avoid a sense of moral obligation[109] to the donor prefer low interest loans to straight gifts. Morocco and India are good examples.[110]

For a weak state to find a patron is also, perhaps unconsciously, to find a scapegoat—a foreign country that can be blamed for domestic failures. Identifying one's state with a prestigious patron state can also be seen as a gratifying experience, permitting the weak country to enjoy the great power's reputation vicariously. Nepal might resent patronage by a country such as India, whose standard of living is even lower than its own, but it might accept as natural the patronage of a distant, materially richer and culturally different country, such as Great Britain or the United States. Albania resented Yugoslav interference, but it sought Russian and Chinese patronage.

When the relationships and alliance systems of great powers and weak states are seen in light of the patron-client model, it becomes apparent that both sides do benefit, even if asymmetrically. And just as in reality weak and powerful states exhibit overlapping characteristics and do not rigidly conform to ideal types, so too not only weak states, but also middle or even great powers (Britain, Canada, Australia) may become client states. Not infrequently Hegel's dialectic of "master" and "servant" persists, with the master needing the servant's services, and being to some degree dependent on the servant.[111] Although the patron is implicitly the superior in the relationship, very frequently, in cost-benefit terms, the client reaps greater benefits, as in the cases of Australia, Canada, South Korea, and Taiwan.

Weak States and the Benefits of Collective (Public) Good

In economics, a collective or public good may be characterized as follows:

Individual interests normally can best be served by individual action, but when a group of individuals has some common objective or collective goal, then an organization can be useful. Such a common objective is a collective good, since it has one or both of the following properties: (1) if the common goal is achieved, everyone who shares this goal automatically benefits, or, in other words, nonpurchasers cannot feasibly be kept from consuming the good, and (2) if the good is available to any one person in a group, it is or can be made available to the other members of the group at little or no marginal cost. Collective goods are thus the characteristic outputs not only of governments, but of organizations in general.

Since the benefits of any action an individual takes to provide a public or organizational good also go to others, individuals acting independently do not have an incentive to provide optimal amounts of such goods.[112]

On a domestic level, examples of collective good are control of air pollution, crime prevention, external defense, and military deterrence. In international relations, collective good accrues to weak states from bilateral or multilateral alliances. As long as a weak state has a reliable defensive arrangement with a great power, a formal alliance is not needed for it to enjoy the collective good originating from its direct or indirect protection by the great power.

In their struggle for primacy and hegemony during the Cold War, both the United States and the Soviet Union tried to recruit as many weaker allies as possible. This scramble for allies, and the readiness on the part of the super powers to pay almost any price to keep their primacy and alliance systems intact, created a situation in which the weak states could enjoy defense and protection while at the same time reducing their own defense expenditures. Such weak NATO states as Norway, Denmark, Iceland, and Belgium (as well as Australia[113] outside NATO), could relax their defensive efforts without fearing a decline in the credibility of their defenses.

> . . . so long as the smaller state is neither coerced by the big one nor offered special incentives, and unless the threat to the small state is very grave indeed—as in actual wartime—the small nation is likely to regard the big country's armed forces as a substitute for its own. The small country will feel able to relax its own efforts because it has obtained great power protection. Thus the big power's success in extending its umbrella works against its other

goals of using the alliance to enhance its own military strength. The small power's effort will vary inversely with its confidence in the big power's guarantee and the disparity in size between the two.[114]

The more *automatic* the security promised to a weak state, the more important that state is to the defense system of the super power, and the fewer of its own resources it has to invest in security. To a large extent it enjoys a free ride. Logically, the more powerful a state is, the less it can rely on the aid of other states for protection. Thus the stronger the nation, the more disproportionate the share of the total military cost it must bear in an alliance. There is a difference, though it should not be exaggerated, between small and large military alliances.

> In small groups [alliances] this effect [collective good] may be mitigated because freeloaders can be spotted, and their laggardness may be highlighted by publicity about members' contributions . . . the larger the group the greater the proclivity for "exploitation" of the big members by the small ones . . . . There are even cases where the small powers will provide nothing.[115]

Iceland, for example, spends almost nothing on defense. Its total contribution to NATO is a few important bases, but in return NATO guarantees its security.[116]

This behavior on the part of weak states is encouraged not only by their perception of their importance to the super power's security, but also by two other facts.

First, they know that whatever they do, they cannot hold out against the onslaught of an attacking super power. Hence *any* investment in their own defense is a waste of resources.[117] This attitude is very strong in Denmark, where certain influential politicians who see no utility in maintaining military power would like to limit the role of their defense department, if war breaks out, to answering the phone in Russian and saying, "We surrender!"

The development of nuclear weapons is a second fact that has encouraged the small states to adopt a strategy of "coercive deficiency." Many of the weak states believe that mutual nuclear deterrence will prevent a war and that therefore it would be foolish to invest in conventional forces that would never be used or would be unhelpful and irrelevant. The nature of modern nuclear deterrence is such that they can feel relatively secure even without the "trip wire" or "hostage" presence of conventional or non-conventional forces of the super power. Intercontinental missiles based in the United States and the Polaris submarines provide the necessary deterrence. Furthermore, the presence of such troops on their soil might put the weak states on the target list of the opposing super power.

Paradoxically, the *failure of burden sharing* is an indication of the faith of the weak state in the super power with which it is allied.[118] Conversely, "A nation which spends *more* than its size would predict is a state that feels the shelter of its bigger allies *less* than do the others, and for some reason the alliance is not providing the expected security."[119] Not surprisingly, studies of burden sharing in NATO indicate that the weak states tend to spend less on defense relative to their GNP than do the great powers.[120] The neutral and non-aligned European states, such as Sweden, Switzerland,[121] and Yugoslavia, are also covered by NATO, though to a lesser extent, and undoubtedly they take this into account in their defense planning. Without being members of NATO, they enjoy *informal* benefits —a collective good—derived from the existence of the alliance. "The NATO states may regard the west European neutrals not as free-loading chiselers but as nations whom they want to protect informally without openly incorporating them in the treaty organization."[122]

Another example of a neutral state enjoying a free ride is Ireland:

> Ireland is not a member of NATO. We were not invited, because the government of the day made it clear that we didn't wish to be invited. But we do not doubt that the American nuclear umbrella —the American system of defense in Europe—applies to Ireland's interests as well as it applies to Holland's.[123]

Sweden's attitude has been similar:

> The Swedish government argued that the interest of the Western countries to prevent Scandinavia to fall under Soviet domination anyhow was so strong that the Scandinavian countries would be

assisted both in war and peace without a clear understanding, and that a clear understanding would be provocative in the sense that it would cast doubt on the neutrality of the Scandinavian pact and thus run the risk of inviting pre-emptive actions from the East.[124]

Clearly, the position of the weak states in the international system is not without its advantages. If the interests of a power and those of a weak state coincide, the weak state can benefit considerably from its collaboration with the great power. If the weak state contributes nothing or very little to the common defense, as is often the case, a situation may develop in which the weak (or small) is exploiting the large one.[125] An alliance of weak states with a super power offers them many benefits which are not available if they choose to ally only with other weak partners. In an alliance of weak states such as the Balkan League of 1912–1913, the Little Entente, or the Arab League, each state of more or less equal power (or weakness) must contribute to the common good. This, of course, means shouldering a much heavier burden and sacrificing more of their own resources.[126] Very rarely can a weak state get a free ride in an alliance consisting entirely of weak states.

Under certain circumstances in a complex balance of power situation the benefit of a collective good can, paradoxically, be given to an enemy or ex-enemy state. For example the Kingdom of Jordan directly and indirectly has been protected by the active support and mere existence of the State of Israel. In September 1970 the movements of Israeli troops saved King Hussein and his kingdom from a Syrian invasion. Hussein knows that under certain conditions Israel's interest in the continued existence of his monarchy can be counted on, despite the situation of war that exists between the two states. He knows that Israel's calculations of the regional balance of power force it to support his regime whether or not it likes the situation.[127]

In a way, weaker states also enjoy the benefits of a collective good in the classic balance of power. Since the rules of this system call for the major power *not* to eliminate weaker states that might be needed in future diplomatic combinations, these states are, up to a point, protected and their survival secured even if their own defensive capacities cannot by themselves secure their continued existence.

Alliances of Weak States

Although opinions differ about the dangers and benefits accruing to weak states that align themselves with great powers, there is a general consensus on the lack of effectiveness of alliances among weak states, especially if directed against a great power.

> An alliance of Small Powers is an instrument of limited utility. It neither can nor is designed to handle major military threats. When Small Powers are threatened by Great Powers, they must turn to other Great Powers for support.[128]
> Statesmen are . . . wrong in assuming that "a combination of Small Powers is equivalent to a Great Power."[129]
> Small Power alliances are a poor instrument if the immediate goal is increased military strength. But they may very well be extremely useful instruments if the goal involves maintaining the status quo, and controlling or removing local grievances without Great Power intervention.[130]
> The combination of any number of weak states does not make one strong one.[131]
> Traditionally, small-state alliances have not been prominent, nor have they been signally successful in dealing with internal instability or external insecurity of lesser states.[132]
> Where only lesser states are involved, the aggregation is more likely to be one of weaknesses, compounded by the non-complementary nature of assets and the divergent nature of interests and apprehensions under stress. Consequently, small-state alliances will fare best against dangers of a special kind.[133]

Alliances of weak states are usually created *ad hoc* for a temporally limited goal or a single issue. An example of the first type was the alliance among the Balkan states to divide the spoils of the European Ottoman Empire. Examples of the second were the Little Entente's effort to contain Hungarian revisionism, and the Arab League's decision to unite against Israel—but not for any other purpose. In all these cases the effectiveness of the alliances was limited by internal tensions and contradictions.

The Balkan states,[134] which were usually at one another's throats, united to fight the "sick man on the Bosphorus." Having successfully eliminated the remnants of the Ottoman Empire in the Balkans, they turned against one another again, and remained divided during and after the First World War. The Little Entente succeeded in containing Hungary only because Hungary was virtually disarmed. For a moment in history the members of the League of Nations coordinated their efforts and appeared as a great power, but they were divided when real pressures confronted them. The Czechs were in conflict or in danger of conflict with the Germans and Poles, the Rumanians cooperated with the Poles but were endangered by the Russians with whom the Czechs were friendly, while the Yugoslavs confronted the Italians and cooperated with the Germans. Hungary served as a limited and weak common denominator or, rather, common enemy. Underlying tensions, diverging interests, and different orientations were much too strong to permit the Little Entente to survive.[135]

The history of the Arab League is not very different.[136] The common denominator was and still is their hatred of Israel, but their attacks on Israel in 1948 were badly coordinated and the League failed to reach its military goals. The Arab states have been continuously at odds with one another. Nasser's ambitions to control the Arab world, his political intervention in Lebanon, Jordan, and Syria, and the domestic strife in these countries which resulted from his intervention further weakened Arab unity. The failure of the unification project between Egypt and Syria, the competition for hegemony between Iraq and Egypt, the war in Yemen, Iraq's confrontation with Kuwait, and the division of the Arab world into Western- and Eastern-oriented countries have put serious obstacles across the road to effective cooperation.

The larger the number of weak states in an alliance, the more difficult it becomes to coordinate military and political actions. In the military sphere, the different sources, and therefore types, of supplies and equipment, different training and procedures, and different doctrines all make coordination a difficult task. In the political sphere, varying hierarchies of interest, conflicting priorities, and competition for leadership and influence within the alliance make it very hard to maintain united and coordinated action for any prolonged period.

Finally, behind every alliance of weak states can be found the great powers. Russian support for the Balkan League was essential to its establishment and success, even though the Russians could not control it. The French stood behind the establishment of the Little Entente, and the withdrawal of that support was one of the reasons for its collapse. Whatever may be the merits of the Arab League, the major support for the Arab war effort and success comes from the USSR.

This chapter has examined some of the ways in which the weak states can strengthen themselves by obtaining power from external sources. In the post-colonial, post-imperial world (at least the *direct* type of imperialism), in which international conduct is increasingly governed by democratic-egalitarian-liberal norms, the dangers for a weak state entering an alliance with a great power have considerably declined. The benefits of such alliances, with the exception of non-voluntary alliances like the Warsaw Pact, are considerable, and they can often favor the weak states. Frequently weak states align themselves to a great power or super power in order to achieve immediate, short-term benefits, such as support in a local struggle. The great and especially the super powers, which seek support from the weak states in order to maintain their hegemonial position, often set their eyes on future rewards that may never be realized. Thus they sometimes find themselves overpaying to maintain their hegemony and actually weaken themselves in the process.[137] The action of the United States in Vietnam is a classic example.

Often weak states that have obtained the support of a great power try to lead the power in their own direction, through manipulation, *faits accomplis,* or tactics of coercive deficiency.

This chapter has also explored the relationship between weak states and great powers on the model of patron-client relationships. Even though the position of a weak state in such a relationship is that of an inferior and is therefore somewhat more difficult, materially or psychologically, nevertheless the benefits can outweigh the costs. The weak states can obtain security and protection as free riders, whereas by "going it alone," they would be unable to achieve any measure of security. By joining in an alliance with a great power, they not only obtain almost fool-proof security, but they also enjoy the benefits of a collective goal supplied by the power—and at little extra cost. On the other hand, when the weak states choose to ally among themselves, many of the advantages accruing to them from a mixed alliance disappear. Their defense costs rise while the efficiency and reliability of their security decline.

NOTES

1. *The Adventures of Tom Sawyer* (New York: Lancer Books, 1967), p. 16.
2. Stanley Hoffmann, *The State of War* (New York: Praeger, 1968), p. 138, n. 1.
3. Morgenthau, *Politics Among Nations*, p. 290.
4. Hoffman, *Gulliver's Troubles*, p. 28.
5. In a study of the military aid furnished by great powers to weak states, Bruce Russett has found that "the analyst who limited his examination to the present cases would be forced to conclude that a small nation was as safe without an explicit guarantee as with one" (p. 100). Examples are U.S. military aid to South Korea in 1950 and the U.S. decision to protect Quemoy and Matsu in 1954–58. Conversely, a formal promise to protect the weak state was not found to be a guarantee that such aid would be forthcoming. See Bruce M. Russett, "The Calculus of Deterrence," *Journal of Conflict Resolution*, 7 (1963), 97–109. This article might have been entitled "The Credibility of Great-Power Military Assistance to Weak States Under Attack."
6. See Rothstein, *Alliances and Small Powers*, p. 177. For weak states in alliance see also a descriptive article by Donald E. Nuechterlein, "Small States in Alliance: Iceland, Thailand, Australia," *Orbis*, 13 (Summer 1969), 600–623; and George Liska, *Alliances and the Third World* (Baltimore: Johns Hopkins Press, 1968).
7. See for a similar approach Nils Örvik, "NATO: The Role of the Smaller Members," *Atlantic Community Quarterly*, 4 (Spring 1960), 92–103. Örvik refers to the weak states in NATO as "B" class members (p. 100).
8. Keohane, "Lilliputians' Dilemmas," p. 302.
9. See Tarulis, *Soviet Policy Towards the Baltic States 1918–1940*, esp. chap. 13.
10. Robert E. Osgood, *Alliances and American Foreign Policy* (Baltimore: Johns Hopkins Press, 1968), p. 62.
11. This is also the opinion of Rothstein in *Alliances and Small Powers*, p. 127. Quantitatively, the number of defense pacts, non-aggression pacts, and ententes among the weak states is higher than the number between weak states and great powers:

Fig. 8

DISTRIBUTION OF ALLIANCE COMMITMENTS, 1946–1965

Combination	Defence pacts	Non-Aggression pacts	Ententes	Totals
Majors with Majors	7	0	1	8
Majors with Minors	21	5	7	33
Minors with Minors	27	2	10	39
Totals	55	7	18	80

Source: Raimo Vayrynen, "On the Definition and Measurement of Small Power States," *Cooperation and Conflict,* 6 (1971), 95, where the table is based on J. David Singer and Melvin Small, "Formal Alliances, 1815–1939," *Journal of Peace Research,* 1 (1966), 1–32.

According to this table the number of treaties made among the weak states is larger than the number made between them and the great powers. The table raises a few questions, however. In the first place, because there are many more weak states than great powers, the probability of their concluding a larger number of treaties and pacts among themselves is higher. Secondly, the importance of treaties varies. Certainly a treaty between a weak state and a great power would carry more weight than one among weak states.

12. This does not mean, however, that the weak states always seek the support of an external power for defensive purposes only. Often it is not clear whether they need external power for the purpose of defense or offense. Russia's support of Serbia was used not only for defensive purposes but also to alter the status quo in the Balkans and the Hapsburg Empire. Taiwan used American support at times to raid the mainland, and the Arab states have used Russian support to attack Israel.
13. "And here it should be noted that a prince ought never to make common cause with one more powerful than himself to injure another, unless necessity forces him to it, as before said; for if he wins you rest in his power, and princes must avoid as much as possible being under the will and pleasure of others." Machiavelli, *The Prince* (New York: Modern Library, 1950), p. 84.
14. Robert Jervis, *The Logic of Images in International Relations* (Princeton, N.J.: Princeton University Press, 1970), pp. 87–88.
15. See also Rothstein, *Alliances and Small Powers,* pp. 119, 269.
16. Quoted in Andres Suarez, *Cuba, Castroism and Communism 1959–1966* (Cambridge, Mass.: M.I.T. Press, 1967), p. 93.
17. *Ibid.,* p. 113.
18. *Ibid.,* p. 115.
19. See Morton H. Halperin and Tang Tsou, "United States Policy toward the Offshore Islands," in *Public Policy,* 15 (1966), 126–127; also

Jonathan Trumbull Howe, *Multicrises: Sea Power and Global Politics in the Missile Age* (Cambridge, Mass.: M.I.T. Press, 1971), pp. 163–176; and Dwight D. Eisenhower, *Mandate for Change* (Garden City, N.Y.: Doubleday, 1963).

20. Trumbull, *Multicrises,* p. 173. The way in which the Chinese Nationalists obtained their mutual security treaty with the United States is also instructive.

    The mutual security treaty with the nationalist government was signed in December, 1954. This was effected by a hoax perpetrated by the Nationalists in regard to the Communist bombardment of Quemoy on September 3, 1954. After the start of the Communist propaganda drive for the "liberation" of the offshore islands, two landing ships were set as a dock on Quemoy by the Nationalists. The dock formed a "T" where supply ships could unload. It was carefully placed within sight and easy range of Amoy—under the Communists' noses. Naturally they bombarded it. The Nationalists presented this action, which had been provoked by themselves, as evidence of impending invasion . . . . Mr. Dulles, who was at the SEATO Conference in Manila at the time, hastened to Formosa and agreed to the mutual security treaty the Nationalists had long been angling for. [Thomas R. Phillips, "The Military Worth of Quemoy," *The Reporter,* 19 (2 October 1958), 15].

21. The idea of penetrated systems is suggested by James N. Rosenau, "Pre-Theories and Theories of Foreign Policy," in R. Barry Farrell (ed.), *Approaches to Comparative and International Politics* (Evanston: Northwestern University Press, 1966) pp. 65–71. He defines a penetrated political system as "one in which *nonmembers of a national society participate directly and authoritatively, through actions taken jointly with the society's members, in either the allocation of its values or the mobilization of support on behalf of its goals"* (p. 65).

22. Keohane, "Lilliputians' Dilemmas," p. 306, and *idem.,* "Big Influence of Small Allies," pp. 161–183. Keohane seems to me to exaggerate the real influence that weak states can obtain by appealing to the public opinion of the great powers. On the one hand, he underestimates the self-will of the great powers and on the other neglects the existence of a common interest between the great powers and weak states. He also neglects the much greater ability of the big power's government to manipulate public opinion by its own actions and control of the mass media. For another critique of his position see Astri Suhrke, "Gratuity or Tyranny—The Korean Alliances," p. 511.

23. Edward C. Thaden, *Russia and the Balkan Alliance of 1912* (University Park, Pa.: Pennsylvania State University Press, 1965), p. 64.

24. Ernst Christian Helmreich, *The Diplomacy of the Balkan Wars 1912–1913* (Cambridge, Mass.: Harvard University Press, 1938), p. 112, also pp. 154, 161. Still the best discussion available of the diplomacy behind the Balkan Wars, this book is a rich source for the study of weak-state diplomacy.

25. Ross Y. Koen, *The China Lobby in American Politics* (New York:

Macmillan, 1960). This book was taken off the market because of pressure from the China lobby.
26. Thomas C. Schelling, *The Strategy of Conflict* (New York: Oxford University Press, 1969), pp. 187–193.
27. See "U.S. Will Pull Out Planes from Taiwan," *The New York Times* (19 May 1974), p. 8.
28. Gelber, *The Australian American Alliance*, p. 27.
29. See Astri Suhrke, "Gratuity or Tyranny—The Korean Alliances," *World Politics*, 25 (July 1973), 513, for the symbolic value the two Koreas have acquired in the Cold War.
30. For a discussion of the German-Soviet Non-Aggression Pact and its impact on eastern Europe, see Gerhard L. Weinberg, *Germany and the Soviet Union 1939–1941* (Leiden: E. J. Brill, 1954); also Tarulis, *Soviet Policy towards the Baltic States 1918–1940*.
31. See, for example, Rothstein, *Alliances and Small Powers*, p. 61; and George Liska, *Nations in Alliance* (Baltimore: Johns Hopkins Press, 1968), p. 13.
32. Philip M. Burgess, *Elite Images and Foreign Policy Outcomes—A Study of Norway* (Columbus: Ohio State University Press, n.d.), pp. 126–127. In 1946 Iceland decided not to allow the United States to maintain bases on Icelandic territory, fearing that such bases, instead of providing for defense, would invite an attack. See Donald E. Nuechterlein, *Iceland, Reluctant Ally* (Ithaca: Cornell University Press, 1961), p. 42.
33. Neuchterlein, *Iceland, Reluctant Ally*, pp. 57, 78, 109, 194.
34. John C. Griffiths, *Modèrn Iceland* (London: Pall Mall Press, 1969), p. 147.
35. The problem of cultural penetration is a difficult one for many weak states to handle. Canada is a good example. At least 25 per cent of all Canadians regularly watch US television stations. The Canadian Radio and Television Commission has stepped in and decreed that at least 60 per cent of Canadian radio and television programs must have a Canadian content. Dobbel, *Canada's Search for New Roles*, p. 67. See also "The Nationalist Dilemma in Canadian Broadcasting," by Frank Peers, in Peter Russell (ed.), *Nationalism in Canada* (Toronto: McGraw-Hill Co., 1966), pp. 252–267. The same problem exists with regard to Canadian newspapers and magazines.
36. The relationship between Serbia and Russia on the eve of the First World War has been described as follows: "This programme [of Pasić against Austria] made Serbia *indivisibiliter atque inseparabiliter* the tail of the Russian dog. Which member attached itself to the other, and which ended by wagging which, are questions to which no answer is, perhaps, possible; but the existence of the compound animal was now irrevocably there, and that before long it would be at grips with Austria was hardly to be doubted." Macartney and Palmer, *Independent East Europe*, p. 34.
37. Morgenthau, *Politics Among Nations*, pp. 545–546.
38. Helmreich, *Balkan Wars*, p. 164.

39. Shirer, *The Rise and Fall of the Third Reich*, p. 466.
40. Rothstein, *Alliances and Small Powers*, p. 119.
41. *Ibid.*, p. 119, n. 146, quoting Taylor's *Struggle for Mastery in Europe*, pp. 29–30.
42. The tactic of coercive deficiency was used by the South Vietnamese leaders in their negotiations with American policy makers. See David Halberstam, *The Best and the Brightest* (New York: Random House, 1972), pp. 484–510.
43. Schelling, *The Strategy of Conflict*, p. 37; also Astri Suhrke, "Gratuity or Tyranny—The Korean Alliance," p. 509. Stanley Hoffmann calls this the "blackmail of weakness." See his *Gulliver's Troubles*, pp. 4, 38, 376; and his "Restraints and Choices in American Foreign Policy," *Daedalus*, 91 (Fall 1962), 677.

    In extreme cases, when the benefits of an alliance go only in the direction of the weak partner, the relationship between the two can be defined as parasitic. A treaty under which both partners enjoy equally important though different benefits could be compared to symbiosis or mutualism. This would be the ideal alliance between equal partners in international relations.
44. This summary is based on the following articles: Robert R. Kaufman, "The Patron Client Concept and Macro-Politics: Prospects and Problems," paper given at American Political Science Association meeting, 1972; René Lemarchand and Keith Legg, "Political Clientelism and Development: A Preliminary Analysis," *Comparative Politics*, 4 (January 1972), 149–178; John D. Powell, "Peasant Society and Clientelist Politics," *American Political Science Review*, 64 (June 1970), 411–425; James C. Scott, "Patron-Client Politics and Political Change in Southeast Asia," *American Political Science Review*, 65 (March 1972), 92–114; Alex Weingrod, "Patrons, Patronage and Political Parties," *Comparative Studies in Society and History*, 10 (July 1969), 376–400; Peter M. Blau, *Exchange and Power in Social Life* (New York: John Wiley, 1964), pp. 115–142; Edward C. Banfield, *The Moral Basis of a Backward Society* (New York: Free Press, 1958), pp. 75–78; Robert Paine, "Theory of Patronage and Brokerage," in Robert Paine (ed.), *Patrons and Brokers in the East Arctic* (Toronto: Memorial University of Newfoundland, 1971).
45. For example: "Because of the stigma attached to acceptance of substantial amounts of aid, recipients of French aid have been reluctant to reveal the full extent of their indebtedness. Perhaps it would be more accurate to say that the full measure of French aid in its various forms is concealed, which poses certain difficulties in research." Henry L. Bretton, *Power and Politics in Africa* (Chicago: Aldine Press, 1973), p. 72.
46. Edward N. Luttwak, *The Grand Strategy of the Roman Empire: From the First Century A.D. to the Third* (Baltimore: The Johns Hopkins Press, 1976).
47. Edward N. Luttwak, *ibid.*, p. 31.
48. Among the few studies are Ernst Badian, *Foreign Clientelae (264–70*

B.C.) (Oxford: Clarendon Press, 1958) and Henry L. Bretton, *Patron-Client Relations: Middle Africa and the Powers* (New York: General Learning Press, 1971). Bretton's book is mainly an economic analysis of the relations between France and her ex-colonies and has little to do with patron-client relations. Norman A. Bailey, *Latin America in World Politics* (New York: Walker and Co., 1967), suggests that all states could be divided into either patrons (paramounts) or clients, but his discussion ends in a conventional study of relations between states. See also Johan Galtung, "A Structural Theory of Imperialism," *Journal of Peace Research,* 8 (1971), 81–118, esp. pp. 85–91. Instead of patron-client relations Galtung speaks of a "Feudal interaction structure."

49. For example, during the Second World War the Finnish government, without being asked to do so, gave the German government information on the effects of German air attacks on London which had been supplied by the Finnish Embassy there. "This somewhat unneutral act was a small token of appreciation." Upton, *Finland in Crisis,* p. 182.

50. "There is, to be sure, extreme sensitivity to Soviet pressure.... There is also a flow of sometimes-nauseating flattery directed toward the Kremlin. Finns are careful to stroke the Bear's fur in the right direction. Its claws are, after all, very close by." William R. Frye, "Finland Tiptoes between East, West," *Boston Globe* (July 15, 1973), p. 59. The Finns have decided not to publish in Finland a translation of Alexander Solzhenitsyn's *The Gulag Archipelago 1918–1956,* in order not to offend the Soviet Union. See *New York Times* (March 6, 1974), p. 43.

51. Caullery, *Parasitism and Symbiosis,* p. 3.

52. For a similar metaphor see E. Bjol, "The Small State in International Politics," in Schou and Brundtland (eds.), *Small States in International Relations,* p. 33.

53. Macartney, *October Fifteenth* (Edinburgh: University Press, 1961), pp. 143–144.

54. Conor Cruise O'Brien, *To Katanga and Back* (New York: Grosset and Dunlap, 1966), p. 25.

55. Singer, *Weak States in a World of Powers,* p. 315.

56. Quoted in Robert Keohane, "Political Influence in the General Assembly," *International Conciliation,* no. 557 (March 1966), p. 18. Marshall Singer has ordered states according to their support of the United States (or USSR) on Cold War issues in the General Assembly between 1955 and 1959. Nine Latin American countries were found to be "most pro-US" and 11 "only pro-US". See Singer, *Weak States in a World of Powers,* pp. 327–329 (Table 8.1).

57. See Keohane, "Political Influence in the General Assembly", pp. 17–28.

58. Knorr, *Power and Wealth,* p. 28. See also Badian, *Foreign Clientelae,* p. 25.

59. R. R. Bettes, "The European Satellite States", *International Affairs,* 21 (January 1945), pp. 15–29.

60. Pano, *The People's Republic of Albania*, p. 12.
61. Albania's permanent position as someone's client has been described as follows:

    "Historically, Albania, like other Balkan states, has sought the protection of a major power to ensure her security. In the period between gaining independence from Turkey in 1912 after until World War II, she was controlled first by Austria then Yugoslavia, Italy, Germany, and again Yugoslavia. After the Stalin-Tito break in 1948 Albania became a fully-fledged Soviet satellite, primarily to protect herself against Yugoslav irredentism, but Khrushchev's decision to move towards a *rapprochement* with Yugoslavia, first in 1955 and later from 1957 to 1960, led to strains in Soviet-Albanian relations which intensified when Albania began to side with China in the Sino-Soviet dispute. Tirana's refusal to renounce his support for China, despite heavy Soviet pressure, led to the dramatic break with Moscow in 1961 and gave the Chinese their first genuine client.

    Since then Albania has remained to all intents and purposes a Chinese satellite, and the patron-client relationship has in general been mutually beneficial. For Albania, the Chinese connection has been a vital source of economic and political support. Internally, Chinese aid has allowed Albania to develop her economy, particularly her extractive industries, at a far faster pace than would otherwise have been possible; externally the tie with China has helped Albania to withstand Soviet pressure."

    F. Stephen Larrabee, *Balkan Security*, Adelphi Papers No. 135 (London: The International Institute for Strategic Studies, 1977), pp. 31–32.
62. Goldhamer, *The Foreign Powers in Latin America*, p. 186.
63. Ibid.
64. Rose, *Nepal's Strategy for Survival*, p. 20.
65. Ibid., p. 195.
66. Ibid., pp. 205–206.
67. Ibid., p. 208.
68. Ibid., p. 215.
69. Ibid., p. 212.
70. Ibid., p. 273.
71. Ibid., p. 247.
72. H. G. Gelber, "Some Western Determinants of Australian Foreign Policy", in Teichmann, *New Directions in Australian Foreign Policy*, p. 89. My emphasis.
73. Gelber, *The Australian American Alliance*, pp. 28, 32.
74. Millar, *Australia's Foreign Policy*, p. 2. See also Millar, *Australia's Defense*, p. 1.
75. Millar, *Australia's Foreign Policy*, p. 247.
76. Ibid., p. 7.
77. Ibid., p. 126.
78. Gelber, *The Australian American Alliance*, p. 121.
79. Ibid., p. 72. See also Millar, *Australia's Foreign Policy*, p. 100, and

Amry and Mary Belle Vandenbosch, *Australia Faces Southeast Asia: the Emergence of a Foreign Policy* (Lexington: University of Kentucky Press, 1967), pp. 108–129.
80. See Richard Kennaway, *New Zealand Foreign Policy 1951–1971* (Wellington: Hicks Smith & Sons Ltd., 1972), p. 76.
81. For a detailed survey of the US-South Korean patron-client-type relationship see Sungjoo Han, "South Korea's Participation in the Vietnam Conflict: An Analysis of the US-Korean Alliance," *Orbis*, 21 (1978), 893–912.
82. *Ibid.*, pp. 897–898.
83. *Ibid.*, pp. 901–902.
84. *Ibid.*, pp. 903; 904.
85. *Ibid.*, p. 898.
86. *Ibid.*, p. 907.
87. Thomas Schelling in "The Bargaining Power of the Small State," in *The Leonard Davis Institute for International Relations: Proceedings of the Opening Conference* (Jerusalem: 1974), p. 58.
88. Charles Hanly, "The Ethics of Independence", in Clarkson, *An Independent Foreign Policy for Canada?*, p. 22.
89. *Ibid.*, p. 23.
90. *Ibid.*, p. 24.
91. Granatstein, *Canadian Foreign Policy Since 1945: Middle Power or Satellite*, p. 1.
92. John W. Warnock, *Partner to Behemoth: The Military Policy of a Satellite Canada* (Toronto: New Press, 1970), pp. 297–298.
93. Granatstein, *Canadian Foreign Policy*, p. 140.
94. Clarkson, *Independent Foreign Policy for Canada?*, p. 27.
95. Quoted in Dobbel, *Canada's Search for New Roles*, p. 149 (emphasis mine). Canada's identity problem *vis-à-vis* the United States has also been demonstrated in recent Canadian fiction. Such novels as *Ultimatum, Exxoneration, The Dirty Scenario*, and the like are devoted to the unequal relationship between the two states. "The Americans look on our resources as being their own. They look on us as being weak-kneed, gray-faced people, and see our country as a colony of the States". (*Exxoneration*). In *Ultimatum* the American President presents an ultimatum to the Canadians in 1980 to yield to the energy-starved Americans their huge reserves of natural gas "which belongs to the American people by right of investment". In *Exxoneration*, the sequel to *Ultimatum*, the Canadians decide to fight back. While these books were not viewed as "inspiring fiction", their sales have been impressive. They reflect the worries of many Canadians. The author of *Ultimatum* and *Exxoneration*, Mr Rohmer, conceded that his books have educational value for Canadians. "It is an attempt to point out and emphasize the growing need for vigilance and concern over Canada's relationship with its good friends, the Americans, whose demands for our natural resources, especially natural gas, are increasing dramatically".

As the fictional Canadian Prime Minister in *Ultimatum* warns

Parliament, during the debate on how to respond to the American President:

'It boils down quite simply to a question of sovereignty. If Canada is to remain an independent nation with its own goals and objectives and a political and judicial system quite different from that of the United States, then it is clear that we must be as free as possible to plan our own economic development and the use to which our natural resources are put'.

From "New Novels in Canada Depict U.S. as Domineering," *The New York Times* October 27, 1974, p. 10.

96. *Ibid.*, p. 149.
97. See "Retaliation: The Price of Independence," in Clarkson, *Independent Foreign Policy for Canada?* pp. 43–56.
98. *Ibid.*, p. 10. Emphasis mine.
99. Quoted in Dobbel, *Canada's Search for New Roles*, p. 150.
100. John Holmes, "Nationalism in Canadian Foreign Policy," in Peter Russell (ed.), *Nationalism in Canada* (Toronto: McGraw-Hill, 1966), p. 204.
101. The identity problem of Canada and Australia is also reflected in what Jean Barrea calls the "counter-core role" of the middle powers: ". . . the demands of the middle power's prestige are satisfied by a hostile attitude towards a process of integration led by a first-rank state." Jean Barrea, "The Counter-Core Role of Middle Powers in Processes of External Political Integration," *World Politics*, 25 (January 1973), 274–287. In the early 1970s Australia adopted similar attitudes toward the United States. See *New York Times* (June 15, 1973), p. 5.
102. See Max Teichmann, "Non-Alignment—A Policy of Australia," in Max Teichmann (ed.), *Aspects of Australia's Defence* (Melbourne: The Political Studies Association, Monash University, 1966), pp. 61–76.
103. Knorr, *Power and Wealth*, p. 180.
104. Richard W. Cottam, *Competitive Interference and Twentieth Century Diplomacy* (Pittsburgh: University of Pittsburgh Press, 1969), esp. pp. 34–77. See also Andrew M. Scott, *The Revolution in Statecraft—Informal Penetration* (New York: Random House, 1965).
105. Cottam, *Competitive Interference*, pp. 155–210.
106. Henry L. Bretton, *Patron-Client Relations: Middle Africa and the Powers*, pp. 1–24.
107. D. Mannoni, *Prospero and Caliban: The Psychology of Colonization* (New York: Praeger, 1956), pp. 39–93.
108. *Ibid.*, p. 85.
109. The Romans stressed the moral nature of their clients' obligation: ". . . the Romans' conception of the freedom of their client states had involved a *voluntary moral subordination* of those states, based on *gratitude* and *pietas*, but had not known any legal restriction of that freedom." Badian, *Foreign Clientelae (264–70 B.C.)*, p. 87. My emphasis.
110. See Knorr, *Power and Wealth*, p. 172.

111. Referred to in John H. Herz, *International Politics in the Nuclear Age* (New York: Columbia University Press, 1967), p. 143.
112. Mancur Olson, Jr. and Richard Zeckhauser, "An Economic Theory of Alliances," in Bruce M. Russett (ed.), *Economic Theories of International Politics* (Chicago: Markham Publishing Co., 1968), pp. 26, 27. See also Bruce Russett and John D. Sullivan, "Collective Goods and International Organization," in Edwin H. Fedder, *The United Nations: Problems and Prospects* (St. Louis: University of Missouri Center for International Studies, 1971), p. 92, also published in *International Organization,* 25 (1973), 845–865; further, Mancur Olson, "Increasing the Incentives for International Cooperation," *International Organization,* 25 (1973), 866–874. Robert A. Dahl and Edward R. Tufte, *Size and Democracy* (Stanford: Stanford University Press, 1978), pp. 122–128.
113. Gelber, *The Australian American Alliance,* p. 94.
114. Bruce M. Russett, *What Price Vigilance?* (New Haven: Yale University Press, 1970), p. 93. See also Jacques van Ypersele de Strihou, "Defense Organizations and Alliances," in Matthew Tuite, Roger Chisholm, and Michael Radnor (eds.), *Interorganizational Decision Making* (Chicago: Aldine Press, 1972), pp. 261–269. See also Ronald S. Ritchie, *NATO: The Economics of an Alliance* (Toronto: The Ryerson Press, 1956), p. 53.
115. Russett, *What Price Vigilance?* p. 96.
116. Donald E. Nuechterlein, "Small States in Alliances: Iceland, Thailand, Australia," *Orbis,* 13, (Summer 1969), 612, 616. The benefit of a collective good obviously existed for the weak state before the age of nuclear weapons and bi-polarity. In the 19th century Holland spent very little on defense, thanks to England's protection.

 What could be more pleasant for a small state? The Netherlands could devote its national income to higher standards of living while a powerful neighbor [England] was under the necessity of regarding Dutch continental territory as within its defense area. So long as British foreign policy, backed by armaments, was successful in maintaining the balance of power on the continent, the Netherlands was secure, at no cost to itself. [Amry Vandenbosch, *Dutch Foreign Policy Since 1815* (The Hague: Martinus Nijhoff, 1959), pp. 58–59].
117. See Knorr, *On the Uses of Military Power in the Nuclear Age,* p. 156.
118. Russett, *What Price Vigilance?* p. 99.

 This is not only the case with weaker states. It can also occur with more powerful states. Japan is a good example. The Japanese have "consistently pursued a policy of committing the United States to protect Japan by means of a mutual defense arrangement—a military alliance . . .". The success of the alliance and the trust in American support is indicated by, among other things, the very low Japanese expenditure on defense. "Since 1960 Japan's defense budget has been less than 10 percent and a declining proportion of the total government budget, and they have been 1 percent or less of the GNP".
 Robert E. Osgood, *The Weary and the Wary: U.S. and Japanese*

Security Policies in Transition (Baltimore: The Johns Hopkins Press, 1972), p. 51.
119. Russett, *Economic Theories of International Politics*, p. 46.
120. Russett, *What Price Vigilance?* pp. 100–112. Among the weak states enjoying the benefits of a "collective good," Bruce Russett has included the Warsaw Pact and Latin American countries. While these countries do indeed spend a smaller percentage of their GNP on security, it is doubtful whether they enjoy a real "collective good." Being included within a sphere of influence of a hegemonial super power, they are "protected" whether they like it or not. But a "collective good" must be desired by the "freeloader" and must add to his security as he defines it. Denmark, the Netherlands, Belgium, and other weak NATO states are interested in any additional free support they can get from the U.S. Hungary, Czechoslovakia, Poland, or Rumania would be happier without Russia's "free protection." The same, though perhaps to a lesser extent, is true for "protected" Central American states. No enforced or undesired help can be considered a "collective good." That the weak states spend less on security is no indication that they enjoy a real "collective good." *What Price Vigilance?* pp. 116–123.
121. See: Bohn, "Neutrality—Switzerland's Policy Dilemma: Options in the New Europe," ". . . even though Switzerland is not a member of NATO, it nevertheless enjoys all the benefits of membership with none of the losts," p. 344.
122. Olson and Zeckhauser, in Russett, *Economic Theories of International Politics*, p. 48.
123. Schou and Brundtland (eds.), *Small States in International Relations*, p. 210.
124. A. O. Brundtland, "The Nordic Countries as an Area of Peace," *ibid.*, p. 134.
125. Mancur Olson, *The Logic of Collective Action*, rev. ed. (New York: Shocken Books, 1971), pp. 3, 29, 35.
126. The defense burden is much easier for a rich great power. "For a rich member [of an alliance] the proportionate sacrifice of $100 is less than for a poor member; for a state with 10,000 taxpayers the per person cost is one cent; for a state with 100 taxpayers the per person cost is one dollar. Hence the big member will feel it is foregoing less to take up a particular burden than will the smaller member." Bruce Russett and John D. Sullivan, "Collective Goods and International Organization," in E. H. Fedder, *The United Nations: Problems and Prospects*, p. 99.
127. William B. Quandt, *Decade of Decisions: American Policy Toward the Arab-Israeli Conflict 1967–1976* (Berkeley: University of California Press, 1977) Chapter 4: The Jordan Crisis: September 1970, pp. 105–127.
128. Rothstein, *Alliances and Small Powers*, p. 169.
129. *Ibid.*, p. 171.
130. *Ibid.*, pp. 174–175. This quotation is included as a good example of the pitfalls of generalizing from a single case study. Rothstein bases his evaluation of weak states' alliances on the study of the Little Entente.

Because of its military ineffectiveness, he reaches the generalized conclusion that all weak states' alliances are militarily unsuccessful. This is logically as well as factually wrong. The Balkan League, for example, had been very successful in the first Balkan War.

131. Alfred Cobban, *The Nation State and National Self-Determination* (New York: Thomas Y. Crowell, 1969), p. 300.
132. Liska, *Alliances and the Third World*, p. 50.
133. *Ibid.*
134. For the Balkan League, see Helmreich, *Diplomacy of the Balkan Wars;* Luigi Albertini, *The Origins of the War of 1914*, I (London: Oxford University Press, 1967), pp. 364–487; and L. C. F. Turner, *Origins of the First World War* (New York: W. W. Norton, 1970), pp. 26–59.
135. For the Little Entente, see Rothstein, *Alliances and Small Powers*, pp. 128–180; and Robert Machray, *The Struggle for the Danube in the Little Entente 1929–1938* (London: Allen and Unwin, 1938).
136. Robert W. Macdonald, *The League of Arab States* (Princeton: Princeton University Press, 1965); also Malcolm H. Kerr, *The Arab Cold War* (New York: Oxford University Press, 1971).
137. See William H. Riker, *The Theory of Political Coalitions* (New Haven: Yale University Press, 1968), pp. 212–216 (section on decline of Empires).

CHAPTER IV

The Position of Weak States in Different International Systems

"I read the other day," said the duchess, "that the Americans are giving away millions to lots of countries and not even asking for the money back. Can't we arrange to get a loan of some kind from the United States?"

"They are giving the money away to countries they are afraid might become Communist, your Grace," replied Benter. "Nobody in Grand Fenwick would ever become a Communist. We all work our own lands. We know how hard it is to make a little profit. Nobody can call himself oppressed. Unless a man suspects that others are getting more than their fair share, there is no reason for him to become a Communist."

"Couldn't we organize a Communist party here—just for the purpose of obtaining a loan?" Gloriana asked. "I don't really mean that we want a true Communist party—just someone who would stand up and tell the people to unite against oppression and throw off their shackles and all those other things. Then we could arrange for the matter to be reported in the American newspapers. An American senator could be invited over and could see some mass meetings. They'd have to be held on Sundays because everybody is busy during the week. But we could get a dispensation from the bishop for holding a political meeting on Sunday. Then the American senator could report to Washington and we could persuade him to recommend a loan to save the duchy from Communism."

Leonard Wibberley[1]

THE TWO CONSTRICTORS

"I don't know about helping you, Adolf, but I *do* understand your point of view!"

From *Punch*, November 8 1939.

Weak States and the Great Powers' Spheres of Influence

In order to enhance their strength and improve their position *vis-à-vis* other states, the weak states must rely on external sources of strength. Their ability to turn to other states and draw on their resources is largely a function of the nature of the particular international system in which they operate. Different types of international systems enhance or weaken their bargaining position or leverage, encourage or discourage them from seeking the aid of other states, or isolate them from other states within the system.

There are two different positions in which the weak states can find themselves, whether they are in a balance-of-power system, a loose or tight bipolar system, or any other. The first is a situation in which the weak state can enjoy complete or almost complete freedom of maneuver and action and can freely align itself with any other country. The second is one in which the weak state is included within a clearly marked sphere of influence of a great or super power; therefore it has little or no freedom of action and cannot align itself with other countries. The international system in which the first situation prevails is called a competitive system; the second is called a hegemonial system.[2]

Here again the phenomena under consideration are relative rather than absolute. The competitive and hegemonial situations or systems are ideal types. In reality, almost no state is completely free to switch allegiances as it pleases, nor can any state change its position too frequently. An uncommitted position gives a state freedom of choice, but once a course has been set, a change of direction becomes difficult. Obviously, states do change their positions, but since such actions cannot be undertaken frequently they require decisions of crucial importance.

In the 1970s, states such as Iceland, Ceylon, Tunisia, Australia, and many others are *almost* completely free to change their alliances. Nevertheless, they are still bound to other states by earlier economic and cultural ties, military connections of various sorts, political tradition, and other commitments which do not allow them complete freedom to shift their positions.

At the other extreme there are countries which are almost

completely excluded from the international system, because they are under the control of a hegemonial power in what is recognized as its exclusive sphere of influence. This is one of the worst situations in which a weak state (or group of states) can find itself. Under such circumstances it loses its freedom of maneuver, cannot ask for the help of other great powers, cannot improve its bargaining position politically or economically by playing one power against another, and cannot freely trade its vote for its best interests in the U.N. or offer strategic bases on its territory to the highest bidder. The small state under the control of one great power which is determined not to loose its grip cannot even request the external help needed to release it from the domination of the hegemonial power.

This has long been the predicament of the South American and especially the Central American countries *vis-à-vis* the United States.[3] The isolation of the Latin American states was clearly one of the results of the Monroe Doctrine, whether or not that was its original intention.

> The Monroe Doctrine, in its broad lines, is a prohibition on the part of the United States against the extension of European influence and power to the New World . . . . But there can be no denial of the fact that it is, in many minds, connected with a more general principle, the principle of separation of the New World from the Old, and that it is regarded as a complement, if you will, as a foil, to the principle of no entangling alliances and no binding political connection with any European power.[4]
>
> . . . the United States has always opposed attempts by Latin American governments to enter into relations with countries outside the western hemisphere which might threaten her interests.[5]
>
> . . . the power of the United States has been a bigger (and ever-present) threat to the genuine independence of Latin America than has that of any extra-continental country or group of countries. Indeed, the unequal distribution of power in the hemisphere has so far limited their freedom of action as to make the Latin American countries in varying degrees satellites of their northern neighbour. Not unnaturally, the United States has striven to maintain the imbalance of power in the western hemisphere by preventing extra-hemispheric powers from intervening to challenge her hegemony. She has rejected the idea that it might be legitimate for a Latin American country to seek the support of an extra-

hemispheric power in a dispute with her, and has jealously watched the development of relations with extra-continental powers by Latin American countries.

From the Latin American point of view, on the other hand, the presence in the hemisphere of extra-continental power to offset that of the United States would seem on the surface to be highly desirable . . . the Latin American countries 'can find protection against the northern neighbor only by using his enemies across the oceans as a balance against him.'[6]

The inability of the Latin American states to borrow or manipulate the strength of extra-hemispheric states for a leverage to improve their positions illustrates the importance of geographic location. Potential competitors of the dominant power (the United States) "are located too far away to counterweigh its influence."[7] Because of the geographic remoteness of the Latin American countries as well as the successful US policy of isolating them from Europe (and vice versa), the United States could consider them "safe,"[8] and invest fewer resources and less attention in them than would otherwise have been necessary. This situation obviously worked against the best interests of the Latin American states. They felt they did not receive their rightful share of the pie of foreign aid, nor derive any benefits from the Cold War competition which was such a bonanza for the Asian and African states. (For the weak states, competition between the great powers is heaven-sent—though this statement will receive some qualification later.)

> They [Latin American states] believed that nothing else could account for the fact . . . that from the end of World War II through 1958 communist Yugoslavia, with only 20 million inhabitants, received more aid in United States public funds than did all of the nations of Latin America, whose populations totalled some 175 million.[9]

As long as the United States could successfully isolate Latin American states from the international system, its attitude toward them was apathetic and uninterested, and it assigned only secondary importance to the region. This is best reflected in a statement attributed to Secretary of State Dulles when he took office in 1953: "I want an imaginative program for Latin America, but one that does not cost any money."[10] When the

Jack Rennert, The Poster Art of Tomi Ungerer (New York: Dover, 1973), p. 26.

Cold War reached the shores of the New World in the form of Castro's revolution, bringing Russian penetration of the United States' preserve, Latin American states suddenly found themselves in a much better bargaining position *vis-à-vis* the United States.[11] Latin Americans have since discovered "that apparently a country will do better if it occasionally sacks the United States Embassy and burns a few United States flags."[12] The great power needs to be reminded not to take the friendship of a weak state for granted; it should be encouraged from time to time to show its interest through economic aid, statements of political support, improving the terms of trade, etc.

Isolation from the international system and its benefits is also the fate of the weak states of Eastern Europe included within the Russian sphere of influence. Russian pressure forced them to reject the offer of the Marshall Plan, and ever since they have been unable to draw on the strength of other states to counter the Russian presence. On occasions the Eastern bloc countries have tried to loosen the Russian grip but with little success. So far only the Rumanians have been able to strengthen their contacts with the West somewhat. Albania broke out of the Russian orbit in order to join the Chinese sphere of influence, but it did not gain much freedom of movement.

Freedom of maneuverability is important for the weak state in all types of international systems. There are three basic types of systems: the balance-of-power or multipolar system,[13] the bipolar system, and the unit veto system.

Weak States in a Balance-of-Power or Multipolar System

A. J. P. Taylor suggests that the balance of power has worked to the benefit of the weak states.

> In fact, Europe has known almost as much peace as war; and it has owed these periods of peace to the Balance of Power. No one state has ever been strong enough to eat up all the rest; and the mutual jealousy of the Great Powers has preserved even the small states, which could not have preserved themselves.[14]

Quincy Wright makes a similar comment: "The smaller states [are] defended by the jealousy of their great neighbors rather than by their own defenses...".[15] And other authorities have put forth the same idea:

> A small state is a vacuum in a high pressure area. It does not live because of its strength but because nobody wants its territory, or because its preservation as a buffer state or as a weight in the balance of power is of interest to a stronger nation. When the balance disappears, the small state usually disappears with it.[16]
>
> For various reasons, Switzerland is not very strongly desired as an object for incorporation. Mutual jealousies existing among neighboring communities of equal strength protect it from this fate.[17]

The weak states, then, are indebted for their survival to the mutual neutralization of the great powers. In periods when the great powers cannot agree on any number of issues, each will try to prevent an uncommitted weak state from being incorporated into the other power's territory or sphere of influence. The weak state exists as a sort of vector of the strength of the great powers, which push in different directions and neutralize one another. Thus the weak states have a negative rather than a positive existence.[18]

The balance-of-power system, whether operating negatively or positively, has not always worked in favor of the weak states for, unlike the great powers, they have not always been considered essential to the continued maintenance of the balance-of-power system. The two following rules, which were accepted when the fate of a great power was at stake, were not applied when the future existence of a weak state was in question.

> Stop fighting rather than eliminate an essential national actor.
> Permit defeated or constrained essential national actors to re-enter the system....[19]

The weak states, in fact, occasionally became the victims of the balance-of-power system and of the unwritten but operative dictum that if two or more major actors can agree to divide up a weaker actor, they probably will.

The accepted norms of international conduct in the postwar world (see Appendix B) restrict the use of direct force against the weak states and inculcate the rule, "Thou shalt not divide weak states." And indeed, actual division of states by the great powers has declined. Now the greatest danger is intervention by a super power within its recognized sphere of influence. Still, several examples of divisions of weak states can be cited from modern history: the four partitions of Poland; the Anglo-French Entente of 8 April 1904, dividing North Africa into spheres of influence (the second of the Triple Entente treaties);[20] the division of Persia into British and Russian zones of influence (the so-called Anglo-Russian Entente of 1907, closing the triangle of the Triple Entente); the Munich Agreement of 1938; the division of the Baltic states into two spheres of influence (or occupation) between the USSR and Germany in the secret protocol of the August 1939 non-aggression pact;[21] and finally the Percentage Agreement between Churchill and Stalin.[22]

An agreement between two or more great powers *always* takes precedence over an agreement between a great power and a weak state or states. Hans Morgenthau quotes Edmund Burke to show what could have happened to the liberties of the small German states in the 18th century if Austria and Prussia had coordinated their policies:

> As long as the two princes [the King of Prussia and the German Emperor] are at variance, so long the liberties of Germany are safe. But if ever they should so far understand one another as to be persuaded that they have a more direct and more certainly defined interest in a proportioned mutual aggrandizement than in a reciprocal reduction, that is, if they come to think that they are more likely to be enriched by a division of spoil than to be rendered secure by keeping to the old policy of preventing others from being spoiled by either of them, from that moment the liberties of Germany are no more.[23]

Until 1936 Austria's integrity was guarded by Italy's desire to prevent it from falling into the German sphere of influence or, even worse, from a process of *Gleichschaltung* or *Anschluss*.[24] If Austria or parts of it could not be under Italian control, it could at least be maintained as a buffer state. Mussolini signed the Rome Protocols with Austria on 17 March 1934, and so in the summer of 1934 he moved several divisions to the Brenner Pass to warn Germany against direct intervention in Austria. However, after the Abyssinian Crisis, when Italy was alienated from France and Great Britain and almost isolated by the League of Nations' sanctions, and when

the balance of power shifted in favor of Germany following Hitler's decision to rearm and remilitarize the Rhineland, Mussolini decided to move closer to Germany. This move sealed Austria's fate as an independent state. These developments have been summarized by Chancellor von Schuschnigg in his memoirs:

> To strike the right balance in these difficulties [maintaining Austria's independence and preventing German intervention], to perform, as it were, this diplomatic tight-rope walking feat, was only possible as long as the international power balance in Europe remained essentially the same as it was in 1934. Then Hitler was forced [by Italy] to retreat after the failure of the Nazi revolt in Austria.
> In the course of 1935 and 1936 this international power balance shifted. Italy began the Abyssinian war, and the resulting conflict with England led to the creation of the Berlin-Rome axis. In this new situation Austrian foreign policy could no longer be based on support from Italy against Germany.[25]

Other examples can be given of the tenuousness of agreements between weak states and great powers. The French, despite their prior agreement with Czechoslovakia, decided at Munich to try to go along with Germany. The United States, because of its interest in a long-delayed rapprochement with the Chinese People's Republic, did not hesitate to sacrifice the interests of Taiwan. Russia's desire to prevent a confrontation with the United States took precedence over its interest in the maintenance of Cuban sovereignty in 1962.

The weak states, of course, recognize the threats to their interests embodied in some of the agreements between the great powers. "When two great powers reach an agreement, it is always to be feared that it will be at the expense of the small."[26] In 1971, for example, the fear of a "deal" between Communist China and the United States probably contributed to the attempts of North and South Korea to achieve a direct understanding.

> The government of the weaker state is inclined to mistrust its larger ally for seeking an agreement with the other large power, in the belief that it may be at its own expense, or for trying to deal with the local adversary in an independent matter.[27]

It must be accepted as axiomatic that when the chips are down and long-range interests of the highest importance are involved, the great powers will not hesitate to sacrifice their weak allies.

The survival of the weak states is not always a function of the mutual strength of the great powers which neutralize one another. On some occasions the exact opposite may be true. The weak states may be able to survive in a situation which could be described as a "balance of weakness." These were the circumstances in which the Baltic States were established at the end of the First World War, when Russia and Germany, the two great Baltic powers, were temporarily defeated and weakened internally, and could not object by force. There is little doubt, however, that in Germany and Russia the existence of these states was not seen as a permanent factor in the Baltic. Indeed, in Germany the Baltic States were referred to as *Saisonsstaaten* ("Seasonal States").[28]

> They came into existence in the years 1919–1920, when both Germany and Russia were exhausted . . . no definite design . . . led to the establishment of the Baltic states, but rather . . . the historically unusual juxtaposition of forces in the post-war, revolutionary, and interventionist vortex of the Baltic produced, within that region's normal pattern of great power strivings, a temporary quiescence which made it possible for the Baltic peoples' feeble efforts to win their nations a short-lived independence. Once British, French and American pressure was withdrawn, and Russia and Germany had regained their strength, the delicate equilibrium could no longer endure and neither could the Baltic states.[29]

The Danubian states also enjoyed considerable freedom of maneuver during the 1920s as a result of the power vacuum left by the weakening of Germany and Russia.[30] This situation changed once German power revived in the mid-thirties, for the Germans began to penetrate the Danubian and Balkan countries economically.[31]

A major practical difficulty with the balance of power is its *uncertainty*—that is, the inability of statesmen to calculate exactly the relative strength of other states.

> This uncertainty of power calculations is inherent in the nature of national power itself. It will therefore come into play even in the most simple pattern of the balance of power; that is, when one

nation opposes another. This uncertainty is, however, immeasurably magnified when the weights in one or the other or in both scales are composed not of single units but of alliances. Then it becomes necessary to compute not only one's own and the opponent's national power and to correlate one with the other, but to perform the same operation on the national power of one's allies and those of the opponent. The risk of guessing is greatly aggravated when one must assess the power of nations belonging to a different civilization from one's own . . . . The crowning uncertainty, however, lies in the fact that one cannot always be sure who are one's own allies and who are the opponent's. Alignments by virtue of alliance treaties are not always identical with the alliances that oppose each other in the actual contest of war.[32]

The existence of uncertainty leads the great powers to compete for the support of the weak states. Such competition often works in favor of the weak states, which, if they are free to offer their allegiance, can raise their price and ask the great powers for more support.

The more tense the relations between the great powers and the more imminent the possibility of war, the more they tend to compete among themselves for the favors of the weak states.

. . . the Small Powers began to be increasingly sought as military allies [on the eve of the First World War] . . . . A Small Power might be able to tip the military balance in a local area, particularly if the opposing Great Powers were equally powerful. It might also facilitate an invasion, or prevent one, by controlling a strategic area. At the very least, it would deprive the other bloc of one potential resource base. These various strategic considerations, buoyed by the traditional notion of equating strength with numbers, led to a struggle among the Great Powers to establish predominance over centrally located Small Powers, particularly those in southeastern Europe.[33]

The two major alliances on the eve of World War I, each desiring to tilt in its favor what looked like an almost equally balanced power relation, courted the loosely committed Balkan states. In this case, the regional competition between the weak Balkan states helped the great powers, which promised support in local conflicts in return for support in the impending European conflict.

The scales were so evenly balanced that it became extremely important on which side the small powers would align themselves, especially if there was the possibility of uniting them. Their combined forces might well have a deciding effect on any trial of strength.

The Balkan states, however, were looking after their own interests and were not to be stampeded into action. Only when the interests of the great powers coincided with their own, or when they stood a chance to gain thereby, were they willing to listen to the advice and promises made to them. The contest for allies was on.[34]

Russian success in helping to establish the first Balkan League advanced the cause of the Triple Entente and seemed to change the European balance of power in its favor.

Such a League, engineered by Russia, meant a decided swing in the balance of power to the Entente. Something would have to be done to rectify that balance—if indeed there was any truth in the theory that the best way to insure the peace of Europe was to maintain an equilibrium among the powers. Led by Vienna the powers of the Triple Alliance—or better Germany and Austria—attempted to accomplish this through peaceful diplomatic means . . . . In this they were unsuccessful, and the tipping scales finally plunged all Europe into war.[35]

The importance, real or perceived, of the Balkan states for the general European balance of power led Russia to support them more strongly than it might have liked, in order not to lose their support if a major European confrontation occurred. The competition between the Triple Entente and the Triple Alliance in the Balkans acquired the nature of a zero-sum game: "What the Triple Alliance lost, the Triple Entente gained."[36]

Was the great effort invested in gaining the support of the Balkan states worthwhile? It is difficult to speculate, but the answer would seem to be yes. The major opening battles were fought on the Marne and in Tannenberg, not on the Balkan front. When the war opened, however, the Austrians mistakenly chose to attack Serbia and Russia simultaneously (Plan B), instead of concentrating on the Eastern Galician front against Russia (Plan R). As a result Austria was decisively beaten on both fronts, not only weakening itself thereby, but exposing the whole German southern flank in Poland and Silesia.[37] The Serbian alliance would have been very valuable had the Russians been able to take advantage of Austria's defeat. In other words, it was important for the great powers to secure the friendship of the weak states not only for their positive support and potential contribution to the war effort, but also to prevent them from *diverting* the strength of the powers to secondary theatres of war and thus reducing their ability to concentrate against the major opponents.[38]

If the great powers have not always followed the classical rules of the balance-of-power system, the same is true of the weak states. Rule 4 of Morton Kaplan's balance-of-power system advises: "Act to oppose any coalition or single actor which tends to assume a position of predominance with respect to the rest of the system."[39] If the balance of power shifts in favor of one of the major actors, a responsible reaction by all others which are free to realign themselves would be to add their power to the weakened side, thus restoring the balance and bringing the system back to equilibrium. Such action has rarely been taken by the weak states. When the balance of power has shifted in favor of one of the participating powers, the reaction of most weak states has been to desert the weakened side (in order not to become the victim of the stronger side should war break out) and to seek the protection of the stronger side. Conducting their policy in this way, the weak states have often acted as a destabilizing element in the European balance of power, further pushing the system out of equilibrium. This policy of the weak states has been rightly referred to by Annette Baker Fox as "anti-balance of power" behavior. Although she speaks of the period after World War II, it is equally applicable after the First World War.

> Postwar changes in the orientation of the countries studied here, as well as the small state's "benevolent neutrality" toward the dominant side during the war, indicate that the decisions made by small states could increase the imbalance between two power constellations. Instead of moving to the side of the less powerful and thereby helping to restore the balance, they tended to comply with the demands of the more powerful and thus to accentuate any shifts in the balance of forces caused by changing fortunes of war or prospects of ultimate victory. Viewed in this way, the small

state's characteristic behavior may be described as "anti-balance of power" while that of a great power is characteristically "pro-balance of power." Where the margin between a self-righting balance and the complete overturn of the balance is very close, this behavior pattern may conceivably be decisive. Ordinarily, however, the small state's weight is unimportant in determining the distribution of power among the great, because the small state follows a pattern already being set and only accents it.[40]

A classical example of this type of anti-balance-of-power behavior by a weak state is Belgium's foreign policy between the two World Wars. Belgium's heroic resistance during the first week of the First World War earned her the respect and gratitude of the great powers at the Versailles peace conference. For the next decade and a half Belgium followed a policy of close political and military cooperation with France. After Locarno, and particularly after Hitler's rise to power, the European balance of power quickly shifted in favor of Germany. Belgium, positioned on the military highway between two equally powerful sides, was in a predicament similar to the one it had faced on the eve of the First World War. The Belgian government was disappointed by the failure of the League of Nations to enforce collective security measures, and it was not confident that Britain would come to its aid in case of attack.[41] Therefore it gradually shifted to a neutral position, which was formally recognized by the powers on 24 April 1937. By following this policy the Belgians further contributed to the weakening of the foundations of the East and Central European alliance system nurtured by France.[42] The Belgians finally notified the French in May 1938 that if they tried to enter Belgium against Germany to support Czechoslovakia they would have to confront the Belgian army.[43]

If Belgium is the most obvious example of the policy of escapism between the two World Wars, it was not the only weak state to pursue such a policy. As the balance of power shifted in favor of Germany and as disappointment over the ineffectiveness of the League of Nations to support the weak states grew, a similar policy was followed by the so-called Oslo group (Norway, Denmark, Sweden, the Netherlands, and Belgium) which in December 1930 decided to improve their economic relations and to unite to protect their mutual interests.

In July 1936 the same group, with the addition of Finland, issued a communiqué declaring that they did not see themselves obliged by Article 16 of the Covenant—i.e., they did not intend to be drawn into any conflict.[44] Similar policies were adopted by Yugoslavia and Rumania as German strength increased. The policies of the weak states, as Professor Fox says, were not detrimental to the European balance of power; they reflected the changes already made in the balance rather than having any substantial influence on it. But their behavior further undermined, even if marginally, the stability of the European balance of power, and contributed to an atmosphere which turned away from cooperation and mutual aid.

The anti-balance-of-power behavior of a weak state forces it to

> continuously trim its sails to the conflicting winds stirred by the great powers. In moments of crisis, the small state is persuaded, or coerced, or patronized, sometimes even consulted, on policies of war, peace, or survival. But it never is allowed to remain aloof; great powers at war do not permit the small states the luxury of neutrality or independent thinking.[45]

Unable to stay aloof in a central conflict (or an approaching conflict) between the great powers, the weak states must side with or at least lean toward one or another of the powers. In times of conflict complete neutrality is practically impossible. Even the avowedly neutral states have to learn to "bend" to the will of the more strongly pressuring power in order to maintain their integrity and prevent an attack.[46]

The choice of the opponents with which to side is a crucial one for the weak states. It poses a serious double dilemma. Due to their own lack of strength, the weak states must usually adhere to the stronger and more powerful side if they do not want to lose their independence. In the first place, though, there is never a guarantee that the stronger side at the beginning of a conflict will win in the end. Secondly, supporting the stronger and often more aggressive side in the first stage may make it more difficult for the weak state to get free of its grip at the end of the conflict, as Machiavelli declared.

In other words, the short-term interests of the weak states can often be contrary to their long-range interests. The need to survive in the short run is usually more immediate and pressing than speculations about who will win in the end.[47] The desire to evade occupation or destruction conflicts with the desire to sit on the right side of the peace table after the war.

To be successful, the diplomacy of a weak state must be conducted in the following manner: it must always side with or placate the stronger and more threatening power at each state of the conflict; it must switch its position when the balance changes, exactly at the moment the declining power with which it originally sided is too weak to retaliate, and while the ascendant power still needs help. The risks in this type of policy are enormous; they can at best be minimized, but never completely eliminated. The weak state has to be extremely cautious, especially with its timing; it must carefully calculate the risks involved at each stage. Thus the weak state faces the same dangers as the inexperienced stockbroker, who buys a certain stock when there is a great demand and the price is rising, and sells it in a recession after it has hit rock bottom. The weak states must avoid the mistake of joining a great power that *seems* to be winning, and then leaving it after it has lost. In this respect the Finns played their cards badly during the Second World War. The Rumanians did somewhat better in both World Wars.

The stakes involved in such situations are always much higher for the weak states than for the strong. A great power, even if it loses a war, has a large population, a distinct culture, and a long political tradition that cannot be easily assimilated or dismembered. Consider, for example, Germany and Japan in 1945, and France in 1814. Weak states, on the other hand, face the danger of disappearing as political entities through integration into the territory of the winning power or its allies (e.g., Estonia, Latvia, Lithuania). The longer the weak state has existed, the longer its tradition, and the longer it has been accepted among the community of nations, the less the danger. It would be difficult to dismember states with a long political tradition, such as the Netherlands or Denmark; but newly established states such as Estonia, Latvia, and Lithuania, which, despite their ancient traditions, had been independent for only a short time, were relatively easily absorbed by the USSR.

The predicament facing weak states drawn into a major conflict between powers has been aptly summarized by Marshal Mannerheim. In a letter to Hitler notifying Germany of the Finnish decision to make a separate peace with Russia, he wrote:

> I wish especially to emphasize that Germany will live on, even if fate should deny you victory in your fighting. Nobody can give such an assurance regarding Finland. If this nation of barely four million be defeated militarily, there can be no doubt that it will be driven into exile or exterminated. I cannot expose my people to such a risk.[48]

In summary, the position of weak states in a balance-of-power system is affected by the following three factors: (a) When the division of strength between the great powers is almost even or the system is in tension and there is a state of conflict, the importance of the weak states rises and the powers are willing to pay a higher price for collaboration and friendship. (b) When a system is oriented toward maintaining the status quo, or when no agreement can be reached between the great powers, they neutralize each other and their mutual jealousy strengthens the position of weak states. However, if one or more of the great powers have revisionist ambitions toward the weak states and can reach an agreement among themselves, such an agreement can work to the disadvantage of the weak states. (c) The weak states within a balance-of-power system tend to pursue a destabilizing policy, contradicting the classical rules of that system by adding their weight to the stronger side.

Weak States in Bipolar Systems[49]

The different kinds of international systems are usually studied as ideal types.[50] In reality, different systems have overlapping characteristics. For example, when two major alliances are formed in a balance-of-power system (such as the Triple Alliance and the Triple Entente on the eve of the First World War), the system acquires many of the traits of a bipolar system, particularly as it is experienced by the weak states. Conversely, a so-called loose (or muted) bipolar system can take on many of the characteristics of a balance-of-power system. What is important to the weak states is not so much the structure or form of the system as its dynamics. A weak state needs to know whether a given system is highly competitive, filled with conflict and tension (a revolutionary system in Hoffmann's terminology), or one in which the great powers can cooperate, pursue status-quo policies, and try to minimize risks (Hoffmann's moderate system).[51] The degree of conflict between the major powers in a bipolar system determines whether it is a *tight bipolar* system or a *loose bipolar* system. The position of the weak states is different in each.

Any bipolar system is characterized by the existence of two major powers, each of which possesses overwhelming strength in relation to all other actors, and which organizes around itself a group of allies or a closely controlled, "recognized" sphere of influence. In a *tight* bipolar system (like that in effect at the height of the Cold War in the 1950s), the ideological competition between the two major powers and the continual danger of war between them created a highly competitive atmosphere. One result is that each major contending power (or bloc leader) tightens its control over its allies, limits their freedom of action, and jealously guards its respective sphere of influence against intruders. In addition, the competition of the major powers over the unaligned states is in the nature of a zero-sum game, as each tries to outbid the other, pays inflated prices for favors, and encourages defection of allies from the opponent's camp.

As the competition between the major contenders escalates, each attaches greater symbolic importance to the states within its alliance or sphere of influence. The major power watches the weak states in its sphere carefully and may intervene in their internal affairs in order to prevent defection to the other camp. After the Second World War, for example, Russia established "recognized" control over the East European states, gradually turning them into satellites with reduced freedom of action in the conduct of their international affairs. In such a situation all major decisions are made in one center, that of the major power. As the tension in the system rises, especially ideologically, the degree of control over the weak states increases—not only in foreign affairs but also in the shaping of their domestic policies.

The clearest statements by the hegemonial powers of their right to intervene, even by force, in what they consider their own spheres of influence are the so-called "Johnson Doctrine" and "Brezhnev Doctrine."

The Johnson Doctrine declares that the "American nations cannot, must not, and will not permit the establishment of another Communist government in the Western hemisphere."[52] The Brezhnev Doctrine states that each of the socialist countries "is responsible not only to its own people, but also to all the socialist countries . . . ." Therefore none of the socialist countries can exercise its full sovereign rights in a way "opposed to the interests of the world of socialism," because the "weakening of any of the links in the world system of socialism directly affects all the socialist countries, which cannot look indifferently upon this."[53]

The Brezhnev Doctrine lays down four principles which support the hegemonial power's right to intervene within its sphere of influence: (1) The members of the system cannot leave the political orbit of the hegemonial power; (2) The hegemonial power (in cooperation with what it considers its loyal allies) sets the proper standards of conduct for the members of the system; (3) It is the sole judge of adherence or non-adherence to these standards; (4) If it finds that a state has violated the code, it can intervene, by force if necessary, to correct the deviant policies of its satellite. Such intervention is considered an act of self-defense.[54]

From the point of view of the great powers, one of the major functions of client (or satellite) states is to legitimize the interventions or other forcible acts of their patrons, by which they set a precedent for possible intervention against themselves in the future. This is done in two ways. In the first place, despite the fact that both the Johnson Doctrine and the Brezhnev Doctrine were established to serve the interests of the United States and the USSR rather than their allies, they were phrased in the plural—"the American nations" and "the Socialist Countries"—as if representing the will of the allies. Secondly, in the intervention in both the Dominican Republic and Czechoslovakia, troops of the client states participated to legitimize the actions of the patron. In the Dominican Republic, troops from Costa Rica, Honduras, Nicaragua, El Salvador, and later Brazil and Paraguay participated. There were 1737 soldiers from client states, most of whom arrived long after the intervention was over, as against 21,500 U.S. troops. The United States tried to legitimize its intervention by transforming it into a regional peace-keeping operation. The Russians did the same by marshalling the forces of East Germany, Poland, and Hungary for the invasion of Czechoslovakia.[55]

In his study of the Peloponnesian Wars, Professor Kagan has distinguished three kinds of relationships between weak states and a major power:

> . . . Sparta's allies were not uniformly treated. We can discern three categories of allies, a decision which was not formal but very meaningful. The first includes small states relatively weak and near enough to Sparta to be easily subject to her discipline . . . . The second category is composed of states that were stronger, more remote, or both, but not so strong or remote as to avoid ultimate punishment . . . . When Sparta was strong she could and did demand obedience from them. When she was weak or distracted they could go their own way, attack their neighbors, who might also be allied to Sparta, adopt democratic constitutions, and even make alliances with another state unfriendly to Sparta. Such independence, however, was always temporary and sometimes costly.
>
> The third category consists of states so remote or so powerful that their independence was rarely tampered with and whose conduct of foreign policy was rarely subordinated to Spartan interests. Only Corinth and Thebes belonged to this group.[56]

The weak states of the 20th century belong to Kagan's first two categories. (In the third category would fall the middle powers.) The crucial difference between the first and second categories is the distance or remoteness of the weak states from the hegemonial power. The closer the weak states are to the major power, the greater their chances of being included in its direct sphere of influence and of being deprived of free maneuvering in the international system. As in ancient times, the intrinsic strength of the weak states is a second important factor in their capability to resist the hegemonial power. This capability is heightened when the hegemonial power is preoccupied in other areas.

While competition in a tight bipolar (or revolutionary)

system endangers the interests of the weak states included within the sphere of influence of one of the super powers, it tends to enhance the position of the non-aligned and non-committed weak states. The greater the competition between the hegemonial powers, the higher the price they are ready to pay for the allegiance of non-aligned and uncommitted states. Under such conditions:
1. The price asked by neutrals or marginal members for their allegiance to one side or another will rise steadily.
2. The tone of politics will become more intense in the sense that each decision will seem to involve the entire future of each coalition.
3. As a result . . . the danger of general warfare will increase.
4. Finally, as a result . . . the two main opposing powers will exhaust their resources in maintaining their alliances and other nations will come to the fore as world leaders.[57]

In a tight, highly competitive bipolar system a hegemonial power not only pays to attract the non-aligned states to its side; it is also ready to pay simply to prevent them from joining the other side. The major power's desire to deny the other power access to the territory of weak states is as important as its wish to have them under its own control. In most cases the weak non-aligned states have taken advantage of the situation by collecting aid and support from both sides.

> By judicious management of the neutralist position, numerous Asian and African governments have been able to wring some side-payments from each coalition for temporary support (as on a vote in the United Nations) without firmly committing themselves to either side. In a sense, both Africa south of the Sahara and many states of north Africa and the Near East have managed to avoid both coalitions, thus reducing the significance of each, and to deploy their mobile diplomacy to their own greatest advantage.[58]

The competition between the super powers, then, has given considerable leverage to the weak non-aligned states, and it has cost the hegemonial powers a fortune in resources. The only way for them to reduce this expenditure is to

> recognize that they are playing not only a zero-sum game against each other but also are playing a sub rosa zero-sum game in which they are allies against the rest of the world.[59]

A rapprochement or détente between the super powers would tend to reduce the competition between them by moving them out of a system in which the free market price is allowed to prevail to one resembling an oligopolistic market.

> ... whenever they try a policy of détente between themselves, bidding for influence on the foreign policy of other states has a tendency to diminish somewhat.[60]

As the competition between the hegemonial powers declines, they will be able, perhaps even unilaterally, to reduce their bidding for the support of the weak non-aligned states and to adopt what Aaron Wildavsky has called the "averaging strategy." "Averaging strategies originate as a response to conditions that make it prohibitively expensive to calculate new policies for each new situation."[61] A hegemonial power using such a strategy would treat all weak states on an equal basis, rather than competing for their favors; ". . . the same policy of friendly benevolence and minimum political involvement is applied to all of them."[62]

The difficulty with the averaging strategy is that its assumptions go against the very nature of the international political system (or any political system), where competition over the authoritative allocation of scarce resources is inevitable. As long as such competition exists, it makes more sense to reward or punish the weak states for their cooperation. An averaging strategy can exist only in an apolitical world. It reflects the feeling of many in the mid-1960s that the weak non-aligned states had taken advantage of the intense competition between the super powers. As the Cold War tensions between the two super powers have eased and their relations stabilized somewhat, the tight bipolar system has gradually been transformed into a loose bipolar system, and this has automatically weakened the bargaining position of many of the weak non-aligned states.

There are at least five reasons for the decline in the weak states' bargaining powers.

(1) The competition between the hegemonial powers for the favor of the weak non-aligned states was partly the heritage of the pre-World-War balance of power. As the super powers developed intercontinental missiles, the importance of foreign military bases (which, for example, had been essential for the

United States' deterrence system) decreased. This trend was further strengthened by the development of nuclear Polaris submarines which serve as mobile missile bases and can stay at sea for long periods without being dependent on friendly ports for refueling and supplies. As the nuclear balance of terror emerged and the probability of a conventional war between the two super powers diminished, the military importance of the weak states for the central balance of power declined. Their strength could add little or nothing to that of the super powers.

> The question of national survival today is dominated by high-yield nuclear weapons, superpowers, and the possibility of central war. Since the concept of central war, in turn, is dominated by intercontinental missiles, submarines, satellites, and aircraft capable of delivering nuclear weapons over long distances, strategic points on the earth's surface are becoming much less significant than they have been. The developing areas lack the capability to engage in or interfere with central war. They are, therefore, increasingly less important in regard to ultimate problems of American survival.[63]

(2) The super powers have discovered that enormous investments do not guarantee the loyal support of the countries receiving them. The difficulty in securing returns on these investments is complicated by the domestic instability of many of the weak underdeveloped countries, and by the ever-present danger of a higher bid from the competing super power. Despite enormous Russian investments in Indonesia and Ghana, Russia could not secure the support or even the neutrality of those states; nor did the United States gain India's sympathy despite many years of extensive aid programs.

(3) Even a country like Cuba, where USSR investments have so far not been lost, and which finds it difficult to turn for help to the opposing super power, has not hesitated to play off the USSR against the People's Republic of China.[64] It has become clear to Russia that despite its enormous investments in Cuba, such support will have to be continued for a very long time. In many ways, Cuba's defection from the West to the East, originally a great symbolic victory, has been more of a liability than an asset to the USSR. Moreover, it has not led to further defections.

(4) From an ideological point of view—assuming that ideology is more than just a tool to further their international position—the competing hegemonial powers have failed miserably. The neutrals or non-aligned states, such as Cuba and Iraq, which received extensive support from the USSR, did not follow orthodox Russian Communism. They put nationalism before internationalism and developed their own brand of local political doctrines—Cuban socialism ("Cuba yes, Russia no." "We are not Communists or capitalists, we are Cubanists.") and Arab socialism.[65] The Russians have supported Egypt, Syria, Iraq, and Indonesia only to have their own comrades thrown into local prisons. The U.S. crusade for democracy and liberalism has not fared any better. It did not bring democracy to Taiwan, South Korea, South Vietnam, the Philippines, or even Greece or Portugal. This situation has increased the difficulty of recruiting domestic support from the American public and mass media for obtaining foreign aid from Congress.

(5) The hegemonial powers have been forced to support their allies in dangerous situations which could have led to undesired confrontations between them. Often the allies have put themselves in situations from which they have had to be bailed out at high cost, both materially and in terms of prestige. Examples are the confrontations in Cuba in 1962, in the Middle East in 1967 and 1973, and the India-Pakistan conflict of 1972. American experience in Korea and Vietnam has demonstrated the prohibitive price, both materially and socially, of supporting weak clients. The USSR's experience is similar though less drastic, for so far it has avoided *direct* support of its protégés. Nevertheless, the economic price of supporting Cuba, the Arab countries, and North Vietnam has been very high.

In summary, two observations may be made. In the first place, the higher the level of tension and competition between the super powers, the higher the price they will be willing to pay for the alliance or continued neutrality of the weak non-aligned states. For such non-aligned states, competition between the super powers is preferable to their cooperation and agreement.[66] Similarly, the more nearly equal the division of strength between the super powers, the greater the need to improve their relative positions, even the small increments of strength obtained by alliances with the non-aligned weak states. Under such circumstances the bargaining position of the weak states is strengthened and they can ask and obtain higher prices for their cooperation.[67]

In the second place, the greater the collaboration and cooperation between the super powers, the lower the price the non-aligned weak states can expect for their cooperative behavior. At best, the weak states' price must decline when the super powers cooperate; at worst, the powers can recognize each other's spheres of influence and divide the territory of a weak state between themselves.

Maneuverability in a Nuclear World

The development of nuclear weapons by the major powers after the Second World War further widened the gap between them and the weak states. To the gap, which hitherto had been basically quantitative, a qualitative dimension of enormous proportions was added. No weak state could even hope to defend itself against a major nuclear power, if such a power chose to use its nuclear weapons. The unique destructive nature of these weapons has, however, imposed a special moral restriction, which has made it much less likely that they will be employed against a weak state. In any case, the super and great powers enjoy an overwhelming conventional military superiority over any weak state, and their own survival is never at risk from a weak state. The ultimate weapons are to be used only when the survival of the major power itself is at stake—in other words, when it is seriously threatened by another nuclear power.

Paradoxically, the acquisition of nuclear weapons has decreased the major powers' desire to intervene conventionally against weak states when there is a chance of confronting another nuclear power and therefore of risking escalation. The result, it may be argued, is that the major powers have intervened less in the affairs of the weak states than they might have done in non-nuclear revolutionary (tight bipolar) systems. When the super powers *have* intervened against weak states within or outside their recognized sphere of influence, they have carefully avoided the possibility of confronting another nuclear power.

Thus the tight bipolar *nuclear* system—and even more the loose system—has given the non-aligned weak states more freedom of action than ever before.

> ... the military forces of the two superpowers are largely structured in relation to one another. They are huge and incredibly complex, capable of meting out destruction on a scale grotesquely disproportionate to what would be appropriate for chastening a small and weak country.... It is in part that the Goliaths do not care for moral reasons to exploit their military superiority; it is largely that the costs of wielding military power are too high in these confrontations in which little is to be gained. There is therefore a gap between the power a state is equipped to exercise and the power it has the incentive to exercise. This leads naturally to an appreciation of the power of the less powerful, and hence the small powers are weak but not meek.[68]
> The factors that inhibit the superpowers' exploitation of their enormous military machines ... *ipso facto* increase the lesser states' capacity to use their own power for denial against the superpowers and their allies.[69]

The dangers of escalation have limited the ability of the great powers to use or take advantage of their superiority over the weak.

> The smaller states, feeling stronger in their defenses against threats from the superpowers, are often able and willing to pursue goals beyond mere survival and security. Conversely, the superpowers, encumbered by their nuclear power, must concentrate as never before on the requirements of security and survival.[70]

The rôles of the two types of states have almost been reversed: "the strong do what they must (and can do only a little more), the weak do a little better than they must."[71]

Under certain conditions the weak states had a large amount of freedom to maneuver in the pre-nuclear balance-of-power and bipolar systems. The major difference, therefore, between those systems and a nuclear bipolar system is that in the latter the relative restrictions and inhibitions which the super powers have imposed on themselves accentuate the freedom of action of the non-aligned states.

The freedom of action of a weak state may also be a function of the support it receives from one of the super powers.

> . . . when defying one big power, many, if not most, militarily weak states have, or count on, diplomatic and perhaps military backing from the other great power . . . . To the extent that this factor is operative, we must of course conclude, not that military power has lost potency in international affairs, but that the possible interposition of large counterpower curbs its exertion.[72]

This might explain why North Korea, North Vietnam, Cuba, and Yugoslavia defied the threats of a super power by drawing on the power of a rival super power.

Problems of Nuclear Weapon Acquisition by the Weak States

> Kokintz chuckled. "And how will these mice tame the lions?" he asked, half mockingly.
> "The biggest of the lions, the United States, is already caught in a trap where all its strength is of no avail," Pierce replied. "We of Grand Fenwick have the Q-bomb, the only one in the world. We are, therefore, suddenly an overwhelmingly powerful nation. We have the means to make others do our will. We can without difficulty form a League of Little Nations, countries such as Finland, Belgium, Uruguay, and El Salvador, Ireland, Lichtenstein, San Marino, Portugal, Norway, Sweden, Denmark, Paraguay, Peru, Chile, Mexico, Liberia, Egypt, Panama, Switzerland—all the small independent nations in the world. Such a League can solemnly demand that the big nations agree to cease the manufacture of nuclear weapons of all kinds and permit international inspection of their plants by teams of scientists from the neutral small nations to ensure that the agreement is adhered to. If they do not agree to do this under moral pressure, we can threaten as a last resource to explode the Q-bomb.
> "I do not put much faith in the power of moral pressure," Dr. Kokintz said. "And as for using the Q-bomb, you would never dare to do that. If it were exploded you would yourself be destroyed . . . . "[73]

The extreme case of nuclear proliferation would be an international system in which all states, including the weakest, had nuclear weapons. Then what Kaplan calls the "unit veto" system would prevail. He likens such a system to the

> ... Hobbesian state of nature, in which the interests of all were opposed—were, in fact, at war—but in which each actor responded to the negative golden rule of natural law by not doing to others what he would not have them do to him. Not only will the unit veto international system not be a political system, but, in a sense, politics will not even take place within the system.... There is only one condition under which such a system is possible, let alone likely. This condition is the possession by all actors of weapons of such a character that any actor is capable of destroying any other actor that attacks it even though it cannot prevent its own destruction.... The unit veto system is a "standoff" system which, as long as it operates according to its inherent rules, perpetuates the existing state of affairs .... The unit system requires that a surprise knockout blow be technically impossible.[74]

In such a world, the position of all states would be equalized militarily. The transformation from a world which accentuates the differences in military power between states to a world of military equality in which the status quo is perpetuated would therefore work in favor of the weak states. Conversely, such a system would reduce the strong states to the level of all other states, and would equalize the international system militarily and politically. "There would be neither strong or weak powers, only mutual respect."[75]

This position has been argued in the sharpest and most extreme form by General Gallois.

> ... thermonuclear weapons neutralize the armed masses, equalize the factors of demography, contract distance, level the heights, limit the advantages which until yesterday the Big Powers derived from the sheer dimensions of their territory (space to retreat into) .... It is easy to prove that countries as different as Switzerland and Communist China are in the same boat when it comes to the nuclear threat.[76]

According to Gallois, weak countries, such as Denmark, which have always been vulnerable to attack by a neighboring power could now hope to defend themselves against such threats.

In the age of the new weapons, however, Denmark could still base its security on the possession of a few nuclear-warhead missiles, whether these weapons are purely national or, as is more likely, if they were placed under the double control of Denmark and the guarantor nation. If, for instance, the Danish government possessed several missile-launching submarines, it would have an effective dissuasion force, because the latter would be difficult to destroy preventively and because the destructive power they represented would greatly exceed the advantage the aggressor might derive from a subjugated Denmark. Who would dare attack this small country, if, in order to depose its government and invade its territory, the aggressor would have to run the risk, in return, of seeing a dozen of his own major urban centers destroyed? . . . [If Denmark decided not to surrender] The aggressor would prove his vulnerability to a small state's power. He would have to bind up his wounds while the rival great nations continued the race toward prosperity.[77]

Gallois and other military analysts have referred to this strategy as *proportional deterrence* or *finite deterrence*. The idea behind it is similar to that behind the "risk theory" presented in Chapter II of this study: for the great power, the price of occupying a weak state is greater than the benefit to be derived from such an operation. The damage a weak state could cause to the great power would be out of proportion to its value as a prize.

In theory, General Gallois' proportional deterrence makes sense; but as any *rational* strategic analysis will show, the theory is still far from being the solution to the defense problems of either the weak states or the great powers.[78] The reason for this is that the basic assumption of the theory—the credibility of deterrence by a small nuclear force—is dubious. The main arguments against the efficiency of proportional deterrence can be summarized as follows:[79]

(1) The number of nuclear warheads is small, both relatively and absolutely.
(2) There is a lack of advanced, sophisticated delivery and command control systems.
(3) The difficulties of hardening such weapons and weapon delivery systems in a weak state, especially when its territory is small, make a second strike highly unlikely.
(4) The small size and dense population of many of the

weak states make them more vulnerable to nuclear attack than the great powers. (This is also true of strong countries like Great Britain, France, Germany, and Japan.)

(5) Because any small nuclear force is necessarily weak, a nuclear attack by a weak power on a super or even a great power would be suicidal (the "bee sting").[80]

Since an attack by a small nuclear force on a super power cannot be successful, the foundations of the proportional deterrence argument must collapse. Small nuclear forces simply cannot reach the necessary threshold of efficacy against a super power. In fact, having such forces could actually reduce the weak state's security—for the following reasons:

(1) It could lead a super power to disengage itself from its earlier military commitments to a state that had acquired nuclear weapons, for fear of being drawn into a nuclear conflict. The weak state, which in the transitory period of building up its nuclear power had relied on the nuclear deterrence of the super power, would then be more vulnerable than before.[81]

(2) A weak state developing nuclear weapons might find itself under overwhelming pressures from one or both of the super powers to dismantle its nuclear force. Such pressures could range from economic sanctions to political and even military intervention.[82]

(3) At worst, if a super power were highly suspicious of the weak state's intentions, it might try to destroy that state's nuclear power by a preemptive strike.

(4) The expense involved in the procurement of nuclear weapons might undermine the conventional military strength of the weak state.[83] A need to develop special delivery systems for nuclear weapons, which can be more expensive than the weapons themselves, might further weaken its conventional force. (A way out would be to develop delivery systems that could also serve its conventional forces, such as the Viggen 35 and the Mirage 4.)

(5) In case of war, the weak state with nuclear weapons could suffer far greater territorial damage than if it had confined itself to the use of conventional weapons. It would be totally destroyed—without causing comparable damage to its major nuclear enemy.[84]

The arguments against the utility of nuclear weapon acquisition by weak states are very convincing. Nevertheless, opponents of this position can adduce arguments to the contrary.

Most of the studies of nuclear proliferation have been conducted by scholars residing in one of the great powers, especially the United States. Their analyses of nuclear weapons proliferation and of the acquisition of nuclear weapons—analyses made from the viewpoint of a super power with an overkill capacity, second-strike capabilities, modern delivery systems, and so on—often have not shown an understanding of the real and very different motives of the weak states. Most of these analyses have been made in relation to the British, French, and Chinese experiences. The lessons derived from these cases are only relevant in part to the problems and decisions involved in the acquisition of nuclear weapons by the weak states. The British, French, and Chinese developed nuclear forces in order to maintain their status as great powers. They intended to deter other major nuclear powers. Failure to produce nuclear weapons would have perhaps reduced them to a position closer to that of the middle powers.

Each of these three states *could* have relied on the deterrence capacity of the super powers. Their cases clearly demonstrate the less rational and non-military elements in the development of nuclear weapons. With the possible exception of the Chinese, none of the three could achieve a credible deterrence posture *vis-à-vis* the super powers. Their second-strike capability is limited and their delivery systems are relatively primitive. Their intention, then, is to maintain their status and influence with the super powers by political and psychological means rather than militarily. If the great powers are finding it difficult to build a credible nuclear force against the super powers (even though they can at least *hope* eventually to develop such an efficient force), it would obviously be beyond the reach of the weak states. The motives for the acquisition of nuclear weapons by weak states are less ambitious and much more limited. Therefore the problems of nuclear proliferation among the weak states cannot be judged by the same criteria as the proliferation process among the great powers.

The objections to nuclear proliferation among the weak

states are related both to the desire of the super and great powers to maintain their nuclear monopoly and their fear of the possible consequences of proliferation. Despite all the rational calculations indicating that the development of small nuclear forces would *not* equalize the great and the weak states, it is certain that the behavior of the big powers in a world in which the weak had acquired nuclear weapons would be different. The weak states would have to be treated more carefully and with more respect, and the fear of nuclear blackmail by a weak state would lurk in the background. "If the capacity of the small state to harm the greater one is increased, reluctance to attack it, all other considerations being equal, will be greater."[85]

> However, where it is the conflict of the aggressive small state with major powers that is in question and it is against one of them that the weapons are, or may be, directed, then a very different set of considerations will surely operate on all sides. It is, for example, hard to believe that the Anglo-French landing in Egypt would have taken place or the attack taken the form it did had Egypt possessed even a small nuclear force at the time.[86]

Or, as Morton Kaplan says, "Had the Czechoslovaks possessed even a few nuclear weapons, the Russians might have considered much more carefully their decision to intervene."[87] Given the historical precedents, it is doubtful that any Czech government would behave suicidally or irrationally in time of crisis. But such a reaction could be expected from other states in certain circumstances. Finland fought against overwhelming odds in a struggle whose outcome was inevitable. Israel has a Massada complex, understandable in the light of the Nazi holocaust. North Vietnam refused to yield under intensified bombing. Given the irrational and unpredictable behavior of Libya's Qaddafi and Uganda's Amin, they could be irresponsible enough to use nuclear weapons (which fortunately they do not possess), even though their own destruction would result.

Certainly the possession of even a small nuclear force by a weak state could inhibit a great nuclear power from threatening it. Although rational calculations indicate the military vulnerability of weak nuclear forces, there are less conventional, less rational ways in which a threat by a weak state could become credible. Even the possibility of hiding some primitive nuclear devices in the capital or a major city of a great power cannot be excluded.[88]

Moreover, the assumption that a weak state cannot develop a serious second-strike capability against a super power, which is usually taken for granted in the "rational" strategic literature, can be questioned. A *massive* second-strike capability *is* out of the question for any weak nuclear force, or even for a medium-sized one. But the possibility of successfully hardening a limited number of nuclear bombs and their means of delivery cannot be ruled out.

Israel, for example, has demonstrated its capacity to refuel its fighter bombers in the air. Such military planes as the A-4 and especially the F-4, when flying a one-way, no-return mission, could easily cover a considerable range (perhaps up to 1300 or 1400 miles)[89] while carrying a nuclear bomb. Out of a force of fifty to one hundred F-4 planes a few could perhaps reach their targets. The same could be said for Sweden:

> . . . it is still plausible that dispersible and therefore invulnerable delivery systems will become cheaply available in the coming decades—for example, the vertical-takeoff (VTOL) or short-takeoff (STOL) airplanes being developed now in Britain and Sweden. If the Swedish Air Force had only 10 atomic bombs, and dispersed some 200 Viggen STOL aircraft to 200 road intersections across Sweden, could the USSR really be assured that it could launch a successful preemptive attack on Sweden and be sure that the Swedes could not hit Leningrad in retaliation?[90]

Such possibilities cast a measure of doubt on all the purely "rational" strategic analyses. Furthermore, there are other factors besides the aspiration to equalize their strength with that of the great powers which may prompt weak states to acquire nuclear weapons.

For some weak states and middle powers the desire to enhance their *prestige* could be central. Countries such as India,[91] Canada, and Brazil, aspiring to move upwards in the international hierarchy, might decide to obtain their own nuclear weapons for non-military reasons.[92]

Related to the desire to enhance their prestige is the important need of states to feel free, to prove that their sovereignty is real and not nominal, and to show that they are able to pursue their own policies. The development of nuclear weapons could be viewed as an assertion of their freedom and identity. Many of the weak and middle states, sensitive to any limits on their freedom of decision, are suspicious of the great powers' objections to nuclear proliferation and see them as an effort to perpetuate the great powers' "thermonuclear duopoly" and "nuclear dictatorship."

> When I can no longer choose the nature and manner of my own defense, even though the material means are available to me, am I still free? Or, to ask the same question differently: are small states with centuries of meaningful political experience to be treated as children who are forbidden to play with matches because only adults can understand how to use them properly?[93]

The major reason, however, for a weak state to obtain nuclear weapons is to secure itself against another weak state rather than against a major power. Since the most dangerous enemies of a weak state are often other weak states, it may be very desirable to acquire what has been called a "neighbor-against-neighbor capacity."[94] Weak states that feel insecure in the *local* military balance of power may have a strong incentive to produce nuclear weapons to deter their neighbors.[95]

No doubt Israel has seriously considered the development of an advanced nuclear option as its last line of defense against a possible Arab attack. Any incentive to develop such weapons in the face of Arab threats must have been strengthened by the October 1973 war. If the Arab states ever reach a clear conventional superiority, the only way for Israel to compensate for its inferiority in numbers would be to acquire nuclear weapons. And that would obviously lead to similar attempts on the part of its neighbors, especially Egypt.[96] China's development of nuclear weapons[97] must have affected India in a similar way.

While a weak state cannot expect to deter a great nuclear power effectively, a small nuclear force can have "some defensive and deterrent value against similarly equipped neighbors . . . ."[98] Nevertheless, the acquisition of nuclear forces by weak states could have a very destabilizing effect on their security.

The confrontation of two relatively small countries, both armed with nuclear weapons, would make for extreme instability unless neither could hope to destroy the enemy's means of retaliation by a pre-emptive strike; otherwise the advantages of aggression become as disproportionately large as the extent of destruction inflicted on the first-strike victim.[99]

Two weak states with roughly equal nuclear forces might feel less secure than before and might actually find themselves in a "balance of terror" due to constant fear of a surprise attack.
Nuclear weapons developed on any militarily rational basis are weapons of last resort. A weak state would rather not produce them unless forced to do so by its neighbors. Instead it would prefer to develop a nuclear option, or what has been called by George Liska "assured seconds,"[100] meaning that it would not be the first to introduce nuclear weapons but would be able to follow immediately. The development of this option by two weak states can have an effect that is almost as destabilizing and dangerous as the actual acquisition of small nuclear forces. In fact, it could mean an even greater temptation for one side to preempt before the other has materialized its option.
The destabilizing effects of small nuclear forces are perhaps the most important reason for the super powers' objections to nuclear proliferation.[101] Rothstein correctly suggests that the effect of acquiring a small nuclear force with only first-strike capability will not be the same for a weak state as for a great power. Despite the destabilizing effect of the British and especially the French nuclear forces, the United States had to maintain its treaty obligations toward them because they were countries of great importance to the balance of power. It did not hesitate to cover them with its nuclear deterrence while they were developing their own weapons. The development of nuclear weapons by a weak state such as Israel would have the opposite effect. Fearful of being drawn into a catalytic war, a great power might terminate all its military obligations, thus creating a situation in which the weak state's security would be in worse shape than before.[102] Moreover, the super powers could neutralize the unilateral acquisition of nuclear weapons by a weak state by guaranteeing its neighboring enemy against a nuclear attack.[103] In that case the weak state's

reason for investing enormous sums of money in the development of nuclear weapons would disappear.

Another motive a weak state may have in considering the acquisition of nuclear weapons is to improve its bargaining position *vis-à-vis* one or more of the super powers.[104] At least in the short run, the weak state is not really interested in actually obtaining nuclear weapons, but rather in getting something in return for *not* producing them.

There is little doubt that this is one of the major reasons why the Israeli government has never officially denied its capability to produce nuclear weapons. In 1966 Israel agreed to an inspection of its nuclear reactor in Dimona, apparently in return for an American agreement to supply A-4 airplanes. Though this explanation of the arms deal has, of course, never been confirmed, the timing implies that it was the *quid pro quo* for U.S. inspection. Similarly, it has been suggested that one of Israel's goals in developing a nuclear option is to "trade" for a U.S. defense treaty or some other form of guarantee.[105]

Such a bargaining position can be achieved only by a weak state that is thought to be capable of producing nuclear weapons. Once a potential option has been converted into reality, however, the weak state may find itself in a weaker position than before. It can no longer exploit its threat to go nuclear, and it may even be pressured to dismantle its nuclear bomb and its bomb-producing capacity.

Another consideration underlying a weak state's decision to develop nuclear weapons could be tactical. The Swiss strategist, Gustav Däniker, asserts that tactical nuclear weapons are the ideal type of weapon to compensate a weak country for its lack of human and material resources. He has calculated that one tactical nuclear warhead is equal to three minutes of fire by 7200 guns, which would require a force of 300,000 soldiers and 800 trucks of ammunition—a force that could never be concentrated by a weak state.[106] This is an absurd calculation, as the two types of weapons are not necessarily military substitutes for each other. The fire of 7200 guns could be directed against many military targets, while a tactical nuclear bomb could be used against one target only. Däniker's lack of understanding of the responsibilities involved in the production and deployment of nuclear weapons is typical of a strategist from a weak state. He ignores the problem of escalation and the difficulty in drawing the line once nuclear weapons have been used, and he does not discuss the possibility that after initiating nuclear warfare, the weak state would suffer much heavier damage than if it had not resorted to nuclear weapons in the first place. He implies that the weak states can dictate the level of escalation on their own terms, which is not true.

Däniker also suggests that in the future, as the price of such conventional weapons as modern aircraft and tanks rises, the weak states will have to spend larger proportions of their GNP on weapon acquisition, without getting commensurate defensive capabilities in return.[107] As a result, he says, nuclear weapons would be the best and cheapest solution for the defense problems of the weak states. Though Däniker may be right in stating that nuclear weapons will become relatively cheaper,[108] the need for conventional forces will not disappear. As long as weak states can continue to deter potential enemies by conventional forces, even at a higher price, it is reasonable for them to do so. The failure of nuclear deterrence would be much more catastrophic than the failure of conventional deterrence. For example, as long as Israel can afford to obtain security by means of conventional forces, it will be better off than if it were to develop nuclear weapons, which would involve moral dilemmas, as well as the risk of total destruction.[109]

There are other, though less important, reasons for the acquisition of nuclear weapons by the weak states. One is the fear of nuclear blackmail by a great power in times of crisis. If this fear can be considered a possibility, the danger would probably originate from another weak state rather than from a great power. On the basis of rational analysis, however, weak states that had acquired nuclear weapons would still be vulnerable to nuclear blackmail by the great powers. The weak states' possession of such weapons might even make the major nuclear powers feel psychologically, morally, and ethically less hesitant about resorting to blackmail.

Yet another reason often cited to explain the development of nuclear programs by Britain and France concerns their wish for greater influence in the Atlantic Alliance. It has been argued that should they feel threatened, but unsure of American help, their own nuclear weapons could work as a detonator for their bigger ally's nuclear arsenal. In fact, Great Britain has not acquired more influence over its bigger partner's decisions.[110] The summit policies of the USSR and the USA regarding the Middle East show clearly that neither Britain nor France has more influence than it had in pre-nuclear days. The impact of these states on the international system is not radically different from that of such non-nuclear powers as West Germany and Japan. Weak and middle states should not expect to have a larger say in alliance matters as a result of acquiring nuclear weapons. On the contrary, they might find the super powers either trying to control their foreign policy and decision-making processes in order to prevent the danger of escalation, or disengaging themselves from their earlier commitments. A small nuclear force would not work as a detonator of a major power's nuclear arsenal if that power had already decided to withdraw from its commitments.

NOTES

1. Leonard Wibberly, *The Mouse That Roared* (Boston: Little Brown, 1955), pp. 16–17.
2. See, for example, Brecher, *Foreign Policy System of Israel*, p. 16.
3. Most of the United States' military interventions have been confined to Central America. The *perception* of most Latin American states, however, has been that if extra-hemispheric powers should try to gain a foothold in South America the United States would intervene to protect its interests. This perception was further strengthened during the Cold War period, and apparently it has been accepted by other powers. See Gordon Connell-Smith, *The Inter-American System* (London: Oxford University Press, 1966), p. 323. Latin American countries have always viewed the Monroe Doctrine not as protection against extra-hemispheric aggression but as an excuse for the United States to establish itself as the hegemonial power in the Western Hemisphere. See Donald Marquand Dozer (ed.), *The Monroe Doctrine* (New York: Alfred A. Knopf, 1965).
4. Dexter Perkins, *A History of the Monroe Doctrine* (Boston: Little Brown, 1963), p. 4.
5. Connell-Smith, *Inter-American System*, p. 2.
6. *Ibid.*, pp. 10–11. See also Lagos, *International Stratification and Underdeveloped Countries*, pp. 119–120.

7. Carlos Alberto Astiz (ed.), *Latin American International Politics* (South Bend, Ind.: University of Notre Dame Press, 1969), p. 21, and F. Parkinson, *Latin America, the Cold War and the World Powers 1945–1973* (Beverly Hills: Sage Publications, 1974), especially chapter 1: Latin America as a Pawn of the World Powers (1945–1950), pp. 11–20.
8. Robert N. Burr, *Our Troubled Hemisphere* (Washington, D.C.: The Brookings Institution, 1967), p. 13.
9. *Ibid.*, p. 22. Latin America's share of United States aid between 1946 and 1960 never exceeded 4.8 per cent. Parkinson, *Latin America, the Cold War and the World Powers*, p. 14.
10. Herbert Q. Mathews, *The United States and Latin America*, 2nd rev. ed. (Englewood Cliffs, N.J.: Prentice Hall, 1963), p. 153.
11. *Ibid.*, p. 161. See also Alberto Conil Paz and Gustavo Ferrari, *Argentina's Foreign Policy 1930–1962* (South Bend, Ind.: University of Notre Dame Press, 1966), p. 196.
12. Goldhamer, *Foreign Powers in Latin America*, p. 278, n. 27.
13. For theoretical studies of the Balance of Power, see Edward Vose Gulick, *Europe's Classical Balance of Power* (New York: W. W. Norton, 1967); Morton A. Kaplan, *System and Process in International Politics* (New York: John Wiley and Sons, 1967), part I; Butterfield, "The Balance of Power," and Wight, "The Balance of Power," in Herbert Butterfield and Martin Wight (eds.), *Diplomatic Investigations* (Cambridge, Mass.: Harvard University Press, 1968), pp. 132–148, 149–175 respectively; Morgenthau, *Politics Among Nations*, pp. 167–224; Taylor, *The Struggle for Mastery in Europe*, introduction; Ernst B. Haas, "The Balance of Power as a Guide to Policy Making," *The Journal of Politics*, 15 (1953), 370–398; Ernst B. Haas, "The Balance of Power—Prescription, Concept, or Propaganda," *World Politics*, 5 (July 1953), 442–477; Per Maurseth, "Balance of Power Thinking from the Renaissance to the French Revolution," *Journal of Peace Research*, 1 (1964), 120–136; Stanley Hoffmann, "Balance of Power," in the *Encyclopedia of Social Sciences* (new), I, 506–509; Sidney B. Fay, "Balance of Power," in the *Encyclopedia of the Social Sciences* (old), II, 395–399; Arnold Wolfers, "The Balance of Power in Theory and Practice," in *Discord and Collaboration* (Baltimore: Johns Hopkins Press, 1962), pp. 117–132; Inis L. Claude, *Power and International Relations* (New York: Random House, 1969), pp. 11–93; William J. Newman, *The Balance of Power in the Interwar Years 1919–1939* (New York: Random House, 1968); Kyung-Won Kim, *Revolution and International System* (New York: New York University Press, 1970); George Liska, *International Equilibrium*, pp. 23–56. Multipolar systems, like balance-of-power systems, have a larger number of power centers, a greater degree of maneuverability for great powers and weak states, and a more complex system of alliances than does a bipolar system. But in a multipolar system, unlike the classical balance-of-power system, the great powers tend to have competitive ideologies, and they do not pursue a policy that will arrive at equilibrium and the

maintenance of a power balance among the major actors. See Hoffmann, *Gulliver's Troubles*, pp. 33–46.
14. Taylor, *Struggle for Mastery in Europe*, p. xix. See also Herbert Butterfield, "The Balance of Power", in Herbert Butterfield and Martin Wight, eds, *Diplomatic Investigations* (Cambridge, Mass.: Harvard University Press, 1968), p. 142.
15. Wright, *Study of War*, I, 267; see also p. 283. In the second volume of *Study of War*, Wright expresses the opposite opinion: "Among the inherent tendencies of a balance-of-power system, sapping its own vitality, has been the cumulative elimination of small states. The balance of power has never functioned sufficiently effectively to avoid this tendency." (pp. 762–763).
16. N. J. Spykman, quoted in Amry Vandenbosch, "The Small States in International Politics and Organization," *The Journal of Politics*, 26 (1964), 294–295.
17. Weber, *Economy and Society*, II, 910.
18. "According to Treitschke, Switzerland, Belgium, and Holland survive not positively, through their own strength, but negatively, as a function of the European balance-of-power." Oscar Bernhard Cappis, *Die Idee des Kleinstaates in Deutschland des 19. Jahrhunderts*, p. 166.
19. Kaplan, *System and Process in International Politics*, p. 23.
20. It is interesting in this context to note Britain's double standard toward the weak states. The British were interested in dividing, dismembering, or controlling weak states outside Europe (especially in Africa and Asia), but claimed to have entered the First World War, as well as the Second, in order to save the weak states from aggression. "We shall never sheathe the sword . . . until the rights of the smaller nationalities of Europe are placed upon an unassailable foundation." This is the oft-quoted declaration of Mr. Asquith in Parliament in August 1914. Quoted in Marriott, *Federalism and the Problem of the Small States*, p. 62. For a similar statement by Sir Edward Grey, see Herre, *Die Kleinen Staaten Europas* p. 476.
21. "It had been regarded as axiomatic that Germany was always bound to resist a Russian attempt to advance in the Baltic area and thus provide Finnish neutrality with a natural cover. This had been proved a fallacy by the Molotov-Ribbentrop pact. As Mannerheim had foreseen, a Soviet-German understanding was the worst thing that could happen: it destroyed the balance of power in the Baltic on which Finnish security had rested." Jacobson, *Diplomacy of the Winter War*, p. 99.
22. See Winston S. Churchill, Triumph and Tragedy, Vol. VI in *The Second World War* (Boston: Houghton Mifflin, 1953), pp. 227–228; also Herbert Feis, *Churchill, Roosevelt, Stalin* (Princeton: Princeton University Press, 1957), pp. 447–451.
23. Edmund Burke, quoted in Morgenthau, *Politics Among Nations*, p. 176.
24. See Gerhard L. Weinberg, *The Foreign Policy of Hitler's Germany: Diplomatic Revolution in Europe 1933–1936* (Chicago: University of Chicago Press, 1970), pp. 87–107; Jurgen Gehl, *Austria, Germany and*

the Anschluss, 1931–1938 (London: Oxford University Press, 1963); Elisabeth Barker, *Austria 1918–1972* (London: Macmillan), pp. 37–105.
25. Kurt von Schuschnigg, *Austrian Requiem* (London: Victor Gollancz, 1947), p. 15.
26. Baron Guillaume, the Belgian ambassador to Paris on the eve of the First World War, quoted in Herre, *Die Kleinen Staaten Europas*, p. 10.
27. Astri Suhrke, "Gratuity or Tyranny: The Korean Alliances," p. 513; see also p. 530.
28. Christopher Thorne, *The Approach of War 1938–1939* (London: Macmillan 1967), p. 2.
29. Stanley W. Page, *The Formation of the Baltic States* (Cambridge, Mass.: Harvard University Press, 1959), p. 184.
30. See Macartney, *October Fifteenth*, chap. 5 ("Foreign Policy in Vacuo"), pp. 81–88.
31. See Antonin Basch, *The Danube Basin and the German Economic Sphere* (New York: Columbia University Press, 1943).
32. Morgenthau, *Politics Among Nations*, p. 205. I have quoted this passage at length because it is fundamental to the study of politics on every level.
33. Rothstein, *Alliances and Small Powers*, p. 212.
34. Helmreich, *Diplomacy of the Balkan Wars*, pp. 12–13.
35. *Ibid.*, p. 59. See also Thaden, *Russia and the Balkan Alliance of 1912*, pp. 133, 135.
36. Helmreich, *Diplomacy of the Balkan Wars*, p. 458.
37. For an excellent and penetrating analysis see Winston S. Churchill, *The Great War*, Vol. I (London: The Home Library Book, 1933), pp. 180–192.
38. See Herre, *Die Kleinen Staaten Europas*, p. 475.
39. Kaplan, *System and Process in International Politics*, p. 23.
40. Fox, *Power of Small States*, p. 187.
41. See Kieft, *Belgium's Return to Neutrality;* Miller, *Belgian Foreign Policy between Two Wars*, esp. pp. 195–300; and Rothstein, *Alliances and Small Powers*, pp. 65–128. It must be stressed that Belgian decisions were not only limited to reactions to the external environment or the changes in the balance of power, but were also a function of domestic political struggles. Kieft writes (pp. vii–viii): ". . . the most common mistake is a failure to discern the close connection between Belgian foreign policy and the structure of Belgian domestic politics. Indeed the decisive factor in the development of the 'policy of independence' was the political crisis which gripped Belgium in 1936 and which momentarily threatened to divide her . . . ." See Appendix A.
42. Miller, *Belgian Foreign Policy between Two Wars*, p. 242. But as Arnold Wolfers has shown, the French never seriously intended to rescue their eastern and central European allies. "France's military policy tends to prove that . . . she was more concerned about receiving than about giving support, more preoccupied with the defense of her

own soil than with the protection of small countries." Wolfers, *Britain and France between Two Wars* (New York: W. W. Norton, 1966), p. 75.
43. Rothstein, *Alliances and Small Powers*, p. 112.
44. See Jones, *The Scandinavian States and the League of Nations*, p. 262. This declaration led to attacks on them for undermining the effectiveness of the League of Nations. This was, of course, unfair.

   The smaller States—often regarded as timid and hesitating in the matter of the application of sanctions—cannot rightly be held responsible for the failure of the League. On the contrary, it is rather the States which in theory uphold Article XVI most strongly [Great Britain and France] that have raised objections to the application and continuance of economic sanctions during these years [i.e. 1931–1937]. [Dr. Unden, quoted in *ibid.*, p. 234].

   See also F. P. Walters, *A History of the League of Nations* (London: Oxford University Press, 1965), pp. 684–685.
45. Hoptner, *Yugoslavia in Crisis*, p. 299. See also Dragisa N. Ristic, *Yugoslavia's Revolution of 1941* (Philadelphia: University of Pennsylvania, 1966), p. 143.
46. See Fox, *Power of Small States*, chaps. 2, 5, 6, for a discussion of the neutrals' position (Turkey, Sweden, Spain) during the Second World War.
47. See Rothstein, *Alliances and Small Powers*, p. 270.
48. Quoted in Fred Charles Ikle, *Every War Must End* (New York: Columbia University Press, 1971), p. 66.
49. For information on the bipolar system, the following works were consulted: Kaplan, *System and Process in International Politics*, pp. 36–45; Hoffmann, *Gulliver's Troubles*, I, pp. 3–87; Knorr, *On the Uses of Military Power in the Nuclear Age;* Kaplan, "The Systems Approach to International Politics," in Morton A. Kaplan (ed.), *New Approaches to International Relations* (New York: St. Martins Press, 1968), pp. 381–404; Riker, *The Theory of Political Coalitions*, pp. 211–247; Kenneth Waltz, "International Structure, National Force and the Balance of World Power," in James N. Rosenau (ed.), *International Politics and Foreign Policy* (New York: Free Press, 1969), pp. 304–314; Richard N. Rosecrance, "Bipolarity, Multipolarity and the Future," in Rosenau (ed.), *International Politics and Foreign Policy*, pp. 325–335; Kenneth Waltz, "The Stability of a Bi-Polar World," *Daedalus*, 93 (Summer 1964), 881–901; Peter J. Fliess, *Thucydides and the Politics of Bipolarity* (Baton Rouge: Louisiana State University Press, 1966); Peter J. Fliess, *International Relations in the Bipolar World* (New York: Random House, 1968).
50. See Hoffmann, *Gulliver's Troubles*, pp. 12–13.
51. For a discussion of moderate and revolutionary systems see *ibid.*, pp. 12–16 and chap. 2. For an excellent analysis of the dynamics of a revolutionary system see also Kyung-Won Kim, *Revolution and International System*.
52. Thomas M. Franck and Edward Weisband, *World Politics—Verbal*

Strategy Among the Super Powers (New York: Oxford University Press, 1971), p. 79.
53. *Ibid.*, p. 33.
54. *Ibid.*, pp. 39–40.
55. *Ibid.*, pp. 89–90. In their book, *World Politics,* Franck and Weisband exaggerate the importance of the Johnson and Brezhnev Doctrines, implying that the verbal politics of the Johnson Doctrine encouraged the Russians to adopt the Brezhnev Doctrine. This *post hoc ergo propter hoc* argument does not seem valid to me. The United States had intervened much earlier in Latin American countries (especially in Central America and the Caribbean) on the basis of the Monroe Doctrine. The Russians had intervened long before in Finland and later in Hungary, and would have intervened in Czechoslovakia with or without an American equivalent. The interpretation of the two *World Politics* authors is part of the post-Vietnam revisionist attempt to equate everything the United States did in the Cold War with what the USSR did.
56. Donald Kagan, *The Outbreak of the Peloponnesian War* (Ithaca: Cornell University Press, 1969), pp. 21–22.
57. Riker, *The Theory of Political Coalitions,* p. 231.
58. *Ibid.,* p. 227.
59. *Ibid.,* p. 239. For a similar idea see Oran Young, *The Intermediaries* (Princeton: Princeton University Press, 1967), p. 380:
    . . . it seems likely that some tacit steps will be taken to reduce the present tendency of the super powers to cancel out each other's power and, therefore, to undermine their usable power when dealing with the so-called uncommitted and non-aligned states. Therefore, as the conflict pattern of the system becomes more complex and as Soviet-American common interests tend to become more influential, the uncommitted states may well find it more and more difficult to play the established superpowers off against each other both profitably and with impunity.
60. Knorr, *On the Uses of Military Power in the Nuclear Age,* p. 65.
61. Wildavsky and Singer, "A Third-World Averaging Strategy," in Wildavsky, *Revolt Against the Masses,* p. 474.
62. *Ibid.,* p. 464.
63. *Ibid.,* p. 467. See also Knorr, *On the Uses of Military Power in the Nuclear Age,* pp. 154–156.
64. Suarez, *Cuba, Castroism and Communism, 1959–1966,* pp. 131–153, 171–185; Maurice Halperin, *The Rise and Decline of Fidel Castro* (Berkeley: University of California Press, 1972), pp. 134–148, 204.
65. See Suarez, *Cuba, Castroism and Communism, 1959–1966,* pp. 107–185, 214–241.
66. Fidel profoundly disliked the "spirit" [of Camp David], since he feared that an improvement of relations between the big two would be damaging to small countries like Cuba. Knowing or suspecting Khrushchev's intentions, he may have decided to make overtures to the United States so as to make it more difficult for Moscow and

Washington to reach agreement behind his back. (Suarez, *Cuba, Castroism and Communism, 1959–1966*, p. 120).
67. "The smaller the margin of power that favors either of two contending parties, the more relevant is the total power of an intrinsically weak third party." George Liska, quoted in Young, *The Intermediaries*, p. 44, n. 59.
68. Knorr, *On the Uses of Military Power in the Nuclear Age*, p. 78.
69. Hoffmann, *Gulliver's Troubles*, p. 53.
70. *Ibid.*, p. 39.
71. *Ibid.*
72. Knorr, *On the Uses of Military Power in the Nuclear Age*, p. 76.
73. Wibberly, *The Mouse That Roared*, pp. 144–48.
74. Kaplan, *System and Process in International Politics*, pp. 50–51. Kaplan's definition of the unit veto system implies rational behavior on the part of all states, but this cannot be taken for granted. It is necessary to differentiate between a unit veto system which assumes rational behavior on the part of all states and an all-nuclear system in which rational behavior by all states is not assured.
75. Pierre Gallois, *The Balance of Terror* (Boston: Houghton Mifflin, 1961), p. 181.
76. Pierre Gallois, as quoted in Raymond Aron, *The Great Debate* (Garden City, N.Y.: Doubleday, 1965), p. 102.
77. Gallois, *Balance of Terror*, pp. 9–10. See also Rothstein, *Alliances and Small Powers*, pp. 280–281.
78. Gallois, *Balance of Terror*, pp. 135–136; Aron, *Great Debate*, pp. 122–125.
79. For detailed discussions see Vital, *Inequality of States*, pp. 159–182; Rothstein, *Alliances and Small Powers*, pp. 265–323; Aron, *Great Debate*, pp. 100–143. For general background Y. Harkabi's *Nuclear War and Nuclear Peace* is still the best work. The subject is also discussed in great detail in the literature on nuclear proliferation.
80. This is Leo Szilard's phrase, quoted in Knorr, *On the Uses of Military Power in the Nuclear Age*, p. 118.
81. See, for example, Rothstein, *Alliances and Small Powers*, pp. 283, 290–291; and George Liska, *Nations in Alliance* (Baltimore: Johns Hopkins Press, 1968), pp. 277, 280.
82. For example, Rothstein, *Alliances and Small Powers*, p. 290; Vital, *Inequality of States*, p. 171.
83. George Liska makes the interesting suggestion that the weak states would actually have to strengthen their conventional forces after acquiring nuclear weapons. The reason is that nuclear weapons are weapons of last resort. Hence the need to develop one's conventional forces in order to widen options and reduce the need to utilize nuclear weapons. Liska, *Nations in Alliance*, pp. 276–277.
84. Vital, *Inequality of States*, pp. 168–170, 173.
85. *Ibid.*, pp. 170–171.
86. *Ibid.*, p. 178.
87. See Morton A. Kaplan, "The Unit Veto Reconsidered," in Richard

Rosecrance (ed.), *The Future of the International Strategic System* (San Francisco: Chandler, 1972), p. 53; also for a similar suggestion, George H. Quester, "The Politics of Twenty Nuclear Powers," in Rosecrance, *The Future of the International Strategic System*, p. 67.
88. See, for example, Yehezkel Dror, *Crazy States* (Lexington, Mass.: D. C. Heath, 1971).
89. J. Bowyer Bell, "Israel's Nuclear Option," *The Middle East Journal*, 28 (Autumn 1972), 382. He suggests a longer range of 2000 miles.
90. Quester, "Politics of Twenty Nuclear Powers," in Rosecrance, *Future of the International Strategic System*, p. 57.
91. In May 1974 (after this chapter was written), India tested its first nuclear bomb. Undoubtedly, its decision to do so was determined to a large extent by prestige politics. This can be deduced from the fact that India is not currently threatened by the Chinese People's Republic, and decisively won its last war against Pakistan.
92. See, for example, Rosecrance (ed.), *Future of the International Strategic System*, p. 2; Rothstein, *Alliances and Small Powers*, pp. 298–299; Vital, *Inequality of States*, p. 178.
93. Däniker, *Strategie des Kleinstaats*, pp. 98–99.
94. Malcolm Hoag, "Superpower Strategic Postures for a Multipolar World," in Rosecrance, *Future of the International Strategic System*, pp. 283–284.
95. Knorr, *On the Uses of Military Power in the Nuclear Age*, p. 120.
96. Handel, *Israel's Political-Military Doctrine*, pp. 48–49. See also J. Bowyer Bell, "Israel's Nuclear Option," *The Middle East Journal*, 26 (Autumn 1972), 379–388.
97. For India's nuclear policy see Rothstein, *Alliances and Small Powers*, pp. 306–312. (See also n. 91 above.)
98. Knorr, *On the Uses of Military Power in the Nuclear Age*, p. 120.
99. Aron, *Great Debate*, p. 134. See also Vital, *Inequality of States*, pp. 174–179; Rothstein, *Alliances and Small Powers*, p. 281.
100. Liska, as quoted in Rothstein, *Alliances and Small Powers*, p. 316.
101. George Liska is one of the few who stress the stabilizing effects of nuclear proliferation. See Liska, *Nations in Alliance*, pp. 269–284.
102. Rothstein, *Alliances and Small Powers*, pp. 283ff.
103. *Ibid.*, p. 290.
104. Hoffmann, *Gulliver's Troubles*, pp. 30, 45. See also Handel, *Israel's Political-Military Doctrine*, pp. 48–49.
105. William B. Bader, *The United States and the Spread of Nuclear Weapons* (New York: Pegasus, 1968).
106. Däniker, *Strategie des Kleinstaats*, p. 162. He does not point out that the same firepower could be achieved by a force of 900 guns firing for 24 minutes, or by a force of 400 guns firing for 48 minutes, which is well within the reach of many weak states. The Swedish Army has long advocated the acquisition of nuclear weapons for the following tactical military reasons:
    (1) A nuclear-armed enemy would be able to concentrate his forces while the Swedes would be forced to disperse their own in order to

minimize the effects of nuclear weapons. Such dispersal would weaken Sweden's ability to defeat the enemy's invasion forces.

(2) On the other hand, if the Swedish forces also possessed nuclear weapons, the enemy would be forced to disperse his own units, and experience from maneuvers indicated that in equal combat of this kind tactical nuclear weapons favored the defenders.

(3) Nuclear weapons were relatively inexpensive in relation to their great destructive power and were therefore both economical and effective.

(4) Sweden would be easy prey for a nuclear power if she maintained a purely conventional defense.

(5) Since Sweden desired tactical nuclear weapons rather than strategic weapons, her nuclear capability would threaten no one.

(6) Sweden's armed forces should not be expected to defend the nation's independence with weapons inferior to those of the enemy.

Jerome Garris, "Sweden's Debate on the Proliferation of Nuclear Weapons," *Conflict and Cooperation*, 8 (1973), 195–196. See also Jan Prowitz, "A Nuclear Doctrine for Sweden," in *Conflict and Cooperation*, 3 (1968), 184–193.

107. Däniker, *Strategie des Kleinstaats*, pp. 27, 37.
108. For example, Vital, *Inequality of States*, p. 162, shows that weak states such as Sweden, Switzerland, Belgium, and the Netherlands could develop nuclear weapons over ten years by an additional yearly allocation of around 1.8 per cent of their yearly GNP. For underdeveloped countries the problem is much more serious, as the absolute sums of money needed would be of a much higher order relative to their total GNP and would undermine both their economies and their conventional forces.
109. See Leonard Beaton, "Why Israel Does Not Need the Bomb," *The New Middle East*, 1 (April 1969), 11.
110. Aron, *Great Debate*, p. 111.

CHAPTER V

The Economic Position of the Weak States in the International System

Most theoretical studies of weak states in international relations are strictly political and military.[1] Such economic studies as exist rarely include any political-military analyses. This is not surprising, for to analyze the economic position of the weak states in the context of a basically political-military study is a very difficult task. In addition to the interdisciplinary problems, the enormous amount of existing research on international trade, primary commodities, markets for raw materials, and economic theory would have to be mastered. It would be a mistake, however, to perpetuate the unnatural separation between the economic and the political and military spheres, which are closely inter-related in reality. Without pretending to undertake an exhaustive or innovative analysis, this chapter will summarize some of the economic problems involved in the relations between the weak and strong states, and will relate them to the subject matter of the preceding chapters.

Some of the most important events in international politics in 1973–74 have been based in economics. For example, OAPEC (Organization of Arab Petroleum Exporting Countries) has placed a successful oil embargo on western Europe, Japan, and the United States. Weak states that export other raw materials, such as copper, tin, bauxite, rubber, and coffee, have been considering similar measures to improve their terms of trade.[2] These activities have demonstrated the growing importance of the economic dimension in the relations between the weak, less developed countries (LDC's) and the economically powerful states, as well as between other states and groups of states, such as the United States and the EEC.

The growing reluctance of the great powers to use their superior military might against the weak states and among themselves has shifted conflict between states to the economic arena and has emphasized, perhaps more than ever before, the economic dimension of international relations.[3] As a result, the question can be raised whether the relative distribution of strength and therefore the relationship between some of the weak states and the great powers has not changed radically in favor of the weak states.

So far in modern history, the great powers in political and military terms have also been the great powers economically. They could take advantage of their military superiority to improve their economic position *vis-à-vis* the weak states. They did so by directly controlling the economies of the weak states through their imperialistic and colonial policies; by exploiting special trade relations with less developed countries dependent on their markets (examples are Germany's dominant trade position in the Danubian and Balkan states between the two World Wars, and Great Britain's and France's trade relations with their former colonies, often referred to as neocolonialism); by explicit or veiled threats of military intervention; by raising the specter of economic sanctions, and later by threatening to withhold positive economic rewards such as loans, financial aid, and private investments.

But now a new breed of states seems to be appearing, states that are militarily weak and technologically underdeveloped but economically strong. Saudi Arabia, Libya, Kuwait, and Iran combine enormous capital revenues with relatively small populations and basically "finite," limited domestic economies which cannot absorb the enormous capital revenues accumulated. Because these "capital surpluses" cannot be invested at home, they must be invested abroad.

Between 1974 and 1977 OPEC countries invested 162 billion dollars in foreign countries. This sum is divided in the following way:

TABLE 8
OPEC FOREIGN INVESTMENT 1974–1977

Investment	%	Billion $
Eurodollar and other banking deposits	63.82	39.4
Bilateral lending	46.33	28.6
Investments	24.78	15.3
U.S. Government Securities	15.22	9.4
Lending to International Organizations	9.88	6.1
U.S. Bank Deposits	6.64	4.1
British Government Securities	1.94	1.2

Note: Figures are rounded off; therefore totals exceed 100% and 162 billion dollars.
Source: *The Economist*, June 10, 1978, pp. 87–88.

For the first time, relatively weak states (in military and political terms) can grant or withhold enormous financial aid and investments, and they can also finance military purchases on the scale of the great powers. For the first time, states which were hitherto considered weak have offered rewards to other countries that will support their causes and have thus carved out their own little spheres of influence.[4]

For the first time, then, the "highest stage of imperialism" is working in reverse. The very large surpluses of capital accumulated by the rich oil-exporting countries are being invested in modern industrialized countries, yielding higher profits. Although Hobson's and Lenin's theories of economic imperialism do not accurately describe the behavior of the industrialized great powers, they may, ironically, prove to be true for some of the *nouveaux riches* countries. A new class of states seems to be emerging in Arabian deserts—"coupon-clipping sheikdoms," to paraphrase Lenin. Such countries will be able to manipulate and disrupt the monetary system of the industrial Western World, and speculate against the currency of any of the great powers.

Can these militarily weak but economically strong states translate their newly acquired economic power into political power? If so, under what conditions? Will their circle be joined by other weak states that do not produce oil, or will it remain an exclusive club of the oil-producing countries? Are the oil-producing countries economically *sui generis?* Under what conditions will their bargaining position be strengthened or weakened? What are the limits to their strength? How vulnerable are they now, in spite of their growing economic might?

Many of the new problems in international economics defy conventional economic wisdom, for they involve highly complicated political, social, and psychological factors. It seems that international economics, at least concerning the relations between the developed and underdeveloped states, has reached a turning point. The definitions of economically weak and strong states are in flux, and it is difficult to predict the focus of future relations between the developed and the underdeveloped states. Therefore the questions raised above can be answered only speculatively. It may well be that many earlier theories of international trade, which were based on the economic relations between the developed and underdeveloped states, will be of little value in understanding international economic developments and may even be misleading. For the present, the best that one can do is to look at the relations between the economically weak and strong states in the light of traditional economic theory.

Sources of Economic Weakness

According to traditional economic theory, a state's territorial size and the size of its domestic market play important roles in determining its economic strength and viability. Economic logic is based on the assumption that all other things being equal (i.e., all states being on the same general level of economic development), the state with a large area and population has an advantage over the small one. Territorially small states are less likely to have diverse and balanced sources of raw materials, and because of climatic uniformity they tend to have a smaller variety of agricultural products.[5]

> There is . . . the possibility that a large geographical size would, other conditions given, connote a richer supply base, and if the supply base is also rich from a potential point of view so that there is a large gap between the actual levels of utilization of resources and their potential supply, a large population might connote the possibility of higher incomes and hence of a larger-sized market. Other conditions given, if resources are abundant in relation to population, productivity levels can potentially rise, and the economy has considerable scope of expansion, the process having increasing returns.[6]

Economically weak states, which frequently produce only a limited number of products, are sometimes referred to as one-dimensional states.[7] It has been found by economists that the "smaller the country . . . the stronger is the concentration in production and exports".[8] This high concentration on one-commodity production is illustrated by the export patterns of Latin American countries and African states, as summarized in Tables 9 and 10.

> The developing countries are heavily dependent on primary products for most of their exports: currently 88 per cent of their

export earnings are derived from primary product sales. Furthermore, these exports are concentrated on a narrow range of products: almost one half of these countries depend on one commodity for more than 50 per cent of their total exports and as many as threequarters derive more than 60 per cent of their total exports from three primary commodities. As a result, the export earnings of the developing countries, with their crucial influence on import capacity and development potential, are heavily dependent on the prices and trading opportunities prevailing in world commodity markets.[9]

Because of this situation, many LDC's are more vulnerable to political pressures from the states which purchase their products (usually the great powers). Their sensitivity to price fluctuations and political pressures varies directly with the demand for their products and the number of countries competing for them in the international markets.

This can be demonstrated by the following table:

TABLE 9

RELATION BETWEEN SIZE OF COUNTRY (POPULATION, GNP) AND COUNTRY EXPORT CONCENTRATION

GROUPS OF COUNTRIES Countries ranked in Increasing Order of Population Size Quartiles	Number of Countries	Average Population (millions)	Median Country Export Concentration
I	20	2.04	55.5
II	20	6.02	42.1
III	20	13.33	40.7
IV	20	74.01	33.1
Countries Ranked in Increasing Order of GNP Size (Quartiles)	Number of Countries	Average GNP ($ billions)	Median Country Export Concentration
I	19	0.405	50.6
II	19	1.35	41.0
III	19	3.48	40.7
IV	20	51.69	31.9

Source: Nadim G. Khalaf, *Economic Implications of the Size of Nations* (Leiden: E. J. Brill, 1971), p. 82.

TABLE 10

PER CENT COMMODITY SHARE IN COUNTRY TOTAL EXPORT BY VALUE, 1965
(FOR AFRICAN STATES)

Country	Product	Per cent	Year (other than 1965)
Algeria	Petroleum (oil)	51.1	
Burundi	Coffee	73.9	
C.A.R. (Central African Republic)	Diamonds	53.8	
Congo (Brazzaville)	Diamonds	42.7	30.1% (1968) registered
	Wood	38.9	50.1% (1968) exports
Ethiopia	Coffee	66.5	
Ghana	Cocoa	61.0	(1970)
Guinea	Bauxite	45.7	(1964)
Ivory Coast	Coffee	37.8	
Kenya	Coffee	22.3	(1970)
	Tea	12.7	(1970)
Liberia	Iron ore	72.5	(1964)
Libya	Petroleum (oil)	99.4	
Malagasy	Coffee	31.5	
Mauritania	Iron ore	95.1	
Nigeria	Petroleum (oil)	57.1	(1970)
	Cocoa	15.0	(1970)
Rwanda	Coffee	50.5	
Senegal	Peanuts	37.3	
	Wood	27.0	
Sierra Leone	Diamonds	60.0	(1970)
Sudan	Cotton	46.5	
UAR	Cotton	44.5	
Uganda	Coffee	59.0	(1970)
Zaire	Copper	60.0	(1968)
Zambia	Copper	97.0	(1970)

Source: Henry L. Bretton, *Power and Politics in Africa* (Chicago: Aldine Publishing Co., 1973), p. 26.

Since their products are less diversified, the economically weak states have little chance to achieve autarky.[10] They depend on foreign trade for many of the goods necessary for their development and improvement in their standard of living.

The rich country can with little effort supply a poor country with implements for agriculture or the chase which doubled the effectiveness of her labor, and which she could not make for herself; while the rich country could without great trouble make for herself most of the things which she purchased from the poor nation or at all events could get fairly good substitutes for them. A stoppage of the trade would therefore generally cause much more real loss to the poor than to the rich nation.[11]

TABLE 11

LATIN AMERICA'S EXPORTS (1959)

Country	Primary Export	Producing % of Total Export Earnings	Second Export	% by Both
Argentina	Meat	26	Wheat	39
Bolivia	Tin	62	Lead	71
Brazil	Coffee	58	Cacao	64
Chile	Copper	66	Nitrates	76
Colombia	Coffee	77	Oil	92
Costa Rica	Coffee	51	Bananas	86
Cuba	Sugar	77	Tobacco	83
Dominican Rep.	Sugar	48	Cacao	65
Ecuador	Bananas	57	Coffee	75
El Salvador	Coffee	72	Cotton	88
Guatemala	Coffee	72	Bananas	85
Haiti	Coffee	63	Sisal	80
Honduras	Bananas	51	Coffee	70
Mexico	Cotton	25	Coffee	36
Nicaragua	Cotton	39	Coffee	73
Panama	Bananas	69	Cacao	72
Paraguay	Wood pulp	24	Meat	46
Peru	Cotton	23	Sugar	38
Uruguay	Wool	54	Meat	68
Venezuela	Oil	92	Iron ore	98

Latin American Average export earnings:
  from one item: 55.3%   from to: 70.3%

Source: John Gerassi, *The Great Fear in Latin America* (New York: Collier Books, 1973), p. 32.

It is not surprising that on the whole the ratio of foreign trade to GNP is higher for the small and economically weak states than for the great powers.

> ... the smaller is the country the larger is the proportion of its exports to its total output. This renders a small country especially vulnerable to changes in its exports, first, because a given percentage change in exports means a relatively large change in the market for its products; and secondly, because the balance of payments deficit, if one comes into being with a decline in exports, is relatively larger ....[12]

The generally high foreign trade (or export) proportions that often characterize small countries are unusually sensitive to fluctuations in their foreign trade. Any shift in demand for their exports will mean, because of the high proportion of exports to national income, a relatively large proportionate change in the demand for the country's total product .... The unavailability of abundant and diversified resources and a limited domestic market obstruct a small country's capacity to accommodate sudden changes in demand for its products.[13]

A small state has already been defined economically

> ... as one which, while depending comparatively heavily upon foreign trade both for supplies and sales markets, makes only a modest contribution to the aggregate flow of international trade.[14]

Marshall Singer has suggested that

> ... if more than 20 per cent of the G.D.P. of any country is accounted for by foreign trade (as was the case in more than two thirds of all the countries in the world in 1967), at least the monetized sector of that country's economy can be considered dependent on foreign trade.[15]

Not only do the economically weak states produce a narrow range of products and export a high percentage of their GNP, but very frequently they export to relatively few states. This means that they often become dependent on the good-will of one great power, and thus a single state can have an extraordinary impact on their economic well-being. Marshall Singer has suggested that

> ... if more than one third of . . .[a] country's total trade is with just one Power . . . then clearly any decisions—public or private —made in the more powerful country that relate to the foreign

trade of the weaker could have a profound effect on the economic well-being of the weaker; and thus the weaker could legitimately be considered economically dependent upon the stronger.[16]

Such a situation enables a great power to extract political support (such as votes in the UN or military bases) from an economically weak state in return for continuing economic support. The strong power can also exploit the economic dependence of the weak state to "retard" its economic development. For example, the great power may encourage the weak state to concentrate on the production of primary commodities, or may refuse to import from it anything but primary commodities. Although trade relations between an economically strong and an economically weak, less developed state usually do not reflect a conscious design on the part of the strong state to retard or contain the development of the weak, this is often the result. Many states, especially in Latin America and Africa, fear a "deliberately planned," conspiratorial development of dependency ("Dependencia") on a great power's economy.[17]

In the 1930s, Germany's trade policy toward the Danubian and Balkan states was aimed at limiting production in its weak trading partners to primary commodities.[18] Later, it was Nazi Germany's deliberate policy to gain an economically dominant position in southeastern Europe and finally to use its economic bargaining position to exact political and economic concessions. The Germans achieved this by offering higher prices for primary commodities than other states. Though the weak states were aware of the dangers involved, they decided to opt for economic gain rather than economic security.[19]

> . . . Germany was ready to trade with Hungary and Yugoslavia and Roumania; and to countries still wallowing in the wake of the Depression, a Great Power which was prepared to modify its economic policy to their benefit was a more attractive partner than a Great Power which talked only of security and the need to preserve the European Order [France]. A secret commercial treaty between Germany and Hungary was signed in February 1934, and the Germans thereafter began to receive almost a quarter of Hungary's total exports, mostly livestock, bauxite and raw materials for industry; and Hungary, in turn, imported from Germany manufactured products and coal and coke, or their

derivatives. The economies of the two countries became so interlocked that had there been an interruption in the supply of machinery or spare parts from Germany, the Hungarian factories would once more have faced disaster . . . and when the Second World War began Germany was receiving more than half of Yugoslavia's exports and was supplying almost as large a proportion of her imported requirements.

Naturally the Germans did not help the Danubian States to solve their economic problems out of sheer kindness of heart. A German Foreign Office memorandum of June 1934 . . . records that both the Hungarian and Yugoslav agreements 'had political significance above their actual commercial content' and were 'designed to create in Hungary and Yugoslavia two points of support for German policy in the Danube region, and above all to counteract French and Italian policy directed against German policy there.' It is significant that when, only three weeks after the Yugoslavs had struck their bargain, the Roumanians sought a commercial agreement, they were told by the German Foreign Minister that Germany 'could make sacrifices only in favor of those states which did not support our opponents politically, as was the case with Roumania.'[20]

The extent of German economic penetration into southeastern Europe within a period of four years is shown on Table 12.

In trade relations between unequal partners,

> If a nation with an absolutely large volume of trade imports from, or exports to, a small trading nation, the trade they conduct together will inevitably result in a much higher percentage for the small than for the large trading nation. German-Bulgarian trade in 1938, for example, represented 52 and 59 per cent of Bulgarian imports and exports respectively, but only 1.5 and 1.1 per cent of the German imports and exports. These figures indicate that although the same absolute amount is involved, it will be much more difficult for Bulgaria to shift her trade with Germany to other countries than it will be for Germany to replace Bulgaria as a selling market and a source of supplies.[21]

Similarly, in the case of

> . . . countries like Sierra Leone or Dahomey, with 45 per cent and 68 per cent of their 1967 total trade accounted for by trade with Britain and France respectively, it must indeed appear that their markets are very important to those European Powers. But for

the British in 1967, Sierra Leone accounted for only .2 per cent of the U.K.'s total foreign trade, while for France in that year, Dahomey accounted for only .1 per cent of total trade.[22]

... the economic relationships of Britain and Sierra Leone and France and Dahomey ... are examples of "one-way" economic dependence. No economic decision in either of those African countries could have more than the most minor effect on the economies of Britain or France. In contrast, any relevant economic decision made in those European countries would have the most profound effect on the economies of those African states.[23]

Although Germany's planned economic penetration of southeastern Europe is an atypical case, it nevertheless illustrates the political and economic dangers awaiting a weak partner which conducts a high percentage of its foreign trade with one economically powerful state.

TABLE 12

GERMANY'S PERCENTUAL SHARE IN THE TRADE OF SOUTHEASTERN EUROPEAN COUNTRIES

Country	Trade	Year	
		1934	1938[a]
Hungary	Import	18.3	40.9
	Export	22.2	40.0
Rumania	Import	15.5	40.0
	Export	16.6	26.5
Yugoslavia	Import	13.9	39.4
	Export	15.4	42.0
Bulgaria	Import	40.2	52.0
	Export	42.8	59.0
Greece	Import	14.7	29.5
	Export	22.5	40.3
Turkey	Import	33.8	47.5
	Export	37.4	43.9

[a]—Includes Austria
Source: C. A. Macartney and A. W. Palmer, *Independent Eastern Europe* (London: Macmillan, 1966), p. 315.

It has often been argued that small states suffer from what is called diseconomics of scale:

> Certain industries must operate at a minimum scale or not at all, presumably because of large indivisibilities of plant. Those countries whose markets are too small to support this "technological" minimum scale will import such products from larger countries. It is contended that nations below a critical size seldom have such industries as an aircraft industry, an integrated automobile industry, or a large-scale chemical industry.[24]

If weak states do succeed in developing large mass-producing industries, they must be export-oriented and hence more dependent on foreign markets.

> ... in a small country, a specialized enterprise, if large, is likely to be large because it is international; and its domestic segment is likely to be a small part of its total size.[25]

For the same reasons, weak states are presumably at a disadvantage in research and development of new industrial products.

> The large country has more funds for research, a field for experiment wide enough to try a greater number of new proposals, and more trained people who may develop new ideas. The statistical probability of a flash of genius is presumably no greater per thousand of population in a big country than in a small one, but there are not only more people to have flashes; there are also the technicians to carry out a systematic programme of research large enough to explore all the variant possibilities implicit in a particular bright idea.[26]

Moreover, because the volume of their exports and imports is small, weak states are of necessity "price-takers." The prices they demand and pay are set entirely by the world market, independent of their domestic conditions of supply and demand.[27]

The major problems of weak states in international trade can be summarized as follows:

(a) They produce a much narrower range of products than the larger states and hence are less likely to achieve autarky. As a result they depend to a larger extent on foreign trade.

(b) They have a much higher ratio of exports (and imports) in relation to their GNP than the economically strong states.
(c) They often tend to conduct their foreign trade with fewer trading partners than do the great powers.
(d) They are relatively disadvantaged with respect to large-scale industries based on mass-production techniques. If they do develop mass-production industries, they are more dependent on external markets. Also, they usually have little to invest (in absolute terms) in research and development.

The foregoing suggests that since economically weak states depend heavily on external market conditions, they are more sensitive to foreign developments beyond their control; their economic dependence on others could easily lead to political dependence as well.

Modifications, Qualifications, and Caveats

While many sources of weakness of the economically small and less developed states which are prescribed by traditional economic theory can be accepted as valid, the economic predicament of the weak states may not be so severe as that theory would suggest. In the first place, some empirical evidence runs counter to the general rules to which, in any case, there are many exceptions. Secondly, the economically weak states can reduce their vulnerability by taking precautionary measures. Thirdly, the political environment that has prevailed since the 1950s tends to work in favor of the economically weak states by restraining the great powers.

It is true that economically weak states, especially the LDC's, tend to produce a limited assortment of products. However, some economically small but *highly developed* states can produce a large and well-balanced variety of commodities (e.g., Switzerland,[28] Sweden, the Netherlands, and Czechoslovakia). Although the production of a small range of goods can be considered a serious disadvantage, the economic position of a country depends also on the nature of the products it exports and the markets in which they are sold.

Saudi Arabia, Kuwait, and Libya, whose single export is

oil, operate in a seller's market. The demand for oil is highly inflexible, the great powers compete for the right to purchase oil, there are no effective substitutes for oil, and the number of large oil-producing countries is relatively small. The oligopolistic conditions in the oil market work to the benefit of the oil-producing states and put them in a unique position *vis-à-vis* consumer states. And they certainly have taken advantage of their newly acquired power. As long as these conditions exist in the oil market,[29] and as long as the OPEC countries can effectively cooperate among themselves, they are in an exceptionally strong position, despite the single-commodity nature of their production.

Similar conditions exist in other markets for primary commodities, or can be created through the cooperation among weak states which are leading producers. In the copper market,

> Four countries control more than 80 per cent of the exportable supply of world copper, have already organized, and have already begun to use their oligopoly power. Two countries account for more than 70 per cent of world tin exports, and four countries raise the total close to 95 per cent. Four countries combine for more than 50 per cent of the world supply of natural rubber. Four countries possess over one-half the world supply of bauxite, and the inclusion of Australia . . . brings the total above 90 per cent. In coffee, the four major suppliers have begun to collude to boost prices.[30]

Nevertheless, there are limits to the ability of countries producing commodities other than oil to collaborate in order to improve their terms of trade and also their political position.[31] Products such as tin and copper often have substitutes, and the demand for them is not as unvarying as the demand for oil. In the case of coffee, cocoa, and sugar, the number of producing countries is relatively large, which makes cooperation more difficult.[32]

Nevertheless, by improving their own coordination, allocating quotas, regulating production, and taking advantage of the growing demand for both food and raw materials, the weak states can improve their terms of trade and, in some markets of great strategic and industrial importance, can even improve their political standing. Although weak states should try to diversify their products, a limited variety does not necessarily mean greater vulnerability.

There is also evidence to indicate that despite their potential vulnerability to external pressures and their sensitivity to fluctuations in the world markets, the weak, less developed states have received a fairly stable income from their export of primary commodities.

> . . . probably the importance of short-term export instability to underdeveloped countries has been exaggerated. There is little evidence to show that in general their economies have been damaged. In most cases fluctuations in income do not appear to be at all closely related to fluctuations in export earnings. Many countries with highly unstable exports have relatively stable incomes.[33]
>
> Commonly accepted explanations of the extra instability of exports of underdeveloped countries—such as specialization in primary products, commodity concentration, geographical concentration—are found to miss the mark . . . . For most underdeveloped countries, variations in the supply of exports seem to have been more important than fluctuations in demand.[34]

Similarly, the common-sense notion that the economically small states tend to have, in absolute terms, only a small share of the primary-commodity market and hence tend to be "price-takers" is not substantiated by empirical evidence. In the oil, copper, tin, rubber, and bauxite markets, they have a very substantial share and hence a substantial impact. This has been found to be true for other markets as well:

> The larger trading countries have, on the average, practically the same commodity-weighted share in world trade as all the rest, save the smallest trading countries . . . many of the smaller economies have a stronger monopolistic position, in this sense, than most of the large countries.[35]
>
> . . . statistics conclusively refute the notion that the export sales of small countries comprise a small share of foreign markets and that therefore small countries are price-takers in their export markets.[36]

Although most weak states have not developed heavy industries—with the notable exceptions of Sweden, Belgium, Czechoslovakia, and Luxembourg—some have developed other types of mass-production industries.

In the first place, as Jewkes has shown, it is not clear that large mass-production industries are always more efficient; in some industries small- or medium-sized firms have proved to be just as efficient or more so.[37]

> "Outside a few exceptional industries most technical economies are exhausted by firms of quite moderate size. Even relatively small and poor countries can have a number of firms of the minimum size to give full, or almost full, technical efficiency." At the outset one should note that there are certain industries whose unit costs are not likely to be affected by the scale of output. One category is the extractive industries located near raw materials; another category includes some products of superior technical quality that require skilled workmanship. Switzerland provides the classical example in the watch and precision instrument and machinery industries which are carried on by small firms, mass production methods being almost totally absent.[38]

Also, there is no positive evidence to indicate that new inventions and research have been more successful in large than in small- and medium-sized firms, though there is some evidence that once a new invention has been made it can be developed more quickly by large firms.[39]

Secondly, small states can compensate for their limited domestic markets by producing for much larger export markets. Countries such as Taiwan, Singapore, Malaysia, Hong Kong, Lebanon, Cyprus, and the Central American countries have grown at rates equal or superior to those of larger countries such as India, Indonesia, and Egypt.[40]

It was once assumed that small states were less likely to develop efficient economies, and that labor and capital were less mobile within them. The fragmentation of a large state into smaller states—smaller economic units—was supposed to be an economic disaster, of which the classic example is the dissolution of the Hapsburg Empire.[41] However, as Leff has convincingly shown, fragmentation can sometimes work to the advantage of the small state that has broken away.

> Surely Lebanon would not have done as well economically if the country were part of Syria. And if Pakistan had remained joined to India, its development, too, would only have been retarded by the weaknesses of Indian economic policy-making.[42]

It would certainly not be in the economic interest of affluent Libya to merge with impoverished Egypt.

Small, autonomous economic units included within a larger political framework can sometimes become the victims of the so-called "internal colonialism" practiced by the dominant region.[43] This was the problem faced by East Pakistan (Bangladesh) within Pakistan. By breaking away, the new small states can benefit economically through becoming eligible for foreign aid. "In terms of aid per capita, the smaller countries have done much better than large ones."[44] Had Lebanon been part of Syria, or Bangladesh remained an integral part of Pakistan, they would not have been able to attract as much aid as they can now, and their regional economic achievements might have been swallowed up in the large, less developed area.

When exporting countries reach an agreement among themselves to sell certain primary commodities at a fixed price, and decide to allocate export quotas to each exporting state, as was the case in the International Coffee Agreement of 1962, the small exporting states enjoy a collective good. The larger producers, such as Brazil and Colombia in the coffee agreement, who have the greatest interest in coordinating their efforts and trying to control the market prices, "will accept a greater burden in providing a collective good—in this case a higher world price for coffee."[45]

Such agreements benefit the smaller producers. The larger producers avoid price competition among themselves, and thus prices do not fall below the profit price of the smaller producers.[46] As has been the case with the International Coffee Agreement, the larger producers may even agree to reduce their own quotas rather than those of the smaller states.[47] OPEC's decision to raise oil prices well above the extraction prices benefited the less efficient and smaller producers, such as Indonesia and Venezuela, which were formerly undersold in the oil market by Saudi Arabia, Kuwait, and Iran.

All these qualifications and exceptions warn against overstressing the connection between size and economic performance.

Many small countries [especially the developed ones] do not in fact have the characteristics that have often been ascribed to them, because the significance which country size may have is swamped by the influence of location, market access, historical ties, the level of the exchange rates, and many other factors. This also means that the group of small developed countries to which most of our attention is confined . . . does not generally have all the trade characteristics which the builders of models believed small countries to have.[48]

One notable feature of the scattered literature on the international trade of small countries is the preponderance of pessimistic arguments. It has been repeatedly suggested that small countries will be particularly unstable and dependent in various senses, that income adjustments will easily overflow into balance of payments problems, and that membership in regional trade groupings may have dire consequences for the industries of small countries. Admittedly some counter advantages of smallness have been put forward, notably that devaluation will readily correct a balance of payments disequilibrium of a small country . . . .

This "size pessimism" is difficult to understand in view of the outstanding stability of export receipts in many small countries and the relatively high rates of economic growth which many of them have had . . . . One explanation may be that most of the small developed countries do have large foreign trade sectors in relation to the aggregate sizes of their economies and may therefore be more aware of actual and possible disturbances in this sector, even though the historical experience of most of these countries in the postwar period gives no cause for their being more concerned over international trade difficulties than other countries.[49]

While economically developed small states have generally done better than abstract models would indicate, the situation of the LDC's is more difficult to evaluate. Lacking enough solid data to analyze the economic position in these countries, economists have focused their attention mainly on the developed small states. They also tend to overlook the political price paid by the LDC's for the stability of their foreign trade.[50]

The former British and, more particularly, the former French colonies in Africa have established stable relations with their one-time masters, and on occasion have even secured higher payments than in the free markets.[51] But stability of income from exports is often achieved at the expense of political concessions to and cooperation with the great powers, which continue their political presence in the African capitals.[52]

It must also be remembered that stability of income from exports can be misleading. Many LDC's would prefer to see an increase in income and an improvement in the terms of trade.

What are some of the precautionary measures the economically weak states can take to reduce their vulnerability to economic pressures and to minimize the risks involved in foreign trade? The following may be suggested:

1. They should diversify their domestic production and try to export a larger variety of products. By following such a strategy they can (a) become less dependent on the income from only a few export items; (b) become more self-sufficient;[53] (c) reduce their dependence on foreign trade in general.[54]
2. They should try to "distribute their foreign trade over many countries differing in political alignments"[55] and seek "many markets of about equal size."[56]
3. They should try to direct their trade to smaller (weaker) trading partners. It is ". . . an elementary principle of the power policy of a state to *direct its trade away from the large to the smaller trading states* . . . trade should be directed toward the poorer countries."[57]
4. They should try not to conduct their trade with only one state, especially not with a great power.

. . . it will be an elementary defensive principle of the smaller trading countries not to have too large a share of their trade with any single great trading country, so that the integration of their economies with those of the great countries (for which no reciprocal integration is forthcoming) may be kept at a minimum compatible with their economic well-being.[58]

It is not easy for economically weak states to follow these suggestions. They must usually be willing to sacrifice some of their political security and their future economic well-being to achieve a short-term, immediate improvement in their economic position. After the long economic crisis experienced by the Balkan and Danubian states in the 1930s, they were happy to accept the possibility of future political dependence on Germany in return for immediate economic relief. Conversely, Cuba under Castro was ready to sacrifice its economic independence in order to be free to determine its form of government. Facing an urgent problem with only a limited freedom of choice, weak states often choose to solve the immediate problem, leaving the new problems thereby created to be coped with somehow in the future.

The Application of Economic Pressure against Economically Weak States

Weak states have sometimes been the victims of economic pressures or sanctions imposed on them by the great powers. They have suffered severe economic setbacks and dislocation as a result, but as long as the great powers have not combined economic pressure with military action, the weak states have survived. The so-called "Pigs' War" between Austria and Serbia is a good example.[59]

In April 1906 the Austro-Hungarian government closed its frontiers to Serbian transit trade and imposed high tariffs on Serbian exports to the Hapsburg Empire. For Serbia, whose main products were agricultural, Austria was not only its major trading partner but the only outlet (through ports and railways) for its transit trade. For thirty years it "had traded almost exclusively with Austria-Hungary. For the five-year period preceding 1906 Austria-Hungary had supplied 53.35 per cent of Serbia's imports and absorbed 83.66 per cent of Serbia's exports."[60]

Prior to the tariff crisis of 1906 the Serbians had attempted to diversify their trade in order to lessen their dependence on Austria-Hungary by forming a Customs Union with Bulgaria and seeking new trade partners and alternative transit routes through Bulgaria and Salonika. But Austria interfered, putting economic pressure on Serbia in order to maintain its dependence. The Serbian government had also refused to buy heavy guns and ammunition from Austria (Skoda), and instead turned to France and Germany for military supplies; an inevitable decision, since Serbia's enemy would otherwise control spare parts and ammunition in wartime. A final reason for the tariff war was that "Magyar landlords found that Serbian products came into competition with their own."[61]

Both the Austrians and Serbians were convinced that Austrian markets were indispensable to Serbia's foreign trade, which would not be able to find new markets for its products. Thus Serbia could either bow to pressure and be reduced to the status of a mere puppet, or it could rebuff Austria and assert its independence. The latter alternative was obviously more costly in the short run, but would be economically and politically advantageous in the long run.

The tariff war which began in April 1906 lasted for nearly two years. Serbia succeeded in obtaining railway transit to Salonika (then under Turkish control) as well as a loading zone in its harbor, despite Austrian protests to Turkey. It also succeeded in finding new markets as a substitute for its lost trade with Austria. As Table 13 indicates, these "proved very satisfactory and accounted in no small part for Serbia's ability to endure the hardships caused by the tariff war with Austria-Hungary."[62] Among the states supporting Serbia was Austria's ally Germany, a fact which "caused not a little hard feeling between Vienna and Berlin which persisted for years."[63]

TABLE 13

SERBIAN EXPORTS IN 1906 AND 1907
(valued in dinars)

Country	1906	1907
Austria-Hungary	30,032,477	12,932,380
Germany	19,053,882	32,925,623
Italy	572,319	4,898,867
Russia	151,650	3,133,719
Belgium	6,259,929	13,010,853

Source: Wayne S. Vucinich, *Serbia between East and West* (Stanford: Stanford University Press, 1954), p. 206.

By the time the "Pigs' War" was over, Serbia had considerably improved its position *vis-à-vis* Austria and had consolidated its economic independence.

The customs war caused a complete change in the ratio of trade with individual foreign powers. Instead of controlling 90 per cent of Serbia's trade, Austria now enjoyed but 30 per cent, and trade with other states increased proportionately.

The customs war forced Serbia to improve her export products both in quality and quantity. The length of export routes necessitated, for example, a transformation in the articles of commerce; raw materials were replaced by semimanufactured goods; live cattle were replaced by fresh and salted meats and animal products of various sorts . . . . In this way Serbia avoided "gravitating exclusively towards the Austro-Hungarian markets, for the transformed products could choose longer ways towards distant markets."[64]

Another case is the economic war waged on Cuba by the United States, which in July 1960 cancelled sugar purchases from Cuba for the remainder of the year. In October there followed an embargo on all exports to Cuba except for medicine and some food products. Finally in 1962, the importation of any products of all or partial Cuban origin was banned.[65]

In 1958, 67 per cent of Cuban exports went to the United States, and 70 per cent of her imports originated there. Most of the equipment in the island's industries was from the United States. Under the Costigan Act of 1934, the United States bought the bulk of Cuban sugar exports at an artificial price substantially above world market prices. In 1958, the bonus resulting from this preferential treatment alone amounted to about $150 million.[66]

TABLE 14

DECLINE IN US-CUBAN TRADE AFTER CASTRO'S RISE TO POWER
(JANUARY 1, 1959)

Year	US Exports to Cuba	US Imports from Cuba
1958	$546,947,000	$527,831,000
1959	438,593,000	474,663,000
1960	223,726,000	357,306,000
1961	13,716,000	35,125,000
1962	13,398,000	6,808,000
1963	36,475,000	55,000

Source: Anna P. Schreiber, *World Politics,* 25 (1973), 395.

The objectives of the American embargo were:

> To reduce Castro's will and ability to export subversion and violence to other American states; to make plain to the people of Cuba that Castro's regime cannot serve their interests; to demonstrate to the peoples of the American Republics that communism has no future in the Western Hemisphere; and to increase the cost to the Soviets of maintaining a Communist outpost in the Western Hemisphere.[67]

Had the United States been able to prevent Cuba from trading with other countries, the Cuban economy might have totally collapsed, and the country might have been coerced into accepting US political demands. But Cuba succeeded, though not without enormous difficulties, in diverting its trade to the Eastern Bloc and also enlarging its market in many Western countries. In 1961 the Communist bloc was already taking 75 per cent of Cuban exports, while 86 per cent of its imports were coming from Communist states,[68] as can be seen from the following table:

TABLE 15

GEOGRAPHIC DISTRIBUTION OF CUBAN EXPORTS
(IN PER CENTAGE BY GROUPS OF COUNTRIES)

Group of Countries	1959	1960	1961	1962	1963	1964*
Socialist countries	2.2	24.2	74.7	82.0	67.4	59.0
Other countries	97.8	75.6	25.3	18.0	32.6	41.0

*Percentage based on the first six months of the year.
Source: K. S. Karol, *Guerillas in Power* (New York: Hill and Wang, 1970), p. 587.

Canada, Spain, Sweden, Japan, Yugoslavia, and other countries considerably expanded their dealings with Cuba despite heavy US pressure,[69] which included blacklisting ships unloading cargoes in Cuba and suspension of foreign aid to countries trading with Cuba.

By mid-1961, Cuba's industrial equipment started to break down. While some spare parts were "cannibalized" from other local factories, thus accelerating the industrial breakdown, and others could be obtained in the black market, the damage to the economy was considerable.[70] The United States embargo, combined with Cuban mismanagement, affected the economy most adversely between 1961 and 1964. Between 1961 and 1968 the total Cuban per capita production dropped by 29 per cent.[71] The standard of living declined and there were serious shortages of food and other consumer goods.[72].

At a very high cost to themselves, the Cubans succeeded in maintaining their political freedom and their chosen course of action. In the process, however, they seem to have traded masters, becoming as economically dependent upon the Soviet Union as they had been on the United States. In 1974 the Cubans conducted most of their foreign trade with the USSR and Soviet bloc countries, obtaining Russian instead of American spare parts for their industrial and military equipment.[73] The Russians, like the Americans before them, have pressured Cuba economically in order to achieve their political ends. In December 1967 and January 1968, after expressing displeasure with Cuba's stand on certain international issues, the Soviet Union froze the level of petroleum deliveries to the island and delayed signing the annual trade protocol.[74] In summer 1968 Cuba was the only state outside the Soviet bloc to give public support to the Russian invasion of Czechoslovakia; in 1974 they paid for Russian support by sending troops to Syria.[75] Cuba's dependency on Russian aid has gradually turned it into a Russian client state.

The United States caused severe economic deprivations in Cuba but did not achieve its goals. It has lost all its investments there, the balance of its Cuban trade, as well as some respect and good will in Latin America and the underdeveloped world. "As an exercise in economic warfare, United States policy hardly rates as a success."[76]

In its relations with other weak states, the USSR has also used the economic weapon quite frequently. It applied an economic embargo of its own (and on behalf of the Soviet bloc) against Yugoslavia in 1948 and again in 1957;[77] against Australia in 1954;[78] against Finland in 1959;[79] and against

Albania in 1961.[80] In none of these cases has it succeeded in effecting a favorable change in the policies of the weak country. After short periods, each of the weak states hit by Soviet economic reprisals successfully directed its trade to other countries, received credits from Russia's political competitors, and finally overcame the effects of Russian economic warfare.

Turning to Rhodesia, the economic sanctions imposed after its unilateral declaration of independence in 1966 caused some initial economic difficulties, but did not undermine Rhodesia's will to continue its existing policies.[81] Rhodesia controls 75 per cent of its own energy resources and continues to receive petroleum through South Africa. After facing some serious trade problems with intermediaries, Rhodesia, until recently, restored its trade to an almost normal level, while the sale of chromium ores (a strategic commodity) to the United States continued. Rhodesia's weaker neighbors, Malawi and Zambia, have had no choice but to continue economic relations.

The Arab League boycott on Israel has been a dismal failure so far. It has encouraged Israel to produce as many of its own products as possible and has led it to diversify domestic production, thus having an opposite effect from that which was intended.[82]

Economic warfare is supposed to be a weapon favoring the economically great powers:

> [economic] vulnerability should be seen more as a property of the small power than as a property of the poor nation. Thus, the general picture is that economic sanctions as a source of power tend to preserve existing power structures.[83]

In actual fact, as long as the imposition of economic sanctions is not accompanied by military action, weak states can usually withstand the pressure by contriving alternative policies.

This leads to conclusions similar to those reached in earlier chapters. Even if weak states are economically weak, they are not helpless. As in the case of political and military weakness, they compensate for *internal* weakness by adding the strength of foreign states. They can take advantage of the competition between great powers, who are ready to offer them economic support in the face of rivalry from another great power. Weak states can usually maneuver easily and change their trade partners quickly.

Another conclusion is that it usually pays to fight back. By resisting economic pressures a weak state can maintain its political integrity and exact a high price from the great power: not only an economic price but a loss of prestige resulting from the appearance of "bullying" a weak state[84] and failing to achieve political ends. The weak states need to prepare themselves for economic warfare as much as for military conflict. By adopting the four precautions suggested above, they should be able to withstand the economic pressure of the great powers. Moreover, the success that weak states have already achieved in resisting economic pressure may eventually deter the great powers from using that weapon against them.

While it is easy to find examples of successful resistance by weak states, there are many types of subtle economic pressures which they have decided not to resist. They have quietly accommodated their positions to the implicit or explicit wishes of the great powers, as has been the case between Cuba and the USSR since 1968.

> Tariff wars and interruptions of trade rarely occur, but the awareness of their possibility is sufficient to test the influence of the stronger country and to shape the policy of the weaker.[85]

Although the application of economic sanctions against weak states has not always been effective, it has nevertheless been one more weapon in the arsenal of the great powers, not available to the weak states. However, in the 1970s for the first time, economic pressure has been applied against the great powers by militarily weak and dependent states. The Arab oil-producing countries placed an oil embargo on the Western great powers and industrialized states in the aftermath of the October 1973 Arab-Israeli war. This action prompts the question: is this embargo the product of unique circumstances favoring oil-producing countries alone, or is it a sign of the growing economic power and leverage of the economically weak and less developed countries?

The changing norms in the conduct of international relations, the mutual neutralization of the super powers, and the reality and mythology of guerrilla warfare have all led to the so-called depreciation of military coercive power possessed by the great Western powers. These inhibitions on the use of force act as intervening variables explaining why militarily weak and vulnerable states (such as the Arab oil-producing countries) can blackmail the great powers economically without being punished. Similar action by weak states only a decade ago would have been highly improbable.

Yet if the economic pressure against the Western powers and industrialized world were to become too severe, it could lead to an economic disaster or even to the extinction of the industrial civilization. In other words, there is a threshold beyond which the great powers will not hesitate to make use of their military might.[86] (Otherwise the term "great power" would have no meaning.) Although this threshold is not clearly delineated, it is nevertheless real, so that the leaders of the weak and less developed states employing the economic weapon must plan their steps with caution.

The economic wealth of the Arab oil-producing countries has created a situation which is in many ways unprecedented. Controlling both vital energy resources crucial for the industrial world and a huge surplus of capital, these countries have a strength, at least on the political-economic level, that has never before been held by militarily weak states. For the first time, they can exert an influence far beyond their own territory and region.

Long before the October 1973 Arab-Israeli War, the Arab oil-producing countries had started to translate their economic wealth into political influence, first within the Arab world itself. Immediately after the Six Days War, at the meeting of Arab governments in Khartoum in August 1967, the oil-producing countries (especially Kuwait, Libya, and Saudi Arabia) decided to give financial support to the so-called confrontation countries (Egypt, Syria, and Jordan), to help them purchase weapons, support their war economies, and compensate for their war losses.[87] But those who have the power to grant also have the power to withhold. Indeed, after the campaign of the Jordanian government against the Palestinian guerrillas in its territory in September 1970, the Arab oil-producing countries abruptly cut back their financial aid to Jordan.

After the October 1973 war the governments of the Arab oil-producing countries pledged financial aid of over $2 billion to the confrontation countries, of which $1,150 million was promised to Syria and $900 million to Egypt.[88] During and after the war, the oil-producing countries also helped the combatants by financing part of the weapon purchases from Russia, and they themselves bought large quantities of weapons which were made available to the confrontation countries. The large sums of money offered by the oil-producing countries give them greater influence on the receiving governments and can be used to pressure them. For example, Libya (under Qaddafi) stopped financial aid to Egypt in order to demonstrate its displeasure with the Egyptian government's decision to sign the disengagement agreement with Israel.[89]

During the summer of 1971, when the government of Malta was bargaining with Britain for higher payments for the use of bases and naval facilities, the Libyan government urged Malta to expel the British from the island, promising financial and military support. On 17 August 1971 Libya actually lent the Maltese government $12 million,[90] which undoubtedly helped it to obtain a better bargain from the British government and NATO.[91]

Before the October 1973 war, Arab pressure on African states to break off diplomatic relations with Israel finally bore fruit, partly because of promises of future financial aid and economic support. Soon after breaking with Israel, some African countries did receive soft loans from Arab countries, notably from Libya and Saudi Arabia.[92]

During and after the October War, Arab oil-producing countries decided to cut oil production to all industrialized nations by 5 per cent a month, whether or not a given country had directly supported Israel; and they tried to impose a total embargo on oil exports to states supporting Israel. Not all countries are equally sensitive to the oil weapon. The United States, then importing between 5 and 10 per cent of its oil from the Arabs, was much less vulnerable than others. Likewise in Sweden and Norway 70 per cent or more of the energy consumed is generated domestically by hydroelectric power.[93] But Japan and the countries of the European Common Market depend more heavily on oil as their major source of energy, and so were much more open to Arab blackmail. In Japan, for example, 70 per cent of all energy produced originates from oil, of which 85 per cent is imported from Arab states.[94] Under this pressure, the EEC countries and Japan changed positions and made statements favorable to the Arab cause.[95]

Robert Dahl defines influence as "a relation among actors in which one actor induces other actors to act in some way they would not otherwise act,"[96] power as "a special case of influence involving *severe losses* for noncompliance,"[97] and coercion as "a form of power that exists whenever A compels B to comply by confronting him *only* with alternatives involving severe deprivation."[98] According to these definitions the Arab governments successfully *coerced* the EEC countries and Japan by means of the October 1973 oil embargo. During this crisis economic power was translated into political power. For the first time the Arabs managed to coordinate their actions, creating a united front based on both economic and political interests.[99]

The EEC countries, on the other hand, failed to cooperate with one another. Each one confronted the Arab governments separately, a process instigated and encouraged by Arab bargaining tactics. In concluding separate bilateral treaties with the EEC countries, the Arabs followed the favorite tactic of the Germans in the Balkans prior to the Second World War.[100] The Europeans suddenly found themselves more dependent on Arab oil than the Arabs were on European goods and industrial products. The terms of trade were reversed, as were political influence and strength. The weak states do not appear to be so weak any more. Over the short range, or perhaps the medium range, the international hierarchy of power seems to have been transformed.

It is very difficult at this stage to evaluate the real power relations involved, to ascertain whether or not the Arab (and other oil-producing) countries can maintain their strength, or to know if the implications of the new power relations are relevant for other weak and less developed states.

Continuation of new power relations depends on many variables. The development of new oil fields in the United States, Europe (the North Sea and the Aegean) and other areas may gradually make the industrialized world less dependent on Arab oil, particularly if reserves prove to be available in larger quantities than expected.[101] The development of new sources of energy would weaken the bargaining power of all the oil-producing states. Also, much of the oil-producing countries' leverage is a function of their ability to cooperate among themselves. Cooperation is easy in a sellers' market. But if over the next decade new and rich oil fields are discovered, or if the oil-producing countries find it more difficult to cooperate for political reasons while consumer countries improve their own cooperation, then the oil-producing states, including the Arabs, will lose a considerable amount of their present leverage.[102]

In the final analysis the oil-producing countries are also dependent on the industrialized world. While they can accumulate a large surplus of capital and can manipulate and damage the currency of any country they choose, they are also dependent on the economic and financial situation within the countries whose economies they can destroy. The two types of economies are interlocked. Because the oil-producing countries cannot invest or spend even a small fraction of their newly acquired capital at home, they have to invest in the industrialized world in order to maintain the value of their assets and maximize their income. Once they do so, their property may be nationalized and their liquid assets frozen; and thus they would become vulnerable to counter pressures and would be less free to employ the oil weapon.[103] On the other hand, it is possible that they might acquire greater influence in Western Europe and the United States by controlling large economic empires and having an impact on employment. If that seemed likely, though, the industrialized countries might pass special legislation in order to retain full control of their economies.

If the oil-producers should invest in the industrialization of their *own* countries, they would become dependent on the technology, machinery, and spare parts of the Western industrialized countries supplying those capital goods.[104]

A similar situation exists in the military sphere. Although the Arab countries and other large oil-producing states spend more money on military hardware than Great Britain, France, or Germany, they do not manufacture weapons themselves and cannot be expected to do so in the foreseeable future.[105] The more they buy Western weapons systems, the more dependent they become on the supply of spare parts, military instruction, and military help from these countries. The greater the sophistication of the weapons they purchase, the greater their dependence. If they should decide to blackmail the Western countries in the future, they could expect to be pressured by the withholding of instruction, spare parts, and military aid. It would therefore be rational for the oil-producing countries to diversify their weapons acquisition by obtaining weapons from countries they do not intend to blackmail or that would support them in the future. It might therefore make more sense for Saudi Arabia and Iran to buy weapons from the Eastern bloc.

Thus, although the oil-producing states are becoming stronger economically and have improved their political bargaining position, they are not and cannot be in full control of their own security and defense, which is a major criterion for classifying a state as a great power. Their military capacity, and hence their security, are derivative, not original. They depend on external military help and the unwillingness of the great powers to use force against them.

For militarily weak but economically rich states, such as Kuwait or even Saudi Arabia or Libya, to say nothing of Abu Dhabi and Qatar, there is a paradoxical danger in becoming richer. Such states may attract the attention of poorer but militarily stronger neighbors and may find themselves in a weaker position than before. As a desert country, Kuwait is unattractive. As a rich but militarily weak country, a power vacuum, it may invite occupation. It required British intervention to save it from occupation by Iraq in June 1961.[106] Not only Iraq but also Iran and Saudi Arabia might like to take over Kuwait. It might even become the target of terrorist blackmail. The great discrepancy between its economic richness and its military weakness makes it very vulnerable.

The position of the Arab oil-producing countries (or of other economically strong but militarily weak states) is in accordance with the ideal type of the weak state. Although they score high in one or two dimensions of strength, they remain weak in others and therefore cannot be considered great powers.

The success of the oil-producing countries in improving their terms of trade and of the Arab governments by using oil as an economic weapon to achieve their political ends is bound to encourage other weak countries that produce primary commodities to strive for the same success *vis-à-vis* the industrialized states. Even without coordinated effort on their part, such a process has already begun with the growing demand for all types of raw materials. The terms of trade in the last few years have gradually "shifted in favour of the primary-producing nations . . . . The third world has actually notched up a balance of trade surplus, and its reserves have almost doubled in the past two years."[107] Recently, though, it has become evident that much if not all of the additional revenue obtained from the improvement of the terms of trade in the primary commodities markets will disappear because of the higher prices for oil.[108]

One thing, however, is clear: no other commodity is in such great demand as oil. Although the industrial world does depend on imported raw materials,[109] many of these have effective substitutes and the demand for them is more flexible. Co-operation among the exporters of raw materials would therefore be more difficult. Not only would they have to coordinate their efforts to create an oligopoly and assign quotas in one market—for copper, bauxite, tin, and so on—but they would also have to coordinate their efforts between different markets so that when the quotas for bauxite were reduced or even completely cut, the countries producing tin would not take advantage of the situation. To reach effective agreements under such conditions would be extremely difficult both politically and economically. Also, unlike the oil-producing countries, the countries producing other primary commodities have much smaller financial reserves and therefore could not afford to stop or considerably reduce their exports.[110] For the same reason, they would not be able to manipulate other currencies and economies, and thereby gain political strength.

Although the countries that produce primary commodities can expect to improve their economic position (their terms of trade) and can move toward coordinating their marketing efforts, they will find the way much more difficult than the oil-producing countries have.[111] They will not experience the "economic miracle" that some of the Arab and other oil-producing countries have managed to bring about.[112]

The economic position of weak states, like their political position, is not simply one of weakness. Historical evidence tends to confirm that despite their smaller economic size, and hence frequent economic weakness, they have succeeded in stabilizing their incomes and, with external help, have been able to resist economic pressures from much stronger states.

In the past the terms of trade tended to work against the LDC's, and they seem to have received less than a fair share for their resources. For economic, political, and moral reasons, this situation is changing. Some of the weak states have become economically strong. Economic strength, however, is not a panacea for lack of strength on the military and industrial levels. Though some weak states have acquired enormous economic wealth, they still score low on other criteria, and while they have climbed upward in the international hierarchy, they cannot yet be considered great or even middle powers.

NOTES

1. There are some exceptions, such as Gustav Lagos, *International Stratification and Underdeveloped Countries;* Singer, *Weak States in a World of Powers;* and R. P. Barston (ed.), *The Other Powers: Studies in the Foreign Policies of Small States* (New York: Barnes and Noble, 1974). All three devote considerable attention to economic relations between the great powers and the weak states, but none is completely satisfactory. Singer, who devotes a long chapter (6) to "economic ties" between the great powers and the weak states, makes no reference at all to the basic literature on the subject of economics. This makes a large part of his work superfluous and sometimes inaccurate. He also seems to write in a vacuum, for he does not refer to earlier books on

weak state-great power relations, such as Robinson (ed.), *Economic Consequences of the Size of Nations;* Peter Lloyd, *International Trade Problems of Small Nations;* Michael Michaely, *Concentration in International Trade* (Amsterdam: North Holland Publishing Co., 1962); Albert O. Hirschman, *National Power and the Structure of Foreign Trade.*

2. See, for example, Theodore H. Moran, "New Deal or Raw Deal in Raw Materials," *Foreign Policy,* No. 5 (Winter 1971–1972), pp. 119–134; C. Fred Bergsten, "The Threat from the Third World," *Foreign Policy,* No. 11 (Summer 1973), pp. 103–124; Zuhayr Mikdashi, "Collusion Could Work," *Foreign Policy,* No. 14 (Spring 1974), pp. 57–68; Stephen D. Krasner, "Oil is the Exception," *ibid.,* pp. 68–84; C. Fred Bergsten, "The Threat Is Real," *ibid.,* pp. 84–90.

3. As Albert O. Hirschman has said, the absence of war or its elimination would not lead to the elimination of economic conflict and dependence relations among states. See *National Power and the Structure of Foreign Trade,* p. 15.

4. The capability to manipulate, induce or seduce, bribe, and aid other countries with positive rewards had previously been confined to the great powers, but now the situation has changed. See Singer, *Weak States in a World of Powers,* p. 60. See also David A. Baldwin, "The Power of Positive Sanctions," *World Politics,* 24 (1971), 19–38.

5. C. N. Vakil and P. R. Brahmananda, in Robinson (ed.), *Economic Consequences of the Size of Nations,* p. 134.

6. *Ibid.,* p. 135. See also Kuznets, *ibid.;* pp. 14, 16, 31, and Edwards, *ibid.,* p. 128.

7. See Benjamin J. Cohen, *The Question of Imperialism* (New York: Basic Books, 1973), p. 155.

8. Nadim G. Khalaf, *Economic Implications of the Size of Nations, with special reference to Lebanon* (Leiden: E. J. Brill, 1971), p. 10.

9. *Stabilization of Prices of Primary Products, Part II: Report of the Executive Directors of the International Bank for Reconstruction and Development IBRD,* Washington, D.C., 1969, p. 11, as quoted in Alton D. Law, "Stabilization of Prices of Primary Products: A Review Article," in *Inter American Economic Affairs,* 24 (Winter 1970), 28–29.

10. See Rothschild in Robinson (ed.), *Economic Consequences of the Size of Nations,* pp. 176–177.

11. Alfred Marshall, quoted in Hirschman, *National Power and the Structure of Foreign Trade,* p. 24.

12. Tarshis in Robinson (ed.), *Economic Consequences of the Size of Nations,* p. 197; also Marcy, *ibid.,* pp. 267, 268. See also Lloyd, *International Trade Problems of Small Nations,* p. 55.

13. Khalaf, p. 9, 10.

14. Marcy in Robinson (ed.), *Economic Consequences of the Size of Nations,* p. 268.

15. Singer, *Weak States in a World of Powers,* p. 238. According to Singer, "Only the U.S. and the U.S.S.R. have less than 10 per cent of their

G.D.P. accounted for by foreign trade and hence are relatively invulnerable to outside foreign trade decisions" (p. 238). See also Johan Galtung, "On the Effects of International Economic Sanctions," *World Politics,* 19 (April 1967), 386–387.

16. Singer, *Weak States in a World of Powers,* p. 328. Economic dependence is related to

    two separate and quite distinct aspects. First, it implies a high measure of sensitivity to external forces: dependent economies are unable to avoid being influenced by events elsewhere. Second, it involves a high measure of irreversibility of impact: dependent economies are unable to override the influence of events elsewhere. Both aspects are essential to the notion of dependence. Together they mean that foreign economies have an implicit veto power over the capability of domestic decision-makers (private or official) to direct the development of the local economy. What happens at home depends on what happens abroad. (Cohen, *The Question of Imperialism,* p. 190.)

    Marshall also suggests "that when as much as 10 per cent of a country's G.D.P. depends on aid from a specific foreign Power, the receiving country is highly dependent economically on that donor." (p. 256).

17. See, for example, Osvaldo Sunkel, "Big Business and 'Dependencia'," *Foreign Affairs,* 50 (April 1972), 517–531; and John Gerassi, *The Great Fear in Latin America,* rev. ed. (New York: Collier Books, 1973), esp. parts I, V, and VI. See also James D. Cockcraft, Andre Gunder Frank, and Dale L. Johnson, *Dependence and Underdevelopment* (Garden City, N.Y.: Anchor Books, 1972).

18. See Basch, *The Danube Basin and the German Economic Sphere,* esp. chaps. 10, 11, 15, 16. See also Hirschman, *National Power and the Structure of Foreign Trade,* pp. 34–40. Hirschman (p. 36) has summarized Germany's policy as follows:

    Germany's attempt to concentrate on exports of finished products, on the one hand, and on exports to agricultural countries, on the other, had obviously the result of giving her exports a quasi-monopolistic position so far as the productive system of her trading partners was concerned. . . . In addition, to maintain this position, it was one of the great principles of German foreign economic policy to prevent the industrialization of her agricultural trading partners. Particular insistence on this point has been noted in all the commercial negotiations of Germany with her southeastern neighbors and even, to some degree and some success, with Italy.

19. Basch, *Danube Basin and the German Economic Sphere,* p. 225. As Palmer and Macartney put it (*Independent Eastern Europe,* p. 315):

    It was precisely because the smaller countries did derive important economic benefits from Germany's system that they accepted it gladly, and even competed for admission to it, in the full knowledge of its political implications.

20. Alan Palmer, *The Lands Between,* pp. 214–215. For Hungary, see also C. A. Macartney, *October Fifteenth,* pp. 136–154; and Mario D. Fenyo, *Hitler, Horthy and Hungary* (New Haven: Yale University

Press, 1972), chap. 5, pp. 79–83. For Yugoslavia, see J. B. Hoptner, *Yugoslavia in Crisis 1934–1941*, pp. 94–108; also Macartney and Palmer, *Independent Eastern Europe*, chap. 8, pp. 301–342.
21. Hirschman, *National Power and the Structure of Foreign Trade*, pp. 30–31.
22. Singer, *Weak States in a World of Powers*, p. 216.
23. *Ibid.*, p. 222.
24. Lloyd, *International Trade Problems of Small Nations*, p. 16. See also Vakil in Robinson (ed.), *Economic Consequences of the Size of Nations*, pp. 136–137.
25. Edwards in *ibid.*, p. 125.
26. *Ibid.*, p. 129.
27. Lloyd, *International Trade Problems of Small Nations*, p. 40.
28. For Switzerland's diversified economy, see W. A. Johr and F. Kneschomek in Robinson (ed.), *Economic Consequences of the Size of Nations*, pp. 54–77.
29. It has frequently been claimed that the OPEC countries are riding on a temporary wave of shortage but that when more oil becomes available in the early 1980s in Alaska, the North Sea, and elsewhere, they will lose much of their monopoly power. M. A. Adelman, "Is the Oil Shortage Real?" *Foreign Policy*, No. 9 (Winter 1972–73), pp. 69–107. See also M. A. Adelman, *The World Petroleum Market* (Baltimore: Johns Hopkins Press, 1972); "Almost Anything for Oil," *The Economist*, November 10, 1973, pp. 11–13.
30. C. Fred Bergsten, "The Threat from the Third World," *Foreign Policy*, No. 11 (Summer 1973), pp. 107–108. See also Theodore H. Moran, "New Deal or Raw Deal in Raw Materials," *Foreign Policy*, No. 5 (Winter 1971–72), pp. 123–127; Zuhayr Mikdashi, "Collusion Could Work," *Foreign Policy*, No. 14 (Spring 1974), pp. 56–68; C. Fred Bergsten, "The Threat Is Real," *Foreign Policy*, No. 14 (Spring 1974), pp. 84–90; Stephen D. Krasner, "Manipulating International Commodity Markets," *Public Policy;* "Bye, Bye Bauxite," *The Economist*, March 2, 1974, p. 94.
31. See Stephen D. Krasner, "Oil is the Exception," *Foreign Policy*, No. 14 (Spring 1974), pp. 68–84.
32. *Ibid., passim.*
33. Alasdair I. Macbean, *Export Instability and Economic Development* (Cambridge, Mass.: Harvard University Press, 1966), p. 339.
34. *Ibid.*, p. 340. See also Lloyd, *International Trade Problems of Small Nations*, pp. 48–49, 125. See also Nadim G. Khalaf, *Economic Implications of the Size of Nations* (Leiden: E. J. Brill, 1971), pp. 45–47; 55–57; 228–229.

> ... size is not a significant source of instability ... dependence on trade, commodity export concentration, and geographic export concentration are not sources of extra instability in income, exports, and imports. Even if small countries turn out to have relatively higher degree of dependence on trade and higher export concentration, small countries are not as a result of these features likely to

experience extra instability in their incomes, exports or imports. These results are contrary to plausible a priori reasoning, and they suggest that small countries need not be very apologetic about their dependence on trade and their export concentration.
Khalaf, p. 229.
35. Michael Michaely, quoted in Lloyd, *International Trade Problems of Small Nations*, p. 41.
36. *Ibid.*, p. 42.
37. Jewkes in Robinson (ed.), *Economic Consequences of the Size of Nations*, pp. 95–116.
38. Lloyd, *International Trade Problems of Small States*, p. 103. E. A. G. Robinson is quoted.
39. Robinson, *Economic Consequences of the Size of Nations*, pp. 108–113; also Lloyd, *International Trade Problems of Small States*, p. 17.
40. Nathaniel H. Leff, "Bengal, Biafra and the Bias of Bigness," *Foreign Policy*, No. 3 (Summer 1971), p. 130.
41. *Ibid.*, pp. 133–135. See also Rothschild in Robinson (ed.), *Economic Consequences of the Size of Nations*, pp. 169–172.
42. Leff. "Bengal, Biafra and the Bias of Bigness," p. 136.
43. *Ibid.*
44. *Ibid.*, p. 137.
45. Krasner, "Manipulating International Commodity Markets," p. 504, n. 12.
46. *Ibid.*, p. 505.
47. *Ibid.*, p. 504.
48. Lloyd, *International Trade Problems of Small Nations*, p. 35. See also Rothschild in Robinson (ed.), *Economic Consequences of the Size of Nations*, p. 177.
49. Lloyd, *International Trade Problems of Small Nations*, p. 126.
50. See a comment on this problem in Alton D. Law, "Coffee: Structure, Control and Development: A Review Article," *Inter-American Economic Affairs*, 27 (Summer 1973), 70.
51. Cohen, *Question of Imperialism*, pp. 218–219.
52. See Henry L. Bretton, "Patron-Client Relations: Middle Africa and the Powers," and also Robin Jenkins, *Exploitation* (London: MacGibbon and Kee, 1970), pp. 106–139.
53. For example, see Knorr, *Power and Wealth*, p. 155.
54. F. J. Wiles, *Communist International Economics* (Oxford: Basil Blackwell, 1968), p. 20; and Knorr, *Power and Wealth*, p. 155.
55. Knorr, *ibid.*
56. Wiles, *Communist International Economics*, p. 20; see also Cohen, *Question of Imperialism*, p. 222.
57. Hirschman, *National Power and the Structure of Foreign Trade*, p. 31.
58. *Ibid.*
59. On this conflict, see Sidney B. Fay, *The Origins of the World War*, 2nd rev. ed., Vol. I (New York: The Free Press, 1966), pp. 359–360; and Wayne S. Vucinich, *Serbia Between East and West* (Stanford: Stanford University Press, 1954), pp. 180–209.

60. *Ibid.*, p. 205.
61. Fay, *Origins of the World War*, I, p. 359.
62. Vucinich, *Serbia Between East and West*, pp. 201–202.
63. Fay, *Origins of the World War*, p. 360.
64. Vucinich, *Serbia Between East and West*, p. 208.
65. Anna P. Schreiber, "Economic Coercion as an Instrument of Foreign Policy: U.S. Economic Measures against Cuba and the Dominican Republic," *World Politics*, 25 (April 1973), 387; and Knorr, *Power and Wealth*, pp. 146–147.
66. See Knorr, *Power and Wealth*, p. 146.
67. Dean Rusk, quoted in *ibid.*, p. 148.
68. Schreiber, "Economic Coercion as an Instrument of Foreign Policy," p. 395.
69. *Ibid.*, pp. 398–399.
70. *Ibid.*, p. 396.
71. *Ibid.*, p. 401.
72. *Ibid.*, p. 397. See also Jorge I. Dominguez, "Taming the Cuban Shrew," *Foreign Policy*, No. 10 (Spring 1973), pp. 111–115.
73. Dominguez, "Taming the Cuban Shrew," pp. 102–104.
74. *Ibid.*, p. 95.
75. See *New York Times*, April 1, 1974, p. 1.
76. Knorr, *Power and Wealth*, p. 148.
77. Wiles, *Communist International Economics*, pp. 499–500.
78. *Ibid.*, pp. 501–502.
79. *Ibid.*, pp. 503–506.
80. *Ibid.*, pp. 499–500. See also Griffith, *Albania and the Soviet Rift*, pp. 171–173.
81. See Johan Galtung, "On the Effects of International Economic Sanctions," pp. 378–416; *New York Times*, January 6, 1974; and Ralph Zacklin, "Challenge of Rhodesia," *International Conciliation*, No. 575 (November 1969).
82. For another appraisal, see Robert W. Macdonald, *The League of Arab States* (Princeton: Princeton University Press, 1965), pp. 118–123.
83. Galtung, "On the Effects of International Sanctions," p. 386.
84. Knorr, *Power and Wealth*, pp. 151–152.
85. Hirschman, *National Power and the Structure of Foreign Trade*, p. 16.
86. See the *Economist*, Dec. 1, 1973, pp. 76–77 ("The Arabs Reach for More"); and also the *Economist*, Jan 13, 1974, p. 80. Defense Secretary Schlesinger has hinted that contingent plans for American military intervention against Arab oil-producing countries were being prepared, though their use would be highly unlikely.
87. See, for example, E. Kanovsky, "The Economic Aftermath of the Six Days War: UAR, Jordan, Syria," part II, *The Middle East Journal*, 22, (Summer 1968), 282.
88. *M.I.S. (Middle East Intelligence Report)*, vol. 1, no. 15 (Nov. 1, 1973), p. 117. (This is a fortnightly published in Tel Aviv, Israel.)
89. See the *Boston Globe*, Apr. 15, 1974, p. 8. Libya cut back its annual

financial support to Egypt of L20 million sterling, as well as oil shipments to Egypt.
90. *New York Times,* Sept. 2, 1971, p. 7.
91. See *New York Times,* June 20, 1971, p. 6; June 28, 1971, p. 6; June 29, 1971, p. 6; June 30, 1971, p. 4; July 4 1971, p. 4 (section IV); Aug. 2, 1971, p. 18; Jan. 5, 1972, p. 2. For a detailed description of the crisis see *Keesing's Contemporary Archives,* XVIII (London: Keesing's Publications, 1971–72), 25151–25154.
92. See the *Economist,* Jan. 5, 1974, p. 68. African and other less developed states may have had second thoughts since then, for they lost a good bargaining card and found themselves paying higher prices for Arab oil. See the *Economist,* "Kicking the Poor," Dec. 8, 1973, p. 80. Less developed non-oil-producing countries may find that they have a common grievance with the industrialized world.
93. For Sweden, see the *Economist,* Jan. 12. 1974, p. 99. For Norway, see the *Economist,* Dec. 29. 1973. p. 56.
94. *Economist,* Nov. 10, 1973, p. 45.
95. For the text of the European Community foreign minister's statement of 6 November 1973, see *Survival,* 16 (January-February 1974), 39. A similar Japanese statement was made 22 November 1973, by the secretary of the Japanese government. For the text, see *Keesing's Contemporary Archives,* 1974, p. 26323.
96. Robert A. Dahl, *Modern Political Analysis,* 2nd ed. (Englewood Cliffs, N.J.: Prentice Hall, 1970), p. 17.
97. *Ibid.,* p. 32.
98. *Ibid.,* p. 33.
99. See Zuhayr Mikdashi, "Cooperation Among Oil Exporting Countries with Special Reference to Arab Countries: A Political Economy Analysis," in *International Organization,* 28 (Winter 1974), 1–30; also Krasner, "Oil Is the Exception," pp. 72–81.
100. See the *Economist,* Jan. 12, 1974, p. 31, and Feb. 16, 1974, p. 73.
101. This is Adelman's position. See M. A. Adelman, "Is the Oil Shortage Real?" *passim,* and *idem., Economist,* Nov. 10, 1973, p. 11.
102. It would be difficult to predict the future relations between the industrialized world and the Arab oil-producing countries. Two scenarios can be suggested. One (A) shows the conditions under which the industrialized countries would be able to improve their bargaining position; the other (B) indicates the conditions which would favor the Arab (and other) oil-producing countries:

Scenario A	*Scenario B*
1. A greater measure of cooperation is reached between the industrial countries; they establish a united front to oppose economic blackmail, perhaps in cooperation with the non-oil-producing LDC's. At the	1. Coordinated economic pressure by the Arabs continues; the industrialized states cannot improve their coordination and continue to conclude bilateral treaties with Arab oil-producing countries.

same time, Arab cooperation is weakened by inter-Arab conflicts.	
2. Western countries become less reluctant to threaten with the use of force or even to apply it. Probably they will also threaten to use economic retaliation.	2. Industrialized states are "psychologically paralyzed"; their inhibitions against the application of force or counter economic pressures increase.
3. New oil fields and oil reserves outside the Arab world are discovered, and/or new alternative sources of energy are developed. They successfully match the growth in the consumption of energy.	3. No adequate new oil fields and reserves are discovered, and/or no new energy sources are successfully developed.

Other scenarios could be suggested that would fall somewhere between these extremes.

103. Robert Mabro and Elizabeth Monroe, "Arab Wealth from Oil: Problems of Its Investment," *International Affairs*, 50 (January 1974), 15–27.
104. *Economist* (comment on Iran's investments in industry). Dec. 29, 1973, p. 22.
105. For example, Iran has super-modern military equipment, part of which is not yet available to the armed forces of the producing countries. *International Defense Review*, 6 (December 1973), 710–729.
106. For Britain's intervention, see James Cable, *Gunboat Diplomacy*, pp. 47–49.
107. The *Economist*, Dec. 8, 1973, p. 80.
108. *Ibid*.
109. The dependence of the United States on certain strategic raw materials is often mentioned. The following raw materials are almost fully imported by the United States: asbestos, 86%; bauxite, 87%; beryl, 89%; chromite, 100%; cobalt, 89%; columbium-tantalum, 100%; manganese ore, 99%; mica sheet, 94%; nickel, 91%; rubber, 100%; tin, 99%. See Hanson W. Baldwin, *Strategy for Tomorrow* (New York: Harper and Row, 1970), app. 2, pp. 342–343. See also Harry Magdoff, *The Age of Imperialism* (New York: Modern Reader, 1969), p. 52.
110. Krasner, "Oil Is the Exception," *Foreign Policy*, p. 80.
111. For a debate on the possibilities of such collusion, see "One Too Many OPEC's?" *Foreign Policy*, No. 14 (Spring 1974), pp. 56–90.
112. The GNP per capita of Qatar would reach the level of $17,400 in 1974, and that of Abu Dhabi would reach $45,000. *New York Times*, March 20, 1974, p. 59 ("Arab Oil Strategy").

Conclusions

Weak states cannot easily be defined or classified. Power/weakness is a continuum, and various types of power must be evaluated (e.g., military, economic). A state may be stronger in some respects than in others. Thus a complex set of criteria is necessary to distinguish the weak states from the great powers, for the differences between them are relative rather than absolute. Above all it must be remembered that the absolute strength of states has not been of primary interest in this work, but rather their strength in relation to their specific interests and needs. The weak and powerful states have many common characteristics and problems. Any attempt to separate out the weak states as a totally different "breed" is artificial. No state is all powerful and no state is completely weak.

The existing literature on weak states in international politics often portrays them as passive pawns owing their continuing existence to the benevolence of the great powers. This has never been the case. A realistic analysis indicates that while the weak states are frequently more vulnerable than the great powers, they are not helpless. Although they cannot defend themselves by their own strength against aggression on the part of a great power, they can and do maneuver within the international system to obtain help from other states.

Unlike the great powers, much of the strength of weak states is *derivative* rather than intrinsic. The diplomatic art of the weak states is to obtain, commit, and manipulate, as far as possible, the power of other, more powerful states in their own interests. Weak states can sometimes manipulate and lead a great power, almost against its own will. This has led some observers to exaggerate their real power and impact on the international system.

The most important condition for the security of the weak states, therefore, is their ability to appeal to other states for help and support. This they can do only if they are free to maneuver in the international system, to choose their allies, to take advantage of the conflicts and tensions between the powers. On the other hand, the conditions most dangerous to security and independence of the weak states are isolation from the international system, or inclusion within the sphere of influence of one of the great powers, where they are closely watched and jealously prevented from developing relations with other powers. From the viewpoint of the weak states, it is not so much the *structure* of the international system that is important, but a certain condition of tension and conflict between the powers and an absence of rigidly defined and mutually respected spheres of influence.

While the weak states usually cannot defend themselves for long against the onslaught of a great power, this does not mean that they can afford to neglect the development of their own strength. The development of their own military power enables them, under certain conditions, to improve their bargaining position, or to deter an attack by a great power which fears it might be weakened *vis-à-vis* another great power (finite deterrence). By developing its military force, a weak state can hold its own against a great power until external help arrives, and it can defend itself effectively against other weak states. The readiness of weak states to defend themselves and fight back (or at least to convey that impression) has, on the whole, worked in their best interests.

Often their very weakness can actually be turned into an asset. In alliance treaties, weak partners frequently enjoy the benefits of a collective (public) good. They contribute proportionately less than the more powerful members but are defended by the alliance as much as any other signatory. Under other circumstances their very weakness and vulnerability can help them to obtain additional aid from a great power which has developed an interest in or staked its prestige on their continued existence.

The development of nuclear weapons, the balance of terror, and the gradual acceptance by the international community of norms that limit and inhibit the use of brute force by the great powers among themselves as well as against the weak states have further contributed to the safety and improved standing of weak states in the international system. Weak states that have been included within a "recognized" sphere of influence of one of the great powers, however, have received much less benefit from these developments.

Nevertheless, normative constraints on the use of force have had much less effect on the weak states, especially the less developed ones, than on the great powers. In the future there might be fewer wars between the great powers and more conflicts between countries such as Iran and Iraq, India and Pakistan, Israel and the Arab states, and perhaps Turkey and Greece.

Similarly, empirical evidence indicates that most weak states are economically more viable and less vulnerable than commonsense economic theories had prophesied. The great powers, on the other hand, have not always been able to translate their economic strength into political gains. When they have tried to use economic pressure to coerce weak states to accept their political demands, they have frequently failed, again due to the external help obtained by the weak states from other weak states or great powers.

In the future many of the weak states will be able to improve their economic position *vis-à-vis* the great powers, due to the increasing demand for primary commodities and the growing recognition on the part of industrial countries that the position of the less developed countries needs to be upgraded.

Some weak states, notably the oil-producing countries, have already been able to gain enormous economic power and to translate it into political gains. It is not clear whether they will continue to enjoy such an impact on a long-term basis, but at least they can exercise considerable short-term political influence on international politics. Yet in spite of their great economic power, and resultant political influence, in the final analysis they are militarily dependent and vulnerable. Thus they cannot be considered as powers in the traditional sense.

In conclusion, although the weak states may not be the principal *dramatis personae* in the world power play, neither are they merely small-part actors.

APPENDIX A

A Note on the Domestic Sources of the Foreign Policy of Weak States

There is no doubt that to a large extent domestic politics determines the foreign policy of any state, weak or powerful. But it seems to me that domestic politics in the weak states, especially during times of international crisis and conflict, have less impact on their foreign policies than would be the case with the great democratic powers. One of the characteristics of the weak states is that they play a much smaller part than the great powers in shaping the nature of the international system. Usually the international system for them is a *datum*. Because of their weakness there are fewer options for action open to them, especially in times of conflict. The United States could decide whether or not it wanted to enter the Second World War, but Norway, Belgium, and Poland had no choice. Because of these limits, the weak states must reach a greater consensus domestically with regard to the policy they should pursue.

Even if opinions differ with regard to the foreign policy to be followed, there is still little room for choice. For example, when Serbia entertained revisionistic aspirations towards the Hapsburg Empire, its only choice was to side with Russia. The Israeli opposition very often criticizes the government for yielding too easily to American pressures, but there is little doubt that if the opposition were called on to form a government, it would have to succumb, willy-nilly, to the same pressures. Whatever the Nepalese feel toward India, the Nepalese government has to follow a cautious policy toward it. As long as Egypt was in conflict with Israel, it sought either Russian or American help, whatever public opinion towards those countries may be. Any Mexican or Canadian government would have to adopt fairly similar positions toward the United States. No Finnish government would dare to change its policy toward the USSR *whatever* the structure of the government and the state of public sentiment. This situation shows that the idea of "*der Primat der Aussenpolitik*" holds good even more for the weak states than for the powers.

A word of caution is necessary. These constraints are often *less* obvious during peace time. Furthermore, the foreign policy of a weak state may take a different course after a radical or revolutionary upheaval, though once changed the government will be constrained again (e.g., Cuba). It is not true that domestic politics have little or no absolute influence on the foreign policies of weak states. But in contrast to the great powers, weak states are less free to influence the course of events and have to learn to adapt themselves to external givens.

The question of the influence of a weak state's domestic politics on its foreign policy is related to the argument that due to its smaller size it can make decisions faster and more efficiently than a great power:

> ... the policy-makers [in the weak state] can themselves become personally familiar with the detail of the topics they are most concerned with. The influence of the bureaucracy is therefore much reduced and decisions are more apt to be taken without or despite its advice and with far less inhibition than might be the case in great powers.... Perception of affairs is more direct, less influenced by, and less dependent on, advisers.[1]

I am not at all convinced that this is a correct distinction between weak (small) states and the powers. In the first place, any leader of a super or great power can become as familiar as he pleases with major foreign policy issues. Here there would be little difference between states on the basis of size. Vital suggests that in weak states bureaucracies would be less influential than individual leaders. The tacit assumption is that larger bureaucracies are more influential. Logically this is incorrect. It is the *politicization of a bureaucracy,* not its size, which influences leaders in any given state. The personality of the leaders involved in the formulation of a state's foreign policy is also important. Henry Kissinger could pursue his policy in total disregard of the huge American bureaucracy, whereas an Israeli prime minister can reach no decision without the agreement of the military high command or the defense ministry.

In other words, one cannot correlate positively the size (or strength) of a state with the shape or form of its decision-making process. My contention is that domestic politics would not influence the direction of foreign policy in markedly different ways in great states or weak ones. A homogeneous population, as contrasted with a divided society, would enhance or weaken the policy of a weak state in the same way as it would that of a powerful one. The more homogeneous the population, the stronger the state. In a weak and small state a bureaucracy might be more expensive and perhaps less efficient because it would not enjoy the benefits of the economies of scale, but that is a different issue altogether.

NOTE

1. Vital, *Inequality of States,* p. 31.

APPENDIX B

The "New" International Norms of Conduct among States and the position of the Weak States

"Heck, Mr. President," he said. "I don't know what all the backing and filling's about. Give me forty parachutists and a plane and I'll go over to that little jerkwater country and get that bomb and this Kokintz back before they know what's happened to them." The President smiled. "That would mean an overt attack on the duchy of Grand Fenwick," he said.

"We aren't scared of them, are we?" the general asked, surprised.

"No," said the President. "But it isn't that simple. Technically we are at war with the duchy, so we would be within our rights to mount any kind of attack we desire against the country. But there's world opinion to be considered. We cannot let it be recorded in history that a nation of our size attacked the smallest country in the world—a state which is only five miles long and three miles wide, and cherishes the same love of freedom that gave us birth. We cannot do that, whatever the provocation. It would be contrary to all the traditions of our country. I do not believe for a moment that our own people would stand for it. And it would completely wreck our relations with the smaller foreign nations, especially the South American republics whose friendship and trust is essential to our own security."[1]

Among the major factors contributing to the relative improvement of the position of the weak states in the international system are the "new norms" guiding the behavior and conduct of states in that system. Since the 19th century these norms have gradually gained influence and importance. They include the right of every nation to self-determination, the sovereign rights of states over their own territory, the growing equality of states in international organizations, the equality of all states in international law,[2] and, perhaps most important, the increasing disapproval of the use of naked force between states. The "new norms" represent "the forward march of history . . . carrying nations from a retarded condition into a new and enlightened era when private standards will become public international rules."[3]

There is, of course, a direct relationship between the rise of democratic, liberal and egalitarian norms in Western society since the 19th century and the growing importance of similar norms in international relations. It is still true, and will be for a long time to come, that in international politics such norms cannot be enforced. For that reason, power politics and the pursuit of national interests will continue to dominate the relations between states. However, the huge gap that existed between the domestically accepted political norms and those governing the conduct of international affairs is slowly closing. Perhaps it will never be closed completely, and even if the utopian moment of world government and world order should ever arrive, conflicts among various groups would hardly disappear. Within the national boundaries of democratic states, conflicts and the struggles for power still continue despite the existence of enforceable justice. What is important here is the tendency for the norms of conduct among states to move slowly towards greater equality. The norms of democratic and liberal conduct seem to be prevailing over the use of force.

During the 19th century, Great Britain, France, and the United States, as well as many lesser states, continuously strove to improve their internal democratic institutions. This trend meant equal voting rights for every citizen, the equality of all citizens before the law, the increasing control by the state of the use of force between individuals, and the growing recognition of the need for greater equality in the distribution of income, for progressive taxation, and for the guarantee of a minimum standard of living.

At the same time, these developments did not hinder those very states from pursuing imperialistic policies abroad. They acquired colonial possessions overseas by force, controlled the fate of other peoples, exploited them without their consent, divided foreign continents into spheres of influence and relegated the weak states to a second-class position, often depriving them of the freedom to conduct their own foreign affairs.

The gap between the two political systems—the domestic and the external—was enormous. The recognized right of the homeland citizens to vote and be heard, while denying the same right to the "natives" in the colonies; the objection to the use of naked force domestically, while applying it mercilessly abroad; the growth of economic equality at home, while exploiting foreign peoples: all these contradictions could not exist side by side indefinitely without creating a situation of cognitive dissonance.

One of the first breakthroughs was the great powers' acceptance of the legal equality of many weak states at the First and Second Hague Conferences (in 1899 and 1907),[4] although the powers still maintained a double standard in regard to countries like Persia, which they could still divide into spheres of influence.[5] Furthermore, not all weak states were equal. At the London Peace Conference held after the Balkan Wars, the great powers insisted that they be given the right of veto on any peace agreements between belligerent weak states following a war in which they themselves did not take part directly. They exercised this right in the creation of Albania and the confrontation with Montenegro. The great powers, however, found it more and more difficult to impose their policies on the weak states, and they were not ready to apply force to back up their demands.

Woodrow Wilson's fight for the right of self-determination for all nations (mainly European, of course, at that stage) was another step toward new international norms. Wilson transplanted the theories of liberal democracy to international affairs:

> The equality of nations upon which peace must be founded if it is to last must be an equality of rights; the guarantees exchanged

must neither recognize nor imply a difference between big nations and small, between those that are powerful and those that are weak.[6]

The League of Nations was an attempt "to apply the principles of Lockeian liberalism to the building of a machinery of international order."[7]

> The Covenant . . . simply carries into world affairs that outlook of a liberal democratic society which is one of the great achievements of our human advance.[8]

Despite the great advance in the equality of states in international politics from the time of the Concert of Powers to the League of Nations, the real influence within the League was still primarily exerted by the great powers. As the prime minister of Ireland observed, "Despite our juridical equality here, in matters such as European peace the small states are powerless."[9] All the important disputes debated in the League of Nations were ultimately decided by agreement among the great powers, but the League supplied the weak states with an important public forum in which to make their grievances heard.

After summarizing the discussion of the Corfu incident before the League's Council in 1923, James Barros concludes:

> The Greek career officials . . . had no illusions about the effectiveness of the League of Nations should the interests of the Great Powers fail to coincide and should these Powers refuse to support the Greek appeal. On the other hand, since Greece was a small Power and without allies, they also realized that the League was an excellent forum which could be used to arouse the small States and keep the issue before public opinion. To achieve this result, the Greeks . . . used the tools that all small nations invariably invoke in any debate against a greater Power: the appeal to international law and morality and to world public opinion.[10]

Nominally, then, the weak states enjoyed a position almost equal to that of the great powers in the League of Nations (and the United Nations), excluding the right to a permanent seat in the League's Council (and the UN Security Council) and the right of veto.[11] They had gained an important access to world public opinion, and their voices could be heard on world issues. In this respect, the new egalitarianism in international organizations was an important step forward. In reality, however, the League (and UN) could not effectively protect the weak against the strong, though it could, of course, bring pressure to terminate conflicts among the weak.

> . . . by its very nature the collective security system, with its privileged role for the great powers, was never meant to be directed against an erring great power, at least through the medium of the organization . . . the experience of the League and the United Nations therefore reflects a dismal series of failures whenever coercion was attempted against a great power . . . the only times it has worked were when smaller powers not allied with any great powers were involved.[12]

The Corfu incident was one of many events between the two World Wars in which naked force—especially against a weak state—proved morally difficult to accept and to justify to both domestic and external audiences. The great powers tried hard to present their use of force in a more acceptable form, a need which had not been felt so strongly in earlier historical periods.[13]

An indication of this need and of the growing moral difficulty of using brute force against weak states was the somewhat absurd attempt on the part of the great powers to present their attacks on the weak states as responses to acts of aggression by the weak. Some examples are the murder of the Italian General Tellini by unknown brigands on the Albanian-Greek border (27 August 1923), which supplied the Italians with an excuse to bombard and occupy Corfu;[14] the Mukden incident (18 September 1931), which served as the Japanese pretext for the occupation of Manchuria;[15] the Wal-Wal incident (5 December 1934), which became the Italian excuse for attacking Ethiopia;[16] the attack by German soldiers disguised in Polish uniforms on their own radio station in Gleiwitz;[17] the unconfirmed Russian claim of a submarine attack on the "Metalist," near Estonian territorial waters, which served as an excuse to pressure Estonia to accept Soviet troops for defense;[18] the Russian accusation that Finland had opened artillery fire on Russian troops; and the so-called Mainila incident (25 November 1939).[19]

It makes very little sense to accuse a weak state of committing acts of provocation when it is facing the danger of attack by a great power. In any case, all such incidents, whether fabricated, provoked, or real, have been blown up out of all proportion and have been used as pretexts by the powers to present a weak state with an ultimatum, in the style of Austria's ultimatum to Serbia on the eve of the First World War.[20] Humiliating demands, which practically require unconditional surrender, make acceptance of such an ultimatum impossible. These incidents demonstrate the need of the great powers for a moral excuse to attack the weak states. No such excuses, however, are necessary when a great power wants to launch an attack on another great power, e.g., the attack by Germany on France or Russia, or by Japan on the United States.

On other occasions, acts of aggression, occupation, or control by a great power over a weak state are disguised by "mutual defense treaties." These treaties supply excuses for many acts by the great powers: stationing (garrisoning) troops on the territory of a weak state; setting up puppet states which are made to appear genuinely independent; and intervening to "save" a great power's citizens or its ambassador residing in a weak state (this is a US favorite—justifying its intervention in Honduras in 1924 and in the Dominican Republic in 1965).[21] Still, whatever cover is used, the employment of force by a great power against a weak state is viewed negatively by other states, and very often by residents of the aggressor power itself. Therefore these excuses have become increasingly difficult to get away with.

The growing moral difficulties in the application of force by a great power against weak states became clearly evident in the 1930s with the initiation of the United States' "good neighbor" policy.

> This policy, in practice and in formal legal statement, renounced "intervention" in the domestic and foreign affairs of other American states, and for several years Washington ceased trying to implement its preferences among presidential aspirants and governmental policies in the Caribbean states by its previously customary methods of influence and diplomatic pressures . . . the fact was evident to all in 1945 that since January 1933 the United States government had not put troops ashore in any Latin American country for other than mutually acceptable measures of hemispheric defense.[22]

An attempt was made by the United States to give the Latin American countries the impression that their relations were symmetrical and based on reciprocity. The United States "could, of course, always employ force at its discretion, a capacity that was not shared by any other state in the Americas."[23] Clearly, therefore, the declared intention not to use force was not a result of military weakness but of moral inhibitions. The US government could not continually denounce other countries for acts of aggression and intervention in the Far East and Europe and then resort to the same methods so close to its own shores. It also became increasingly difficult to gain support for such activities from American public opinion.

No doubt the spirit of the good neighbor policy worked in favor of the Latin American states. It must be remembered, however, that while the use of naked force became more ugly, unacceptable and less likely, at the same time the United States

> ... was able to offer or withhold economic rewards, and this capacity, which it alone possessed among the American states in adequate measure, underlined the fact that the "system" comprised one wealthy power and twenty states of varying, but vastly lower, levels of economic resources. The discovery of the potentialities of the rewards technique was itself novel in inter-American affairs, for loans, grants, and technical assistance to Latin American governments by governmental agencies in Washington began to be offered on any significant scale only in 1939, and from the beginning they had a political tinge. The exploitation of the possibilities and limitations of the technique became a continuous process when its potentialities were realized.[24]

The formulation of the United States good neighbor policy foreshadowed a trend that became universal after the Second World War and especially after the end of the 1950s. While renouncing the use of naked force, the great powers began to resort to less offensive, less visible, but no less effective means of influence. They began to utilize economic rewards and punishments to obtain the cooperation of the weak states. The indirect took the place of the direct approach. Still, although the weak states have not yet freed themselves from the pressure of the great powers, they feel more secure from military threats and violent interventions. Knowing that the military threat has been curbed, they have gained confidence and a new freedom to maneuver in the international system.

This moral threshold can be quite effective under certain conditions. Part of the explanation for the failure of the British-French Suez expedition in 1956 lies in the half-hearted, reluctant, and guilt-ridden military effort of the British government. Similarly, after Castro had taken over in Cuba, the United States, despite its hostility, avoided using force and applied only economic pressure.

Since the mid-1950s, neither Great Britain nor the United States has used its overwhelming power against Iceland, Chile, Ecuador, or Peru in order to resolve the disputes concerning territorial waters and fishing rights. The ships of the two great powers have been taken into custody by these weak countries, their catches have been confiscated, they have been shot at, and they have had to pay heavy fines for the release of their boats. This "gunboat diplomacy in reverse" would have been impossible before the Second World War, but now it is accepted as part of international life. The great powers have developed a thicker skin, though not without some growing pains, and have stopped reacting to minor or "medium" provocations.

After the Second World War—a war fought to free Europe from German domination and occupation—it became increasingly difficult for the great powers to justify their own presence in Africa and Asia. The contradiction between fighting a war of liberation from tyranny on one continent and fighting colonial wars on others became too obvious. How could occupied Holland try to assert its control over Indonesia after the colony had been freed from Japanese occupation?[25] The largest colonial powers, Great Britain and France, were too exhausted to fight prolonged wars overseas. Furthermore, they depended on aid from the United States, which did not look favorably upon their overseas ventures. Public opinion in the two European states could not be expected to remain enthusiastic about colonial wars. In France a substantial part of public opinion was consistently against the wars in Indo-China and Algeria,[26] while in Great Britain there was considerable opposition to the Suez Expedition.[27]

Public opinion in the Western democratic powers could no longer be expected to support wars, especially prolonged ones where the direct interest of the power did not seem to be involved. The public opposition to the French military activities in Indo-China and North Africa only hinted at the difficulties to be faced by the United States government during the Vietnam war. Public opinion in the Western democracies would make it very difficult to mobilize the large conscript armies necessary to fight prolonged major wars against weak states. Such wars could perhaps be fought by relatively small mercenary or regular professional armies, such as the British Forces in Malaya, Singapore, Cyprus, and Aden, or the French Foreign Legion in Algeria,[28] but once larger conscript forces became necessary, the government would run into considerable difficulties.

The Second World War contributed to the demise of the myth that the possession of colonies strengthens the colonial power. Germany, which possessed no overseas territories, fought Britain, France, and Russia all at the same time and came close to victory. There were also good economic reasons for the declining interest in overseas conquests.

> A world that has understood Keynes and post-Keynesian economics has no need to conquer territory for the sake of national economic gain.[29]

> It also seems that world economic development and technological progress have rendered highly developed countries less dependent on foreign sources of supply than was still true half a century ago or less.[30]

As the economic benefits to be derived from the direct possession of colonies have diminished, or have become obtainable at a lower cost through normal trade, the price of colonial war and military intervention has risen by leaps and bounds. No such war can be justified on an economic basis. Guerrilla warfare, especially when it is waged in favorable terrain by a determined opponent receiving external support and sanctuaries in neighboring countries, has enormously raised the costs for any intervening power in both human and material terms.

The war in Indo-China cost the French at least ten billion dollars, in addition to American aid totaling $954 million at that time.[31] The number of soldiers killed in the operations related to Dien Bien Phu alone was 13,050.[32] The Suez expedition cost the British between £100 and £328 million sterling.[33] The war in Vietnam cost the United States 53,813 soldiers killed in action, and 153,302 seriously wounded, while the price tag was at least $108 billion.[34] And this enormous investment got the United States nowhere. The days when a hundred United States Marines disguised as legation guards in Nicaragua could control and maintain peace in a weak country are over.[35]

Since the 1950s the weak states have improved their standing in the United Nations. The U.N. General Assembly has a greater impact and voice in international affairs than did its predecessor in the League of Nations. Thanks to the Uniting for Peace Resolution, the General Assembly has more official responsibility and is capable of acting in time of crisis. Its decisions are not legally binding, but they carry considerable moral weight. The General Assembly has had a marked impact on the management of international crises, especially in the Suez and in the Congo. Yet its impact is dependent upon super- and great-power cooperation with the weak states.[36] Despite the great advance towards accepting egalitarian norms, James Barros' conclusions regarding the unequal influence of the great powers and the weak states are still almost as valid for the U.N. as for the League of Nations.

The distinction between the formal and the real status of the weak states still exists, though the gap has narrowed.[37] The growing tendency to transplant domestic egalitarian-liberal norms to the international system, combined with the increasing moral inhibitions on the great powers limiting the application of brute force against weak states, and the rising costs of applying such force, have all contributed to the improvement of the international milieu from the point of view of the weak states. Although the weak states cannot rely solely on the great powers' adherence to these norms, the experiences of the 1950s and the 1960s would indicate that the norms are gaining acceptance as the rules governing international conduct.

NOTES

1. Wibberly, *The Mouse That Roared*, pp. 126.
2. See E. H. Carr, *The Twenty Years' Crisis* (New York: Harper and Row, 1964), pp. 22–40, and pp. 163–166; Edwin DeWitt Dickinson, *The Equality of States in International Law* (Cambridge, Mass.: Harvard University Press, 1920); Thomas Fleiner, *Die Kleinstaaten in den Staatsverbindungen des Zwanzigsten Jahrhunderts* (Zurich: Polygraphischer Verlag, 1966).
3. Kenneth W. Thompson, *Political Realism and the Crisis of World Politics* (Princeton: Princeton University Press, 1960), p. 136.
4. See Rudolf Lüthi, *Die Europäischen Kleinstaaten und die Haager Friedenkonferenz von 1899* (Winterthur: Verlag P. G. Keller, 1954).
5. See Firuz Kazemzadeh, *Russia and Great Britain in Persia 1864–1914* (New Haven: Yale University Press, 1968), esp. pp. 516–680.
6. Quoted in Alfred Cobban, *The Nation State and National Self-Determination* (New York: Thomas Y. Crowell, 1969), p. 76. For a similar quote from Woodrow Wilson, see Gustav Lagos, *International Stratification and Underdeveloped Countries* (Chapel Hill: University of North Carolina Press, 1963), p. 22.
7. R. H. S. Crossman, quoted in Carr, *Twenty Years' Crisis*, p. 28.
8. General Ian Smuts, quoted in *ibid*.
9. Eamon De Valera, quoted in *ibid.*, p. 104.
10. James Barros, *The Corfu Incident of 1923* (Princeton: Princeton University Press, 1965), p. 301.
11. For the attempts of the weak states to limit or even abolish the right of veto of the great powers, see, for example, H. V. Evatt, *Australia in World Affairs* (Sydney: Angus and Robertson, 1946), p. 133.
12. James Barros, *The Aaland Islands Question: Its Settlement by the League of Nations* (New Haven: Yale University Press, 1968), p. 335.
13. Robert E. Osgood and Robert W. Tucker, *Force, Order and Justice* (Baltimore: Johns Hopkins Press, 1967), part II, chap. 1, pp. 195–219.
14. See Barros, *Corfu Incident of 1923*, pp. 20–32.
15. See Christopher Thorne, *The Limits of Foreign Policy* (New York: Capricorn Books, 1973), pp. 3, 131–133; also T. Yoshihashi, *Conspiracy at Mukden* (New Haven: Yale University Press, 1963).
16. See George W. Baer, *The Coming of the Italian-Ethiopian War* (Cambridge, Mass.: Harvard University Press, 1967), pp. 45–61.
17. Shirer, *Rise and Fall of the Third Reich*, pp. 518–520, 599.
18. Tarulis, *Soviet Policy towards the Baltic States*, p. 152.
19. Anatole G. Mazour, *Finland Between East and West* (Princeton: D Van Nostrand, 1956), pp. 108–109.
20. See the discussion of the Austrian ultimatum to Serbia in Albertini, *Origins of the War of 1914*, vol. II, *The Crisis of July 1914*, pp. 170–175, 254–289; also Sidney B. Fay, *The Origins of the World War*, vol. II, *After Sarajevo*, rev. ed. (New York: Free Press, 1966), pp. 183–273. Another example is the Italian ultimatum to Greece. See Barros, *Corfu Incident of 1923*, pp. 33–73.

21. Bryce Wood, *The Making of the Good Neighbor Policy* (New York: Columbia University Press, 1962), pp. 5, 41–47.
22. Bryce Wood and Minerva Morales, "Latin America and the United Nations," in Norman Padelford and Leland M. Goodrich, *The United Nations in the Balance* (New York: Praeger, 1965), p. 351.
23. Wood, *Making of the Good Neighbor Policy*, p. 351.
24. *Ibid.*, p. 334.
25. See Arend Lijphardt, *The Trauma of Decolonization: The Dutch and West New Guinea* (New Haven: Yale University Press, 1966).
26. See, for example, John Steward Ambler, *Soldiers Against the State* (Garden City, N.Y.: Anchor Books, 1968), pp. 107–109.
27. Hugh Thomas, *Suez* (New York: Harper and Row, 1967), pp. 138–140.
28. Ambler, *Soldiers Against the State*, pp. 374–375.
29. Knorr, *On the Uses of Military Power in the Nuclear Age*, p. 26. This attitude can be traced to the classical free trade arguments that preceded Keynes. "From the [free trade] argument it follows not only that free trade is the correct policy but also that attempts to enlarge the territory of the state, whether by annexing neighbors or acquiring colonies, are foolish. The expenses of conquering and holding cannot be balanced by advantages in trade, for the same advantages can be had, without expense, under a policy of free trade." Kenneth N. Waltz, *Man, the State and War* (New York: Columbia University Press, 1968), p. 99 (referring to Bentham's work, "Emancipate Your Colonies"). See also Waltz, pp. 145–146.
30. Knorr, *On the Uses of Military Power in the Nuclear Age*, p. 24.
31. Bernard Fall, *Hell in a Very Small Place* (New York: Vintage Books, 1966), pp. vii–viii.
32. *Ibid.*, p. 484.
33. Thomas, *Suez*, p. 151.
34. *Time*, Aug. 27, 1973, p. 34.
35. Wood, *Making of the Good Neighbor Policy*, p. 26.
36. For the position of the weak states in the United Nations see Norman J. Padelford and Leland M. Goodrich, *United Nations in the Balance*, esp. pp. 350–410; and David A. Kay, *The New Nations in the United Nations 1960–1967* (New York: Columbia University Press, 1970).
37. See Lagos, *International Stratification and Underdeveloped Countries*, pp. 22–30.

APPENDIX C

The Potential Impact of Modern Military Weapons Technology on the Military Position of Weak States

Recent developments in modern conventional weapons technology may, in the future, enhance the military strength of the weaker and smaller states relative to that of the great powers. The so-called precision guided munitions (or PGM's in short) tend to favor the defense over the offense, and considerably increase the effectiveness and firepower of small but highly mobile and flexible combat teams.[1]

> By improving defensive capabilities, the new weaponry is thought to make weaker states better able to resist invasion from stronger neighbours and intervention by outside powers. The systems thus seem particularly relevant to states with special defensive problems, such as Yugoslavia, Sweden, Pakistan or Japan, which must coexist with far more powerful neighbours. For nations like Israel, which have a high degree of technical competence, the new technologies might enable armed forces to use technological advantage to counter less sophisticated but numerically stronger adversaries.[2]

> [The effectiveness of PGM's] not only reverses the previous advantage of the "offense" against the "defense", but also allows for a small defensive force and one which requires less and less sophisticated support and logistics backup because the defensive units can operate as independent units and because fewer munitions will be necessary to destroy an equivalent amount of enemy hardware.[3]

The ratio of attacking to defending forces may have increased from the traditionally accepted one of three to one in favour of the defense to as much as six, or even seven, to one. In other words, the so-called PGM's act as a force multiplier, improving the defensive capabilities of states which are relatively short in both human and economic resources.

PGM's have an accuracy "ten to a hundred times greater"[4] than that of earlier unguided conventional munitions. Their accuracy is often over 50 per cent for the most modern PGM's and comes close in effectiveness to "one shot one kill". This quantum jump in the accuracy of modern conventional weapons has had an important impact on the financial, logistical, and troop level requirements of modern warfare.

Weaker states which have found it increasingly difficult to obtain and deploy modern tanks and aircraft in large quantities, may yet find some comfort in the latest trends in the development of modern weapons. The price tag of a modern tank is around half a million dollars, while the price of the future main battle tank designed for the 1980s will be close to a million dollars per unit.[5] In addition to the prohibitive price of modern tanks, they require a crew of 4 to 5 highly trained soldiers in order to operate, and an even larger number of maintenance and logistical personnel. They also consume very large amounts of fuel and ammunition. In comparison, the highly mobile vehicles necessary for carrying anti-tank missiles cost only $25,000 per unit and can be operated by soldiers who have undergone minimal training. These vehicles can be maintained by civilian autoshops and can travel more than ten times as far as a tank on a given portion of fuel.[6]

Until recently, the odds have usually been placed in favour of the tank. Oddly enough, while the cost of modern tanks has skyrocketed in recent years, the vulnerability of these tanks has also increased considerably with the advent of modern anti-tank missiles.[7] The odds have now been reversed in favour of the anti-tank missile. While the price of the modern tank is close to a million dollars, the price of a very sophisticated and highly effective anti-tank missile such as the American TOW (not including its launch vehicle and platform) is only $3,000 dollars.[8] In other words, for the price of one modern tank many anti-tank missile systems could be purchased. Even if the anti-tank missiles have a one out of two or one out of three chance of hitting their target, it appears preferable to invest relatively more in cheap anti-tank weapons rather than in expensive tanks for both cost/benefit and tactical military considerations.

Anti-tank missiles, like the less expensive and more efficient vehicles which carry them, can offer additional benefits: they are light and highly mobile, require little or no maintenance, require less highly trained personnel, and can be operated by smaller teams. For countries short on manpower, they thus offer the triple advantage of smaller operating teams, little maintenance, and minimally trained personnel.[9]

In the age of conventional unguided munitions and imprecise area weapons, very large quantities of munitions were often required to attain only meager results. These enormous quantities of imprecise munitions were very costly and required considerable logistical support (trucks, fuel, drivers, large depots and so on).

In actual engagements which pitted artillery against tanks, for example, roughly 2,500 artillery rounds were fired per tank destroyed.[10] Certainly, the two, three or even four antitank missiles required to knock out a tank would cost much less than the price of 2,500 conventional ballistic free flight shells, although the unit price of the anti-tank missile is much higher. During the Second World War, 30,000 bullets were needed to score one hit. During the Vietnam War, the U.S. Army had to fire no less than 400 shells to cause one casualty, and well over one thousand shells to cause one fatal injury.[11] The modern Cannon Launched Guided Projectiles (CLGP's in short), which are designated and directed to their target by laser beams, are highly accurate even against moving targets.[12] Thus, while the unit price of each PGM is considerably higher than that of conventional unguided munitions, their much greater accuracy makes them more effective, and hence cheaper in the long run. (For example, "smart bombs" do not necessarily cost *much more* than "dumb bombs", though their efficiency is between at least 145 to 4000 times higher.)

In addition, many smart bombs can be dropped from higher altitudes and greater ranges, often out of the range of antiaircraft guns and missiles. "This means less risk to the aircraft and thus a lower attrition rate. The extra cost of 'smart bombs' —quite apart from their extra effectiveness—is cancelled out if the attrition rate is only about ½ per cent per sortie less."[13] A comparison between the number of planes required to deliver smart bombs and dumb bombs reveals that the highly accurate smart bombs require much fewer planes to perform the same mission. It was estimated that over a period of twenty years, the cost of using standard bombs to achieve a given objective would be almost three times the cost of using precision guided munitions. This price discrepancy is primarily due to the high cost of aircraft maintenance and operations.[14] PGM's "sound like an economist's dream come true".[15] "Precision weapons (are) tailor-made for any nation with adequate technology but limited resources, desperately seeking a shortcut to combat power."[16]

The great advantages offered to weaker states are, however, mainly in the military rather than the economic sphere. New weapons technologies extend the military capabilities of these states far beyond their previous limits. The PGM's compensate for a shortage in manpower in a way which money could not. In an above quote it was said that "One Finn may be worth ten Russians, but what do we do when the eleventh comes along?" The use of PGM's may alter the statement to read, "One Finn may be worth twenty-five Russians, but what do we do when the twenty-sixth comes along?" This is a considerable and meaningful improvement in the power of weaker states—though it is still no panacea. There is, of course, an upper limit, even if on a higher level, to the power of a weaker state.

The utility of military force for a weak state in conflict (as discussed in chapter two) will thus increase. Its ability to exact a much higher price from a great power during a *conventional* conflict will also clearly increase its conventional deterrent credibility. A weaker state's indication that it will meet force with force will further reduce a great power's incentive to attack or intervene.

In the future, more exotic weapons technologies will even further compensate for a weak state's shortage of manpower. One such weapon which is currently being tested in the United States is the SADARM (Sense and Destroy Armor). This is designed as a "low cost" missile that can be fired from any howitzer now in service. This missile is fired toward an area of a massive tank attack, and, once over the target, the missile splits into three submunitions. Each submunition is a true PGM that can independently home in on a different target.[17] The trend in the design of PGM's is therefore toward "one shot many kills", a quality which makes them even cheaper to use, and increases the firepower of a given military unit by giving it a higher "tooth to tail ratio".[18] Thus, small units on the defensive will be able to undertake larger and larger attacking units. Modern technology will, in this manner, stretch the power of numerically weaker states, (including NATO vis-a-vis the numerically superior Warsaw Pact).

PGM's offer yet another advantage to the weaker states. While few of the weaker states can design and build tanks and aircraft from scratch, they do have the capacity to produce PGM's in large quantities. The R&D requirements involved in the production of PGM's and RPV's (Remotely Piloted Vehicles) are well within the means and scientific capabilities of many of the weaker states. A glance in the annual Jane's Weapons Systems can demonstrate the successful efforts of weaker states in the development of these weapons. Countries such as Israel, Norway, Belgium, Australia, Italy and South Africa, as well as many others, have successfully produced one or two such weapons systems, although none of them have been able to produce a complete array of PGM's.[19] The Israeli efforts to develop PGM's in each of the major areas of warfare illustrate the importance which weaker countries ascribe to such weapons. They have successfully developed a sea to sea missile (the Gabriel—now going into its second generation), an air to air missile (the Shafrir), and also an electro-optical air to ground missile. It can be safely assumed that they will also develop a longer distance anti-tank missile, and perhaps even a longer range ground to ground missile. In addition, the Israelis have already developed, and started production on, a small battlefield reconnaissance RPV to be used at the battalion level.

A further benefit of the new weapons technologies is that the PGM's enable the weaker states to stretch the useful life of older platforms at a time when the platforms for major weapons such as aircraft, ships and tanks have become prohibitively expensive. Since many of the so-called "smart weapons" can be fired "stand off", or out of the range of the enemy's defense, their superior performance compensates for the inferior performance of the platforms carrying them.

Aside from the obvious military advantages which accompany the use of PGM's, they may also have an important political impact on prospects for stability in the international system.

The selective sale of defense-oriented PGM's to weaker states in the Middle East, Africa or Latin America, for example, can strengthen the defensive posture of those states vis-à-vis each other. The existence of PGM's could reduce the incentives for anti-status quo policies by raising the attrition rate of any attacker and considerably reducing his chances for a quick victory, and ultimately stabilize regional politics. For the United States and Europe, this could stabilize the flow of primary commodities and trade, minimize the risk of a super-power confrontation between the U.S. and the USSR, and lower the conflicting demands of their client states. A policy which aims at establishing regional stability is feasible, and can succeed under the assumption that the great powers will carefully consider their weapons supply policies to the Third World and weaker states. They should symmetrically sell defensive and second strike stabilizing weapons such as anti-tank and anti-aircraft weapons, instead of offensive, destabilizing weapons such as missile boats, smart bombs, tanks, modern fighters and long range "stand off" missiles. So far, however, such a policy has not been pursued because of the buyer's market for sophisticated weapons and the economic and political competition for influence between the great powers.[20]

Given the highly accurate PGM's and the new, more powerful conventional explosives, it can be argued that a careful weapons export policy of the great powers could also substantially reduce the regional incentives for nuclear proliferation. Of course, such a development could be viewed positively by the great powers. The existence of greater conventional defensive deterrence and stability would reduce the incentive of some weaker states to produce nuclear weapons. In the future, the accuracy and high yield of conventional munitions, as well as the fact that they are less expensive and equally effective, could cause them to be substituted for tactical nuclear weapons. In any event, even if regional nuclear proliferation continues as projected by many observers, the *threshold* of using them will be higher given the substitute capabilities of PGM's.[21]

APPENDICES

NOTES

1. This is not the place to go into a detailed discussion of the technological aspects of PGM's and their impact on military tactics and strategy. For our purposes, PGM's can be defined as a weapons system with a probability of hitting its target which is well over 50%, and whose flight to the target can be corrected in mid-course either by itself (a "true PGM") or by an operator directing it to its target. For some of the recent literature on PGM's see:

Books and Monographs:

Richard Burt, *Developments in Arms Transfers: Implications for Supplier Control and Recipient Autonomy* (Santa Monica: the Rand Corporation P-5991, September, 1977).

Richard Burt, *New Conventional Weapons Technologies: Debate and Directions,* Adelphi Papers No. 126 (London: IISS, 1976).

Steven Canby, *The Alliance and Europe: Part IV: Military Technology,* Adelphi Papers No. 109 (London: IISS, 1975).

Paul Dickson, *The Electronic Battlefield* (Bloomington: Indiana University Press, 1976).

James Digby, *Precision Guided Weapons,* Adelphi Papers No. 118 (London: IISS, 1976).

James Digby, *New Weapons and the Dispersal of Military Power* (Santa Monica: the California Seminar on Arms Control and Foreign Policy, Discussion Paper No. 78, September, 1978).

Johan Holst and Uwe Nerlich (eds.), *Beyond Nuclear Deterrence* (New York: Crane, Russak and Co., 1977).

G. Kemp, R. L. Pfaltzgraff, U. Raanan (eds.), *The Other Arms Race* (Lexington, Ma.: Lexington Books, 1975).

New Conventional Weapons and East-West Security, Parts I & 2, Adelphi Papers No. 144–145 (London: IISS, 1978).

Articles

Frank Barnaby, "Precision Warfare", *New Scientist,* (8 May 1975), pp. 304–307.

Saadia Amiel, "Deterrence by Conventional Forces", *Survival,* (March/April 1978), pp. 58–62.

John T. Burke, "Smart Weapons: A Coming Revolution in Tactics", *Army,* Vol. 23 No. 2 1973, pp. 14–20.

"The Precision Revolution", *The Economist,* (March 27, 1976), pp. 60–61.

"Tomorrow's Wars", *The Economist,* (December 4, 1976), pp. 100–101.

John W. Finney, "Guided Bombs Expected to Revolutionize Warfare", *The New York Times,* (March 18, 1974), pp. 1; 8.

Collin Gray, "New Weapons and the Resort to Force", *International Journal* (Toronto, Spring 1975), pp. 238–259.

James L. Foster, "The Future of Conventional Arms Control", *Policy Sciences,* Vol. 8, No. 1, 1977, pp. 1–19.

Phillip Karber, "The Soviet Anti-Tank Debate", *Survival,* (May/June 1976), pp. 105–111.

John Marriott, "Precision Guided Munitions", *NATO Fifteen Nations*, Vol. 20, (October/November 1977), pp. 112–121.

Ferdinand Otto Micksche, "PGM's Are Changing the Combat Picture", *Military Review*, Vol. 58, No. 7, (July 1978), pp. 10–18.

Phillip Morrison and Paul F. Walker, "A New Strategy for Military Spending", *Scientific American*, Vol. 239, No. 4, (October, 1978), pp. 48–61.

Palmer Osborn and William Power, "How to Defend Western Europe?", *Fortune*, (October 9, 1978), pp. 151–156.

Kosta Tsipis, "Cruise Missiles", *Scientific American*, Vol. 236, No. 2, (February 1977), pp. 20–29.

2. Richard Burt, *New Weapons Technologies: Debate and Directions*, Adelphi Papers No. 126 (London: IISS, 1976), p. 9.
3. James L. Foster, *New Conventional Weapons Technologies: Implications for the Third World*, (Mimeo), 1976, p. 4.
4. Burt, *New Weapons Technologies*, p. 3.
5. For prices of modern weapons systems see:

    Tom Gervasi, *Arsenal of Democracy: American Weapons Available for Export* (New York: Grove Press, 1977).
6. See Palmer Osborn and William Bowers, "How to Defend Western Europe", *Fortune*, (October 9, 1978), p. 153.
7. See Phillip Karber, "The Soviet Anti-Tank Debate", *Survival*, (May/June 1976), pp. 105–111.

    Richard M. Ogorkiewicz; "The Future of the Battle Tank", *Survival*, (May/June 1976).

    Kemp, Pfaltzgraff and Raanan, op. cit., pp. 43–56.

    Steven Canby, *The Alliance and Europe: Part IV Military Doctrine and Technology*, Adelphi Papers No. 109 (London: IISS, 1975).

    Similar arguments also hold for other modern weapon platforms such as aircraft and ships, whose prices have skyrocketed over the years at the same time that their vulnerability has increased. For example, the price of modern fighter aircraft is now at least ten to fifteen million dollars apiece (the F–15, F–14, F–16, Tornado and others). Anti-aircraft missile systems cost considerably less, and the modern sophisticated air to air missiles can compensate for the less than optimal performance of older generation aircraft such as the F–4, F–104, MIG 21, MIRAGE–3. Israel's purchase of 25 F–15's from the United States from 1975/1976 onward has cost Israel well over half of the total U.S. massive military aid program (over 600 million dollars!)
8. See Gervasi, *Arsenal of Democracy*.

    Burt, *New Weapons Technology*, p. 9; 17.
9. Burt, *New Weapons Technology*, p. 9–10; 18.
10. Osborn and Brown, "How to Defend Western Europe", *Fortune*, p. 151.
11. John Marriott, "Precision Guided Munitions", *NATO Fifteen Nations*, Vol. 20, (October/November 1977), p. 115.
12. For CLGP's, see for example, R.D.M. Furlong, "The U.S. Army's

Cannon Launched Guided Projectile", *International Defense Review* No. 1, 1976, pp. 117–119.

Phillip H. Morrison and David S. Amberntson, "Guidance and Control of a Cannon-Launched Guided Projectile", *Journal of Spacecraft*, Vol. 14, No. 6, pp. 328–334.

John S. Phillip, "True Magic for the Artilleryman", *Aerospace International*, (January/February 1976), pp. 22–26.

Col. Frank P. Regano, "Smart Projectiles for the Sharpshooting Artillery", *National Defense*, Vol. 60, No. 332, (September/October 1975), pp. 120–123.

Major Robert A. Doughty, "Armor Copperhead", (March/April 1978), pp. 65–67.

Clarence A. Robinson, "Wings to Boost Guided Projectile Range", *Aviation Week and Space Technology*, (October 13, 1975), pp. 55–57.

13. Canby, *Military Doctrine and Technology*, p. 30.
14. Osborn and Brown, "How to Defend Western Europe", p. 154.
    Philip Morrison and Paul F. Walker, "A New Strategy for Military Spending", *Scientific American*, Vol. 239, No. 4, (October 1978), pp. 48–61.
15. Marriott, "Precision Guided Munitions", p. 115.
16. Col. John T. Burke, "Precision Weaponry: The Changing Nature of Modern Warfare", *Army*, Vol. 24, (March, 1974) as quoted in James C. Foster, *New Conventional Weapons Technologies Implications for the Third World* (Mimeo, Tufts University Conference on Implications of the Military Build-Up in Non-Industrial States 1976).
17. See *Army Research and Development News Magazine*, (October/November 1977), p. 5.
18. These new types of weapons are referred to in professional literature as WAAM—Wide Area Anti-Armor Munitions.
19. For a partial and somewhat dated list of weaker states producing PGM's, see Burt's "New Weapons Technologies", p. 4.
    George Copley, "Third World Arms Production: Less Power to the Superpowers", *Defense and Foreign Affairs Digest*, (September 1976), p. 24.
    George Copley, Michael Moodie and David Harvey, "Third World Arms Production: An End to Embargoes?", *Defense and Foreign Affairs Digest*, (August, 1978).
    David Harvey, "The Law of Supply and the Armed: Industry and the U.S. Arms Control Policies", *Defense and Foreign Affairs Digest*, (September 1978).
    Frank Barnaby, "World Arsenals in 1977", *The Bulletin of Atomic Scientists*, Vol. 34, No. 5, (May 1978), pp. 10–19.
20. "For weaker states in other regions the possibility of improved defensive capabilities carries the connotation of greater deterrence, and hence greater stability. In the Middle East, South Asia or the Korean Peninsula, waging aggressive wars might become more difficult, thus raising the chances of peaceful settlements to outstanding disputes being reached . . . bolstering the confidence of states in the ability to

defend themselves with conventional arms might reduce incentives to acquire nuclear weapons."

Burt, "New Weapons Technologies", pp. 10; 26.

These developments may have been among the most important incentives behind the Sadat peace initiative in the winter of 1977.

See also, S. J. Dudzinsky, Jr. and James Digby, "New Technology and the Control of Conventional Arms: Some Common Ground", *International Security,* (Spring 1977), pp. 143–146, esp. p. 155).

Yair Evron, *The Role of Arms Control in the Middle East,* Adelphi Papers, No. 138, (London: IISS, 1978).

Philip T. Farley, Stephen S. Kaplan and William H. Lewis, *Arms Across the Sea,* (Washington D.C.: the Brookings Institution, 1978).

Anne Hessing Cahn, Joseph J. Kurzel, Peter M. Dawkins, Jacques Huntzinger, *Controlling Future Arms Trade,* (New York: McGraw-Hill, 1977).

21. For a debate on this question, see

Col. T. N. Dupuy, "Weapons Lethality and the Nuclear Threshold", *Armed Forces Journal,* (October 1978).

Burt, "New Weapons Technologies", pp. 23; 26.

Richard Burt, *Nuclear Proliferation and Conventional Arms Transfers: The Missing Link,* (Santa Monica, California: California Seminar on Arms Control and Foreign Policy Discussion Paper No. 76).

Bibliography

Books

Abrahamsen, Samuel. *Sweden's Foreign Policy.* Washington, D.C.: Public Affairs Press, 1957.

Adcock, Sir Frank and D. J. Mosley. *Diplomacy in Ancient Greece.* New York: St. Martin's Press, 1975.

Adelman, M. A. *The World Petroleum Market.* Baltimore: Johns Hopkins Press, 1972.

Agmon, Tamir and Charles P. Kindelberger. *Multinationals From Small Countries.* Cambridge, Mass.: The MIT Press, 1977.

Albertini, Luigi. *The Origins of the War of 1914,* Vol. I. Trans. Isabella M. Massey. London: Oxford University Press, 1967.

Albrecht, Ulrich. *Der Handel mit Waffen.* München: Carl Hasner Verlag, 1971.

Alker, Hayward R. and Bruce M. Russett. *World Politics in the General Assembly.* New Haven: Yale University Press, 1965.

Allison, Graham T. *Essence of Decision.* Boston: Little Brown, 1971.

Ambler, John Steward. *Soldiers Against the State.* Garden City, N.Y.: Anchor Books, 1968.

Andrén, Nils. *Power Balance and Non Alignment.* Stockholm: Almquist and Wiksell, 1967.

Andreski, Stanislav. *Military Organization and Society.* Berkeley: University of California Press, 1968.

Andrew, Arthur. *Defence By Other Means: Diplomacy for the Underdog.* Toronto: Canadian Institute of International Affairs, 1970.

Aron, Raymond. *The Great Debate.* Trans. Ernst Powell. Garden City, N.Y.: Doubleday, 1965.

——————. *Peace and War.* Trans. Richard Howard and Annette Baker Fox. New York: Frederick A. Praeger, 1967.

——————. *On War.* Trans. Terence Kilmartin. London: Secker and Warburg, 1958.

Art, Robert J. *The Influence of Foreign Policy on Sea Power: New Weapons and Weltpolitik in Wilhelminian Germany.* Beverly Hills: Sage Publications, 1973.

Astiz, Carlos Alberto, ed. *Latin America International Politics: Ambitions,*

Capabilities and the National Interests of Mexico, Brazil and Argentina. South Bend, Ind.: University of Notre Dame Press, 1969.
Azar, Edward E. *Probe for Peace: Small State Hostilities.* Minneapolis, Minnesota: Burgess, 1973.
Bader, William B. *The United States and the Spread of Nuclear Weapons.* New York: Pegasus, 1968.
Badian, E. *Foreign Clientelae (269–70 B.C.).* Oxford: Clarendon Press, 1958.
Bailey, Norman A. *Latin America in World Politics.* New York: Walker, 1967.
Bailey, Sydney D. *Voting in the Security Council.* Bloomington: Indiana University Press, 1969.
Baldwin, Hanson W. *Strategy for Tomorrow.* New York: Harper and Row, 1970.
Banfield, Edward C. *The Moral Basis of a Backward Society.* New York: Free Press, 1958.
Barber, James. *South Africa's Foreign Policy, 1945–1970.* London: Oxford University Press, 1973.
Barker, Elisabeth. *Austria 1918–1972.* London: Macmillan, 1973.
Barros, James. *The Aaland Islands Question: Its Settlement by the League of Nations.* New Haven: Yale University Press, 1968.
——————— *The Corfu Incident of 1923: Mussolini and the League of Nations.* Princeton: Princeton University Press, 1965.
Barston, R. P. *The Other Powers: Studies in the Foreign Policies of Small States.* New York: Barnes and Noble, 1973.
Basch, Antonin. *The Danube Basin and the German Economic Sphere.* New York: Columbia University Press, 1943.
Bendict, Burton, ed. *Problems of Smaller Territories.* London: The Athlone Press, 1967.
Bendl, Judith Janoska. *Methodologische Aspekte des Idealtypes: Max Weber und die Soziologie der Geschichte.* Berlin: Duncker und Humblot, 1965.
Blair, Patricia Wohlgemuth. *The Ministate Dilemma.* New York: Carnegie Endowment for International Peace, 1967.
Blau, Peter M. *Exchange and Power in Social Life.* New York: John Wiley, 1964.
Blood, Hilary. *The Smaller Territories: Problems and Future.* London: The Conservative Political Center, 1958.
Board, Joseph B. *The Government and Politics of Sweden.* Boston: Houghton Mifflin, 1970.
Bonjour, Edgar. *Geschichte der Schweizerischen Neutralität,* Vol. II. Basel: Helbing und Lichtenhahn, 1963.
Bonsal, Stephen. *Suitors and Suppliants: The Little Nations at Versailles.* New York: Prentice Hall, 1946.
Branch, William. *India, Pakistan and the Great Powers.* New York: Praeger, 1972.
Brecher, Michael. *Decisions in Israel's Foreign Policy.* London: Oxford University Press, 1974.
——————— *The Foreign Policy System of Israel.* New Haven: Yale

University Press, 1972.
Bretton, Henry L. *Patron-Client Relations: Middle Africa and the Powers.* New York: General Learning Co., 1971.
────────── *Power and Politics in Africa.* Chicago: Aldine, 1973.
Brewin, Andrew. *Stand On Guard: The Search for a Canadian Defence Policy.* Toronto and Montreal: McLelland and Stewart Limited, 1965.
Breyer, Siegfried. *Battleships and Battle Cruisers 1905–1970.* Trans. Alfred Kurti. Garden City, N.Y.: Doubleday, 1973.
Encyclopaedia Britannica, Vol. XXI. Chicago: Encyclopaedia Britannica Inc., 1970.
Brockhaus Enzyklopadie, Vol. X. Wiesbaden: F. A. Brockhaus, 1970.
Brühl, Helmut. *Probleme Westeuropäischer Kleinstaaten: Volk und Staat in Holland, Belgien, Luxemburg und der Schweiz.* Berlin: Dietrich Reimer, 1940.
Budurowycz, Bodhan B. *Polish-Soviet Relations 1932–1939.* New York: Columbia University Press, 1963.
Burgess, Philip M. *Elite Images and Foreign Policy Outcomes: A Study of Norway.* Columbus, Ohio: Ohio State University Press, n.d.
Burr, Robert N. *By Reason or Force: Chile and the Balance of Power in South America 1830–1905.* Berkeley: University of California Press, 1965.
────────── *Our Troubled Hemisphere: Perspectives on United States-Latin America Relations.* Washington, D.C.: The Brookings Institution, 1967.
Burrell, R. M. *The Persian Gulf.* The Washington Papers, No. 1. New York: Library Press, 1972.
Butterfield, Herbert and Martin Wight. *Diplomatic Investigations.* Cambridge, Mass.: Harvard University Press, 1968.
Cable, James. *Gunboat Diplomacy.* London: Chatto and Windus, 1971.
Campbell, John C. *Tito's Separate Road.* New York: Harper and Row, 1967.
Campen, S. I. P. Van. *The Quest for Security.* The Hague: Martinus Nijhoff, 1958.
Cappis, Oscar Bernhard. *Die Idee des Kleinstaats in Deutschland des 19. Jahrhunderts.* Basel: Franz Mehr, 1923.
Carey, James C. *Peru and the United States.* Notre Dame, Indiana: University of Notre Dame Press, 1964.
Carmi, M. *The Economies of Small Developed States.* Jerusalem: The Jerusalem Group for National Planning, 1975. (Mimeographed).
────────── *Research and Development in Small Developed States with Special Reference to Israel.* Jerusalem: The Jerusalem Group for National Planning, 1977. (Hebrew, mimeographed).
Carr, Edward Hallett. *Conditions of Peace.* New York: Macmillan, 1943.
────────── *The Twenty Years' Crisis 1919–1939.* New York: Harper, 1964.
Caullery, Maurice. *Parasitism and Symbiosis.* Trans. Averil M. Lysaght. London: Sidgwick and Jackson, 1952.
Chubin, Sharam, and Sepher Zabih. *The Foreign Relations of Iran: A Developing State in a Zone of Great-Power Conflict.* Berkeley: University

of California Press, 1974.
Churchill, Winston. *The Gathering Storm*, Vol. I in *The Second World War*. Boston: Houghton Mifflin, 1948.
————— *The Great War*, Vol. I. London: The Home Library Book Co., 1933.
————— *Triumph and Tragedy*, Vol. VI in *The Second World War*. Boston: Houghton Mifflin, 1953.
Cienciala, Anna M. *Poland and the Western Powers 1938–1939*. London: Routledge and Kegan Paul, 1968.
Clarkson, Stephen, ed. *An Independent Foreign Policy for Canada?* Toronto: McClelland and Stewart, 1968.
Claude, Inis L. *Power and International Relations*. New York: Random House, 1969.
—————*Swords Into Plowshares*, 2nd rev. ed. New York: Random House, 1961.
Cline, Ray S. *World Power Assessment 1977: A Calculus of Strategic Drift*. Boulder, Colorado: Westview Press 1977.
Cobban, Alfred. *The Nation State and National Self-Determination*, rev. ed. London: Collins, 1969.
Cockcraft, James D., Andre Gunder Frank and Dale L. Johnson, *Dependence and Underdevelopment*. Garden City, N.Y.: Anchor Books, 1972.
Cohen, Benjamin J. *The Question of Imperialism*. New York: Basic Books, 1973.
Cole, J. P. *Geography of World Affairs*, 4th ed. Harmondsworth, Middlesex: Penguin Books, 1972.
Condon, Richard W. *The Winter War*. New York: Ballantine Books, 1972.
Connell-Smith, Gordon. *The Inter-American System*. London: Oxford University Press, 1966.
Connelly, Owen. *Napoleon's Satellite Kingdoms*. New York: Free Press, 1965.
Cottam, Richard W. *Competitive Interference and Twentieth Century Diplomacy*. Pittsburgh: University of Pittsburgh Press, 1969.
Craig, Gordon A. and Felix Gilbert. *The Diplomats 1919–1939*. Princeton: Princeton University Press, 1953.
Cuthbertson, Brian. *Canadian Military Independence in the Age of the Superpowers*. Toronto: Fitzhenry and Whiteside, 1977.
Dahl, Robert A. *Modern Political Analysis*. 2nd rev. ed. Englewood Cliffs, N.J.: Prentice Hall, 1970.
Dahl, Robert A. and Edward R. Tufte. *Size and Democracy*. Stanford: Stanford University Press, 1973.
Däniker, Gustav. *Strategie des Kleinstaats*. Frauenfeld: Verlag Huber, 1966.
Leonard Davis Institute for International Relations. *Proceedings of the Opening Conference at the Hebrew University of Jerusalem*. Jerusalem: n.p., 1974. Session Two: Small State Policies in the International System, pp. 51–84.
De Kadt, Emamuel, ed. *Patterns of Foreign Influence in the Caribbean*. London: Oxford University Press, 1972.
Debicki, Roman. *Foreign Policy of Poland 1919–1939*. London: Pall Mall

Press, 1962.
Demas, William G. *The Economics of Development in Small Countries with Special Reference to the Caribbean.* Montreal: McGill University Press, 1965.
Derry, T. K. *The Campaign in Norway.* London: HMSO, 1952.
Deutsch, Karl W. *The Analysis of International Relations.* Englewood Cliffs, N.J.: Prentice Hall, 1968.
Deutsche Gesellschaft für Auswärtige Politik, Bonn. *Mittlere Mächte in der Weltpolitik.* Opladen: C. W. Leske, 1969.
Diamond, William. *Czechoslovakia Between East and West.* London: Stevens, 1947.
Dickey, John Sloan, ed. *The United States and Canada.* Englewood Cliffs, N.J.: Prentice Hall, 1964.
Dickinson, Edwin DeWitt. *The Equality of States in International Law.* Cambridge, Mass.: Harvard University Press, 1920.
Dobell, Peter C. *Canada's Search for New Roles: Foreign Policy in the Trudeau Era.* London: Oxford University Press, 1972.
Doenitz, Karl. *Memoirs: Ten Years and Twenty Days.* Trans. R. H. Stevens. Cleveland, Ohio: The World Publishing Co., 1959.
Dörfer, Ingemar. *System 37 Viggen: Arms, Technology and the Domestication of Glory.* Oslo: Universitetsforlaget, 1973.
Dozer, Donald Marquand. *The Monroe Doctrine.* New York: Alfred A. Knopf, 1965.
Dror, Yehezkel. *Crazy States.* Lexington, Mass.: Heath, 1971.
Dürrenmatt, Peter Ulrich. *Der Kleinstaat und das Problem der Macht.* Basel: Helbing und Lichtenhahn, 1955.
Eggleston, F. W. *Reflections on Australian Foreign Policy.* Melbourne: F. W. Cheshire, 1957.
Ehrhardt, Dieter. *Der Begriff des Mikrostaats.* Marburg: Scienta Verlag Aalen, 1970.
Eisenhower, Dwight D. *Mandate for Change.* Garden City, N.Y.: Doubleday, 1963.
Ernst, Fritz. *Die Sendung des Kleinstaats.* Zurich: Atlantis Verlag, 1940.
Evatt, H. V. *Australia in World Affairs.* Sydney: Angus and Robertson, 1946.
——— *Foreign Policy of Australia.* Sydney: Angus and Robertson, 1945.
Fall, Bernard. *Hell in a Very Small Place.* New York: Vintage Books, 1966.
Falls, Cyril. *The Great War 1914–1918.* New York: Capricorn Books, 1959.
Farrell, R. Barry, ed. *Approaches to Comparative and International Politics.* Evanston: Northwestern University Press, 1966.
Fay, Sidney B. *The Origins of the War,* Vols. I–II, 2nd rev. ed. New York: The Free Press, 1966.
Fedder, Edwin H., ed. *The United Nations: Problems and Prospects.* St. Louis: University of St. Louis Center for International Studies, Monograph No. 3.
Feis, Herbert. *Churchill, Roosevelt, Stalin.* Princeton: Princeton University Press, 1957.

Fenyo, Mario D. *Hitler, Horthy and Hungary: German Hungarian Relations 1941–1944.* New Haven: Yale University Press, 1972.
Fisher, Bart S. *The International Coffee Agreement: A Study of Coffee Diplomacy.* New York: Praeger, 1972.
Fisher, Herbert. *Studies in History and Politics.* Oxford: Clarendon Press, 1920.
Fitzgerald, Ernest. *The High Priests of Waste.* New York: W. W. Norton, 1972.
Fleiner, Thomas. *Die Kleinstaaten in den Staatenverbindungen des Zwanzigsten Jahrhunderts.* Zurich: Polygraphischer Verlag, 1966.
Fliess, Peter J. *International Relations in the Bipolar World.* New York: Random House, 1968.
——— *Thucydides and the Politics of Bipolarity.* Baton Rouge: Louisiana State University Press, 1966.
Fontaine, Roger W. *On Negotiating With Cuba.* Washington D.C.: American Enterprise Institute for Public Policy Research, 1975.
Fox, Annette Baker. *The Power of Small States: Diplomacy in World War II.* Chicago: University of Chicago Press, 1959.
——— *The Politics of Attraction: Four Middle Powers and the United States.* New York: Columbia University Press, 1977.
Fox, William T. R., ed. *Theoretical Aspects of International Relations.* South Bend, Ind.: University of Notre Dame Press, 1959.
Frank, Thomas M. and Edward Weisband. *World Politics: Verbal Strategy Among Super Powers.* New York: Oxford University Press, 1971.
Funke, Manfred, ed. *Hitler, Deutschland und die Mächte.* Dusseldorf: Droste Verlag, 1977.
Furniss, Edgar S., ed. *The Western Alliance: Its Status and Prospects.* Columbus, Ohio: Ohio State University Press, 1965.
Gallois, Pierre. *The Balance of Terror.* Trans. Richard Howard. Boston: Houghton Mifflin, 1961.
Garner, William R. *The Chaco Dispute.* Washington, D.C.: Public Affairs Press, 1966.
Gehl, Jurgen. *Austria, Germany and the Auschluss, 1931–1938.* London: Oxford University Press, 1963.
Gelber, H. G. *The Australian American Alliance: Costs and Benefits.* Baltimore: Penguin, 1968.
———ed. *Problems of Australian Defence.* Melbourne: Oxford University Press, 1970.
Gerassi, John. *The Great Fear in Latin America.* New York: Collier Books, 1973.
Gitelson, Susan A. *Israel's African Setback in Perspective.* Jerusalem: Jerusalem Papers on Peace Problems, 1974.
Glassman, John. *Arms For the Arabs: the Soviet Union and War in the Middle East.* Baltimore: The Johns Hopkins Press, 1975.
Goldhamer, Herbert. *The Foreign Powers in Latin America.* Princeton: Princeton University Press, 1972.
Gordon, Walter L. *A Choice for Canada.* Toronto: McClelland and Stewart, 1966.

Gould, Julius and William L. Kolb. *A Dictionary of the Social Sciences*. New York: The Free Press, 1967.

Granatstein, J. L., ed. *Canadian Foreign Policy Since 1945: Middle Power or Satellite?* Rev. ed. Toronto: The Copp Clark Publishing Company, 1970.

Grewe, Wilhelm G. *Spiel der Kräfte in der Weltpolitik*. Düsseldorf: Econ Verlag, 1970.

Griffith, William E. *Albania and the Sino-Soviet Rift*. Cambridge, Mass.: The MIT Press, 1963.

Griffiths, John C. *Modern Iceland*. London: Pall Mall, 1969.

Grünwald, Constantin de. *Baron Stein, The Enemy of Napoleon*. London: Jonathan Cape, 1936.

Gulick, Edward Vose. *Europe's Classical Balance of Power*. New York: W. W. Norton, 1967.

Halberstam, David. *The Best and the Brightest*. New York: Random House, 1972.

Halley, Irving Brinton. *Buying Aircraft: National Procurement for the Army Air Forces*. United States Army in World War II, Special Studies. Washington, D.C.: Department of the Army, 1964.

Halperin, Maurice. *The Rise and Decline of Fidel Castro*. Berkeley: University of California Press, 1972.

Handel, Michael I. *Israel's Political-Military Doctrine*. Occasional Papers, No. 30. Cambridge, Mass.: Harvard Center for International Affairs, 1973.

Harkabi, Y. *Nuclear War and Nuclear Peace*. Jerusalem: Israel Program for Scientific Translations, 1966.

Harlow, C. J. E. *The European Armaments Base: A Survey*. Part I: *Economic Aspects of Defence Procurement*. London: The Institute for Strategic Studies, 1967.

————— *The European Armaments Base: A Survey*. Part II: *National Procurement Policies*. London: The Institute for Strategic Studies, 1967.

Hastings, Stephen. *The Murder of the TSR–2*. London: Macdonald, 1966.

Heckscher, Gummar. *The Role of the Small Nations Today and Tomorrow*. London: University of London, The Athlone Press, 1966.

Hellmann, Ronald G. and Jon H. Rosenbaum, eds. *Latin America: The Search for a New International Role*. New York: John Wiley, A Sage Publication, 1975.

Helmreich, Ernst Christian. *The Diplomacy of the Balkan Wars 1912–1913*. Cambridge, Mass.: Harvard University Press, 1938.

Herre, Paul. *Die Kleinen Staaten Europas und die Entstehung des Weltkrieges*. München: C. H. Beck'sche Verlagsbuchhandlung, 1937.

Herz, John C. *International Politics in the Nuclear Age*. New York: Columbia University Press, 1962.

Himmelfarb, Gertrude. *Darwin and the Darwinian Revolution*. New York: W. W. Norton, 1962.

Hirschman, Albert O. *National Power and the Structure of Foreign Trade*. Berkeley: University of California Press, 1969.

Hobbes, Thomas. *Leviathan.* Ed. Michael Oakeshott. New York: Collier Books, 1966.
Hoffmann, Stanley. *Contemporary Theory in International Relations.* Englewood Cliffs, N.J.: Prentice Hall, 1960.
————— *Gulliver's Troubles.* New York: McGraw Hill, 1968.
————— *The State of War.* New York: Fredrick A. Praeger, 1968.
Hofstadter, Richard. *Social Darwinism in American Thought.* Boston: Beacon Press, 1971.
Holbraad, Carsten. *The Concert of Europe.* London: Longmans, 1970.
Holst, Johan Jørgen, ed. *Five Roads to Nordic Security.* Oslo: Universitetsforlaget, 1973.
Hoptner, J. B. *Yugoslavia in Crisis 1934–1941.* New York: Columbia University Press, 1962.
Horthy, Nicholas. *Memoirs.* New York: Robert Speller, 1957.
Howe, Jonathan Trumbull. *Multicrises.* Cambridge, Mass.: The M.I.T. Press, 1971.
Hugo, Grant. *Appearance and Reality in International Relations.* London: Chatto and Windus, 1970.
Ikle, Fred Charles. *Every War Must End.* New York: Columbia University Press, 1971.
Institute for Strategic Studies. *The Military Balance 1973–1974.* London: The Institute for Strategic Studies, 1973.
Jackson, O. Bruce. *Castro, the Kremlin, and Communism in Latin America.* Baltimore: The Johns Hopkins University Press, 1969.
Jakobson, Max. *The Diplomacy of the Winter War.* Cambridge, Mass.: Harvard University Press, 1961.
————— *Finnish Neutrality.* New York: Fredrick A. Praeger, 1968.
Jenkins, Robin. *Exploitation.* London: MacGibbon and Kee, 1970.
Jha, Braj Kishore. *Indo-Nepalese Relations 1951–1972.* Bombay: Vora, 1973.
Johnson, Chalmers. *Autopsy on People's War.* Berkeley: University of California Press, 1973.
Johnstone, William C. *Burma's Foreign Policy—A Study in Neutralism.* Cambridge, Mass.: Harvard University Press, 1963.
Jones, S. Shepard. *The Scandinavian States and the League of Nations.* Princeton: Princeton University Press, 1939.
Jukic, Ilija. *The Fall of Yugoslavia.* New York: Harcourt Brace Jovanovich, 1974.
Kaegi, Werner. *Historische Meditationen,* Vols. I–II. Zurich: Fretz und Wasmuth Verlag. 1942, 1946.
Kagan, Donald, *The Outbreak of the Peloponnesian War.* Ithaca: Cornell University Press, 1969.
Kahn, Herman and Anthony J. Wiener. *The Year 2000.* New York: The Macmillan Company, 1967.
Kaplan, Abraham. *The Conduct of Inquiry.* Scranton, Pa.: Chandler, 1964.
Kaplan, Morton A. *System and Process in International Politics.* New York: John Wiley, 1967.

Karol, K. S. *Guerillas in Power: the Course of the Cuban Revolution.* New York: Hill and Wang, 1970.
Karpat, Kemal H. *Turkey's Foreign Policy in Transition 1950–1974.* Leiden: E. J. Brill, 1975.
Kay, David A. *The New Nations in the United Nations 1960–1967.* New York: Columbia University Press, 1970.
Kazmadeh, Firuz. *Russia and Great Britain in Persia 1864–1914.* New Haven: Yale University Press, 1968.
Keatinge, Patrick. *A Place Among the Nations: Issues of Irish Foreign Policy.* Dublin: Institute of Public Administration, 1978.
Keenleryside, Hugh L., James Eayrs, Gaddis Smith, et al. *The Growth of Canadian Policies in External Affairs.* Durham, N.C.: Duke University Press, 1960.
Kennaway, Richard. *New Zealand Foreign Policy 1951–1971.* Wellington: Hicks Smith, 1972.
Keohane, Robert A. and Nye, Joseph S. *Power and Interdependence: World Politics in Transition.* Boston: Little Brown, 1977.
Kerner, Robert J., ed. *Czechoslovakia.* Berkeley: University of California Press, 1940.
Kertesz, Stephen D. *Diplomacy in a Whirlpool: Hungary between Nazi Germany and Soviet Russia.* South Bend, Ind.: University of Notre Dame Press, 1953.
─────────── and M. A. Fitzsimons, eds. *Diplomacy in a Changing World.* South Bend, Ind.: University of Notre Dame Press, 1959.
Khalaf, Nadim G. *Economic Implications of the Size of Nations with Special Reference to Lebanon.* Leiden: E. J. Brill, 1971.
Kieft, David Owen. *Belgium's Return to Neutrality: An Essay in the Frustrations of Small Power Diplomacy.* Oxford: Clarendon Press, 1972.
Kim, Kyung-Won. *Revolution and the International System.* New York: New York University Press, 1970.
Klein, Burton H. *Germany's Preparation for War.* Cambridge, Mass.: Harvard University Press, 1959.
Klein, Robert A. *Sovereign Equality Among States: The History of An Idea.* Toronto: University of Toronto Press, 1974.
Klenberg, Jan. *The Gap and the Straits: Problems of Nordic Security.* Occasional Paper No. 18. Cambridge, Mass.: Harvard Center for International Affairs, 1968.
Knorr, Klaus. *Military Power and Potential.* Lexington, Mass.: D. C. Heath, 1970.
─────────── *Power and Wealth: The Political Economy of International Power.* New York: Basic Books, 1973.
─────────── *On the Uses of Military Power in the Nuclear Age.* Princeton: Princeton University Press, 1966.
─────────── *The War Potential of Nations.* Princeton: Princeton University Press, 1956.
─────────── and James N. Rosenau, eds. *Contending Approaches to International Politics.* Princeton: Princeton University Press, 1969.

Koen, Ross Y. *The China Lobby in American Politics.* New York: Macmillan, 1960.
Korbel, Josef. *Poland Between East and West.* Princeton: Princeton University Press, 1963.
Lagos, Gustav. *International Stratification and Underdeveloped Countries.* Chapel Hill: The University of North Carolina Press, 1963.
Lamont, Archie. *Small Nations.* Glasgow: William Maclellan, 1944.
Larrabee, F. Stephen. *Balkan Security.* Adelphi Papers No. 135. London: The International Institute for Strategic Studies, 1977.
Ledermann, László. *Considérations sur le Petit État.* Neuchâtel: Editions de La Baconnière, 1946.
Levitt, Kari. *Silent Surrender: The American Economic Empire in Canada.* New York: Liseright, 1971.
────── *Silent Surrender: The Multinational Corporation in Canada.* Toronto: Macmillan of Canada, 1970.
Liddell Hart, B. H. *A History of the World War 1914–1919.* Boston: Little Brown, 1935.
Lijphardt, Arne. *The Trauma of Decolonization: The Dutch and West New Guinea.* New Haven: Yale University Press, 1966.
Lindgren, Carl-Ivar. *Small States' Freedom of Action and Responsibility for International Stability under the Super Powers' Nuclear Umbrella.* Mimeographed. Cambridge, Mass.: Harvard Center for International Affairs, 1968.
Liska, George. *Alliances and the Third World.* Baltimore: The Johns Hopkins Press, 1968.
────── *International Equilibrium.* Cambridge, Mass.: Harvard University Press, 1957.
────── *Nations in Alliance.* Baltimore: The Johns Hopkins Press, 1968.
Littauer, Raphael and Norman Uphoff, eds. *The Air War in Indochina,* rev. ed. Boston: Beacon Press, 1972.
Lloyd, Peter J. *International Trade Problems of Small Nations.* Durham: Duke University Press, 1968.
Lukacs, John A. *The Great Powers and Eastern Europe.* New York: American Book Co., 1953.
Lüthi, Rudolf. *Die Europäischen Kleinstaaten und die Haager Friedenkonferenz von 1899.* Winterthur: Verlag P. G. Keller, 1954.
Luttwak, Edward N. *The Grand Strategy of the Roman Empire: From the First Century A.D. to the Third.* Baltimore: The Johns Hopkins Press, 1976.
Macartney, C. A. *October Fifteenth: A History of Modern Hungary 1929–1945.* 2nd ed., Vol. I. Edinburgh: Edinburgh University Press, 1961.
────── and A. W. Palmer. *Independent Eastern Europe.* New York: St. Martins Press, 1966.
Macbean, Alasdair I. *Export Instability and Economic Development.* Cambridge, Mass.: Harvard University Press, 1966.
Macdonald, Robert W. *The League of Arab States.* Princeton: Princeton University Press, 1965.

Machiavelli, Niccolo. *The Prince and the Discourses.* New York: The Modern Library, 1950.
Machray, Robert. *The Struggle for the Danube and the Little Entente 1929–1938.* London: George Allen and Unwin, 1938.
Madariaga, Salvador de. *Latin America Between the Eagle and the Bear.* New York: Fredrik A. Praeger, 1962.
Magdoff, Harry. *The Age of Imperialism.* New York: Modern Reader, 1969.
Mannerheim, Carl Gustav. *The Memoirs of Marshal Mannerheim.* Trans. Eric Lewenhaupt, New York: E. P. Dutton, 1954.
Mannoni, O. *Prospero and Caliban: The Psychology of Colonization.* Trans. Pamela Powesland. New York: Fredrik A. Praeger, 1956.
Marder, Arthur J. *From Dreadnought to Scapa Flow 1904–1914,* Vol. I. London: Oxford University Press, 1966.
Markus, Joseph. *Grandes Puissances, Petites Nations.* Neuchâtel: Éditions de La Baconnière, 1947.
Marriot, J. A. R. *Federalism and the Problem of the Small State.* London: George Allen and Unwin, 1943.
Martin, William. *Switzerland From the Roman Times to the Present.* New York: Praeger 1971.
Masaryk, T. G. *The Problem of Small Nations in the European Crisis.* London: University of London, The Athlone Press, 1966.
Mathisen, Trygve. *The Functions of Weak States in the Strategies of the Great Powers.* Oslo: Universitetsforlaget, 1971.
Matthews, Herbert L., ed. *The United States and Latin America,* 2nd ed. Englewood Cliffs, N.J.: Prentice Hall, 1963.
Mazour, Anatole G. *Finland Between East and West.* Princeton: D. Van Nostrand, 1956.
McEntee, Girard Lindsley. *Military History of the World War.* New York: Charles Scribner, 1937.
McKean, Roland N., ed. *Issues in Defense Economics.* New York: Columbia University Press, 1967.
McLin, Jon B. *Canada's Changing Defense Policy, 1957–1963: The Problems of a Middle Power in Alliance.* Baltimore: The Johns Hopkins Press, 1967.
McSherry, James E. *Stalin, Hitler and Europe,* Vol. II. Cleveland: World Publishing Co., 1970.
Merchant, Livingston, ed. *Neighbors Taken for Granted.* New York: Praeger, 1966.
Michaely, Michael. *Concentration in Economic Trade.* Amsterdam: North Holland Publishing Co., 1962.
Millar, T. B. *Australia's Defence,* 2nd ed. Melbourne: Melbourne University Press, 1969.
——————— *Australia's Foreign Policy.* Sydney: Angus and Robertson, 1968.
Miller, Jane Kathryn. *Belgian Foreign Policy Between Two Wars 1919–1940.* New York: Bookman Associates, 1951.
Montgomery, John Flournoy. *Hungary the Unwilling Satellite.* New York:

Devin-Adair, 1947.
Morgenthau, Hans J. *Peace, Security and the United Nations.* Chicago: Chicago University Press.
────────── *Politics Among Nations,* 5th ed. New York: Alfred A. Knopf, 1973.
Munli, S. D. *Foreign Policy of Nepal.* Delhi: National, 1973.
Nakhleh, Emile A. *Arab American Relations in the Persian Gulf.* Washington, D.C.: American Enterprise Institute for Public Policy Research, 1975.
Newman, William J. *The Balance of Power in the Interwar Years 1919–1939.* New York: Random House, 1968.
Nilson, John. *Russian Tanks 1900–1970.* Harrisburg, Pa.: Stackpole Books, 1970.
Northedge, F. S., ed. *The Use of Force in International Relations.* London: Faber and Faber, 1974.
Nuechterlein, Donald E. *Iceland, Reluctant Ally.* Ithaca: Cornell University Press, 1961.
O'Brien, Conor Cruise. *To Katanga and Back.* New York: Grosset and Dunlap, 1966.
Olson, Mancur. *The Logic of Collective Action,* rev. ed. New York: Schocken Books, 1971.
Osgood, Robert E. *Alliances and American Foreign Policy.* Baltimore: The Johns Hopkins Press, 1968.
────────── *The Weary and the Wary: U.S. and Japanese Security Policies in Transition.* Studies in International Affairs, No. 16. Baltimore: The Johns Hopkins Press, 1972.
────────── and Robert Tucker. *Force, Order and Justice.* Baltimore: The Johns Hopkins Press, 1967.
Padelford, Norman and Leland M. Goodrich, eds. *The United Nations in the Balance.* New York: Fredrick A. Praeger, 1965.
Page, Stanley W. *The Formation of Baltic States.* Cambridge, Mass.: Harvard University Press, 1959.
Paine, Robert, ed. *Patrons and Brokers in the East Arctic.* Toronto: Memorial University of Newfoundland, 1971.
Palmer, Alan. *The Lands Between: A History of East-Central Europe Since the Congress of Vienna.* New York: The Macmillan Co., 1970.
Pano, Nicholas C. *The People's Republic of Albania.* Baltimore: The Johns Hopkins Press, 1968.
Papagos, Alexander. *The Battle of Greece 1940–41.* Trans. Pat Eliascos. Athens: J. M. Scazikis, "Alpha", 1949.
Parkinson, F. *Latin America, The Cold War, and The World Powers, 1945–1973: A Study in Diplomatic History.* Beverly Hills: Sage, 1974.
Paz, Alberto Conil and Gustavo Ferrari. *Argentina's Foreign Policy 1930–1962.* Trans. John J. Kennedy. South Bend, Ind.: University of Notre Dame Press, 1966.
Peckert, Joachim. *Die Grossen und Die Kleinen Mächte.* Stuttgart: Deutsche Verlags-Anstalt, 1961.
Perkins, Dexter. *A History of the Monroe Doctrine.* Boston: Little Brown, 1963.

——————— *The United States and Latin America.* Baton Rouge: Louisiana State University Press, 1961.

Petras, James, ed. *Latin America: From Dependence to Revolution.* New York: John Wiley, 1973.

Plischke, Elmer. *Microstates in World Affairs: Policy Problems and Options.* Washington D.C.: American Enterprise Institute for Public Research, 1977.

Popper, Karl R. *The Poverty of Historicism.* New York: Harper, 1964.

Poston, M. M. *British War Production.* London: HMSO and Longmans Green, 1952.

Prasad, Khirendra Mohan. *Ceylon's Foreign Policy Under the Bandaranaikes, 1956–1965.* New Delhi: S. Chand, 1973.

Preston, Richard A., ed. *The Influence of the United States on Canadian Development.* Durham, N.C.: Duke University Press, 1972.

Purnell, Robert. *The Society of States: An Introduction to International Politics.* London: Weidenfeld and Nicolson, 1973.

Radvanyi, Janos. *Hungary and the Superpowers: The 1956 Revolution and Realpolitik.* Stanford: Hoover Institution Press, 1972.

Ramazani, Rouhollah K. *The Foreign Policy of Iran 1500–1941.* Charlottesville: University Press of Virginia, 1966.

Rangel, Carlos. *The Latin Americans: Their Love-Hate Relationship with the United States.* New York: Harcourt Brace Jovanovich, 1977.

Rapaport, Jacques, Ernst Muteba, and Joseph J. Therattil. *Small States and Territories: Status and Problems.* New York: Arno Press, 1971.

Rechigl, Miloslav, ed. *Czechoslovakia Past and Present,* Vol. I, *Political, International, Social and Economic Aspects.* The Hague: Mouton, 1968.

Redford, Robert W. *Canada and Three Crises.* Toronto: The Canadian Institute of International Affairs, 1968.

Reid, George L. *The Impact of Very Small Size on the International Behavior of Microstates.* Sage Professional Papers, International Studies Series. Beverly Hills: Sage, 1974.

Regling, Horst. *Militärausgaben und Wirtschaftliche Entwicklung.* Hamburg: Verlag Weltarchiv, 1970.

Rich, Norman. *Hitler's War Aims,* Vol. I. New York: W. W. Norton, 1973.

Richardson, Neil R. *Foreign Policy and Economic Dependence.* Austin: The University of Texas Press, 1978.

Riekhoff, Harold von. *German-Polish Relations 1918–1933.* Baltimore: The Johns Hopkins Press, 1971.

Riker, William H. *The Theory of Political Coalitions.* New Haven: Yale University Press, 1968.

Ripka, Hubert. *Small and Great Nations: The Conditions of a New International Organization.* London: Czechoslovak Ministry of Foreign Affairs Information Service, 1944.

Ristić, Dragiša N. *Yugoslavia's Revolution of 1941.* University Park: The Pennsylvania State University Press, 1966.

Roberts, Adam, ed. *Civilian Resistance as a National Defense.* Baltimore: Penguin Books, 1967.

Robinson, E. A. G., ed. *Economic Consequences of the Size of Nations.*

New York: St. Martins Press, 1960.
Rose, Leo E. *Nepal Strategy for Survival*. Berkeley: University of California Press, 1971.
Rosecrance, Richard N. *Action and Reaction in World Politics*. Boston: Little Brown, 1963.
——————, ed. *The Future of the International Strategic System*. San Francisco: Chandler, 1972.
—————— *International Relations: Peace or War*. New York: McGraw Hill, 1973.
Rosenau, James N., ed. *International Politics and Foreign Policy*. New York: Free Press, 1969.
Rothstein, Robert L. *Alliances and Small Powers*. New York: Columbia University Press, 1968.
—————— *The Weak in the World of the Strong: The Developing Countries in the International System*. New York: Columbia University Press, 1977.
Rotstein, Abraham and Gary Lax. *Independence—The Canadian Challenge*. Toronto: Committee for an Independent Canada, 1972.
Rousseau, Jean-Jacques. *The Government of Poland*. Trans. Willmoore Kendall. Indianapolis, Ind.: Bobbs-Merrill, 1972.
Rout, Leslie B. *Politics of the Chaco Peace Conference 1935-1939*. Austin: University of Texas Press, 1970.
Rubinstein, Alvin Z. *Yugoslavia and the Non Aligned World*. Princeton: Princeton University Press, 1970.
Russel, Peter, ed. *Nationalism in Canada*. Toronto: McGraw-Hill Company of Canada, 1966.
Russett, Bruce M., ed. *Economic Theories of International Politics*. Chicago: Markham, 1968.
—————— *What Price Vigilance?* New Haven: Yale University Press, 1970.
Safran, Nadav. *From War to War*. New York: Pegasus, 1969.
Sampson, Anthony. *The Arms Bazaar*. New york: The Viking Press, 1977.
Schelling, Thomas C. *Arms and Influence*. New Haven: Yale University Press, 1966.
—————— *The Strategy of Conflict*. New York: Oxford University Press, 1969.
Schou, August and Arne Olav Brundtland, eds. *Small States in International Relations*. Stockholm: Almquist and Wiksell, 1971.
Schottelius, Herbert and Wilhelm Deist, eds. *Marine und Marinepolitik in Kaiserlichen Deutschland 1871-1914*. Düsseldorf: Droste Verlag, 1972.
Schuschnigg, Kurt von. *Austrian Requiem*. Trans. Franz von Hildebrand. London: Victor Gollancz, 1947.
Schwarz, Urs. *Confrontation and Intervention in the Modern World*. Dobbs Ferry, N.Y.: Oceana Publications, 1970.
Schweizer Lexikon. Zurich: Encyclios Verlag, 1947. Vol. IV.
Scott, Andrew M. *The Revolution in Statecraft—Informal Penetration*. New York: Random House, 1965.
Senn, Alfred Erich. *The Emergence of Modern Lithuania*. New York:

Columbia University Press, 1959.
─────────── *The Great Powers: Lithuania and the Vilna Question 1920–1928.* Leiden: E. J. Brill, 1966.
Sharp, Daniel A., ed. *U.S. Foreign Policy and Peru.* Austin: University of Texas Press, 1972.
Sharp, Gene. *The Politics of Nonviolent Action.* Boston: Porter Sargent, 1973.
Shirer, William L. *The Collapse of the Third Republic.* New York: Simon and Schuster, 1969.
─────────── *The Rise and Fall of the Third Reich.* New York: Simon and Schuster, 1960.
Sieber, Edward. *Die Idee des Kleinstaats bei den Denkern des 18. Jahrhunderts in Frankreich und Deutschland.* Freiburg in Baden: C. A. Wagner, 1920.
Singer, Marshall R. *Weak States in a World of Powers.* New York: The Free Press, 1972.
SIPRI (Stockholm International Peace Research Institute). *The Arms Trade with the Third World.* Stockholm, 1971.
Skumik, W. A. E. *The Foreign Policy of Senegal.* Evanston: Northwestern University Press, 1972.
Smith, Stanley A. de. *Microstates and Micronesia.* New York: New York University Press, 1970.
Spector, Sherman David. *Rumania at the Paris Peace Conference: A Study in the Diplomacy of Ioan I. C. Bartianu.* New York: Bookman Associates, 1962.
Spence, J. E. *Republic Under Pressure: A Study of South African Foreign Policy.* London: Oxford University Press, 1965.
Stafford, Roy William. *Signaling and Response: An Investigation of Soviet-American Relations with Respect to the Crisis in Eastern Europe in 1968.* Unpublished Ph.D. dissertation written at the Fletcher School of Law and Diplomacy 1976. Medford, Massachusetts.
Steinberg, Jonathan. *Yesterday's Deterrent: Tirpitz and the Birth of the German Battle Fleet.* New York: Macmillan, 1965.
Stoessinger, John G. *The Might of Nations,* 3rd ed. New York: Random House, 1969.
Strach, Harry R. *Sanctions: The Case of Rhodesia.* Syracuse, N.Y.: Syracuse University Press, 1978.
Suarez, Andre. *Cuba: Castroism and Communism 1959–1966.* Cambridge, Mass.: The M.I.T. Press, 1967.
Sveics, V. V. *Small Nation Survival: Political Defense in Unequal Conflicts.* New York: Exposition Press, 1969.
Tanner, Väino. *The Winter War: Finland-Russia 1939–1940.* Stanford: Stanford University Press, 1950.
Tanter, Raymond and Richard H. Ullman. *Theory and Policy in International Relations.* Princeton: Princeton University Press, 1972.
Tarulis, Albert N. *Soviet Policy Toward the Baltic States 1918–1940.* South Bend, Ind.: Notre Dame University Press, 1959.
Taylor, A. J. P. *The Origins of the Second World War,* 2nd ed. Greenwich,

Conn.: Fawcett Primer Book, 1968.
────────── *The Struggle for Mastery in Europe 1848–1918*. Oxford: Clarendon Press, 1965.
Teichmann, Max, ed. *Aspects of Australia's Defence*. Monash: The Political Studies Association, Monash University, 1966.
────────── , ed. *New Directions in Australian Foreign Policy: Ally, Satellite, or Neutral?* London: Pelican, 1969.
Thaden, Edward C. *Russia and the Balkan Alliance of 1912*. University Park: The Pennsylvania State University Press, 1965.
Theberge, James D. *Latin America in the World System: The Limits of Internationalism*. The Washington Papers No. 27. Beverly Hills: Sage, 1975.
Thomas, Hugh. *Suez*. New York: Harper and Row, 1967.
Thompson, Kenneth W. *Political Realism and the Crisis of World Politics*. Princeton: Princeton University Press, 1960.
────────── and Joseph E. Black, eds. *Foreign Policies in a World of Change*. New York: Harper and Row, 1963.
Thorne, Christopher. *The Approach of War 1938–1939*. London: Macmillan, 1967.
────────── *The Limits of Foreign Policy*. New York: Capricorn Books, 1973.
Thucydides. *The History of the Peloponnesian War*. Trans. Richard Crowley. New York: E. P. Dutton, 1950.
Tingsten, Herbert. *The Debate on the Foreign Policy of Sweden 1918–1939*, London: Oxford University Press, 1949.
Treitschke, Heinrich von. *Politics*. Trans. Blanche Dugdale and Torber de Bille. New York: Macmillan, 1916.
Trevor-Roper, H. R., ed. *Blitzkrieg to Defeat: Hitler's War Directives, 1939–1945*. New York: Holt, Rinehart and Winston, 1971.
Treverton, Gregory F. *Latin America in World Politics: The Next Decade*. Adelphi Papers, No. 137. London: Institute of Strategic Studies, 1977.
Triepel, Heinrich. *Die Hegemonie*. Stuttgart: Verlag W. Kohlhammer, 1938.
Tucker, Robert W. *The Inequality of States*. New York: Basic Books, 1977.
Tuite, Mathew, Roger Chisholm, and Michael Randor, eds. *Interorganizational Decision Making*. Chicago: Aldine Press, 1972.
Turner, L. F. C. *Origins of the First World War*. New York: W. W. Norton, 1970.
Udgaard, Nils Morten. *Great Power Politics and Norwegian Foreign Policy*. Oslo: Universitetplaget, 1973.
United Nations Statistical Yearbook 1972. New York: Statistical Office of the United Nations Department of Economic and Social Affairs, 1973.
United States Arms Control and Disarmament Agency. *World Military Expenditures 1971*. Washington, D.C.: Bureau of Economic Affairs, U.S. Arms Control and Disarmament Agency, 1972.
Upton, A. F. *Finland in Crisis 1940–1941: A Study in Small-Power Politics*. Ithaca: Cornell University Press, 1965.
Ustinov, Peter. *Five Plays*. Boston: Little Brown, 1965.

Vandenbosch, Amry. *Dutch Foreign Policy Since 1815: A Study in Small Power Politics*. The Hague: Martinus Nijhoff, 1959.
——— and Mary Belle. *Australia Faces Southeast Asia*. Lexington, Ky.: University of Kentucky Press, 1967.
Vasener, Adalbert Krieger and Javier Pazos. *Latin America: A Broader Role*. London: Ernest Benn, 1973.
Vital, David. *The Inequality of States: A Study of the Small States in the International System*. Oxford: Clarendon Press, 1967.
——— *The Survival of Small States: Studies in Small Power/Great Power Conflict*. London: Oxford University Press, 1971.
Vondracek, Felix John. *The Foreign Policy of Czechoslovakia 1918–1935*. New York: Columbia University Press, 1937.
Vucinich, Wayne S. *Serbia Between East and West: The Events of 1903–1908*. Stanford: Stanford University Press, 1954.
Wagner, R. Harrison. *United States Policy Toward Latin America*. Stanford: Stanford University Press, 1970.
Wallace, Michael David. *War and Rank Among Nations*. Lexington, Mass.: Lexington Books, D. C. Heath, 1973.
Walters, F. P. *A History of the League of Nations*. London: Oxford University Press, 1965.
Waltz, Kenneth N. *Man, the State and War*. New York: Columbia University Press, 1968.
Wandycz, Piotr S. *France and Her Eastern Allies 1919–1925: French-Czechoslovak-Polish Relations from the Paris Peace Conference to Locarno*. Minneapolis: The University of Minnesota Press, 1962.
Warnock, John W. *Partner to Behemoth: The Military Policy of a Satellite Canada*. Toronto: New Press, 1970.
Watt, Alan. *The Evolution of Australian Foreign Policy 1938–1965*. Cambridge: Cambridge University Press, 1967.
Weber, Max. *Economy and Society*, Vol. II. Ed. Guenther Roth and Claus Wittich. New York: Bedminster Press, 1968.
Wegener, Wolfgang. *Die Seestrategie des Weltkrieges*. Berlin: Mittler, 1929.
Weinberg, Gerhard L. *The Foreign Policy of Hitler's Germany: Diplomatic Revolution in Europe 1933–1936*. Chicago: Chicago University Press, 1970.
——— *Germany and the Soviet Union 1939–1941*. Leiden: E. J. Brill, 1954.
Whitaker, Arthur P. *The United States and the Southern Cone*. Cambridge, Mass.: Harvard University Press, 1976.
Wibberley, Leonard. *The Mouse That Roared*. Boston: Little Brown, 1955.
Wildavsky, Aaron. *The Revolt Against the Masses*. New York: Basic Books, 1971.
Whetten, Lawrence L. *The Arab-Israeli Dispute—Great Power Behavior*. *Adelphi Papers* No. 128. London, Institute of Strategic Studies, 1976.
Wiles, P. J. D. *Communist International Economics*. Oxford: Basil Blackwell, 1968.
Wilkes, John. *Australia's Defense and Foreign Policy*. Sydney: Angus and Robertson, 1964.

Wolfe, Thomas W. *Soviet Power and Europe 1945–1970.* Baltimore: The Johns Hopkins Press, 1970.
Wolfers, Arnold. *Britain and France Between Two Wars.* New York: W. W. Norton, 1966.
——————— *Discord and Collaboration.* Baltimore: The Johns Hopkins Press, 1962.
——————— *The Small Powers and the Enforcement of Peace.* New Haven: Yale Institute of International Studies, 1963. (Mimeographed).
Wood, Bryce. *The Making of the Good Neighbor.* New York: Columbia University Press, 1962.
Woodhead, A. Geoffrey. *Thucydides on the Nature of Power.* Cambridge, Mass.: Harvard University Press, 1970.
Woodward, E. L. *Great Britain and the German Navy.* London: Frank Cass, 1964.
Wright, Quincy. *A Study of War.* 2 Vols. Chicago: The University of Chicago Press, 1942.
Wythe, George. *The United States and Inter-American Relations.* Gainesville, Fla.: University of Florida Press, 1964.
Young, Oren R. *The Intermediaries: Third Parties in International Crises.* Princeton: Princeton University Press, 1967.
Zartman, I. William. *International Relations in the New Africa.* Englewood Cliffs, N.J.: Prentice Hall, 1966.
Zea, Leopold. *Latin America and the World.* Trans. Frances K. Hendricks and Beatrice Berler.
Ziedonis, Arvidis, Rein Taagepera and Mardi Valgemäe. *Problems of Mininations, Baltic Perspective.* San José: Association for the Advancement of Baltic Studies, Inc., 1973.
Ziemke, Earl F. *The German Northern Theater of Operations 1940–1945.* Washington, D.C.: Department of the Army Pamphlet No. 20–271, 1959.
Zook, David H. *The Conduct of the Chaco War.* New Haven: Bookman Associates, 1960.

Articles

Abbott, George C. "Size, Viability, Nationalism and Politico-Economic Development," *International Journal,* 25 (1969–70), 56–68.
Adelman, M. A. "Is the Oil Shortage Real?: Oil Companies as *OPEC* Tax Collectors," *Foreign Policy* (Winter 1972–73), No. 9, 69–107.
Albrecht, Ulrich. "The Costs of Armamentism," *The Journal of Peace Research,* 10 (1973), 265–282.
Amstrup, Niels. "The Perennial of Small States: A Survey of Research Efforts," *Conflict and Cooperation,* 11 (1976), 163–182.
Amuzegar, Jahangir. "The Oil Story: Facts, Fiction and Fair Play," *Foreign Affairs,* 51 (1973), 676–689.
Anderson, Elam J. "Is the Small State Doomed?" *Proceedings of the*

Institute of World Affairs (Eighteenth Session), 17/18 (1940), 250–259.

Axline, W. Andrew. "Underdevelopment, Dependence, and Interpretation," *International Organization,* 31 (Winter 1977), 83–106.

Baehr, Peter J. "Small States: A Tool for Analysis," *World Politics.* 27 (1975), 457–465.

Bailey, Sydney D. "Veto in the Security Council," *International Conciliation* (January 1968), No. 566.

Baldwin, David A. "The Power of Positive Sanctions," *World Politics,* 24 (1971), 19–38.

Barrea, Jean. "The Counter-Core Role of Middle Powers in Process of External Political Integration," *World Politics,* 25 (1973), 274–287.

Beaton, Leonard. "Why Israel Does *Not* Need the Bomb," *The New Middle East,* 1 (1969), 7–11.

Bell, J. Bowyer. "Israel's Nuclear Option," *The Middle East Journal,* 26 (1972), 379–388.

Belassa, Bela. "Country Size and Trade Patterns: Comments," *American Economic Review,* (March 1969), 201–204.

Bergsten, C. Fred. "The Threat from the Third World,: *Foreign Policy* (Summer 1973), No. 11, 103–124.

——————— "The Threat is Real," *Foreign Policy* (Spring 1974), No. 14, 84–90.

Betts, Richard K. "Paranoids, Pygmies, Pariahs and Nonproliferation," *Foreign Policy,* 26 (Spring 1977), 157–183.

Betts, R. R. "The European Satellite States," *International Affairs,* 21 (1945), 15–29.

Bjol, Erling. "The Power of the Weak," *Cooperation and Conflict,* 3 (1968), 157–168.

Bohn, David E. "Neutrality: Switzerland's Policy Dilemma: Options in New Europe," *Orbis,* 21 (1977), 335–352.

Brown, J. Seyom. "The Changing Essence of Power," *Foreign Affairs,* 51 (1973), 286–299.

Bruell, Christopher. "Thucydides' View of Athenian Imperialism," *American Political Science Review,* 68 (1974), 11–17.

Brummer, Karl. "The New International Economic Order: A Chapter in a Protracted Confrontation," *Orbis,* 20 (1976), 103–122.

Bundy, P. "Elements of Power," *Foreign Affairs,* 56 (1977), 1–26.

Cable, Vincent. "The 'Football War' and the Central American Common Market," *International Affairs,* 45 (1969), 658–671.

Campbell, John C. "Oil Power in the Middle East," *Foreign Affairs,* 56 (1977), 89–110.

Caporaso, James A. "Dependence, Dependency, and Power in the Global System: A Structural and Behavioral Analysis," *International Organization,* 32 (1978), 13–45.

Churba, Joseph. "Weighing the Middle East Balance on a Different Set of Scales," *Armed Forces Journal,* 115 (1977), 17–27.

Cohen, Raymond. "Israel and the Soviet-American Statement of October 1, 1977: the limits of Patron-Client Influence," *Orbis* 22 (1978), 613–34.

Cooper, John F. "Taiwan's Strategy and America's China Policy," *Orbis,*

21 (1977), 261–276.
Cordesman, Anthony. "How Much is Too Much?" *Armed Forces Journal,* 115 (1977), 32–39.
Davis, Jerome D. "The Arab Case of Oil October 1973–July 1974," *Cooperation and Conflict,* 11 (1976), 56–67.
Dominguez, Jorge I. "Mice That Do Not Roar: Some Aspects of International Politics in the World's Peripheries," *International Organization,* 25 (1971), 175–208.
─────────── "Taming the Cuban Shrew," *Foreign Policy* (Spring 1973), No. 10, 94–116.
─────────── "The Cuban Operation in Angola: Cost and Benefits for the Armed Forces," *Cuban Studies,* January 1978.
─────────── "Cuban Foreign Policy", *Foreign Affairs,* (Fall 1978), Vol. 57, No. 1, 83–108.
Donaldson, Robert H. A review article on Robert L. Rothstein, *Alliances and Small Powers. American Political Science Review,* 63 (1969), 609–611.
Dror, Yehezkel. "Small Powers Nuclear Policy: Research Methodology and Exploratory Analysis," *The Jerusalem Journal of International Relations,* 1 (1975), 29–50.
East, Maurice A. "Foreign Policy-Making in Small States: Some Theoretic Observations Based on a Study of the Uganda Ministry of Foreign Affairs," *Policy Sciences,* 4 (1973), 491–508.
Fagen, Richard R. "The Realities of U.S.-Mexican Relations," *Foreign Affairs,* 55 (1977), 685–700.
─────────── "Size and Foreign Policy Behavior: A Test of Two Models," *World Politics,* 25 (1973), 556–599.
Fox, Annette Baker. "Intervention and the Small State," *International Affairs,* 22 (1968), 247–256.
─────────── "The Small States in the International System 1919–1969," *International Journal,* 24 (1969), 751–764.
─────────── "The Small States of Western Europe in the United Nations," *International Organization,* 13 (1965), 774–786.
─────────── . A review on Arthur Andrew's *Diplomacy for the Underdog* and V. V. Sveics' *Small Nation Survival. International Organization,* 26 (1971), 792–794.
─────────── A review on David Vital's *The Inequality of States. International Journal,* 23 (1971), 623–624.
─────────── Alfred E. Hew, Jr., and Joseph S. Nye, eds. "Canada and the United States: Transnational and Transgovernmental Relations," *International Organization,* 28 (1974).
Francis, Michael J. "United States Policy Toward Latin America: An Immoderate Proposal," *Orbis,* 20 (1977), 991–1006.
Furlong, O. M. "Iran—A Power To Be Reckoned With," *International Defense Review,* 6 (1973), 719–729.
Galbraith, Francis J. "Indonesia's Worldview and Foreign Policies," *Orbis,* 19 (1975), 1102–1114.
Galtung, Johan. "On the Effects of International Economic Sanctions," *World Politics,* 19 (1967), 378–416.

———. "A Structural Theory of Imperialism," *The Journal of Peace Research*, 8 (1971), 81–118.
Garris, Jerome. "Sweden's Debate on the Proliferation of Nuclear Weapons," *Cooperation and Conflict*, 8 (1973), 189–208.
German, F. Clifford. "A Tentative Evaluation of World Power," *Conflict Resolution*, 4 (1960), 138–144.
Gitelson, Susan A. "Why Do Small States Break Diplomatic Relations With Outside Powers?" *International Studies Quarterly*, 18 (1974), 451–484.
Goldmann, Kjell. "Notes on the Power Structure of the International System," *Cooperation and Conflict*, 12 (1977), 1–20.
Grinter, Laurence E. "Bargaining Between Saigon and Washington: Dilemmas of Linkage Politics During War," *Orbis*, 18 (1974), 837–867.
Guy, James John. "Canada and Latin America," *The World Today*, 32 (1976), 376–386.
Haagerup, Niels J. "Are Small Nations Being Left Out?" *NATO Review*, 24 (1976), 13–17.
Haas, Ernst B. "The Balance of Power as a Guide to Policy Making," *The Journal of Politics*, 15 (1953), 370–398.
——————— "The Balance of Power—Prescription, Concept or Propaganda?" *World Politics*, 5 (1953), 442–477.
Halle, Louis J. "Does War Have a Future?" *Foreign Affairs*, 52 (1973), 20–34.
Halperin, Morton H. and Tang Tsou. "United States Policy Toward the Offshore Islands," *Public Policy*, 15 (1966), 119–138.
Hambro, Carl J. "The Role of the Smaller Powers in International Affairs To-Day," *International Affairs*, 15 (1936), 167–182.
Hambro, Edward. "Small States and a New League—From the Viewpoint of Norway," *American Political Science Review*, 37 (1943), 903–909.
Han, Sungjoo. "South Korea's Participation in the Vietnam Conflict: An Analysis of the U.S.-Korean Alliance", *Orbis*, 21 (1978), 893–912.
Hansen, Peter. "Adaptive Behavior of Small States: The Case of Denmark and the European Community," in *Sage International Yearbook of Foreign Policy Studies*, Vol. II, ed. Patrick J. McGowan. Beverly Hills: Sage, 1974.
Harris, Owen, "Australia's Foreign Policy Under Whitlam," *Orbis*, 19 (1975), 1090–1101.
Hart, Jeffrey. "Three Approaches to the Measurement of Power in International Relations," *International Organization*, 30 (1976), 289–309.
Herbert, Joseph R. "The Behavior of the Ministates in the United Nations," *International Organization*, 30 (1976), 109–128.
Hirsch, Mario. "Influence Without Power: Small States in European Politics," *The World Today*, 32 (1976), 112–128.
Hoffmann, Stanley. "Restraints and Choices in American Foreign Policy," *Daedalus*, 91 (1962), 668–704.
Holbraad, Carsten. "The Role of the Middle Powers," *Cooperation and Conflict*, 6 (1971), 77–90.
Holsti, K. J. "Canada and the United States," in *Conflict in World Politics*,

eds. Steven Speigel and Kenneth Waltz. Boston: Winthrop, 1971.
Irani, Robert G. and Standenmaier, William O. "Microstates and the Balance of Power in the Contemporary International System," *National War College Review*, 31 (1978), 76–96.
Johnson, A. Ross, "Yugoslav Total Defence," *Survival*, 15 (1973), 54–58.
Jonsson, Agnar Kl. "Iceland's Place in the World—The Foreign Policy of Iceland," *NATO Letter*, 14 (1966), 10–11.
Kaegi, Werner. "Der Typus des Kleinstaaten im Europäischen Denken," *Neue Schweizer Rundschau*, 6 (1938), 257–271, 345–361, 414–431.
Kende, Istvan. "Twenty Five Years of Local Wars," *The Journal of Peace Research*, 8 (1971), 5–22.
Kende, Istvan. "Wars of Ten Years 1967–1976", *Journal of Peace Research*, Vol. 15, No. 3, 1978, 227–241.
Keohane, Robert O. "The Big Influence of Small Allies," *Foreign Policy* (Spring 1971), No. 2, 161–182.
——————— "Lilliputians' Dilemmas: Small States in International Politics," *International Organization*, 23 (1969), 291–310.
——————— "Political Influence in the General Assembly," *International Conciliation* (March 1966), No. 557.
Kinter, William R. "Thailand Faces the Future," *Orbis*, 19 (1975), 1126–1140.
Klicka, Otta. "Small States and Big Problems," *Survival*, 8 (1966), 162–165.
Knorr, Klaus. "On the International Uses of Military Force in the Temporary World," *Orbis*, 21 (1977), 5–28.
Knovsky, E. "The Economic Aftermath of the Six Days War: UAR, Jordan, Syria," Part II, *The Middle East Journal*, 22 (1968), 278–296.
Koht, Haldvan. "Neutrality and Peace: The View of a Small Power," *Foreign Affairs*, 15(1937), 280–289.
——————— "The Role of Small Nations," *The Annals* (1945), No. 240, 86–89.
Krasner, Stephen D. "The Great Oil Sheikdown," *Foreign Policy* (Winter 1973/74), No. 13, 123–138.
——————— "Manipulating International Commodity Markets: Brazilian Coffee Policy 1906 to 1962," *Public Policy*, 21 (1973), 493–522.
——————— "Oil Is the Exception," *Foreign Policy* (Spring 1974), No. 14, 68–84.
——————— "State Power and the Structure of International Trade," *World Politics*, 28 (1976), 317–347.
Lang, William W. "Can Sweden Defend Itself?" *U.S. Naval Institute Proceedings*, 93 (1967), 47–57.
Larrabee, F. Stephen. "The Rumanian Challenge to Soviet Hegemony," *Orbis*, 17 (1973), 227–246.
——————— "The Soviet Union and the Non-Aligned," *The World Today*, 32 (1976), 467–475.
——————— "Whither Albania?" *The World Today*, 34 (1978), 61–79.
Laux, Jeanne Kirk. "Small States and Inter-European Relations: An

Analysis of the Group of Nine," *The Journal of Peace Research*, 9 (1972), 147–160.
Law, Alton D. "Coffee: Structure, Control and Development: A Review Article," *Inter-American Economic Affairs*, 27 (1973), 69–86.
—————— "Stabilization of Prices of Primary Products: A Review Article," *Inter-American Economic Affairs*, 24 (1970), 27–42.
Leff, Nathaniel H. "Bengal, Biafra and the Bigness Bias," *Foreign Policy*, (Summer 1971), No. 3, 129–139.
Lemarchand, Rene and Keith Legg, "Political Clientelism and Development," *Comparative Politics*, 4 (1972), 149–178.
Levy, Walter J. "Oil Power," *Foreign Affairs*, 49 (1971), 652–668.
Mabro, Robert and Elizabeth Monroe. "Arab Wealth From Oil: Problems of Its Investment," *International Affairs*, 50 (1974); 15–27.
Mack, Andrew. "Why Big Nations Lose Small Wars: The Politics of Asymmetric Conflict," *World Politics*, 27 (1975), 175–200.
Malmgren, Harold B. "Coming Trade Wars? (Neo Mercantilism and Foreign Policy)," *Foreign Policy* (Winter 1970–71), No. 1, 115–143.
Mande, George. "Finland's Security," *The World Today*, 31 (1975), 406–414.
Marriott, J. A. R. "The Problem of the Small State," *Fortnightly*, 161 (1942), 132–138.
Maurseth, Per. "Balance of Power Thinking from the Renaissance to the French Revolution," *The Journal of Peace Research*, 1 (1964), 120–136.
McGowan, Patrick J. and Klaus-Peter Gottwald. "Small State Foreign Policies: A Comparative Study of Participation, Conflict and Political and Economic Dependence in Black Africa," *International Studies Quarterly*, 19 (1975), 469–500.
Mikdashi, Zuhayr. "Collusion Could Work," *Foreign Policy*, (Spring 1974), No. 14, 57–68.
—————— "Cooperation Among Oil Exporting Countries with Special Reference to Arab Countries: A Political Economy Analysis," *International Organization*, 28 (1974), 1–30.
Miller, J. D. B. "Australian Foreign Policy I," *International Affairs*, 50 (1974), 229–241.
—————— "Australian Foreign Policy II," *International Affairs*, 50 (1974), 425–438.
Milsten, Donald E. "Small Powers—A Struggle for Survival: A Review," *The Journal of Conflict Resolution*, 13 (1969), 388–393.
Moran, Theodore H. "New Deal or Raw Deal in Raw Materials," *Foreign Policy* (Winter 1971–1972), No. 5, 119–134.
Murray, J. Alex and Mary C. Gerace. "Canadian Attitudes Toward the U.S. Presence," *Public Opinion Quarterly*, 36 (1972), 388–397.
Nansen, Fritjof. "The Mission of the Small States," *The American-Scandinavian Review*, 6 (1918), 9–13.
Nuechtelein, Donald E. "Small States in Alliances: Iceland, Thailand, Australia," *Orbis*, 13 (1969), 600–623.
Øberg, Jan. "Arms Trade with the Third World as an Aspect of Imperialism," *Journal of Peace Research*, 12 (1975), 213–234.

O'Leary, James P. "Envisioning Interdependence: Perspectives on Future World Orders," *Orbis*, 22 (1978), 503–538.
Olson, Mancur. "Increasing the Incentives for International Cooperation," *International Organization*, 25 (1973), 866–874.
────────── and Richard Zeckhauser. "An Economic Theory of Alliances," *The Review of Economics and Statistics*, 48 (1966), 266–279.
Orvik, Nils. "NATO, NAFTA and the Smaller Allies," *Orbis*, 12 (1968), 455–464.
──────────"NATO—The Role of the Small Members," *Atlantic Community Quarterly*, 4 (1966), 92–103.
──────────"Defense Against Help—a Strategy for Small States", *Survival*, 15, No. 5, Sept./Oct. 1973, pp. 228–231.
Paarlberg, Robert L. "Food, Oil and Coercive Resource Diplomacy", *International Security*, (Fall 1978), Vol. 3, No. 2, 3–19.
Park, Chang Jin. "The Influence of Small States Upon the Superpowers: United States-South Korean Relations as a Case Study 1950–53," *World Politics*, 28 (1975), 97–117.
Parkinson, F. "Latin American Foreign Policies," *International Affairs*, 50 (1974), 439–450.
Paterson, William E. "Small States in International Politics," *Cooperation and Conflict*, 4 (1969), 119–123.
Pipinelis, Panayotis. "Integration, Detente, and the Smaller Countries," *NATO Letter*, 15 (1966), 8–13.
Powell, John Duncan. "Peasant Society and Clientelist Politics," *American Political Science Review*, 64 (1970), 411–425.
Powelson, John P. "The Terms of Trade Again," *Inter American Economic Affairs*, 23 (1970), 3–11.
Rappard, William E. "Small States in the League of Nations," *Political Science Quarterly*, 49 (1934), 544–575.
Remington, Robin Alison. "Yugoslavia and European Security," *Orbis*, 17 (1973), 197–226.
Rogers, Robert F. "Korea: Old Equation, New Factors," *Orbis*, 19 (1975), 1115–1125.
Rose, Leo E. and Roger Dial. "Can a Ministate Find True Happiness in a World Dominated by Protagonist Powers?" *The Annals* (November 1969), No. 386, 89–101.
Rosen, Steven J. "A Stable System of Mutual Nuclear Deterrence in the Arab-Israeli Conflict," *American Political Science Review*, 71 (1977), 1367–1383.
Rothstein, Robert L. "Foreign Policy and Development Policy: From Non-Alignment to International Class War," *International Affairs*, 52 (1976), 598–616.
────────── "Inequality, Exploitation and Justice in the International System: Reconciling Divergent Expectations," *International Studies Quarterly*, 21 (1977), 319–358.
Russett, Alan de. "Large and Small States in International Organizations," *International Affairs*, 30 (1954), 463–475; 31 (1955), 192–203.
Russett, Bruce M. "The Calculus of Deterrence," *The Journal of Conflict*

Resolution, 7 (1963), 97–109.

─────────── and John D. Sullivan. "Collective Goods and International Organization," *International Organization,* 25 (1973), 845–865.

Rustow, Dankwart A. "Who Won the Yom Kippur and Oil Wars?" *Foreign Policy,* 17 (1974/5), 166–175.

Salmore, S. A. and C. F. Hermann. "The Effect of Size: Development and Accountability in Foreign Policy," *Peace Research Society Papers,* 14, 17–30.

Sawyer, Jack. "Dimensions of Nations: Size, Wealth and Politics," *American Journal of Sociology,* 72 (1967), 145–172.

Schreiber, Anna P. "Economic Coercion as an Instrument of Foreign Policy: U.S. Economic Measures Against Cuba and the Dominican Republic," *World Politics,* 25 (1973), 387–413.

Scott, James C. "Patron Client Politics and Political Change in Southeast Asia," *American Political Science Review,* 66 (1972), 91–113.

Seers, Dudley. "Big Companies and Small Countries: A Practical Proposal," *Kyklos,* 15 (1963), 599–608.

Singer, J. David and Melvin Small, "The Composition and Status Ordering of the International System: 1815–1840," *World Politics,* 18 (1966), 236–282.

─────────── "The Diplomatic Importance of States An Extension and Refinement of the Indicator," *World Politics,* 25 (1973), 577–599.

─────────── "Formal Alliances 1815–1939," *The Journal of Peace Research,* 3 (1966), 1–32.

Singleton, F. B. "Albania and Her Neighbors: The End of Isolation," *The World Today,* 31 (1975), 383–390.

Skagestad, Gunnar. "Small States in International Politics: A Polar-Political Perspective," *Conflict and Cooperation,* 2/3 (1974), 133–141.

"Small Power Policy," *Times Literary Supplement,* (October 25, 1959).

Smith, Tony. "Changing Configurations of Power in North-South Relations Since 1945," *International Organization,* 31 (1977), 1–28.

Spiegel, Steven. "The Fate of the Patron: American Trials in the Arab Israeli Dispute," *Public Policy,* 21 (1973), 175–202.

Starr, Harvey. "A Collective Good Analysis of the Warsaw Pact After Czechoslovakia," *International Organization,* 28 (1974), 521–532.

Sucor, Vladimir. "The Limits of National Independence in the Soviet Bloc: Rumania's Foreign Policy Reconsidered," *Orbis,* 20 (1976), 701–732.

Suhrke, Astri. "Gratuity or Tyranny: The Korean Alliances," *World Politics,* 25 (1973), 508–532.

Sunkel, Osvaldo. "Big Business and 'Dependencia'," *Foreign Affairs,* 50 (1972), 517–531.

Tägil, Sven. "Wegener Raeder and the German Naval Strategy: Some Viewpoints on the Conditions for the Influence of Ideas," *Cooperation and Conflict,* 2 (1967), 102–112.

Tucker, Robert W. "Further Reflections on Oil and Force," *Commentary,* 59 (1975), 45–56.

Tucker, Robert W. "Egalitarianism and International Politics", *Commentary* (September 1975), 27–40.

——————— "Oil: The Issue of American Intervention," *Commentary*, 59 (1975), 29–31.
Vandenbosch, Amry. "The Small States in International Politics and Organization," *The Journal of Politics*, 26 (1964), 293–312.
Väyrynen, Raimo. "Finland's Role in Western Policy Since the Second World War," *Cooperation and Conflict*, 12 (1977), 87–108.
——————— "On the Definition of Small Power Status," *Cooperation and Conflict*, 6 (1971), 91–201.
——————— "The Position of Small Powers in the West European Network of Economic Relations," *European Journal of Political Research*, 2 (June 1974), 143–178.
——————— "A New International Order," *Commentary* (February 1975).
——————— "Stratification in the System of International Organizations," *The Journal of Peace Research*, 7 (1970), 291–310.
Vellut, Jean-Luc. "Smaller States and the Problem of War and Peace: Some Consequences of the Emergence of Smaller States in Africa," *The Journal of Peace Research*, 4 (1967), 252–269.
Vernon, Raymond, ed. "The Oil Crisis in Perspective," *Daedalus*, 104 (1975).
Vital, David. A review article on Robert L. Rothstein, *Alliances and Small Powers*. *International Journal*, 24 (1968/1969), 823.
Waltz, Kenneth N. "The Stability of a Bi-Polar World," *Daedalus*, 93 (1964), 881–901.
Weingrod, Alex. "Patrons, Patronage and Political Parties," *Comparative Studies in Society and History*, 10 (1969), 379–400.
Werner, Pierre. "Luxemburg's Challenge of Smallness," *Atlantic Community Quarterly*, 15 (1977), 80–84.
Wheelock, Thomas R. "Arms for Israel: the limit of leverage," *International Security*, (Fall 1978), Vol. 3, No. 2, 123–137.
Wilcox, Wayne A. "The Influence of Small States in a Changing World," *The Annals* (July 1967), No. 372, 80–92.
Wilson, Carroll L. "A Plan for Energy Independence," *Foreign Affairs*, 51 (1973), 657–675.
Wolfers, Arnold. "In Defense of Small Countries," *The Yale Review*, 33 (1944), 201–220.
Woolf, Leonard. "The Future of the Small States," *Political Quarterly*, 14 (1943), 209–214.
Young, Oran R. "Political Discontinuities in the International System," *World Politics*, 20 (1968), 369–392.
Zabih, Sepeh R. "Change and Continuity in Iran's Foreign Policy in Modern Times," *World Politics*, 23 (1971), 522–543.
Zacklin, Ralph. "Challenge of Rhodesia," *International Conciliation* (November 1969), No. 575.

Index

Abu Dhabi, 247
Afghanistan, 75
African States, 22, 86, 88, 132, 177, 220ff, 235, 244
African/Asian States, 5, 121, 138, 147, 173, 191, 272
Aggressions; limits on great powers' use of force, 39f, 176, 195f, 217, 242f, 258, 265–274; alleged provocations, 50, 269f; by weak states, 38ff
Albania, 46, 50, 90, 267; client state, 135, 137, 139, 148; and USSR, 40, 74, 175, 241
Alliances and Ententes; Anglo-French, Anglo-Russian, 177; ANZUS, 121; cat and mouse, 72, 121f, 127f; CENTO, 121; Little Entente, 121, 152, 153f, 155; NATO, 121, 145, 149f, 151, 208, 244, 281; SEATO, 121; Triple Alliance, 182, 187; Triple Entente, 177, 182, 187; Warsaw Pact, 120f, 155, 281
Allison, Graham, 3f
Andorra, 75
Arab League, 152, 153ff, 241
Arab States; foreign investments, 218f, 246; foreign relations, 22, 37, 46, 139, 204, 259; military purchases, 246f; oil producers (OAPEC), 42, 51, 217ff, 242, 243—249, 255 (n 102), 259; and USSR, 88, 89, 194
Aron, Raymond, 10, 68
Australia, 230, 240; client state, 30, 127, 139ff, 144–148; defense, 84f, 89, 102, 149, 281
Austria, 28, 39, 95f, 177–179, 182f, 236ff, 270
Averaging Strategy, 192

Balance of power, 13, 171, 175–187, 188; anti-balance of power, 183ff; balance of weakness, 180

Balkan League, 29, 121, 152, 153f, 182
Balkan (Danubian) States, 124, 180, 181ff, 218, 225–227, 235f
Balkan Wars, 37, 91, 130
Baltic States, 7, 51, 72, 77, 121, 127f, 139, 177, 180, 186
Bangladesh, 28, 31, 233
Barros, James, 268, 274
Barston, R. P., 31
Bases, extra-territorial, 40, 42, 126f, 128, 129, 136f, 192f, 244
Belgium; defense, 28, 76, 85, 149, 281; foreign relations, 38, 184f; geography, 61, 71, 72, 74, 102, 128f; heavy industry, 231; training foreign armies, 88; in World Wars, 77f, 97, 261
Bipolar systems, 130, 171f, 187–197
Blair, Patricia, 48
Bolivia, 37
Bonjour, Edgar, 101
Brazil, 12, 13, 23, 139, 190, 203, 233
Brecher, Michael, 44
Brezhnev Doctrine, 189
Bulgaria, 24, 37, 226, 236
Bureaucracy, 262
Burke, Edmund, 177
Burma, 88

Cambodia, 90
Canada, 14, 23, 84, 203; and USA, 30, 40, 51, 139, 143–148, 261
Ceylon, 41, 137, 171
Chaco War, 37, 91
Chad, 10
Chile, 6, 72, 75, 272
China (People's Republic); defense, 19f, 40, 79, 83, 201; foreign relations, 137, 138, 179; population, 13
China (Taiwan), 22, 122, 232; and USA, 51, 124, 126, 127, 128, 136, 148, 179, 194
Cold War, 149, 173, 175, 188, 192

313

Colombia, 233
Colonialism, 22, 39, 55 (n 12), 147f, 267, 272f; neo-colonialism, 218, 234f
Competition for weak state support, 181ff, 190–195
Corfu incident, 268f
Costa Rica, 189
Cuba; foreign relations, 45, 46, 197, 262; geography, 75, 128; sends troops abroad, 132, 240; status, 29; and USA, 40, 50, 272; and USSR, 41, 132, 175, 193f, 240, 242
Cuban Missile Crisis, 30, 123f, 179, 194
Cultural; penetration, 145, 159 (n 35); shock, 129
Czechoslovakia; defense, 85; economics, 229, 231; foreign relations, 37, 124, 126, 154; geography, 6, 71, 72, 73, 75; status, 23; in WW II, 106, 107; and see Munich Crisis
Czechoslovak invasion 1968, 30, 40, 41, 51, 104, 105, 189f, 202, 240
Cyprus, 232

Dahl, Robert, 245
Dahomey, 226f
Däniker, Gustav, 206f
Defense, see Military
Defense Nihilism, 77, 150
Denmark; defense, 28, 76, 149, 150, 198f; foreign relations, 38, 44, 77, 184f; geography, 74; status, 186; in WW II, 78, 91, 105
Deterrence, 78, 90, 92, 94f, 100ff, 104, 150f, 201; finite, 258; proportional, 95, 199f
Doenitz, Karl, 77
Dominguez, Jorge, 39
Dominican Republic, 190f, 270
Dulles, John Foster, 173f

East, Maurice, 54
East European States, 7, 22, 120f, 122, 127f, 134, 137, 155, 175, 188, 239, 281

Economic factors, 217–256; defense spending ratio, 89f, 103, 151, 207; embargoes, 238–242; foreign trade ratio, 224, 229; GNP, 13f, 24, 28, 31; penetration, 225–227; pressure by weak states, 219, 242–246, 248; structure, 14ff, 25ff, 46f, 49
Ecuador, 272
Egypt; defense, 12, 89, 90, 204; economics, 14, 232f; foreign relations, 121, 122, 139, 154, 194, 243f; 261; geography, 74; status, 29, 42; and see Middle East
Eisenhower, President, 123, 124, 126
El Salvador, 189
Entente, see Alliances and Ententes
Estonia, 269
Ethiopia, 88, 132; Abyssinian War, 91, 95, 269
European Economic Community, 217, 244f
Exports, 217, 220–233, 237ff

Finland, 6, 7, 28, 85, 185; and USSR, 43, 51, 72, 77, 127, 135, 147, 240, 261f, 269; in war, 93, 106, 186, 187, 202; and see Winter War
Fisher, H. A. L., 37f
Fox, Annette Baker, 31, 42, 72, 183f, 185
France; democratization, 266f; foreign relations, 45, 130, 155; and former colonies, 218, 226f, 272ff; and Israel, 88, 121, 126, 135f; military equipment, 83, 89, 236; nuclear weapons, 19, 200, 201, 205, 207f; patron, 135, 147; status, 13, 22, 23, 186; in WW II, 77f; and see Munich Crisis

Gallois, Pierre, 198f
Gelber, H. G., 141
Geographical factors; border pressure, 75f; location, 6, 45, 51, 68, 70ff, 76, 79, 101ff, 128, 173; terrain, 74f; territorial size, 10, 47f, 70f, 198, 220, 233f; and see Population

German-Soviet Non-Aggression Pact, 128, 130, 177
Germany; armed forces, 81, 94, 97, 99; Austrian Anschluss, 177–179; and Balkan (Danubian) States, 218, 225–227, 235f; and Baltic States, 180; and Czechoslovakia, 73, 93, 154; as occupying power, 72f, 77f, 99, 105; as patron, 137; and Scandinavia, 77f, 91; and Serbia, 236f; shift of power to, 184f; WW II campaigns, 97, 99, 269, 270; after WW II, 186
Germany (FRG); defense, 40, 83, 85, 200; status, 13, 22, 23f, 208
Germany (GDR), 190
Ghana, 45, 88, 193
Great Britain; colonial power, 134, 272f; and democratization, 266f; foreign relations, 126, 129, 130, 177; and former empire, 139, 141, 218, 226f, 244; military equipment, 81f, 83; navy, 94f; nuclear weapons, 19, 200, 201, 205, 207f; patron/client, 139, 141, 148; status, 13, 22, 23; and see Munich Crisis
Greece; defense, 28, 37, 87; foreign relations, 43, 194, 259, 268f; in WW II, 74, 80, 82, 95, 97
Grewe, Wilhelm G., 41
Guatemala, 41
Guerrilla War, 81, 99f, 105f, 273

Haushofer, Karl, 6
Hegel, G. W. F., 148
Herre, Paul, 11
Hitler, Adolf, 77, 111 (n 39)
Hobbes, Thomas, 50, 198
Hoffmann, Stanley, 188
Holbraad, Carsten, 28f
Holland, see Netherlands
Honduras, 41, 189, 270
Hong Kong, 47, 232
Hungary, 6, 24, 37, 72, 135, 153f, 190, 225; invasion 1956, 41, 104
Huntingdon, Samuel, 4
Hussein, King of Jordan, 87f, 152

Iceland, 39, 42, 71, 78, 129, 149f, 171, 272
India; defense, 37, 85, 203, 204; economics, 14, 232; foreign relations, 193, 259; as patron (Nepal), 137ff, 147, 148; population, 13; war with Pakistan, 88, 90, 194
Indonesia; economics, 232, 233; foreign relations, 45, 137, 193, 194; status, 13, 23, 28
Iran (Persia); economics, 218, 233; foreign relations, 37, 147, 177, 247f, 259, 267; military purchases, 87; and USSR, 122, 128
Investment and aid programs, 193f, 219, 243f
Iraq, 37, 90, 154, 194, 247, 259
Ireland (Eire), 52, 72, 151
Israel; and Arab States, 152, 153; armed forces, 52, 79, 81, 89, 203; defense, 37, 90, 106; economics, 14, 241, 244; foreign relations, 43, 46, 122, 126, 202, 259; and France, 88, 121, 135f; geography, 71, 72, 75; military equipment, 12, 84ff, 88, 277, 281; nuclear weapons, 204, 205, 206, 207, status, 23, 29; training foreign armies, 88; and USA, 51, 126, 261; and see Middle East
Italy: defense, 40, 85, 154, 281; foreign relations, 135, 137, 154, 177, 179, 268f; and Greece in WW II, 74, 80, 82, 95, 97; status, 13, 23

Jacobson, Max, 95
Japan; and Cuba, 239; military equipment, 40, 81ff, 85, 200, 277; and oil, 244f; status, 13, 20, 22, 23f; 186, 208; wars, 269, 270
Johnson Doctrine, 189
Jordan, 87f, 90, 152, 154, 243

Kagan, Donald, 190
Kaplan, Morton, 183, 198, 202
Kenya, 88
Keohane, Robert O., 21, 29
Khrushchev, Nikita, 123
Knorr, Klaus, 90

Korea, North, 39, 79, 90, 179, 197
Korea, South; army, 79, 143; foreign policy, 128, 179; and USA, 121, 122, 126, 129, 136, 142f, 148, 194
Korean war, 91, 93
Kuwait, 37, 42, 154, 218, 229f, 233, 243, 247f
Kuznets, Simon, 31

Laos, 90
Latin America, 135, 172–175, 220f, 223, 232, 270f
League of Nations, 5, 22, 135, 154, 184, 268f
Lebanon, 41, 154, 232f
Leff, N. H., 232
Less Developed Countries, 217, 221, 229, 234, 235, 249
Libya, 10, 202, 218, 229f, 233, 243, 244, 247
Liska, George, 205
Luxembourg, 41, 231

Machiavelli, Niccolo, 121, 126, 185
Malawi, 241
Malaysia, 232
Malta, 42, 244
Manchukuo, 137
Manipulation of great power, 46, 51, 70, 120, 129ff, 155; bargaining power, 7, 87f, 128; coercive deficiency, 131, 150; economic pressure, 219, 242–246, 248; Lafayette syndrome, 141f; lobbying, 124, 126; moral obligation, 141f, 148; pre-emptive selling, 87f; reverse potentiality, 130f; strengthening of commitment, 122f, 127
Mannerheim, Carl Gustav, 79, 187
Mannoni, O., 147f
Marriott, J. A. R., 31
Marshall Plan, 175
Masaryk, Thomas Garrigue, 31
Mass production, 229, 231f
Mauritania, 10, 48, 71
Mexico, 13, 23, 51, 75, 145, 261

Middle East, 82f, 88, 89, 91, 204, 243f, 247; Arab-Israeli wars, 43, 92f, 154, 194; Suez War, 40, 126, 202, 272, 273f
Military equipment; precision guided munitions, 277–282; pre-emptive supply, 86f, 246f; production of, 81f, 83ff, 85f, 281; purchase of, 83–89, 219, 236, 246f, 278, 282; tanks 278f
Military expenditure, 83f, 89f, 102f, 149ff; and see Military equipment, purchase of
Military Participation Ratio, 78ff
Military strength, 13, 15ff, 19ff, 25ff, 28, 32, 36ff, 70, 76ff, 90–107; and see Aggression, Nuclear weapons
Mongolian People's Republic, 10, 75
Monroe Doctrine, 172
Montenegro, 29, 267
Morgenthau, Hans, 50, 130, 177
Morocco, 148
Mussolini, Benito, 95, 177
Munich Crisis, 93, 126, 177, 179

Nasser, Gamel abd-el, 154
NATO, see Alliances
Nepal, 75, 137ff, 147, 148, 2ʋ1
Netherlands, 13, 23, 28, 38, 76, 77, 85, 102, 184f, 229, 272
Neutrality, 77, 129, 151f, 184f
New Zealand, 6, 45, 72, 141f
Nicaragua, 189, 274
Nigeria, 13
Nobel Prizewinners, 113 (n 58)
Non-Aggression, see Passivity
Norway, 43, 244; defense, 28, 149, 281; neutrality 77, 129, 184f; in WW II, 78, 91, 99, 105, 111 (n 39)
Nuclear weapons, 12f, 19, 20, 30, 40, 46, 150f, 193, 197–208, 258, 282; tactical, 206f

Occupation; by Germany, 72f, 77f, 99, 105; detrimental to victor, 97ff
Oil; OPEC, 218, 219, 229f, 233; and see Arab States

INDEX

Pakistan, 23, 28, 37, 232f, 259, 277; war with India, 88, 90, 194
Panama Canal Zone, 74
Paraguay, 37, 41, 139, 190
Passivity, 37f, 43ff, 257
Patron-Client relationship, 131–148, 155, 189f
Peace conferences, 21f, 97, 267
Peru, 39, 272
Philippines, 142, 194
"Pigs' War", 236ff
Poland; foreign relations, 124, 130, 139, 154, 190; geography, 6, 51f, 72, 75, 102; partitions, 177; status, 24; in WW II, 97, 105, 261
Population; effective population, 13f, 78ff; homogeneity, 106f, 263; size, 13f, 24, 28, 31, 47f, 49, 68, 141, 220
Portugal, 6, 38, 72, 74, 194
Power vacuum, 73, 77f
Prussia, 13, 79, 177

Qatar, 247
Quemoy and Matsu, 124

Rapaport, Jacques, 48
Resistance; advantages of, 92–97, 110f; against occupying power, 105, 106, 118 (n 124); economic, 242; passive, 104–107; and see Deterrence, Guerrilla war, Occupation
Risk Theory, 94f, 199
Rhodesia, 241
Roman Empire, 133f
Roosevelt, Franklin Delano, 97
Rothstein, Robert L., 130f, 205
Rumania; foreign relations, 37, 154, 175, 185, 186, 225f; and USSR, 28, 40, 50, 102
Russia (Tsarist), 124, 130, 154f, 182f

Salonika, 236f
San Marino, 75
Santo Domingo, 40, 41
Saudi Arabia, 5, 10, 42, 87, 90, 218, 229f, 233, 243, 244, 247f
Scandinavia, 77f, 91, 151

Schelling, Thomas C., 7, 143
Schuschnigg, Kurt von, 179
Serbia, 29, 37, 124, 261, 270; and Austria, 39, 95, 182f, 236ff
Shirer, William, 97, 99
Sierra Leone, 226f
Singapore, 47, 232
Singer, Marshall R., 28, 136, 224f
Smith, Stanley de, 48
South Africa (Republic of), 23, 281
Spain, 23, 31, 43, 99f, 239
Sparta, 190
Spheres of influence, 5, 21f, 29, 42f, 171–175, 177, 188, 267
Super powers, definition, 19
Sveics, V. V., 104–107
Sweden; defense capability, 28, 76, 78, 79, 92, 100ff, 106, 277; economics, 229, 231, 239, geography, 6; neutrality, 77, 151f, 184f; population, 13, 106; status, 23; weapons, 12, 85, 89, 215f (n 106)
Switzerland, 176; defence, 12, 28, 78, 79, 92, 100ff, 106, 151; exports, 229, 232; geography, 74ff
Syria, 29, 90, 152, 154, 194, 232f, 243f

Tanzania, 137
Taylor, A. J. P., 131, 175
Tibet, 138
Tirpitz, Alfred von, 94
Treitschke, Heinrich von, 6
"Trip wire", 126f, 151
Tunisia, 171
Turkey, 23, 31, 37, 74, 79, 87, 127, 259

Uganda, 29, 41, 45, 88, 202
United Nations, 22, 135f, 268f, 274
USA; and Australia, 30, 84, 127, 139ff; and Canada, 29f, 40, 84, 143–148, 261; and China, 126, 179; and China (Taiwan), 124, 126, 127, 179; and Cuba, 40, 41, 123, 238ff, 272; democratization, 266f; economic relations, 193f, 217, 244; foreign bases, 126, 127, 129;

foreign policy, 43, 46; intervention and pressure, 41, 51, 270ff; and Israel, 88, 89, 93, 126, 206; and Jordan, 87f; and Latin America, 172–175, 189f; military equipment production, 81f, 83ff; and Panama, 74; as patron, 139–148, 172–175, 194, 205, 265; UN support, 135f; entry into WW II, 261; and see Cold War, Cuban Missile Crisis, Vietnam War

USSR; and Albania, 40, 74, 137; and Arab states, 87f, 89, 121, 122, 128, 155; "cat and mouse" alliances, 121f, 127f; and Cuba, 123f, 126f, 132, 193, 240, 242; economic relations, 193f, 240f; and Finland, 43, 72, 74, 127, 135, 147; foreign policy, 43, 175, 177, 189; geography, 73; and Germany, 95, 97, 128, 130, 177; intervention, 41, 51, 104; military equipment production, 82, 84; patron state, 261; and Rumania, 102, 154; and Turkey, 74; weak state provocation, 50; and Yugoslavia, 102, 128, 139; and see Baltic States, Cuban Missile Crisis, Czechoslovak invasion, East European States, Winter War

Vellut, Jean-Luc, 24, 28, 31

Venezuela, 233
Vietnam (North), 79, 90, 93f, 194, 197, 202
Vietnam (South), 79, 90, 122, 128, 129, 136, 194
Vietnam War, 30, 40, 41, 50, 51, 82, 89, 91, 93f, 95, 100, 141ff, 155, 274
Vital, David, 31, 107ff (n 2), 262
Vlekke, B. H. M., 54

Waltz, Kenneth, 3
War; war potential, 81ff; weak state involvement, 91ff, 259; world wars, 77f, 91, 182f
Weapons, see Military equipment
Wildavsky, Aaron, 192
Wilson, Woodrow, 267f
Winter War (Russia/Finland 1940–41), 74, 79, 82, 91, 92, 93f, 95
Wright, Quincy, 39, 175f

Yemen, 154
Yugoslavia; border pressure, 75f; defense, 87, 102, 151, 277; economic relations, 173, 225f, foreign relations, 37, 46, 126, 137, 139, 185, 197, 239; status, 23; training foreign armies, 88; and USSR, 50, 128, 240; in WW II, 97, 99, 105, 107

LIBRARY OF DAVIDSON COLLEGE